DOGGER BANK
FIRST PHASE
0630 –1000

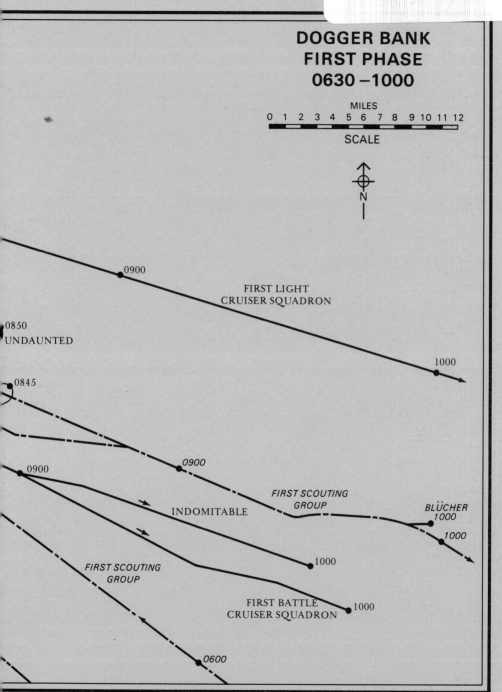

MILES

0 1 2 3 4 5 6 7 8 9 10 11 12

SCALE

N

0900

FIRST LIGHT
CRUISER SQUADRON

1000

0850
UNDAUNTED

0845

0900

FIRST SCOUTING
GROUP

0900

BLÜCHER
1000

INDOMITABLE

1000

0900

1000

FIRST SCOUTING
GROUP

1000

FIRST BATTLE
CRUISER SQUADRON

1000

0600

The King's Ships
Were at Sea

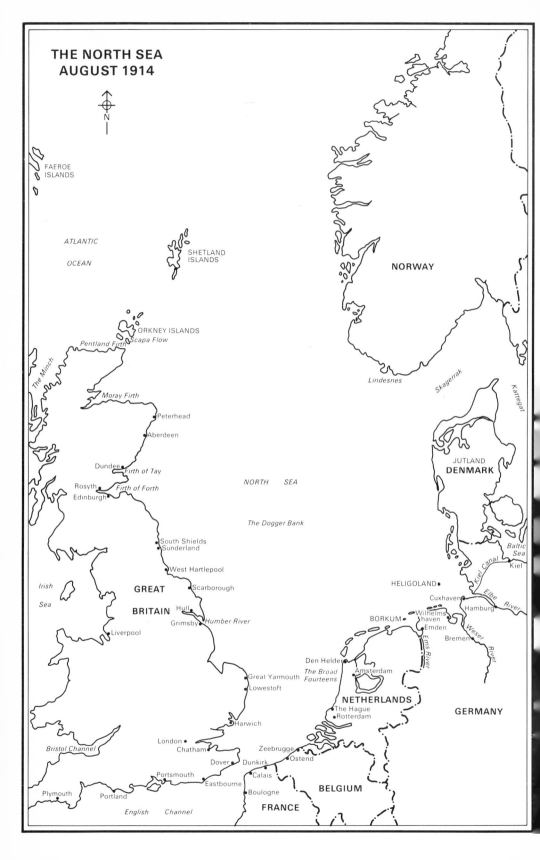

JAMES GOLDRICK

The King's Ships Were at Sea

THE WAR IN THE NORTH SEA
AUGUST 1914–FEBRUARY 1915

Naval Institute Press
Annapolis, Maryland

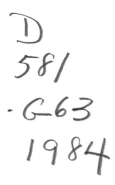
Library of Congress Cataloging in Publication Data
Goldrick, James.
  The king's ships were at sea.

  Bibliography: p.
  Includes index.
  1. World War, 1914–1918—Naval operations, British.
2. World War, 1914–1918—Campaigns—North Sea. I. Title.
D581.G63   1984   940.4'54   83-63436
ISBN 0-87021-334-2

Printed in the United States of America

For
My Father
and
Stephen Wentworth Roskill

Contents

Preface

This book seeks to present a comprehensive history of operations in the North Sea between August 1914 and February 1915. The question that must be asked when considering such a work is, Is it a necessary book? Despite the fact that skillfully written and extensively researched official histories have been available for decades, I believe that the answer is, Yes.

The authors of *Naval Operations*, Sir Julian Corbett and Sir Henry Newbolt, operated under three major constraints. First, the German side of the story was still shrouded in doubt and confused by the propaganda of the war. Second, although the vast majority of Admiralty documents were made available to Corbett and Newbolt, certain elements—notably those concerned with cryptographic analysis—were not. Third, and perhaps most important, both historians had to face formal censorship by the Admiralty and attempts at self-vindication by the politicians and senior naval officers who had been involved. In his recent biography of Sir Julian Corbett, D. M. Schurman treated in some detail Corbett's difficulties with the Admiralty over the publication of the early volumes, as well as an encounter with Winston Churchill before the first volume was finally issued.[1]

In addition, the unofficial activities of senior officers cannot be discounted. Corbett was under extreme pressure from more than one admiral. The Sturdee papers, for example, contain a lengthy exchange between Corbett and Admiral of the Fleet Sir Doveton Sturdee on the Falklands Battle, with Sturdee urging amendments to the text in order to show his performance in a better light.

Corbett resisted all these pressures as best he could, and in many ways Schurman is right to praise both the integrity and subtlety of the text. Nevertheless, in retrospect, the official historians' task was little short of impossible. Although the several volumes of *Naval Operations* are reliable enough in their detailing of fact, they are incomplete and often ingenuous in their interpretation of events. Vice Admiral Sir Peter Gretton put the matter in a nutshell when he wrote:

> The more one reads *Naval Operations*, Vols. I and II, the more one realises how the author was shackled by the Admiralty which resented any criticism of its work or indeed that of senior officers afloat. There are many omissions of errors and no candid comment.[2]

There is another reason for this history. Although affairs such as Coronel and Falklands, the Dardanelles and Jutland have been admirably dealt with by a number of historians, there has been little or no attempt to treat the naval war as a continuum. This has been done for the conflict on the western front, but there has been little coverage of the equally dreary, though less bloody, war at sea. Such an incident-oriented approach distorts the total picture. In 1914, for example, too many in Britain had a mistaken concept of their country's sea power, fed as they had been on the glories of the Royal Navy in the Napoleonic Wars but not on their accompaniment—twenty years of blockade.

No action fought in the North Sea was a chance happening. Some train of events always brought about the meeting, and it is the analysis of these events and their linkage that leads to a proper understanding of the conflict.

The difficulty with any work that sets out to be directly revisionist is that it almost inevitably becomes destructive in its criticism. No true historian can ever believe that he or she has written the last word on a subject. Conversely, he or she should not despise the efforts of predecessors or seek to detail their faults without granting equal exposure to their merits. Therefore, early in my research, and having access first to the necessary *Naval Staff Monographs* and then to the Public Record Office (PRO) files, I made the decision not to refer to Corbett directly or to model this book in any way upon *Naval Operations*. In particular, the *Naval Staff Monographs* constitute fundamental source material. Written after *Naval Operations* and without the necessity for public release (although still under considerable official restraint), these skillfully constructed texts deserved a wider audience than they gained during their years of circulation in the Royal and Commonwealth navies.

The King's Ships Were at Sea is not intended as a revision of the late Professor A. J. Marder's *From Dreadnought to Scapa Flow*. As Professor

Marder himself declared, the "War behind the War" could well be the subtitle for those of his volumes which dealt with the years 1914 to 1918.[3] This book is conceived, rather, as an operational history.

The Battle of the Dogger Bank set the pattern of maritime conflict until the Battle of Jutland. The six months between the outbreak of war and the destruction of the *Blücher* constitute a period of extraordinary interest for the naval historian because of the unparalleled novelty of the situation in which the opposing navies found themselves. A situation unparalleled, that is to say, until the present day. Perhaps there are lessons for the navies of the missile age in the history of the reaction of the Royal and Imperial navies to the strategic and tactical problems created by the technology they employed.

Acknowledgments

I am indebted first and foremost to the late Captain Stephen Roskill and to the late Mrs. Roskill for all the kindness and hospitality which they gave me. Captain Roskill put me right on a vast number of matters, gave me introductions to a number of extremely helpful authorities, and made some trenchant criticisms of my chapter on the Battle of the Dogger Bank.

To Vice Admiral Sir Peter Gretton, RN; Vice Admiral B.B. Schofield, RN; Captain A.B. Sainsbury, RNR; Commodore J.A. Robertson, RAN; Commander D.J. Campbell, RAN; Mrs. F.M. McGuire; Commander A.W. Grazebrook, RANR; Commander George Nekrasov, RAN; Professor Jack Sweetman; Dr. Jon Sumida; Mr. Jurg Meister; Lieutenant Commander S.P. Lemon, RAN; Father Michael Head, SJ; and Lieutenant Mark Sexton, AARes—all of whom read the manuscript in part or in whole—go my sincere thanks, as well as that for all their other help and hospitality.

Mr. J.D. Brown, head of the Naval Historical Library, Mr. Roderick Suddaby of the Imperial War Museum, and Dr. N.A.M. Rodger of the Public Record Office all took me in and gave me the greatest help in their departments. To the Master and Fellows of Churchill College Cambridge, for their hospitality, and for permission to make use of and quote from the College Archives, go my thanks, as well as to Mrs. Patricia Bradford, Archivist, for her considerable help.

Lieutenant Commander Patrick Beesly, RNVR; Commander A.J. Bull, RN; Dr. N.J.M. Campbell; Lieutenant S.J. Firth, RAN; Lieutenant P.A. Gardiner, RAN; Lieutenant W.T.V. Gobert, RAN; Lieutenant R.M.O. Hawke, RAN: Lieutenant and Mrs. G.P. Lunn; Commander and Mrs. J.A.A. McCoy; Vice Admiral Sir Ian and Lady McGeoch; Lieutenant P.J. Murray, RAN; the late Professor A.J. Marder; the late Admiral of the Fleet the Earl Mountbatten of Burma; Rear Admiral J.R.D. Nunn; Mr. Richard Ollard; Mr. Anthony Pollen; Dr. Jurgen Rohwer; Lieutenant D.M. Stevens, RAN; and Mr. John Winton all gave me much advice and assistance.

My particular thanks go to Lieutenant P.D. Jones, RAN, not only for the drawings which he has contributed, but for his unfailing encouragement.

Admiral Sir William and Lady Staveley not only made available the papers of the late Admiral of the Fleet Sir Doveton Sturdee, but offered me the hospitality of their home, as did Mrs. Oswald Frewen when I was reading the diaries of her husband, the late Captain Frewen. To them I give my deepest thanks.

Mrs. George Nekrasov translated and typed a number of articles from German, for which I am very grateful.

Ruth Wilson was kind enough not only to look up a number of articles and details which I was otherwise unable to obtain but also indexed this work for me.

Finally, my sincere thanks to Mrs. Mary Kooyman for her beautiful typing of the manuscript and to Mrs. Bridget Coles for accomplishing the revisions in short order.

Despite the enormous assistance which I was rendered at every stage of the work, all errors within the text are entirely my responsibility and I would be delighted to hear from anyone kind enough to point them out.

Grateful acknowledgment is made to the following authors, literary estates and publishers for permission to quote from the works cited. The literary estate of Admiral Sir Henry Pelly and Chatto & Windus Ltd for *300,000 Sea Miles*; the literary estate of A.H. Pollen and Chatto & Windus Ltd for *The Navy in Battle*; the literary estate of Brigadier C.F. Aspinall-Oglander and The Hogarth Press for *Roger Keyes*; the Misses King-Hall and Faber and Faber Ltd for *My Naval Life 1906–1929*; Mr. Winston Churchill, MP, the Hamlyn Publishing Group Ltd and Charles Scribner & Sons for *The World Crisis*; the Hutchinson Publishing Group Ltd for *Admiral von Hipper*; Mrs. A.J. Marder and Jonathan Cape Ltd for *Portrait of an Admiral* and *Fear God and Dread Nought*; Verlag E.S. Mittler & Sohn for *Dur Krieg zur See*; Vice Admiral Sir Peter Gretton and Cassell Ltd for *Former Naval Person*; the Earl Jellicoe and Cassell Ltd for *The Grand Fleet 1914–16*; Cassell Ltd for *The Riddle of Jutland, With the Battle Cruisers* and *Germany's High Sea Fleet in the World War*; Captain G.M. Bennett and B.T. Batsford Ltd for *Naval Battles of the First World War*; the literary estate of Rear Admiral W.S. Chalmers and Hodder &

Stoughton Ltd for *Max Horton and the Western Approaches*; the literary estate of Rear Admiral W.S. Chalmers and A.P. Watt Ltd for *The Life and Letters of David Earl Beatty* and *Full Circle*; the literary estate of Captain Taprell Dorling and A.P. Watt Ltd for *Swept Channels* and *Endless Story*; MacDonald & Co for *The Kaiser and His Court*; Sir Reginald Tyrwhitt, Professor A. Temple Patterson and MacDonald & Co for *Tyrwhitt of the Harwich Force*; Lord Chatfield for *The Navy and Defence*; the literary estate of Admiral Sir Lewis Bayly and Harrap Ltd for *Pull Together*; the literary estate of Admiral Sir Dudley de Chair and Harrap Ltd for *The Sea is Strong*; Constable Publishers for *Cruisers in Battle*; the literary estate of Admiral Sir William James and Methuen & Co Ltd for *The Sky Was Always Blue* and *The Eyes of the Navy*; the Misses King-Hall and Methuen & Co Ltd for *A Naval Lieutenant 1914–1918*; Victor Gollancz Ltd for *The Navy From Within* and *Sea Saga*; Mrs. A.J. Marder and the Oxford University Press for *From Dreadnought to Scapa Flow*; Admiral Sir Desmond Dreyer for *The Sea Heritage*; Lt. Cdr. W.H. Plunkett-Ernle-Erle-Drax and the Viscount Hood for their father's papers; Mrs. M. Godfrey for the papers of Admiral John Godfrey; Sir Reginald Tyrwhitt for the papers of Admiral of the Fleet Sir Reginald Tyrwhitt.

Abbreviations

BCF	Battle Cruiser Force/Fleet
BCS	Battle Cruiser Squadron
BEF	British Expeditionary Force
BS	Battle Squadron
Captain (D)	Captain of a Destroyer Flotilla
C in C	Commander in Chief
Commodore (S)	Commodore Commanding Submarines
Commodore (T)	Commodore Commanding Torpedo Craft
COS	Chief of Staff
CS	Cruiser Squadron
DF	Destroyer Flotilla
DID	Director of the Intelligence Division
DOD	Director of the Operations Division
DSO	Distinguished Service Order
GF	Grand Fleet
HMAS	His Majesty's Australian Ship
HMS	His Majesty's Ship
HSF	High Sea Fleet
LCS	Light Cruiser Squadron
RA	Rear Admiral
RAN	Royal Australian Navy
RN	Royal Navy
RNAS	Royal Naval Air Service
RNR	Royal Naval Reserve
S/M	Submarine
SMS	His Majesty's Ship (German)
TB	Torpedo Boat
TBD	Torpedo Boat Destroyer (Destroyer)
VA	Vice Admiral
W/T	Wireless Telegraphy

Table of Equivalents

GUNS

Metric	British
75 mm	3″
88 mm	3.4″
105 mm	4.1″
150 mm	5.9″
210 mm	8.3″
28 cm	11″
30.5 cm	12″
38 cm	15″

TORPEDOES

450 mm	17.7″
457 mm	18″
500 mm	19.7″
533 mm	21″

The King's Ships
Were at Sea

CHAPTER 1

The Beginning

The weather of early summer, 1914, was brilliant. It was as though the very sunshine mirrored the dawning hope in Europe that peace on the continent could be preserved. For the first time in a decade the Balkans were quiet, the major powers appeared capable of resolving their differences and, most important, the armaments race that had gripped the entire world since the turn of the century seemed at last to be coming to an end as civilized nations everywhere realised the folly of their indulgence.

In Germany it was Kiel Week, celebration of the young empire's maritime success. An annual event, the festivities at Kiel had grown larger and more magnificent as Germany's prosperity and the size of her merchant and naval fleets had grown apace. This year there was a special reason for German rejoicing. The high point of the week was to be the reopening of the Kiel Canal, which had been dredged and widened so as to be capable of taking the largest and most modern battleships direct from the Baltic to the North Sea ports and back without the time consuming—and dangerous—passage through the Kattegat and around Denmark. At 1300 on 24 June, the Imperial Yacht *Hohenzollern* cut the ribbon suspended across the entrance to the main locks. Not only was the bulk of the magnificent German High Sea Fleet laid out in review, but present also, as a gesture of friendship and trust, were four British battleships and three light cruisers.

The *King George V, Ajax, Audacious*, and *Centurion* were the most powerful dreadnoughts Britain possessed. The cruisers *Southampton, Birmingham*, and *Nottingham* were also the most modern and best equipped of their type. They, as much as the German ships around them, were products of the sixteen-year-old naval race between Great Britain and Germany. Hostility and doubt had for a decade surrounded the naval activities of each power. To bring their best units together under the public eye in peace would, it was to be hoped, go some way toward defusing the dangerous rivalry.

Despite the hectic round of official calls, parties, dances, sports matches, and sailing races, despite the fraternization between the officers and men of the two countries, the atmosphere was a little tense. Both Germans and British commented on the yachtlike appearance of the German warships in their light grey paint, compared to which the British units in their battleship grey looked sombre indeed. The officers attempted to see as much as they could of the other's navy. The Germans were disappointed to find that the British had swathed all their gunnery instruments in canvas, while for their part they could not help noticing the interest which the British displayed in the Kiel Canal and the new submarine classes.

On 28 June, all festivities came to an abrupt end. Whilst on a tour of Bosnia, the pro-German heir to the Austro-Hungarian throne, the Archduke Franz Ferdinand, was assassinated together with his wife. The murders cast a pall of gloom over Kiel as the German Court went into mourning and all remaining functions were hurriedly canceled. Few realized then the political ramifications of the assassination, and there was little mention of the possibility of war. It was another "damned little incident" in the Balkans which might end in a threatening exchange of notes, or even a minor local war, but could not possibly involve Britain or Germany.

As a gesture of friendship, it was suggested that the British light cruisers might prefer to return to Britain through the Kiel Canal. The offer was immediately accepted. The parting was amicable. When, on 30 June, the British ships left Kiel, Sir George Warrender, the Vice Admiral Commanding, was so moved as to make the signal to the Imperial Navy, "Friends in the past, friends for ever."

The assassinations were having their effect on the rigid European alliances. Austria-Hungary, with its own ethnic problems, felt threatened by the emergent nationalism of the Slavic states in the Balkans and the increasing Russian interest in the area. Austria-Hungary was especially suspicious of Serbia. The countries had been estranged since the Austro-Hungarian annexation of Bosnia-Herzogovina in 1908. The provinces, because of their Serbian population, had long been a source of concern to Serbia, many of whose people wanted to wrest them from Austria-Hungary. The assassin had been a

Bosnian Serb and the Austro-Hungarian government was quick to see a conspiracy involving the Serbian government.

For several weeks Austria-Hungary considered her move. The danger was that Russia, the self-styled "protector of the Slavs" might enter the ring to support Serbia. On 5 July the Austro-Hungarian Chargé d'Affaires in Berlin asked what Germany's position would be in the event of an Austro-Serbian war with the threat of Russian intervention. Wilhelm II did not believe that Russia would enter, nor that she could, since Serbia had compromised her own position by the assassination. He instructed his Chancellor to inform the Austro-Hungarians that Germany would stand by them whatever their decision as to the Serbian question. This message had since been called the "blank check," for its effect was to convince the Austro-Hungarians that they had complete freedom of action.

The High Sea Fleet maintained its peacetime routine. All activity was concentrated on preparations for the fleet cruise to Norway planned for mid-July. There were, however, some doubts as to the German position. Whilst the politicians and the army saw little risk of hostilities with Britain, the Imperial Navy saw matters rather differently. The Admiralstab held that the High Sea Fleet would be running a considerable risk in moving out of German waters at a time of international tension. During the Norwegian cruise, the fleet would be split into squadrons to visit various ports. Such a scattering of forces would leave the fleet especially vulnerable to a surprise attack by the British.

The Germans had never forgotten that "Copenhagening" the High Sea Fleet by making surprise attacks while the German ships were at their anchorages had been publicly advocated in Britain. It did not escape the attention of the Admiralstab that at the time the High Sea Fleet was in Norway the Royal Navy would be unusually well prepared for war. On 5 July, Admiral Hugo von Pohl, Chief of the Admiralstab, remarked that the Kaiser's decision to let the cruise proceed was wise only if the international situation had calmed down.

But to cancel the cruise would be an inflammatory step which could be construed by the British as a hostile action. Germany's alliance with Austria-Hungary would only come into effect in the event of a war with Russia. To all but the navy that prospect seemed remote enough; the possibility of hostilities with Britain was even more distant. On 10 July, the High Sea Fleet sailed to begin exercises in the Skagerrak before continuing north to Norway. The situation now appeared quiet, so calm in fact that most of the Imperial Navy's staff and senior officers went on their summer leaves.

Across the North Sea the Royal Navy seemed to take the international situation even less seriously. Attention was focused upon the Irish Question. The Liberal Government's decision to give Home Rule to Ireland had brought the nation close to civil war. Rival factions in Ireland were already armed and Conservative circles in both Ireland and England were declaring that they would fight to prevent the implementation of Home Rule. The Government's decision to send troops in to prevent bloodshed and ensure that the decision would be carried out had misfired. Army officers at the Curragh had resigned en masse, declaring that they could not fire upon their own people. Since the army was thus not to be relied upon, how would the navy react? Warships were lying in Irish ports, but there was some doubt whether their crews could be used. Perhaps the discipline of the Royal Navy would have held good, for in the *Southampton*,

> As far as we were concerned "Barge" (Commodore William Goodenough) had all the officers into his cabin, told us that we might have to bombard Belfast and that would be that.[1]

The Royal Navy's major activities for 1914 were to be the test mobilization and the accompanying fleet review at Spithead. In previous years general maneuvers had been conducted in late July, but the Admiralty now felt that enough had been learnt from these exercises. The maneuvers of 1913, wherein one fleet had attempted to land raiding forces on the English coast, had been so successful for the "invaders" that the Admiralty ordered the exercises stopped in order to prevent the Germans learning too much.

Activation of all the reserve ships would test the system of mobilization, at the same time being a measure of economy, for the scheme was far cheaper than the six-week maneuvers. The idea of cost-paring was attractive to the Liberal Government, and, in addition, the exercise would provide a useful demonstration of Britain's naval strength.

On 12 July, the operation began. Junior flag officers were sent to each of the major ports to observe and identify any defects in the system, but the mobilization proceeded smoothly and they found little to report. There was one problem in that, since no state of emergency had been proclaimed, the reserves could not be called up, but some twenty thousand men came in as volunteers to the various manning depots and this enabled every ship in the War Plan to be put into service. The difficulty was that very few ships sailed with their assigned war complements.

Much work needed to be done, since the ships had all been laid up for at least twelve months with their machinery and equipment concealed under layers of grease and other preservatives. Nevertheless, it took but five days, from 12 July until 17 July, for the last ships of the Second and Third Fleets to depart their home ports and proceed to the review.

The assembly of ships which lay at Spithead for three days was the largest and most powerful ever seen: 24 dreadnought battleships and battle cruisers, 35 predreadnoughts, and 123 smaller vessels lay together under the White Ensign. The three fleets—the First, composed of the most modern operational ships; the Second, those ships which normally lay in harbor with reduced complements as an operational reserve; and the Third, the oldest vessels—comprised almost the entire Royal Navy. Only three battle cruisers, two predreadnoughts, and a few armored cruisers were absent on foreign stations. When the preparations for sea were complete, the fleets sailed on 20 July, passing the Royal Yacht *Victoria and Albert* as they left.

The situation in Europe still appeared relatively calm, but on that very day the Austro-Hungarian government warned Germany of its intention to issue a stiff ultimatum to Serbia on 23 July, an ultimatum couched in such terms that it was unlikely that Serbia would ever accept, for to do so would mean the virtual loss of that country's independence. The Kaiser still believed that Russia would not act, but he ordered that the German merchant marine be warned to take precautions with its ships abroad. The commanders on foreign stations were also informed of the situation while the Kaiser directed that the High Sea Fleet not disperse around the ports but remain concentrated in Norway.

The remaining German preparations were disjointed and confused. There was a division between the Foreign Ministry and the navy as to what Britain could do if war broke out between Russia and France and the Triple Alliance. The Foreign Ministry believed that Britain would remain neutral at least for a time, but the Admiralstab was still greatly concerned by the possibility that a preemptive attack would be made on the High Sea Fleet. What made the situation doubly confusing was the fact that not all the senior personnel in either department had been informed of the contents of the Austrian ultimatum. Not until the day after its issue would Admiral Frederick von Ingenohl, Commander in Chief of the High Sea Fleet, learn of the demand.

For a time the decision to send the fleet on to Norway hung in the balance, but the protests of the Foreign Ministry that its recall would aggravate the situation won the day and, late on 23 July, the Admiralstab ordered von Ingenohl to take the battle squadrons into Sogne Fiord. The gesture was wasted, for events began to move quickly. No mobilizations had yet occurred, but the possibility of war with Russia loomed large. At 1800 on 25 July, the Kaiser, who was in Sogne Fiord aboard the *Hohenzollern*, interviewed Admiral von Ingenohl and ordered him to take the fleet to the Baltic to prepare for war against Russia. Von Ingenohl was more realistic, predicting that war between the Triple Alliance and Russia would inevitably drag France and eventually Britain in on the side of the latter. He noted:

> I received verbal orders from the Kaiser . . . to take the fleet to the Baltic in order, in the event of war, to be able to strike the first blow at Russia. When I pointed out the danger of England taking part in the war, and the consequent necessity for having, at all events, the battleships in the North Sea, the Kaiser answered emphatically that there was no question whatever of England's intervention. In spite of repeated representations I could only succeed in obtaining permission to send the various units to their home ports, thus, at all events, enabling the larger proportion of the heavy ships and scouting craft to enter the North Sea.[2]

The High Sea Fleet started south.

For three days the British fleets had taken part in combined exercises. They finally parted company on 23 July, the date of issue of the Austro-Hungarian ultimatum. Sir George Callaghan took the First Fleet to Weymouth Bay, while the Second and Third Fleets left to return to their home ports. On the 24th, the Admiralty signaled to Callaghan, "First Fleet Squadrons all disperse on Monday 27th in accordance with your approved programme."[3]

Already the dreadnought *Bellerophon* had been detached to refit at Gibraltar, but the rest of the First Fleet had been kept together to give their crews some relaxation and to coal before the squadrons began their gunnery exercises. The Admiralty had therefore three days in hand before any decision had to be made on the disposition of the First Fleet.

The First Fleet was the most powerful naval force in the world, by itself larger than the entire Imperial Navy. The Second and Third Fleets were, when all was said and done, merely useful reinforcements. Although the Cabinet was first appraised of the ultimatum to Serbia at a meeting on 24 July, the First Lord, Winston Churchill, was content to let matters ride. He avoided taking precautions that were not yet wholly necessary and might only inflame the situation in Europe still further.

Meanwhile, the auxiliary branches of the Royal Navy which had been placed on a war footing for the test mobilization were disbanding and the ships involved returning to care and maintenance. The light cruiser *Amethyst* and the First and Second Destroyer Flotillas were sent into Portsmouth to give leave, while the Third Flotilla went to Harwich and the Fourth remained in the Irish ports. Were the situation to deteriorate further, it would be necessary for these ships and the three armored and four light cruisers also dispersed around the ports to be recalled to the fleet.

The German Naval Attaché noted the lack of warlike activity and reported it to Germany, where the news was greeted with much relief, especially in the Admiralstab. As if to emphasise the British desire for peace, on Sunday the 26th the First Lord went down to Cromer to be with his family. The First Sea Lord, Admiral Prince Louis of Battenberg, remained at the Admiralty to keep a watch on events. By noon that day the increasing tension between Russia and Austria-Hungary, accompanied by threats of mobilization, had caused the situation to deteriorate to such an extent that Churchill decided to return to London. Meanwhile, at 1600, on his own initiative, the First Sea Lord sent to the Commander in Chief, the order, "No ships of First Fleet or Flotillas are to leave Portland until further orders."[4] By the time Churchill returned to the Admiralty that night, the first restrictions on leave had been applied and the First Fleet was completing with coal.

The Russians, completely unprepared and in the midst of reorganizing their armies, did not want war. At Russia's advice, Serbia sent a conciliatory reply to the Austro-Hungarian ultimatum on 26 July. So conciliatory was this reply that when the Kaiser was informed of its general tenor he declared that Austria-Hungary had been given all she wanted. He ordered Chancellor von Bethmann Hollweg to dispatch a congratulatory telegram to the Austro-Hungarians. Unfortunately, the telegram was transmitted incomplete and the Austro-Hungarians did not receive the declaration included in the text that Germany could now see no reason for war.

The Germans did not comprehend quite how bent on war the Austro-Hungarians were. While the Admiralstab and the Imperial Foreign Ministry continued their soul searching over the movement of the High Sea Fleet back into German waters, the British Admiralty was taking a more realistic view. The silence of Austria-Hungary was ominous, the risk of war very high. As 27 July dawned, further measures were being applied. A press statement was issued:

> The Secretary of the Admiralty begs to state that it has been decided not to re-open the Schools after the maneuvers for the present; consequently the balance crews of the Second Fleet ships and vessels will remain in their ships.[5]

Orders were issued to bring the Second Fleet to full complement and to complete all ships with coal, ammunition, and stores. The remaining destroyers and torpedo boats were ordered out of reserve. The Admiralty specifically ordered that all these actions were to be carried out as unobtrusively as possible. The vast machinery of mobilization was beginning to move as orders were issued for patrols around the Scottish coast, major ports, and anchorages. A warning was sent out to Senior Naval Officers abroad that war between the Triple Alliance and the Triple Entente was becoming an increasing possibility:

> . . . This is not the warning telegram, but be prepared to shadow possible men-of-war, and consider dispositions of HM Ships under your command from this point of view. Measure is purely precautionary. The utmost secrecy is to be observed and no un-necessary person is to be informed.[6]

The aim of the Admiralty was to ensure that the Royal Navy was in its war stations well before it appeared inevitable that Britain would have to enter any war with Germany.

On 28 July Austria-Hungary rejected the Serbian note and declared war. In Russia the General Staff were urging the Tsar to mobilize. In an attempt to keep the war restricted to the Balkans, the Tsar ordered that the mobilization be confined to the units allocated against Austria-Hungary. The Kaiser, however, was thrown into a fury by the news that Russia would act. On the same day, the Naval Attaché in London informed the Admiralstab of what he knew of the Royal Navy's preparations.

The British had only a vague idea of the whereabouts of the High Sea Fleet and, with the deteriorating situation and the vulnerability of Portland to torpedo attack, the First Lord and the First Sea Lord determined to move the First Fleet to a position of safety. The Admiralty telegraphed the C in C:

> The First Fleet is to leave Portland tomorrow, Wednesday, for Scapa Flow. Destination is to be kept secret. . . .[7]

Sir George Callaghan was called to the Admiralty for consultations and the Grand Fleet, as it was henceforth to be known, was placed under the command of Vice Admiral Sir George Warrender for the operation. The destroyer flotillas were recalled, the Fourth hastening back from the Irish coast and the First and Second Flotillas recalling their men from leave as they prepared to depart Portsmouth. The Third was ordered to remain at Harwich, since the port was its war station. Even as Sir George Callaghan boarded his train to London, the ships of the Grand Fleet were moving out of the anchorage.

The conference at the Admiralty made several important changes to the plans for the Grand Fleet. Scapa Flow had been intended only as a preliminary base, to be used only in the period that war threatened, while Rosyth was to be the principal fleet base. Since neither had any submarine defenses, and because Scapa was the better anchorage—less prone to fog and largely protected from submarine penetration (it was thought) by its strong tides and numerous navigational hazards—the conference decided that the Grand Fleet was to remain in the Flow.

The second alteration was caused by a change of plans for the army. The Imperial General Staff had planned that the expeditionary force to France should begin crossing within hours of a declaration of war, but the government had not yet made the decision that any troops were to go. The political situation was complex and would not resolve itself until war had broken out.

While the Grand Fleet moved into the Channel, the Admiralty was putting its affairs into order. By now Germany had given Russia the ultimatum that, unless she end her mobilization against Austria-Hungary, Germany would in turn mobilize and declare war. All British leave was canceled on 29 July and, at the same time, the Warning Telegram was issued. This provided for most preparations and precautions short of actual war. The examination service for merchant ships was complete, awaiting only the final direction of the Admiralty to go into operation. As the last of this series of measures, the War Signal Stations and Naval Centers were connected to the general telegraphic network, thus putting the communications system onto a war footing.

Meanwhile, the German concern was primarily with the Russians, who were beginning to lay defensive mine fields in the Baltic. On 30 July the Kaiser ordered that precautionary measures be taken. Reports came in that day of the disappearance of the Grand Fleet and, though the British Foreign Secretary, Sir Edward Grey, informed the German Ambassador that the fleet's "movements were wholly free from any offensive nature and that it would not approach German waters," the Germans were certain that the Grand Fleet had gone to its war station—wherever that might be.

On 31 July, the most modern units of the High Sea Fleet were ordered to move to the North Sea ports through the Kiel Canal. The oldest predreadnoughts and armored cruisers would be sufficient to deal with the Russian Fleet. Patrols of light cruisers, torpedo boats, and submarines were set up around the Heligoland Bight and the Germans began to activate their own port defenses and examination service.

In the hope that Britain could still be kept out of the conflict, the Commander in Chief was ordered to keep the movements of all warships as quiet as possible. Not until 1 August was a general naval mobilization ordered, to start the next day, and still the Foreign Ministry insisted that no measures be taken which would risk war between Britain and Germany. The primary effect of this policy was that none of the merchant ships allocated as commerce raiders was allowed to begin its conversion, let alone sail, disrupting a major part of the Imperial Navy's war plans.

On 2 August, war broke out between Russia and Germany. The British Third Fleet ships began to receive their assigned war complements, the examination service went into operation, and the official chartering of trawlers for minesweeping began. The various supply ships needed to serve the Grand Fleet in its distant bases were being called up for service. Merchant ships had already been forbidden to use wireless inside British waters and the local defense and patrol flotillas were ordered to commence nighttime patrols. The order, "Mobilize Naval Reserves," went out—the final stage in the preparations. The Royal Navy was as ready as it could be for war.

The next day Germany declared war on France, and for twenty-four hours the position of Britain hung in the balance. The British government might not be willing to involve itself in a Continental war. The Germans seemed ready to agree not to attack the French northern coasts—an area which Britain had agreed to protect. The Government had, in fact, reassured the French of their support. On 2 August, Sir Edward Grey handed this note to the French Ambassador, Cambon:

> I am authorised to give an assurance that, if the German Fleet comes into the Channel or through the North Sea to undertake hostile operations against French coasts or shipping, the British Fleet will give all the protection in its power. . . .[8]

It was possible that this might have been enough. The German plan of attack against France, however, depended upon being able to move armies across Belgian territory. Such a movement would be clear violation of that country's neutrality; a neutrality which Britain had long promised by treaty to protect. As early as 31 July, the German government had been informed that Britain would not countenance any violation. The hope of peace lessened as Germany failed to make any reply. On 1 August, Sir Edward Grey repeated the warning to the German Ambassador. War between Britain and Germany could not be long delayed.

Churchill early saw the writing on the wall. As First Lord, the dispositions of the War Plan made, his attention now turned upon the problem of the fate of those warships completing in Britain for foreign powers. The Royal Navy was indeed larger than the Imperial Navy, but it was not so much more powerful that the addition of further units would not be of immense value. What is more, there was a possibility that some of these ships might eventually come under the control of hostile powers. While Britain would not receive such a clear windfall as Germany from the ships the latter had been building for Russia, there were several vessels very near to completion.

The most important units, and those with which Churchill was most concerned, were the battleships being completed for Turkey. The *Reshadieh* and the *Sultan Osman V* were very powerful ships, the former modeled on the *Iron Duke* class and the latter a design originally conceived for Brazil, carrying no less than fourteen 12″ guns. The First Lord insisted that the Turks, whose loyalties in the coming conflict were, at best, doubtful, could not be permitted to take the ships out of British hands.

On 2 August, Churchill and the Admiralty Board agreed to seize the ships. They were politely but firmly occupied by local troops and the Turks requested to leave, with the promise that the British would pay the Turkish government adequate compensation, as well as return the ships fully repaired after the emergency.

A number of smaller units being built for other countries were also requisitioned, including three Chilean flotilla leaders, four Greek destroyers, and three monitors for Brazil. Nevertheless, not all the ships under construction for foreign powers were immediately taken over. The Admiralty delayed some months before moving in on two 14″ gunned dreadnoughts building for Chile, and two light cruisers for Greek order were not taken over until 1915.

Churchill has since been accused of sacrificing the prospect of Turkey remaining neutral, or even becoming an ally of Great Britain, in exchange for the addition of these two battleships to the Royal Navy. In hindsight, it seems safe to say that Turkey's ancient hatred of Russia, the strong German political and economic influence in Turkey, and the later arrival in Turkish waters of Vice Admiral Wilhelm Souchon's famous squadron, the *Goeben* and *Breslau*, would all have combined to tip the balance in favor of the Central Powers. Perhaps, too, the decision was of value because it indicated the firmness with which Britain intended to deal with the situation.

The North Sea was to be the critical theater of operations for both British and Germans. Other engagements, such as the activities of Vice Admiral Maximilian von Spee's East Asiatic Squadron, and Souchon's escape to Turkey, might be important, but the crux of the matter was that Britain's eventual victory, however tardy that might be, depended upon preserving command of the sea and maintaining the blockade of the Central Powers.

Time was on Britain's side. As one by one the conventions of blockade were discarded and the definition of belligerent materials extended, the blockage would draw tighter about Germany, cutting off essential supplies of raw materials, oil, and food. By one means or another Germany had to render the Grand Fleet ineffective and destroy the blockade.

The blockade question had exercised the staffs of each navy for some years. The British had planned to institute a close blockade of Germany, setting up continuous patrols within sight of the German coasts which would attack any German sally or else, should the High Sea Fleet emerge in force, fall back upon battle squadrons in the vicinity. Exercises had, however, demonstrated that the capabilities of modern defensive weapons and the problems of fuel and wear on men and machinery would make close blockade costly and probably ineffective.

In consequence, the British drew the lines of the "distant" blockade around the perimeters of the North Sea. Patrols in the English Channel, supported by the Channel Fleet, closed off the North Sea to the south. Cruiser patrols were instituted in the various passages between the British Isles, the Faeroes, Iceland, and Greenland which gave access to the Atlantic. The Grand Fleet's anchorage at Scapa Flow was well positioned to support these northern patrols.

The problem for the British was that there were no first-class bases on the east or north coasts of Great Britain. Historical preoccupation with the French and more recent procrastination and false economies meant that Portsmouth, Devonport, and Chatham continued to be the major dockyards. The latter was well situated for the Channel Fleet, but the Grand Fleet had nothing at all. A badly damaged battleship might well be faced with a long passage to the southern dockyards west-about around the British Isles. In addition, the east coast had few patrols of any strength and fewer modern fortifications around its ports and harbors. The Royal Navy could not guarantee its safety from German raids.

On the other hand, the Germans were unable to attempt a military invasion in strength, for any such sortie would bring out both the Grand and Channel Fleets within twenty-four hours. And the landing of a German army sufficient to take over Britain (even assuming that the German army would provide the troops and the German merchant marine the ships) would take much longer than the time Napoleon had demanded from his admirals in 1802. The danger to the British lay rather in surprise bombardments, limited raids ashore, and mining operations.

The small German North Sea coast was much more completely fortified than the British and presented a formidable proposition to anyone contemplating amphibious operations on any scale. The outpost island of Heligoland, once a British possession, was perfectly situated in the Heligoland Bight to cut off attempts to penetrate the High Sea Fleet's anchorages. Nevertheless, elements in the Royal Navy, not least among whom was the First Lord, contemplated either an invasion in the Baltic, supported by the Russians, or else securing an island off the Frisian coast, such as Borkum, as a base for further operations. These schemes satisfied the Royal Navy's intense desire for offensive action, but they shared the defect of close blockade in that they were likely to prove a heavy drain on British strength.

The dominant feeling on both sides was one of uncertainty: uncertainty as to the outcome and uncertainty as to the capabilities of ships and men. The Royal Navy had not fought a major war at sea since 1815; the Germans, never. It had yet to be seen how the new weapons would perform and whether all the theorizing and exercising had produced practical policies in strategy and tactics.

CHAPTER 2

The British

Control of the Royal Navy was vested in the Lords Commissioners for executing the Office of the Lord High Admiral, jointly known as the Board of Admiralty. The system by which the Admiralty operated bears some explanation. At the head of the Board sat the First Lord, the minister responsible to Cabinet and to Parliament for the overall running of the navy. Two Civil Lords handled such matters as contracts and public works. The professional side of the Royal Navy was represented by the four Sea Lords. The First was responsible for the operations and fighting efficiency of the navy; the Second for personnel; the Third, or Controller, for warship design and construction; and the Fourth Sea Lord for stores, supply, and transport. The two other senior Admiralty officers were the Permanent Secretary, who was also a member of the Board and in charge of the administration of the department, and the Financial and Parliamentary Secretary, a junior member of Parliament (MP) who acted as assistant to the First Lord.

The peculiarity of the organization was this. Although in the evolution of the parliamentary system the politician acting as First Lord came to possess both the ultimate authority and responsibility for the navy, he could not act alone. The Admiralty had to function as a board. The First Lord, assisted by an officer who acted as his Naval Secretary, could appoint and dismiss the other Lords Commissioners by himself, but he could do little else. In consequence the Sea Lords possessed a powerful, though drastic, weapon in resignation. Were a First Lord to exceed his competence he might possibly find himself without colleagues and without anyone willing to take their place.

In practice the system normally worked well. As Professor Marder wrote, "the First Lords generally have been able men, skillful parliamentarians and possessed of the common sense to listen to professional advice and of the skill in human relations needed to get along with the Admirals."[1]

For their part, the Sea Lords accepted the First Lord's overall authority without question. They would protest, however, if the latter were to act without consulting them and if he were to interfere with professional matters or attempt to disrupt the properly constituted chain of command between the Admiralty, the commanders in chief, and their subordinates.

The present First Lord, Winston Leonard Spencer Churchill, was in many ways the most difficult—though certainly not the least competent—character conceivable for the job. At forty-one he had already served in government for nearly a decade, and as First Lord since 1911. He came to the Admiralty in the wake of the Agadir crisis, which had revealed an appalling lack of coordination between the war plans of the army and those of the navy and the complete lack of a proper staff organization within the Admiralty. Churchill had been charged by the Government to rectify the situation. Coming thus intent upon change and well known for championing social reform at the expense of the services' budgets, Churchill had been regarded with apprehension by the navy, and his reputation was not much improved by the passage of time. Although the new First Lord was soon persuaded of the need to build up the navy against the German menace, he was a difficult man with whom to work. Slightly contemptuous of senior officers, an attitude probably engendered by his experiences as a war correspondent in the Sudan and South Africa, with a highly retentive memory and a passionate interest in both the operational and material aspects of the navy, it was inevitable that Churchill should come into conflict with the admirals.

After failing with Sir Arthur Wilson and Sir Francis Bridgeman, Churchill was wise in his choice of Battenberg as First Sea Lord in 1912. The latter's tact and appreciation of the First Lord's tremendous desire to be up and doing smoothed over many dangerous conflicts, and where senior officers were infuriated by Churchill's interference in their jobs Battenberg commanded sufficient authority and respect to be able to still their complaints. Nevertheless, Churchill's relations with the Board were never comfortable. Sir John Jellicoe, when Second Sea Lord and prospective C in C First Fleet, complained that he sat "on a volcano here and may fall out so seriously with the First Lord any day that even if he did at one time intend offering me the command he might change his mind."[2]

Churchill was occasionally bested by the admirals, particularly when he forgot that he possessed no military authority as First Lord unless at least two members of the Board were assembled and in agreement. At sea a ship carrying two or more members of the Board of Admiralty would fly the distinguishing fouled anchor flag of the Lord High Admiral. Stephen King-Hall noted an incident during the 1913 maneuvers, when Winston Churchill

> proceeded to sea in a destroyer of exceptional speed called the *Swift* and made a considerable nuisance of himself rushing about the North Sea and alternately joining up with one of the two fleets. I was on the bridge of the *Neptune* when suddenly the *Swift* appeared over the horizon and Churchill began to send signals to the CinC (Sir George Callaghan) telling the latter what he thought his movements should be. The CinC became very annoyed and seizing a telescope examined the *Swift*. Then with a satisfied smile on his face he sent a signal: "C-in-C to *Swift*: What are those signals from the Board of Admiralty? I do not see Admiralty Flag." The *Swift* disappeared over the horizon at thirty knots.[3]

The First Sea Lord, Admiral Prince Louis Battenberg, was one of the most able officers of his generation. Connected by birth or marriage to almost every royal family in Europe, he was clever, charming, handsome, and athletic. Combining an admirable intellect, technical expertise, and a rare breadth of outlook, he also possessed considerable abilities as a strategist and tactician.

Unfortunately, although much respected in the service, Battenberg was regarded with suspicion by many in Britain for his German birth and intimate connections with that country. That he should have to fight Germany was a source of anguish for Prince Louis, but he was intensely loyal to Britain and to the Royal Navy. There was no love lost between the House of Hohenzollern and the Battenbergs and, in any case, as Prince Louis once tartly remarked, he had joined the Royal Navy before a united Germany existed. The problem was that, should the Royal Navy suffer any reverses in the coming war, Prince Louis would immediately be singled out by the popular press as the cause.

The First Sea Lord was also not physically well. He suffered from gout, a complaint that caused him considerable pain and greatly reduced his strength. The duties of the First Sea Lord were monumental in both peace and war, particularly because the system of command was so centralized, and required enormous energy. Study of the Admiralty documents of 1914 reveals that Prince Louis was rarely the initiator of plans or orders. Rather he judged what was presented to him, leaving the original thought to his subordinates. Given a properly organized naval staff and Battenberg's inherent soundness of judgment this might have worked very well, but it was not to be the case.

A War Staff had, in accordance with Churchill's direction, been established, but it was not functioning properly. Authority continued to be centralized at the highest level. Where, as had Prince Louis, the First Sea Lord devolved any of his functions to the Chief of the War Staff, the latter was unlikely to allow his subordinates any exercise of authority. As a result, the Chief of the War Staff was also overwhelmed by a mass of detail and thus less able to deal with the broad sweep of affairs.

Had Battenberg been a centralizer even the Chief of the War Staff would have had little power, for the difference between the Naval War Staff and the Imperial General Staff—indeed, most general staffs—was that the organization held no executive authority over operations. It existed only to advise the Board in theory and the members of the Board in practice. Legally, Battenberg had no authority to delegate any authority upon the Chief of the War Staff, although this did not deter him from so doing. A greater problem than the Chief of the War Staff's lack of power was that there was no one to whom the First Sea Lord could delegate administrative authority—a Deputy First Sea Lord, for example.

It was also true that few of the subordinate officers on the War Staff properly understood its functions and those who did, such as Captain Herbert Richmond, the Assistant Director of the Operations Division, tended to overreact in frustration. The navy was neither used to the staff principle nor educated in its purposes. The lack of education, of preparing officers to be "captains of war," as Churchill termed them, also meant that intellectual activity was not a feature of the Grand Fleet.

That an appreciation of the functions of a staff was lacking is indicated by the fact that Vice Admiral Sir Frederick Doveton Sturdee had taken over as Chief of the War Staff from Admiral Sir Henry Jackson in July 1914. Ostensibly he was suited to the position. He was a capable and innovative tactician well known in the service for his studies of naval history. He had enormous sea experience and had been not only Assistant Director of Naval Intelligence and Head of the 1911 Admiralty Submarine Committee but had also served as Admiral Lord Charles Beresford's Chief of Staff during the latter's command of the Channel Fleet. His strategic understanding, however, was faulty, and he was to display a singular misunderstanding of the lessons of history which he had studied so closely. He seemed convinced, for example, of the invulnerability of the capital ship, despite his acquaintance with submarines and his service as a torpedo specialist.

Worse, Sturdee was not one to make proper use of his subordinates. Rear Admiral Henry Oliver, the Director of Naval Intelligence, later described Sturdee as "a pompous man who would never listen to anyone else's opinion."[4] Richmond complained in August that "Sturdee goes about looking very important & mysterious & none of the naval assistants . . . is allowed to know what great issues are in contemplation. The result is that no one can help."[5]

It seems, in hindsight, that Sturdee was a man convinced of his own rectitude. When he was guiding discussion to his satisfaction no one could be more considerate to his juniors (he was described by a midshipman in the Channel Fleet in 1906 as "a dear"[6]), and Sturdee was at times far quicker than many of his contemporaries to keep his subordinates informed and involved. A formidable presence at the conference table, he had the confidence of both Churchill and Prince Louis. With the inexperience of the former and the preoccupations of the latter, Sturdee was to be responsible for much of the Admiralty's day-to-day policy in the early months of the war.

The junior Sea Lords, Vice Admiral Sir Frederick Hamilton, Rear Admiral Frederick Tudor, and Commodore Cecil Lambert, were distinguished more by their general competence and common sense than by any particular brilliance. They took little part in the normal direction of operations at sea but were always available to give advice and had to be consulted over and concur with decisions made by the Admiralty Board as a whole. In the absence of the First Sea Lord it was the Second Sea Lord who acted for him. All, particularly Sir Frederick Hamilton who had flown his flag afloat for four years, had much sea experience and it was especially galling for Lambert that he should be employed ashore at such a time.

There were a number of subordinate flag officers in the Admiralty, including Rear Admiral Horace Hood, the First Lord's Naval Secretary; Rear Admiral Alexander Duff, the Director of the Mobilization Division; Rear Admiral Arthur Leveson, Director of the Operations Division; and Rear Admiral Henry Oliver.

Horace Hood had been promoted rear admiral at the age of forty-two, the youngest flag officer since Sir David Beatty, and a great friend of the latter with a similar record of bravery in action. Although a hard worker and of a considerably greater intellect than Beatty, Hood was not finding his appointment as Naval Secretary a happy one. Having had a very pleasant relationship with Beatty between 1911 and 1913, Churchill had employed Hood at the first opportunity, but the earnest and conscientious Hood could not cope with the First Lord's passions and enthusiasms. He was, with Churchill's agreement, to seek the first opportunity for sea service.

Alexander Duff possessed one of the best minds in the Admiralty of 1914. An exceedingly competent sea officer, he had also rendered great service at the Admiralty in the Controller's Department and latterly in the Mobilization Division. The success of the recent test mobilization had in large measure been due to his work. He was due for relief, Rear Admiral Sidney Fremantle having been nominated, but the decision had been taken that Duff was to remain until matters settled down. Duff was regarded with tremendous respect throughout the navy, acknowledged as a leader of great presence and intellect. Despite the fact that his principal task had already been completed, little further use was to be made of his abilities in the months ahead.

Arthur Leveson was not a man well suited to his appointment. He did not enjoy staff duties and wanted to be at sea. In addition, he was neither eloquent in discussion nor fluent on paper. A firm believer in loyalty and obedience to his seniors, he was irritated by the attempts of his juniors (particularly Richmond) to initiate unsolicited proposals and was unlikely to question any directives from the First Sea Lord or the Chief of the War Staff. Leveson was typical of his generation in that, although there was no doubt of his moral courage or, indeed, his ability to make decisions when placed in independent command, he was convinced that the primary duty of the subordinate was obedience.

The redoubtable Henry Oliver had lately been installed as Director of Naval Intelligence, having served as naval secretary to Churchill for a few months. With an immense capacity for hard work, Oliver was as much an overcentralizer as any in the navy, famous for keeping his own counsel from seniors and juniors alike. On the other hand, he was a very shrewd and modest man, with a great tactical brain and the uncommon ability to demolish, with a few quietly spoken words, any ill-considered proposals with which he might be presented.

Despite the undoubted talent at the Admiralty and the legal responsibilities of the Board, there came into being an informal "War Group," consisting of the First Lord, First Sea Lord, Chief of the War Staff, and, for the first weeks, the Second Sea Lord. Though this arrangement was probably an inevitable solution and recognized the preeminent interest of the personnel involved in operations, it denied the responsibility of the junior Sea Lords and did nothing either to coordinate the activities of the various departments or to utilize the experience and ability available. Too often, for example, the War Group was to act as its own staff, its members involved in planning details which should have been left to more junior officers.

The command of the Grand Fleet was one of the first matters to be tackled by the First Lord in the crisis. Admiral Sir George Callaghan had been C in C of the First Fleet since 1911, having had his appointment extended by a year in December 1913. Vice Admiral Sir John Jellicoe had been nominated to succeed Callaghan at the end of 1914 but at the conference at the Admiralty on 29 July, Churchill and Battenberg suggested to the C in C that Jellicoe join the fleet immediately as his Second in Command.

Callaghan welcomed the idea. What he did not realize was that the Admiralty had decided to relieve him in the event of war. Churchill felt that Callaghan was getting too old and that his already fragile health would not stand the strain. Jellicoe was interviewed by the First Lord before his departure for sea and handed a sealed envelope containing his orders to take over as C in C. Churchill warned Jellicoe, who knew perfectly well what the contents were, that he would be instructed to open the envelope should war become imminent.

Jellicoe left on 31 July and by the time he arrived at the Scottish port of Wick, to be taken from there to Scapa Flow by the light cruiser *Boadicea*, he was having serious doubts as to the wisdom of the move. He telegraphed to Churchill and Battenberg that "the step you mentioned to me is fraught with gravest danger at this juncture." Jellicoe was well aware that the change of command would come as a grave shock to all concerned and could have a marked effect upon the morale of the fleet. On 2 August, after hoisting his flag in the *Centurion*, Jellicoe repeated his warning. But Churchill was determined to carry the thing through. "I can give you 48 hours after joining Fleet. You must be ready then." That night, Jellicoe replied,

> . . . am certain step contemplated is most dangerous. . . . Am perfectly willing to act onboard Fleet Flagship as assistant. . . . Hard to believe it is realised what grave difficulties change Commander-in-Chief involves at this moment. Do not forget also long experience of command of Commander-in-Chief.

Throughout 3 August, Jellicoe sent further messages attempting to change Churchill's mind, but the die was cast. The First Lord signaled,

> . . . I am telegraphing to the Commander-in Chief directing him to transfer command to you at earliest moment suitable to the interests of the Service. I rely on him and you to effect this change quickly and smoothly, personal feeling cannot count now, only what is best for us all, you should consult with him frankly.

It must have come as a terrible shock to Callaghan to be roused early on the morning of 4 August with the bald message that

Their Lordships have determined upon, and H.M. The King has approved, the appointment of Sir John Jellicoe as Commander-in-Chief. You are to strike your flag forthwith, embark in the *Sappho* or other cruiser, and come ashore at Queensferry, reporting yourself at the Admiralty thereafter at your earliest convenience. These orders are imperative.

Though he knew Jellicoe was intended as his successor, Callaghan had no idea that his appointment would be cut short, and it was all the more surprising because he had been given absolutely no intimation of the proposed change at his conference at the Admiralty only a few days before. The matter might well have been dealt with far more gently by Churchill, but it is to the credit of both Callaghan and Jellicoe that they accomplished the transfer of command without delay and that their old friendship remained unimpaired, so much so that Callaghan was to stand godfather to Jellicoe's son four years later.

When the news was broken to the fleet the reaction was one of shock and surprise. Callaghan was much admired by his subordinates, and they felt it grossly unfair that he who had trained and prepared the navy for war should be dismissed in such a cavalier fashion. Captain C. J. Wintour, commanding the Fourth Destroyer Flotilla, noted in his journal that the supersession would "cause widespread indignation."[7] Of the flag officers, Beatty, Warrender, and Acting Vice Admiral Sir Lewis Bayly were moved so far as to send messages of protest to the Admiralty.

In the event, the fleet's indignation was short-lived. The two officers concerned behaved with such propriety that there was really nothing to be said. The Admiralty for its part did no more than gently reprove the senior officers for making their protest, and Jellicoe quickly gained the respect and confidence of all. Perhaps, too, the ill feeling was tempered by the realization that Callaghan, a "grand old man" at the end of his sea-going career, would not have stood up to the enormous mental and physical strains of wartime command.

When Acting Admiral Sir John Jellicoe assumed the appointment of Commander in Chief Grand Fleet, he came to the post as the culmination of a career that seemed entirely devoted to preparing him for this task. Jellicoe was born in 1859, the son of a merchant captain, and joined HMS *Britannia* as a cadet in 1871. He soon distinguished himself in the service as an unusually able and hard-working officer, popular with both subordinates and contemporaries, modest and unassuming, but very much a leader.

He came early to the attention of Admiral of the Fleet Lord Fisher, for Jellicoe made gunnery his specialization and did splendid work in both training and technical development. Fisher realized Jellicoe's potential and, by the time he was First Sea Lord, Fisher began to think of Jellicoe as Britain's future "Admiralissimo" in the event of a war with Germany. Unlike many of Fisher's other selections, his choice of Jellicoe was not to be faulted by other factions in the service, despite the fact that Jellicoe had been intimately involved with the introduction of many of Fisher's technical innovations.

Alternating between successively more important Admiralty appointments such as Director of Naval Ordnance, and Controller, and commands at sea, Jellicoe continued to build up a reputation for quiet brilliance in all he did. He remained untarnished by the Fisher-Beresford controversies and was probably, after Prince Louis of Battenberg, the most popular senior officer in the service at large.

That Jellicoe was a chronic overcentralizer and addicted to detail was not at this time remarkable. He was not, as was to be the case later in the war, physically and mentally worn out. He was a very easy man for whom to work, for Jellicoe possessed great natural courtesy and was above all consistent in decision. In the relatively simple and spacious days of the early twentieth century, it was considered natural for senior officers to involve themselves with the most minute details in their command. In a service of overcentralizers, Jellicoe was not unusual.

The new Commander in Chief crowned his growing reputation as the coming "man of the hour" during the 1913 naval maneuvers. It was he who handled his command, which represented an invading German naval force, so well that the exercises were hastily curtailed lest the Germans learn too much from them.

Having been responsible in previous years for many of the material aspects of the Royal Navy, Jellicoe knew all the strengths and weaknesses of his fleet; perhaps he knew them too well, for his dispositions of the Grand Fleet were rarely to give any indication of the flair and style of 1913.

There was no doubt that Churchill had chosen the right man and the appointment was well received in Britain. Lord Fisher, of course, was particularly delighted and Churchill was wise enough subsequently to treat Sir George Callaghan as kindly as he could, ensuring that he went as C in C The Nore as soon as that command became vacant at the end of 1914. (The Nore is the sandbank in the center of the estuary of the Thames River, which gave its name to the naval command embracing the estuary and the adjacent coast.)

Churchill arranged for Rear Admiral Charles Madden to join the Grand Fleet as Chief of Staff. Madden's and Jellicoe's wives were sisters, and the two officers were old friends who worked well with each other. Madden was an austere but efficient officer with a formidable capacity for hard work. Not without a sense of humor, he was an admirable second to

Jellicoe and was to be a great support to the latter in the years ahead. Apart from his secretary, Jellicoe determined to retain Callaghan's staff, who included Commodore First Class Alan Everett, Captain of the Fleet and a steady man who was to render the C in C much good service.

Acting Vice Admiral Sir Lewis Bayly was commander of the First Battle Squadron. Aggressive and energetic, Bayly had extensive experience at sea, having already commanded successively the Home Fleet Destroyers, the First Battle Cruiser Squadron, and the Third Battle Squadron, appointments broken only by command of the War College. He was a keen student of naval strategy and would be a leading advocate of the active employment of the large numbers of predreadnoughts which the Royal Navy had at its disposal in 1914.

To his detriment, he thought of sea power only in terms of major units. Well versed in the exploits of the British fleets in the continental wars of the eighteenth and nineteenth centuries, he did not appreciate that technology had ended the invulnerability of the capital ship and had invalidated many of the historical "lessons" he held so dear. In consequence, Bayly's arguments went unheeded in the Grand Fleet and his ideas were dismissed by most, including Jellicoe, as impractical. This was unfortunate, for Bayly's eagerness to be at the enemy's throat might otherwise have acted as an effective counterpoise to his new Commander in Chief's perhaps excessive prudence.

Bayly's second in command in the squadron was Rear Admiral Hugh Evan-Thomas, a quiet and efficient officer who was much more to Jellicoe's taste than his chief.

The urbane and popular Vice Admiral Sir George Warrender commanded the Second Battle squadron, which consisted of the most modern 13.5″ gun dreadnoughts. He had a reputation in the service as a tactician and thinker and was certainly more aware than most of the political and strategic aspects of the war. Warrender was suffering, however, from increasing deafness and ill-health and his performance at sea was to be disappointing. His second in the squadron was the redoubtable Rear Admiral Sir Richard Arbuthnot. The latter was a formidable disciplinarian who possessed a single-minded belief in the merits of physical training. He was hard on all who served under him and permitted no deviation from the King's Regulations and Admiralty Instructions except his own. A humorless and severe character, he survived in the navy only because he never subjected his subordinates to any experience he would not undergo himself.

Vice Admiral Edward Bradford and Rear Admiral Montague Browning led the *King Edward VII* class predreadnoughts of the Third Battle Squadron. Bradford was a calm and resolute officer with much sea experience who had been employed afloat almost continuously since he was promoted rear admiral in 1908.

The Fourth, smallest of the battle squadrons, had as its commander Vice Admiral Sir Douglas Gamble, who flew his flag in the *Dreadnought*. Gamble had headed the naval mission to Turkey in 1909 and had done much good work there. He was unusually experienced in staff work, having also served in the Intelligence Division and as a naval attaché. At fifty-seven, however, Gamble was one of the oldest flag officers afloat and was not to remain at sea for long.

The Third Battle Squadron joined the Grand Fleet a few days after the outbreak of war. This squadron consisted of three predreadnoughts, formerly of the Second Fleet, under Rear Admiral Stuart Nicholson.

Jellicoe had every operational dreadnought battleship in the Royal Navy under his command, a total of twenty—ten of the 13.5″ gunned "super" dreadnoughts and ten with 12″ guns. In the few weeks he could expect to be joined by two more *Iron Duke* class battleships, as well as the two ex-Turkish units.

Attached to the Grand Fleet proper were two squadrons of armored cruisers, the Second under Rear Admiral Somerset Gough-Calthorpe, and the Third under Rear Admiral William Pakenham. Gough-Calthorpe was a modest and reserved officer, but he had an acute brain, having rendered distinguished service as a torpedo specialist, as Captain of the Fleet to Admiral Sir William May, and as the Admiralty's representative at the *Titanic* enquiry.

William Pakenham was one of the Royal Navy's great characters. As British observer in the Japanese fleet during the war with Russia, he had astonished even the Japanese by his imperturbability and coolness under fire. Absolutely fearless and the soul of honor, he also possessed an immense sense of humor. He was a good cruiser admiral and a fine leader of men.

The Grand Fleet's six large light cruisers were formed into the First Light Cruiser Squadron, commanded by Commodore Second Class William Goodenough. Goodenough was a sea officer in the finest sense of the term. Apart from one or two lapses in the early months of the war, he was to handle his squadron with consummate skill and great distinction. Goodenough really understood tactics and the proper functions of his ships, and he could draw loyal and wholehearted service from his subordinates.

Two other cruiser squadrons, the Sixth, consisting only of the armored cruisers *Drake* and *King Alfred* under Rear Admiral William Grant, and the Tenth, under Rear Admiral Dudley De Chair, were allocated to the northern patrols. De Chair's eight *Edgar* class cruisers were among the oldest in service and were, because of their age and condition, only in the area as a stop-gap. Dudley De Chair was a competent officer with a strict sense of propriety and duty. A friend of Jellicoe, he served for a time as Churchill's Naval Secretary, but the relationship had not been a happy one. De Chair later came to command all the forces assigned to the patrols for the northern blockade and his abilities well suited him for that arduous and thankless duty.

In total, the Grand Fleet had eight modern and ten elderly armored cruisers on its strength, as well as Goodenough's six light cruisers, and four older and smaller vessels of the latter type which were attached to each of the principal battle squadrons. Two destroyer flotillas were directly attached to the Grand Fleet. These were the Second, under Captain J. R. P. Hawksley in the light cruiser *Active*, with twenty H class destroyers, and the Fourth, under Captain C. J. Wintour in the leader *Swift*, with twenty K class destroyers.

At this time, still an integral part of the Grand Fleet was the First Battle Cruiser Squadron under Acting Vice Admiral Sir David Beatty. This consisted only of four battle cruisers, all that were immediately available. Three more were in the Mediterranean, the RAN's *Australia* in the Pacific, and the last, the *Invincible*, was hastily completing a major refit.

The youngest flag officer since Nelson and the darling of the popular press, David Beatty had enjoyed a meteoric career in the navy since he first distinguished himself as a gunboat captain on the Nile in 1898. Promotion to Commander and award of the DSO had followed. During the campaign after the Boxer Rebellion in China, Beatty again displayed great gallantry and was promoted captain well before his time. Marriage to Ethel Tree, divorced daughter of the American millionaire Marshall Field, had earned him a certain notoriety, but he continued to flourish in cruiser commands and as the Naval Liaison Officer on the Army Council. Command of the predreadnought *Queen* in the Atlantic Fleet followed, and during this time Beatty came under the eye of Prince Louis of Battenberg.

By 1909, Beatty had arrived at the top of the Post List. Yet because of his service with the Army Council and because of time spent on half-pay recovering from wounds, he had not served the necessary six years in command at sea which was the requirement for promotion. An exception was made and a special Order-in-Council promulgated allowing his promotion to rear admiral on the Active List—at the age of 39.

In 1910, Beatty was offered the appointment of Second in Command of the Atlantic Fleet. He refused it. Whatever reasons Beatty had, this decision caused a great deal of bitterness amongst his seniors and contemporaries. Sea commands were scarce and valuable and to reject one, perhaps in the hope of better things, smacked of arrogance of the worst kind. Beatty, the rumor went, would not be offered another job and would soon be retired under the unemployment clauses.

But Beatty was introduced to Winston Churchill shortly after the latter became First Lord. The young politician and the young admiral appealed enormously to each other. Beatty became the First Lord's Naval Secretary. As such, Beatty acted as liaison officer for the political head of the navy. Although far junior to most of the members of the Admiralty Board, propinquity ensured that the Naval Secretary was likely to have great influence on the First Lord. Most important, the Naval Secretary was the man responsible for arranging flag officers' appointments. Unless he crossed Churchill, Beatty could pick his next post.

In 1913, with Churchill's wholehearted approval, Beatty was appointed Rear Admiral Commanding the First Battle Cruiser Squadron. It was the finest job available for a junior flag officer. The carping comments which were the inevitable accompaniment were soon settled by Beatty's undoubted competence at handling his ships.

With the outbreak of war, Beatty received yet another advancement. It had been the Admiralty's intention that the officer commanding the battle cruisers attached to the Grand Fleet should be the senior cruiser admiral and directly responsible to the C in C for the tactical employment of the fleet's scouting forces. This logical arrangement had (much to Beatty's rage) been placed in jeopardy by the appointment of Rear Admiral Grant, next above Beatty on the flag list, to the Sixth Cruiser Squadron. To remedy this unsatisfactory situation, on 2 August 1914, Beatty was appointed an Acting Vice Admiral, at least a year before he could expect a promotion to that rank.

As soon as the *Invincible* completed her refit, Rear Admiral Sir Archibald Gordon Moore was to hoist his flag in her as second flag officer in the battle cruisers. Moore was an assiduous worker who had achieved a considerable reputation when Director of Naval Ordnance for his championship of the 15″ gun. Though a competent enough officer, he did not get on at all well with Beatty—a situation which was to bring about unfortunate results in later months.

The forces in the south were much more loosely organized. Eighteen predreadnoughts under Vice Admiral Sir Cecil Burney constituted the Channel Fleet. Burney was a steady officer and a fine seaman who had distinguished himself in the Mediterranean by the tact and forbearance he displayed during international naval operations connected with the end of the Second Balkan War. Burney was an old and trusted friend of Jellicoe's, and the latter had every confidence in the commander of the

Channel Fleet. Burney, however, was no great thinker or man of action. Being content to follow where others led and execute rather than initiate plans, he was a far better subordinate than an independent commander.

Burney, who also commanded the Fifth Battle Squadron from the *Lord Nelson*, had two divisional commanders, Rear Admiral Bernard Currey and the competent Rear Admiral Cecil Thursby. Vice Admiral the Hon. Sir Alexander Bethell commanded the Eighth Battle Squadron in the *Prince George*, assisted by Rear Admiral Henry Tottenham in the *Albion*. By a narrow margin, Bethell was the oldest officer in command afloat in home waters, but he was a shrewd and experienced officer who as Commandant of the War College in 1913 had done much to encourage the growth of that establishment.

The only light forces directly attached to the Channel Fleet were four light cruisers, one of which was soon to be detached. The intention was that the destroyer flotillas based on Harwich could support the predreadnoughts if they ventured into the North Sea and, if the fleet should move south, destroyers from Dover or the home ports could do the job.

Between Jellicoe and Burney was interposed a collection of units the Admiralty later came to describe as the "Southern Force." Rear Admiral Arthur Christian was named as the officer in command on 16 August. The heavy units consisted of five old armored cruisers, designated Force C, under Christian in the *Euryalus* and Rear Admiral Henry Campbell in the *Bacchante*. Despite their age, these ships were intended as the heavy support for all the light forces which operated out of Harwich.

Commodore Second Class Reginald Tyrwhitt, flying his broad pendant in the light cruiser *Amethyst* as Commodore (T), commanded the flotillas which were soon to become famous as the "Harwich Force." The First and Third Flotillas, led by the light cruisers *Fearless* and *Amphion*, consisted of a total of thirty-five destroyers. Tyrwhitt was to prove himself one of the finest sea commanders in the navy. A skilled seaman, with an acute tactical brain and an interest in modern technology and its practical application to naval warfare, he was also an immensely popular leader.

Roger Keyes, another commodore second class, was the Superintending Commodore of the Submarine Service, known as Commodore (S). He also had direct charge of the Eighth (or Overseas) Submarine Flotilla, consisting of a depot ship and sixteen D and E class submarines, as well as the Sixth Flotilla, which was based on the Humber with six of the most modern C class boats. Keyes was in a peculiar position in the navy because he was responsible direct to the Admiralty for the Submarine Service as a whole, but also to Rear Admiral Christian and to the C in C

Grand Fleet for the operational employment of his submarines. Keyes was an intensely energetic officer who had displayed signal bravery as a Lieutenant during the Boxer Rebellion. Young for his rank, he was always thinking up new means for using his submarines and attacking the Germans. A fellow spirit to and close friend of Tyrwhitt and Beatty, he was to make every use of his relationship with the Admiralty for putting his plans before the First Lord and the War Group.

The next major operational command was that of Commodore First Class George Ballard, the Admiral of Patrols. As such, Ballard was responsible for the coordination of the operations of all light forces not directly attached to the fleets or otherwise under the immediate orders of the C in C Grand Fleet or the Commanders in Chief of the home ports. The idea behind the creation of this post before the war had been to ensure that resources devoted to coastal defense and local patrols were not disposed of by competitive commands in counterproductive ways.

Assisted by Captain Edward Lowther-Crofton, Ballard had forces scattered around the east coast under his command. The principal base was Dover, which had temporarily a total of four light cruisers, twenty elderly destroyers, and fourteen small submarines operating from the port. These ships were principally occupied with the protection from the north of the shipping lanes between Britain and France. Four predreadnoughts of the *Majestic* class were assigned to Ballard for the protection of the Humber. They were led by Captain Roland Nugent in the *Victorious*.

The Nore, under Admiral Sir Reginald Poore, had twelve old destroyers and twenty torpedo boats. Apart from local patrols, these ships also provided some protection for the Channel Fleet when it was at its anchorages. There were also six C class submarines allotted for coastal defense. Admiral Sir Hedworth Meux at Portsmouth had at his disposal six destroyers and twenty-three torpedo boats, while at Devonport, under Admiral Sir George Egerton, which was furthest to the west and least involved in operations, there were only four destroyers and eight torpedo boats.

There were considerable forces involved in commerce patrols in western waters and the Channel. The bulk of these were in fact French, working out of the Atlantic ports and assigned for the protection of the all-important shipping routes to Britain. The French ships involved were under the overall command of Rear Admiral Rouyer and consisted of a total of fourteen cruisers, thirty-one destroyers, twenty-three submarines, and a large number of smaller units.

In addition, Cruiser Force G, made up of four *Talbot* class cruisers under Rear Admiral Rosslyn Wemyss, was allocated to the Channel. Wemyss, a clever and cultivated officer who spoke fluent French, had been specially appointed to the duty for his ability to deal with his country's ally.

Five more old cruisers constituted the Eleventh Cruiser Squadron, Cruiser Force E, under Rear Admiral Robert Phipps Hornby. These ships patrolled the southern approaches to the Irish Sea.

Finally, of the forces already operational, seven cruiser minelayers, under Captain Mervyn Cobbe, were temporarily stationed at Dover. These ships were antique third class cruisers which had been converted to carry mines. Their operational capabilities were as uncertain as those of the weapons they carried.

By the outbreak of war, mobilization of auxiliary units was in full swing. A large number of merchant ships had been taken up for conversion to armed merchant cruisers and twenty-one would be in commission by the end of August. The bulk of these ships was sent to reinforce the cruiser squadrons employed on blockade duties, where they proved far more efficient and weatherly than the old cruisers. More than two hundred trawlers were being hired or requisitioned outright and sent to the major ports and anchorages for examination duties, local patrols, and minesweeping.

In the matter of personnel, those of the Royal Navy were generally of the highest quality, with the important exception that the abilities of senior officers frequently left much to be desired. There were a variety of reasons for this situation, but two major factors may be isolated. The first was that the navy's establishment had expanded enormously between 1889 and 1914; as a consequence, a large percentage of the officers who entered before 1880 had been promoted to post and flag rank. The size of the selection pool was not sufficient to ensure that all who received advancement possessed adequate ability.

The second point concerned the frequent lack of initiative on the part of senior officers. The presence of an Admiral, it seemed, paralyzed the initiative and common sense of the British commanders at sea. Added to this came frequent Admiralty interference by wireless. Left to his own devices, the British officer almost without exception would rise to the occasion admirably. With a flag officer present the doctrine, "Follow the senior officer's movements," seemed to apply without exception. Even subordinate flag officers would, it soon proved, rarely be persuaded to act without reference to their seniors.

Why this should be so is a complex question and one outside the scope of this book. It could not be because the Royal Navy no longer had so many small units scattered worldwide under independent commanders, because the era of the gunboat fleets had ended only ten years before. Perhaps the reason was that promotion to captain depended upon success as the commander of a big ship, and he who succeeded was the first to have his ship follow the senior officer's movements. Or perhaps the situation had come about as a result of the nineteenth-century system of officer training. It seems, however, that the phenomenon was manifested in the Royal Navy only in the 1914–18 War and that the syndrome was confined to officers above a certain age—Beatty, at forty-three, seems to have marked the beginning of a return to the old ways.

If the admirals were, with some exceptions, an unremarkable group, the same could not be said for the Captains' List. There were some talented officers in command of ships or at the Admiralty in 1914. Apart from Goodenough, Keyes, and Tyrwhitt, they included Reginald Hall, the brilliant Captain of the *Queen Mary* who was to make his name as Director of the Intelligence Division; Ernle Chatfield of the *Lion*, future First Sea Lord and Minister of Defence; and William Wordsworth Fisher, Captain of the *St Vincent*, a formidable and outspoken all-rounder who was one of the youngest captains on the list. There were more: J. S. Dumaresq of the *Shannon*; Osmond de B. Brock of the *Princess Royal*; Francis Kennedy of the *Indomitable*; Richmond in the Operations Division; the list goes on. Perhaps the misfortune of the Royal Navy was that these officers were not ten years older in 1914.

The more junior officers were equally good. The training and education systems had improved over the years and expert "deep" specialists were available in abundance. The traditional preeminence of the gunnery school was being challenged at last by the torpedo specialists and the renascent navigation branch.

The situation with the lower deck was similarly satisfactory. Royal Navy ratings were entered, after training, on a twelve-year engagement. On completion of this time, many remained in the service for further, shorter engagements in order to qualify for pensions. In consequence, and also because ships normally did a two- or three-year commission with the same crew, the levels of expertise and efficiency were very high indeed. They were to remain high for the duration of the war, despite a considerable leavening by reservists.

There were problems. The arrangements whereby seamen could gain commissions were inadequate and the conditions under which ratings worked and lived were barely acceptable. Captain Reginald Hall did much to improve the situation in *Queen Mary* by easing discipline, installing proper washing facilities, and introducing a host of other small but welcome amenities. It was, however, to be some years before all other ships followed suit. Perhaps the greatest deficiency was that inadequate use was made of the abilities of warrant and chief petty officers, especially the latter. Except in the smallest ships, junior officers

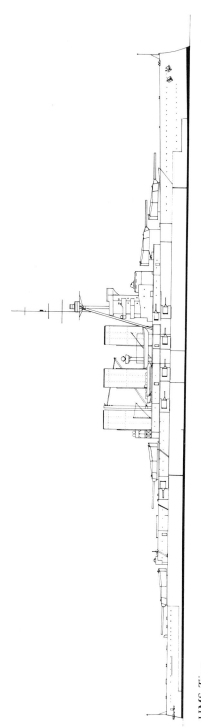

HMS *Tiger*

were inclined to oversupervise evolutions and failed to make proper use of their senior ratings.

The Royal Navy seemed in terms of ships available to be reasonably well prepared for war. The situation was likely to improve in the long term, for there were ten 15″ gun battleships in hand and a 13.5″ gun battle cruiser, the *Tiger*, only a few months from completion. In addition, two 14″ gun battleships building for Chile could be requisitioned. Large numbers of light cruisers and destroyers were building and the Admiralty also felt confident that many of the ships deployed to foreign stations could be recalled as soon as they had dealt with the German forces at large.

Since the war was adjudged likely to be short, there seemed as yet no necessity to embark upon a program of war construction. Orders were put out that construction already in hand was to be expedited, but other contracts were to be canceled. The latter included the four battleships proposed in the 1914 program and a variety of other units.

British ships were on the whole well designed and constructed, being good sea boats with a reasonable balance of the various qualities required of warships. There were, however, drawbacks, particularly with the battle cruisers. With the possible exception of the brand new *Tiger*, all were independently armored over their vital regions and suffered further from the fault that flash from an explosion in a turret could penetrate to the magazines and cause the loss of the ship. The battleships shared this latter design defect, but were to be protected from its consequences in war by their thicker armor.

The Royal Navy had also not mastered the complexities of designing underwater protection, and this was the greatest universal defect. Even the most modern battleships were to display alarming weaknesses to damage by mine or torpedo. Ton for ton, the British ships were not as efficient fighting units as the German ships they faced. On the other hand, they were larger and more heavily armed. Half the battle line of the Grand Fleet carried 13.5″ guns, but the largest German weapon was only 30.5 cm. The Imperial Navy's units required all their extra armor and more complete subdivision to face the British guns.

The newer British armored cruisers, especially the *Warrior* class, were well-balanced and efficient designs, although they had been rendered largely obsolete by the battle cruisers. The oldest cruisers were often liabilities, with poor protection, great coal consumption, and dubious seaworthiness. In many, the casemates containing the 6″ guns of the secondary armament were sited so near to the waterline that they were unworkable in a seaway.

The *Town* class light cruisers were splendid ships, the finest of their type in the world. Well armed and adequately armored, weatherly and with a good turn of speed, they contradicted Lord Fisher's thesis that cruisers were of little use in modern warfare. It was as a result of Fisher setting his face against cruisers during his term as First Sea Lord between 1904 and 1910 that the Royal Navy did not have nearly as many modern cruisers as it wanted. A new class of smaller light cruisers was nearing completion. Designed at Churchill's behest specifically for operations in the North Sea, the *Auroras* were to prove very effective units.

The destroyer force was not nearly as large as the commanders, particularly Jellicoe, would have liked, but it was probably adequate for the demands of the war. From the completion of the first of the type in 1893, the British had led the world in destroyer design, and they continued to do so with the new L and M classes. The maximum speed of the new destroyers had risen to 36 knots, and with three 4" guns and four 21" torpedo tubes, they were powerful indeed.

The situation was equally satisfactory with regard to the submarine forces. The E class submarines were without doubt the best in the world in 1914 and their capabilities had been recognized by the designation of the Eighth as the "Overseas" Submarine Flotilla. Within months the E class submarines were to demonstrate their efficiency not only in the North Sea but in the Baltic and the Bosporus as well. The standard 21" torpedo was not, however, a particularly effective weapon; the contact pistol and the depth-keeping mechanism were unreliable, and the weapon's explosive power left much to be desired.

The minor arms of warfare were not well equipped. The only operational minelayers were the elderly excruisers lying at Dover. Converted between 1909 and 1910, these ships were completely unsuitable for offensive minelaying operations, being nearly a quarter of a century old and with a sustained speed of less than 20 knots. The mines they carried were equally bad. Little or no attention had been devoted by the Admiralty to the subject and, as a result, in 1914 British moored contact mines possessed little destructive power, were unlikely to explode if struck, and often broke their cables and went adrift within days of being laid. The British had little enthusiasm for mine warfare, principally because of the indiscriminate destruction which a mine field could cause and the resultant complications of international law. A hesitant Government refused to allow the navy to risk annoying the neutral nations until the Germans had done so.

Similarly, although a number of old torpedo gunboats had been converted to minesweepers, there were not enough units to protect the major ports and anchorages. Large numbers of trawlers were soon being converted to sweepers, but the Royal Navy possessed little expertise in the subject and was forced to rely upon the seamanship of the thousands of fishermen in the reserve.

The gun reigned supreme in the Royal Navy of 1914, but although the weapons themselves were sound enough, their control system and the shells they fired were inadequate. For just over twenty years the British had been engaged in a search for the solution to the gunnery problem. That is, they sought a method by which, whatever the movements of the gunnery platform and its target, an accurate firing solution could be derived out to the extreme visible range of the guns. The first step had been made in the 1890s when Captain Percy Scott demonstrated the enormous improvements in accuracy which were possible by improving the training of gunlayers.

Matters had come a long way since, but there was still much to do. The 12" or 13.5" guns were ballistically capable of accurate shooting out to 16,000 yards or more, but this was beyond the capabilities of the individual turret captains and gunlayers to achieve. Two things were required. The first was a system by which all guns could be controlled from one position in the ship; the second, a means by which the future position of the target could be predicted to determine the range setting for the next salvo.

The first problem was well in hand, for Sir Percy Scott, now an admiral, had devised a "director" which laid and controlled the entire main armament from one point high up in the ship. Although only a few battleships and battle cruisers had yet been fitted, use of the director was to be extended to all heavy ships as they came in for refit.

The second matter was a source of much controversy. The gunnery problem was extremely complex, for it involved not only the course and speed of the firing ship and the course and speed of the target, but also a host of other factors such as the lateral and vertical movement of the firing platform in a seaway, and the humidity and resultant denseness of the air. A perfectly adequate computer, known as the Argo System, which was to form the substantial basis of the Royal Navy's visual fire control systems twenty years later, had already been produced by a civilian inventor, Arthur Pollen. The Argo System was in fact one of the first really practical analogue computers.

For a variety of reasons, however, Pollen's apparatus had been rejected in favor of that of Captain Frederick Dreyer, a protégé of Jellicoe's who had a great name as a gunnery expert. The Dreyer Table was a vastly inferior system, the better points of which had been plagiarized from Pollen. Few heavy ships that had been fitted with the Dreyer Table during the war were to make much use of it, because results from even the primitive pre-1914 firing practices had demonstrated that a skilled

Admiral Sir John Jellicoe on
board HMS *Iron Duke*. (IWM)

Vice Admiral Sir Cecil Burney.
(Pictured as an admiral) (IWM)

Admiral His Serene Highness Prince Louis of Battenburg. (IWM)

Commodore Reginald Tyrwhitt and Mrs. Tyrwhitt. (Pictured on board HMS *Centaur* in 1918) (IWM)

Commodore William Goode-
nough. (IWM)

Vice Admiral Sir David Beatty.
(Pictured as an admiral) (IWM)

Admiral Sir George Callaghan

Vice Admiral Sir Doveton Sturdee (pictured as an admiral) and Commodore Roger Keyes (pictured as a rear admiral) in 1917. (IWM)

The Right Honorable Winston
Churchill. (IWM)

spotting officer was a more efficient computer. Only a few ships carried
the Argo apparatus and their gunnery was always good.

The system of firing practices did not help matters. Up until the
outbreak of the war only shoots conducted were at stationary targets
in good visibility at ranges of no more than 10,000 yards. Beatty, with
Callaghan's permission, had conducted firings at a towed target at a
range of 16,000 yards in 1914, but these were experimental. In any case,
the results had been appalling.

The gunnery problem was one very close to Jellicoe's heart and,
despite his misguided faith in Dreyer (who soon became Flag Captain in
the *Iron Duke*), he was to do a tremendous amount to raise the gunnery
standards of the Grand Fleet. What no one realized was that the quality
of the heavy armor-piercing shells was extraordinarily poor. Although
fighting ranges had greatly increased in the previous twenty years, there
had been little or no research to determine the resultant effect upon
projectiles. In fact, the British shells were designed to strike their target
perpendicular, or nearly so, to the vertical. Firing at long ranges,
however, resulted in projectiles arriving at an oblique angle—at which
they did not penetrate but broke up harmlessly on the armor.

A poor system of quality control meant that other defects were common. Jellicoe himself, when Controller, had some inkling of the problems but the Admiralty had determined that the insufficient terminal velocity of heavy armor-piercing shells would prevent their penetration at long ranges in any case. In consequence, the problem of oblique strike was ignored, and the cheerful recommendation was made that high explosive or common shell be used at ranges over 10,000 yards.

The Royal Naval Air Service was in good condition, the largest in the world. The failure of lighter-than-air machines had caused the Admiralty to concentrate its attention upon seaplanes and airplanes. A large number of both types were stationed in support of the patrols around the major ports. The RNAS would, however, be incapable of offensive action at sea until it was provided with carriers for its aircraft. The Admiralty had already requisitioned a number of large and fast cross-Channel ferries for conversion to seaplane carriers. Other elements of the RNAS were allocated for the defense of the United Kingdom against air attacks and still more were being considered as accompaniments to any Royal Flying Corps aircraft which were to go to France.

In total, the Royal Navy in 1914 was no perfect organization but it was reasonably well prepared for war and, overall, its ships were the most efficient in the world. That there were deficiencies was manifest but the British had risen as well to the challenge as any.

CHAPTER 3

The Germans

The organization of the German command possessed no coherence comparable to that of the British. The machinations of both the Kaiser and Grand Admiral von Tirpitz had ensured that power remained divided amongst various naval authorities in such a way as to ensure the preeminence of Wilhelm II as the Supreme War Lord and Alfred von Tirpitz as State Secretary of the Imperial Naval Office.

There were no less than eight separate officials with the right of direct access to the Kaiser. The first of these was the Chief of the Naval Cabinet (*Marine Kabinett*), Admiral George Alexander von Muller. He was responsible to the Kaiser for senior naval promotions and appointments, the transmission of the Kaiser's orders within the navy, and for the reception and dispatch of all correspondence. Von Muller had been in the appointment since 1906 and, as von Tirpitz was later to complain, he had become more astute court politician than sailor. The Chief of the Naval Cabinet had, by a combination of propinquity—he attended all inperial audiences with naval authorities—and Wilhelm's unfortunate tendency to make decisions under the influence of the last person to talk to him, become very powerful and did not hesitate to intervene in any naval discussions.

By several degrees the most powerful figure was von Tirpitz, who had served as State Secretary of the Imperial Naval Office (*Reichs Marine Amt*) since 1897. His subordinate departments were responsible for all matters of construction and design, stores and supply, and personnel training and education. Tirpitz had been the real commander of the peacetime navy for, apart from matters handled by the Naval Cabinet, the only elements outside his jurisdiction were operational command and control. The Imperial Naval Office prepared the annual budgets and determined not only the size of the fleet but the specifications of all designs. Clearly, the German fleet bore the mark of Tirpitz, since its ships were built according to his personal determination of the strategic situation and the High Sea Fleet's wartime role.

Nevertheless, the Grand Admiral possessed no operational authority. This was vested in other officers, and the Inspector-General of the Navy, the Chief of the Baltic Station, the Chief of the North Sea Station, the Commander of the Asiatic Squadron, and the Commander of the High Sea Fleet all had rights of audience with the Kaiser.

Practically none of these officers offered any real competition to von Tirpitz, for all were to one degree or another isolated by their geographical situations and by the requirements of their commands. It seems that Tirpitz had envisaged himself created a supreme commander in time of war with all others subordinated to him. Apart from his rivalry with von Muller and the Kaiser's determination to remain in control himself, the State Secretary had reckoned without one most important body.

The Admiralstab (Admiralty Staff)[1] under Admiral Hugo von Pohl had originally been created in 1899 with the function of planning and conducting naval operations under the direction of the Kaiser. In peacetime the Admiralstab had maintained a largely advisory role, concerned with the war plans and the accumulation of intelligence. With the declaration of war, however, the situation changed dramatically. The Admiralstab was the only organization with the machinery to conduct the naval war, and its direct subordination to Wilhelm II ensured that the Kaiser was likely to make the greatest possible use of it.

The result of this fragmented command system was that the Imperial Navy's strategic planning left much to be desired. Tirpitz himself had preached the theory that possession of a sufficiently large navy would mean that Britain would not dare declare war on Germany for fear of injuring herself so much that she would, whatever the outcome, be vulnerable to any of the other great powers. This ingenious but unsound concept had been christened the "Risk Fleet" theory.

Tirpitz had allowed for a period during which Britain would be tempted to attack Germany before the High Sea Fleet could be strong enough to constitute such a threat, but this period had practically ended in June 1914 with the reopening of the Kiel Canal. In consequence, since the theory was a supposed guarantee for the *prevention* of war, the Secretary of State had not been greatly concerned for the employment of the fleet in wartime and had made little or no attempt to create detailed policy.

There is no doubt that, despite saber-rattling declarations and the enthusiastic toasts of their juniors to *Der Tag*, few of the senior officers involved wanted or were prepared to fight the British in 1914. It seems that the Germans were preoccupied with the greater strength of the Royal Navy and doubted the value of operations against it.

Not until 28 July was Tirpitz briefed on the war plans of the Admiralstab. He found that the latter expected that the British would take the offensive immediately on the outbreak of war, instituting a close blockade of the German coast. As a result, the role of the High Sea Fleet would be entirely defensive. The Admiralstab felt that judicious use of coastal defenses and patrols of torpedo boats and U-boats would be sufficient to wear the British down without risking the more important German units. The Kaiser agreed and, in the course of his operation orders for the North Sea, went so far as to allow only the U-boats to be "pushed as far as the British coasts." These orders repeated the expectation that the British would conduct a close blockade and that the limited measures allowed would be enough to achieve the desired equality of forces.

The politicians were also keen on the preservation of the heavy units. Apart from the High Sea Fleet's value as a bargaining counter in any negotiations, Chancellor von Bethmann Hollwegg believed that the British could more easily be persuaded to make peace if they had not been angered by heavy losses.

Finally, the tentative suggestion that the High Sea Fleet could attack the Channel transports and prevent the passage of the BEF was rejected not only because of the difficulties and risks involved but because the Army High Command was confident that the British could be so easily dealt with in the field that they were not worth such an effort at sea. It is difficult to escape the impression that the army was also keen to ensure that the navy could not share overmuch in the glory the soldiers expected.

In sum, all concerned had too much to lose for the Germans to admit that they should do anything other than wait for the British to come to them. The light forces of the High Sea Fleet were too small to permit sustained operations at long range, the submarines were still an unknown quantity, and, above all, the British appeared to possess so overwhelming a superiority in battleships that the High Sea Fleet could not afford to risk meeting the Grand Fleet in battle.

During these first days after the British entry into the war, the German authorities were for the first and probably the only time in the war unanimous in their approval of the Admiralstab's policy. Tirpitz proposed on 29 July that a naval high command be established with himself as its head, but he received a rude rebuff not only from the Kaiser but from the other flag officers as well. Even the Grand Admiral's protégés now serving in command did not seem to relish the prospect of Tirpitz as their supreme commander.

The Germans also had cause to be concerned with the situation in the Baltic. Although Russia was by no means a first-rate naval power, her naval forces had improved greatly in efficiency since their disastrous performance against the Japanese in 1905. The Baltic Fleet included two reasonably modern predreadnoughts, as well as three older battleships and six armored cruisers, the latter including the splendid British-built *Rjurik*, which, with four 10″ and eight 8″ guns and a speed of 23 knots, was easily a match for the *Blücher*. In addition, the Russians possessed quite reasonable strength in their light cruisers, destroyers, and submarines.

Matters were not likely to improve for the Germans since the Russians had a large construction program in hand, at the head of which were four dreadnoughts just completing. Russian progress was to be impeded by the loss of German technical assistance and equipment which had been on order from Germany, but there was every chance that they would not only be able to commission the heavy ships but also complete a number of light cruisers and destroyers.

The Germans were convinced that in a simultaneous war with Britain and Russia they had to take the risk of leaving the latter's naval forces relatively unopposed in order to concentrate their strength in the North Sea. Above all, the High Sea Fleet could not afford the losses which the Admiralstab realized must attend even the most successful operations in the shallow, easily mined waters of the Baltic.

Admiral Prince Heinrich of Prussia, appointed in command of the Baltic, had at his disposal only a few cruisers, torpedo boats, and U-boats. More powerful units would be provided as necessary, but they were to be only such ships as the High Sea Fleet could easily spare. On the other hand, the Prussian coast was vulnerable to amphibious assaults. In order that the Russians not become aware of the ease with which they could obtain temporary command of the sea, Prince Heinrich was authorized to allow frequent raids by light forces into the Gulf of Finland, as well as occasional demonstrations of strength by heavier units.

The hidden advantage which the Germans possessed was that the Russians for their part were unsure of the strength which would be deployed against them and were unwilling for the moment to hazard their forces in the western Baltic. Furthermore, the overall Russian plan was basically defensive, envisioning the creation of defensive mine fields in the Gulf of Finland and the positioning of the fleet behind them to await German attacks. The Commander in Chief, Admiral Nikolai von Essen, urged more offensive measures and declared that his forces, by judicious use of mine fields and patrols, could control the Baltic west to a line between Karlskrona and Danzig.

The Russian High Command was unwilling to allow von Essen's scheme until the fleet had been greatly strengthened. The C in C's concept was thought sound, especially as the Russians were as afraid of amphibious assaults against them as the Germans, but defended bases had yet to be established in the Gulf of Riga and at Libau. In consequence, the fleet was to use Helsingfors and Reval as its home ports, remaining in the "Central Position" behind the mine fields in the Gulf of Finland.

The senior German flag officers were as a body no more remarkable than the British. Apart from being hampered by a general feeling of inferiority to the Royal Navy, they seemed to lack the competence and confidence at sea possessed by their British contemporaries. The accusation leveled by contemporary British observers that senior German officers were happier at their desks than at sea had an element of truth in it, although this was not the direct result of the German staff system. The cause probably lay in the method by which Tirpitz organized his budget campaigns. He drew about him a coterie of talented junior officers with whom he repaired to his country estate every summer to prepare each annual budget. In addition to the months involved in this activity, Tirpitz's disciples devoted much of their time to industrialists, politicians, courtiers, and other interests, lobbying them to gain their support when the budget came before the Reichsrat and pitting their talents against the interests of the Army.

Both von Pohl, Chief of the Admiralstab, and von Ingenohl, C in C of the High Sea Fleet, came from Tirpitz's planning group, as had the majority of the flag officers in command at sea and many of the senior captains. These officers had learned the rules of the game well from Tirpitz. They were far more politically aware than the British admirals and were quite prepared to lobby and intrigue at the highest levels without hesitation. There was certainly not the same feeling of corporate solidarity—a situation probably aggravated by the divided system of command and administration—as could be found in the RN, even the RN after Lord Fisher.

It was also apparent that the younger officers were the more ruthless in their employment of intrigue as a means of attaining their ends. Apart from the Kaiser, the senior commanders were likely to receive their subordinates' support and loyalty for only so long as they were successful and Tirpitz himself was to find that he was not invulnerable to the attentions of his former pupils. The divided system of command allowed, for example, subordinate officers in the fleet to address memorandums to the Chief of the Admiralstab concerning the performance of the C in C and other senior commanders.

Admiral Friedrich von Ingenohl had been Commander in Chief of the High Sea Fleet since April 1913. Ennobled in 1909, he had enjoyed a very successful career, combining the best shore and sea appointments. It seems in retrospect, however, that he did not possess a strong enough character for the task ahead. Though extremely competent and very sound in discussion, he was to be so buffeted by the demands of von Tirpitz and the tantrums of the Kaiser on one hand and the pleas of his eager juniors on the other that the operation of the fleet under his command was to be conducted in a vague, inept, and confused manner.

Georg von Muller, the Chief of the Naval Cabinet, was a very capable administrator and a shrewd judge of the Kaiser's mind. Tirpitz's accusation, already mentioned, that von Muller was more of a politician than a sailor was a fair one, although the Grand Admiral was hardly the officer to be pointing that particular finger of scorn. Nevertheless, von Muller retained an abiding interest in every aspect of naval activity and was a realistic judge of what it was possible for the High Sea Fleet to achieve.

Admiral Hugo von Pohl, a dour and reserved officer of much experience, was particularly suited to his role as Chief of the Admiralstab. Very pessimistic concerning the possibility of success against the British, he was insistent in his determination that the fleet should not be risked unduly. Since von Pohl combined technical expertise with a great reputation as a tactician and was next in line for command of the High Sea Fleet, he was, as von Tirpitz was to find, a formidable opponent in argument.

Admiral Prince Heinrich of Prussia was a sound enough officer, although his birth had perhaps ensured his promotion beyond that which his capabilities entitled him. He did, however, possess (unlike his elder brother) a large measure of common sense and was not only popular with his juniors but receptive to their ideas and suggestions. A known Anglophile, he was probably more happily employed in the Baltic than the North Sea.

Prince Heinrich's immediate subordinates were Rear Admiral Behring, who was assigned in command of sea-going forces for operations in the eastern Baltic shortly after the outbreak of war, and Rear Admiral Mischke, Chief of Coastal Batteries and responsible for the defense of the German Baltic coast.

Commanding the Second Squadron, which consisted of the more modern predreadnoughts, Vice Admiral Reinhard Scheer was widely regarded as one of the most talented officers in the navy. He combined technical competence, practical ability, and the highest qualities of leadership. Typically, he was one of the first to realize the vast possibilities and benefits inherent in the new arms of air and submarine operations. His subordinate in the Second Squadron was Rear Admiral Franz Mauve. The First Squadron, consisting of the older dreadnoughts, was commanded by Vice Admiral Wilhelm von Lans, who also acted as second in command of the fleet. Rear Admiral Gadeke served as his deputy.

The new *König* class battleships were being collected in the newly formed Third Squadron under Rear Admirals Funke and Schaumann. Both were very competent and well considered officers, as would be expected in such appointments, and Funke was in fact soon to be promoted vice admiral.

The Fourth Squadron comprised the remaining useful predreadnoughts under Vice Admiral Ehrhardt Schmidt and Rear Admiral Alberts, while the oldest heavy ships, which could only be of practical service in the Baltic or as coastal defense units, were in the process of recommissioning into the Fifth (Vice Admiral Grapow and Commodore Begas) and Sixth Squadrons (Rear Admiral Eckermann). These three squadrons were not yet operational, since all their units had been in various states of refit or reserve when the mobilization was ordered. None would be effective for at least two weeks more.

Rear Admiral Franz Hipper, commanding the battle cruisers and Senior Officer of the Scouting Groups, seemed a man more cast in the British mold than the German. A fine seaman with extensive experience in torpedo boats, he loathed paperwork and was unique amongst his contemporaries in that he had spent no time whatsoever in staff or shore appointments. Reticent in the extreme, he disdained intrigue but was shrewd enough to employ an extremely competent staff, including Commander Erich Raeder (later C in C of the German navy), some of whom did not hesitate to politick on their master's behalf.

Although Hipper was Senior Officer, the five Scouting Groups themselves were practically divided into two forces—the battle cruisers and light cruisers being in the First, Second, and Third Scouting Groups, and the armored cruisers in the Fourth and Fifth. The armored cruisers were intended for service in the Baltic as required, while the more modern units were to remain with the High Sea Fleet in the North Sea. Rear Admiral Leberecht Maass commanded the Second Scouting Group and also acted as Senior Officer of the torpedo boats, assisted by Captain

Hartog of the *Rostock*. Rear Admiral Tapken acted as Hipper's deputy in the battle cruisers, commanding a division consisting of the *Derfflinger* (still completing) and *Von der Tann*, with his flag in the latter. Rear Admiral Hubert von Rebeur-Paschwitz commanded the Fourth Scouting Group, with his flag in *Roon*. Like the predreadnought squadrons, none of the Fourth's ships would be fully operational until mid-August, for all had been either laid up or in use as school ships. The Fifth Scouting Group, which was also being brought forward from reserve, had as its commander Rear Admiral Jasper in the *Hansa*.

Rear Admiral Paul Behncke was serving as von Pohl's deputy in the Admiralstab. A most efficient officer, he was soon responsible for running affairs in Berlin when his chief was absent, as was normally the case, at Army General Headquarters (GHQ). Behncke also was the authority for explaining the navy's actions to politicians and other interests in the capital. A firm friend of von Pohl's, he was a master of staff work and politics and did much to consolidate the Admiralstab's position in the early days of the war. Behncke's assistant, the Chief of Operations, was Captain Hans Seebohm.

There was a concentration of talent among the commanding officers of the battle cruisers who included Captains Magnus von Levetzow (*Moltke*), Hans Zenker (*Von der Tann* and later to serve as C in C of the German navy), Ludwig von Reuter (*Derfflinger*) and Mathias von Egidy of the *Seydlitz*. These officers were very much products of the 1898 Navy Law and the expansion of the Imperial Navy which followed. Enormously confident of the quality of their service and their own abilities, they constituted an alternative and highly critical naval staff. Their fault, despite their technical expertise, enthusiasm, and eagerness to be at the enemy, lay in a lack of sympathy with their crews. If German officers were more at ease with the grand design than their British contemporaries, they were also sometimes dangerously ignorant of the demands of leadership under stress.

The German torpedo boat flotillas were of a more workable size than the British, consisting as they did of eleven vessels made up of a leader and half flotillas for operational purposes. Eight flotillas, with a total of ninety vessels, were at the disposal of the High Sea Fleet, together with twenty older and smaller units disposed at Heligoland and the various North Sea anchorages for local patrols and harbor defense.

Two U-boat flotillas, the First under Commander Hermann Bauer and the Second under Commander Otto Feldman, were attached to the High Sea Fleet. Together with the cruisers *Hamburg* and *Stettin* and four torpedo boats, the strength of the flotillas totaled nineteen submarines.

Six more were being brought forward for service but could not be expected to join until at least the beginning of September.

Apart from the minesweepers and the smallest patrol vessels, the forces in the North Sea were completed by the older light cruisers allocated for the defense of the Ems, Elbe, and the Jade and Weser Estuary anchorages. At this stage, the mine-laying forces were very weak, since all the purpose-built mine-layers were occupied in the Baltic and the only unit immediately available was the auxiliary *Königin Luise*.

Admiral Prince Heinrich could call upon seven cruisers of varying ages in the Baltic. These included the modern *Augsburg*, which was to hoist the flag of Rear Admiral Behring, and *Magdeburg*. In addition, fourteen torpedo boats, four U-boats, and four mine-layers were permanently assigned to the Baltic Command. The latter ships were already laying defensive mine fields off the German coasts and they had been joined temporarily by the High Sea Fleet's *Nautilus*, *Albatross*, and *Pelikan*.

Only one zeppelin, L-3, and twenty-four seaplanes and airplanes were ready to support naval operations in the North Sea, while the Baltic had been allotted only two small airships and eight aircraft. Other zeppelins were being put into service, together with requisitioned aircraft of various types. Like so many other units, these would not be operational until well into the autumn.

The *Kaiser Wilhelm der Grosse* was the lone auxiliary cruiser preparing to sail for commerce operations. Many more ships intended as raiders had been caught in foreign waters by the emergency than had been expected in prewar planning. Two more ships, *Berlin*, and *Viktoria Luise*, were fitting out.

In sum, the German mobilization had been neither as prompt nor as efficient as that of the British. The High Sea Fleet not only had much the inferior battle line, but was dangerously understrength in those units—torpedo boats and submarines—which were intended to wear down the Grand Fleet. There was no doubt that the Germans required time to put their house in order and that large-scale offensive operations were not, at least for the first weeks of August, practicable.

In the matter of material, German ships were smaller than their British contemporaries, carried a lighter armament, and were often rather slower. On the other hand, they were more adequately subdivided and robustly built. The newest *König* class battleships were, for example, more heavily armored than the contemporary *Iron Duke* class, but the fact that their British opponents carried 13.5″ guns as opposed to their own 30.5 cm meant that they needed all their extra protection.

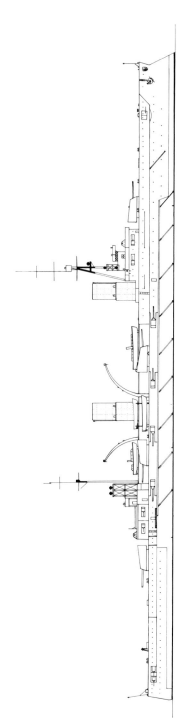

SMS *Blücher*

The German battle cruisers were particularly well designed. The newest, *Derfflinger*, could more accurately be described as a fast, though lightly gunned (eight 30.5 cm) battleship which was quite capable of standing up to all but the newest British dreadnoughts and certainly a match for any British battle cruiser.

The armored cruisers were not so satisfactory. The hybrid *Blücher* which had been designed in response to carefully planted rumors from Britain that the *Invincible* was to carry 9.2" guns, was a magnificent ship. However, with only 21 cm guns and 25 knots speed she suffered in comparison with the battle cruisers with which she operated. The fact that there were only four battle cruisers in the North Sea meant that *Blücher* was used to make up the numbers in the First Scouting Group. Her proper place was in the Baltic, as a counter to the Russian *Rjurik*. Two good earlier units, *Scharnhorst* and *Gneisenau*, were in von Spee's East Asiatic Squadron, but the remaining armored cruisers had evil reputations in the Imperial Navy, being cramped, overgunned, bad steamers, and poor sea boats. Certainly they could not stand against the more modern armored cruisers of the Grand Fleet.

The light cruisers, especially the newer units, were very satisfactory ships but were armed only with 10.5 cm guns. The latter, though a splendid weapon, was no match for the British light cruisers' 6" in either range or weight of metal.

A similar situation prevailed in respect to the torpedo boats, which were little more than half the size, carried a far smaller gun armament, and were 4 knots slower than British destroyers in action. All the minor war units had been designed specifically for the North Sea and Baltic and in consequence were small and possessed a limited radius of action. Their designers had, however, neglected to realize that the British need to build vessels with greater range and sea-keeping ability would necessarily result in their producing better weapon platforms.

The German heavy ships' gunnery standards were high but not remarkably so. They had some idea of the British experiments with director and fire-control systems and the long-range firings, but the High Sea Fleet had not yet advanced beyond practices at a range of 10,000 metres. On the other hand, these were conducted on a much more ambitious basis than those to which the British were used, including shoots in poor visibility and at high speed.

The gunnery of the cruisers and torpedo boats was particularly good and markedly better than that of the British. A notable feature was the German skill at sustaining concentrated and controlled fire in the heat of action.

The High Sea Fleet was thus well skilled in the use of the guns it had

Grand Admiral Alfred von Tirpitz. (BZ)

Admiral Hugo von Pohl. (BZ)

Vice Admiral Reinhard Scheer.
(Pictured as an admiral) (BZ)

Rear Admiral Franz Hipper
with his staff. (USNI)

to hand. German gunnery was probably less scientific but, for the moment, more practical than the British. No capital ship yet carried director firing, although some units operated a hybrid system which still left most of the responsibility in the hands of the turret captains. Although a great deal has been said on the subject of German stereo-scopic sights as opposed to the British prismatic rangefinders, it seems that the advantages of the former at extreme range and in poor visibility were balanced by its inherent disadvantages in that the range taker needed perfect sight in both eyes and great concentration when using the instrument—not an easy thing in action.[2]

Certainly, however, the gunnery problem exercised as great an in-fluence over tactics as in the Royal Navy and ensured a continued emphasis on the stability of the battle line in long- or medium-range actions. While the Imperial Navy did not labor under the crippling but as yet undiscovered British problem of faulty shells, its own projectiles were not perfect and were to include a number of duds or incomplete bursts in action.

The Germans had always had a particular interest in torpedoes, indeed the officers of that branch maintained a primacy in their service comparable with that of the gunnery officers in the Royal Navy. The weapons were efficient and, for their size, powerful, although the tendency to lose such advantages was again manifest in that the German standard torpedo was only 50 cm as opposed to the British 21″.

The same could not be said for mines. The German moored contact mine remains the model for the subtype today. The British themselves were to abandon their own inefficient weapons for a version patterned after a captured copy. The High Sea Fleet's problem lay rather in the fact that there were all too few fast mine-layers available to make adequate use of the weapon.

The German submarine force was far smaller than the British and not as well equipped. Certainly none of the operational U-boats were compa-rable to the E class. On the other hand, there was little to choose between the professional competence of the crews. The advantage which the Germans possessed was that the situation inevitably gave their sub-marines more opportunities than it did the British.

Antisubmarine warfare was no more advanced than in Britain; that the Germans were not to suffer the same heavy losses in the first weeks of the war was probably due to the fact that their heavy units did not spend the same time at sea. It is clear that the U-boats had yet to prove themselves in the eyes of senior officers. German staff definitely regarded submarines with much the same feelings as many British flag officers, tempered by the admission that the submarines could be very useful in wearing down the strength of the British battle line.

The Germans did not have so much foreign construction as the Royal Navy at hand. Two light cruisers were building for Russia, and these were immediately seized. Armed with 15 cm guns, they were to prove a valuable addition to the Scouting Groups when they completed in 1915 and 1916. Four large torpedo boats for Argentina were also taken over, as well as four smaller units building for the Netherlands.

One error of judgment that had particularly serious consequences for the Imperial Navy was the decision concerning the fate of destroyer machinery which had been ordered by Russia from Germany. The Shichau yard of shipbuilders made an offer to build nine large torpedo boats for the Imperial Navy using the Russian engines and boilers but this was refused on the grounds that the ships could not be completed for another eighteen months. Not until October 1914, by which time it had become clear that the German torpedo boats were too small for the duties demanded of them, would large-scale orders be placed for such vessels.

One fast battleship, the *Salamis*, was building at the Vulkan shipyard in Hamburg for Greece. Three months from launching, and nearly two years from the earliest possible completion, *Salamis* could be considered no more than a useful reserve unit. Vulkan was allowed to continue construction until launching stage, the decision as to whether the ship should be completed being reserved until the end of the year. Unfortunately for the Imperial Navy, any such decision was to prove completely impractical, since the 14″ guns intended for the *Salamis* were being built in America. The British would never let them past the blockade and, indeed, it was not long before the weapons passed into British hands. Construction of the ship would eventually be abandoned, since it was far better for the Germans to build another hull to their own specifications, rather than fabricating heavy guns specifically for the "odd number" *Salamis*.

In the matter of personnel, there was little remarkable about the German naval officer corps, which was as profoundly middle class an organization as that of the Royal Navy, leavened only by a small percentage of the poorer Prussian nobility.

Officers were entered only on completion of their secondary education and underwent a very comprehensive and technically oriented training program. They tended, since very few German units served overseas, to have less acquaintance with the world at large than the British and generally less sea-going experience than the latter. One particular difference was that very few German officers, married or unmarried, lived onboard when ships were in their home ports—a habit that seemed to result in far less propriety interest on the part of the officers in their crews and ships than seemed to be the case in the RN.

There was also a greater division between the executive, engineering, and other specialist branches. The engineers in particular were badly treated in the Imperial Navy and there was in 1914 a great shortage of trained engineer officers. Similarly the German "Deckoffizieres" were treated with less respect by their seniors than warrant officers in the Royal Navy. It was a natural consequence that they were neither as useful nor as reliable.

The German system of conscription for three year's service was, though the most practicable solution, given the enormous expansion of the Imperial Navy over such a short period, not nearly so satisfactory as the British long-service system. On the other hand, the Germans ensured that the conscripts did as much of their service in the one ship as possible, which ensured the greatest levels of efficiency and expertise.

The Imperial Navy was in fact suffering from shortages of trained personnel in almost every field. The situation was preserved first by the fact that entrants to all ranks and branches were of extremely high quality and second because the training offered was very thorough indeed. The real fault was not inexperience, but the wide gulfs which lay between the executive officers and the specialists and between the officers and men.

In total, the Imperial Navy was little more ready for war than the Royal Navy. The Germans made up in quality of material much of what they lacked in quantity in comparison with the British but there was, except in mine warfare, no extraordinary technological edge. Clearly there was also no marked superiority of strategic or tactical thought. The Imperial Navy lacked unity of command and suffered friction and divisions at many levels within the service. The greatest merit of the navy was the determination of its personnel, feeling themselves to be not only the products but the champions of their proud new empire, to prove themselves and their service in action.

CHAPTER 4

First Blood

At 1830 on 4 August, a state of war existed between Great Britain and Germany. Germany had determined to declare war on Great Britain immediately, even though the British ultimatum to leave Belgium did not expire until midnight. The Grand Fleet was already at sea. The previous day, the Admiralty had been alerted by intelligence that three German transports had left the Baltic on 1 August. It had long been a fear of the British that the Germans would attempt to invade the sparsely inhabited and ill-defended Shetland Islands and establish a base there. Callaghan had sent a light cruiser and four destroyers to patrol the islands two days before. On being informed of the German movement, however, the C in C hastily ordered out the Third Cruiser Squadron, as well as *Achilles* and *Cochrane* of the Second. Beatty, too, was sent out with the battle cruisers to act as a covering force.

Despite the fact that they found nothing—there was no truth in the intelligence report and even the battle cruisers' encounter with two unidentified warships was resolved when it realized that "it was only old Packs"—the cruisers and battle cruisers were ordered to remain at sea.[1] The Admiralty was still not satisfied that the Shetlands were clear of enemy forces, and the decision was finally made to send out the entire Grand Fleet.

News was also coming through that German armed merchant cruisers were being sent to break out into the Atlantic by the northern route. Jellicoe took the fleet to sea, heading east to within 100 miles of the Norwegian coast, while the cruiser squadrons separated to sweep south into the North Sea and west around the coast of Scotland. At 2300 on the night of 4 August, the Admiralty issued the War Telegram.

The sweep had little result, principally because it kept too far to the west. A German armed merchant cruiser, the *Kaiser Wilhelm der Grosse*, Cruiser D, had left Bremen on the 4th, and on her passage north came within thirty miles of the Grand Fleet. Cruisers under the command of Rear Admiral Gough-Calthorpe did make a sweep farther to the east along the coast, but they were nearly a day too late, and by that time the German raider, which from intercepted wireless traffic had a good idea of the presence of British ships, was able to get well clear.

This latter movement by the British cruisers had been ordered by Jellicoe to investigate reports that the Germans had established a secret base in Norway. Again, however, intelligence proved to be false and they found nothing. Reports continued to flow in that the Germans were collecting merchant ships off the Lofoten Islands to convert them into raiders. It seemed credible enough, especially since the British had long suspected that certain German merchant ships were not only strengthened to carry guns, as was the British practice, but carried their armaments secretly stowed away. The desperate attempts made to arm such fast liners as the *Cap Trafalgar* which had already been cut off from Germany prove this to be untrue, but it was some time before the British could rid themselves of the belief. On 7 August, the Third Cruiser Squadron and the Second Destroyer Flotilla were sent into Norwegian waters to search. Again, nothing was found. Formal protests and apologies were made for the breach of neutrality that the movement involved, but fortunately the Norwegian government did not seem unduly disturbed.

It was manifest to Jellicoe that the northern blockade would remain insecure until the cruisers assigned to it arrived on station. Even to examine the few trawlers and merchantmen met during the sweep involved stopping the entire Grand Fleet, leaving ships vulnerable to submarine attack. Furthermore, it was obvious that irregular sweeps could not have the effectiveness of regular patrols in visual contact with each other. Not one German had been seen but Jellicoe found it very difficult to believe that this meant that the Germans were making no attempt to send commerce raiders out into the Atlantic.

The *Edgars* were on their way north. Read Admiral Dudley De Chair, hoisting his flag in the *Crescent* at Portsmouth, managed to get her and two other cruisers away on 3 August. This feat had only been accomplished by De Chair working his men around the clock and a fourth cruiser had to be left at Portsmouth to follow when she completed. The three cruisers, and the three which left Devonport the next day, were delayed on their progress to Scapa by the need to intercept and examine various German and neutral merchant ships, but they arrived on the 6th and began coaling immediately.

Since the Grand Fleet was, for the time being, filling the Shetland-Norwegian passage well enough, Jellicoe did not yet order any of De Chair's cruisers into that area. As a consequence, on the 7th De Chair took his six ships into the Orkney-Shetland passage. Not until the Grand Fleet began to move clear on 8 August did the cruisers divide and the *Edgar*, *Theseus*, and *Gibraltar* begin patrols off the Norwegian coast.

Although the squadron would be brought to full strength by the arrival of the *Hawke* and the *Royal Arthur* on the 10th, as a blockading force the *Edgars* could not be considered as anything more than a temporary measure. They were too old to face the northern weather, and though conditions were likely to remain good for about a month, the season of the equinoctial gales would soon begin. Their numbers, too, were only just sufficient, for in even the finest visibility four ships—which would be the maximum available to patrol each passage—would be only just enough to watch the entire Shetlands-Norwegian passage over its breadth of 150 miles.

For the moment, they were better than nothing. The German reaction to the threat of war—ordering all their ships to shelter in neutral ports—meant that the normally busy shipping lanes were almost clear. Even the ships of the neutral Scandinavian and European countries were keeping away from the area, for in the days leading up to the declaration of war most sailings had been canceled while shipping companies awaited the outcome. What would strain the squadron over the next few weeks would be the continuous reports of German bases on the Norwegian coast and among the islands which would need to be checked. Such activities bore particularly hard on the *Edgars* since they necessitated continuous high-speed steaming, which taxed the cruisers' aged machinery.

In the south, the decision had been made to send the Expeditionary Force to France. All the plans made before the war had provided for the cavalry division and all six infantry divisions in the regular field army to be sent across the Channel, but the War Cabinet would not immediately allow this. The worry was that the Germans would be able to land an invasion force unopposed during the weeks between the dispatch of the Expeditionary Force and the mobilization of the Territorials. Consequently, although on 4 August it was decided to send troops to France, the forces allocated next day for the BEF were reduced by two infantry divisions, which were to stay in Britain.

The movement of eighty thousand infantry and twelve thousand cavalry was nonetheless a mammoth undertaking, and it was fortunate that much thought had gone into the planning. The preliminary movements were to begin on 6 August, the embarkation was scheduled for 9 August, while the disembarkation of the main body and its stores was to finish on the 19th, with only base detachments requiring to be moved until the 23rd and the entire operation to be completed on that day. The process was further complicated by the decision made on 18 August to send another infantry division, but it was included in the program with little or no dislocation. The entire operation was conducted without the loss of a ship or man, and was remarkable as the first time an army had been dispatched to the Continent in anything like fighting condition.

Some 240 vessels had to be requisitioned. The lists of the vessels needed had been prepared some years before the war, and the Admiralty—indicating the importance attached to the matter by the British departments—had kept watch day by day on the movements and cargo state of each vessel. Many of the ships needed conversion, especially those required as horse-carriers or temporary ambulance ships, but although such work could take up to six days, it was all accomplished on time.

Because the numbers were so large and the reserve transport capacity so small, and because only two ports in both Britain and France would be used for the vast bulk of stores, animals, and men (nearly 90 percent), it was decided not to organize the transports into convoy but to sail them from their ports as soon as they were ready. As was to prove, this was a wise decision. The troops were to go from Southampton to Le Havre, and the stores from Newhaven to Boulogne.

Protection of the transport routes involved almost every ship in home waters, but the forces in the south bore the principal burden, and these ships spent many days at sea. The Admiralty was relieved of the need to provide forces to close off the southern entrances of the Channel as the French were willing to employ their Atlantic forces on the necessary patrols. Consequently, only Cruiser Force G, with its four old *Talbot* class cruisers, was allocated to the area.

The French were providing ten armored and four light cruisers under the command of Rear Admiral Rouyer. The whole force was to patrol along a line from Land's End to Ushant, the British watching to the north-west and the French to the south-east. Four armored cruisers of the latter were deployed to act as a heavy covering force. The Admiralty did not think that any major German thrust was likely from this direction, but they did fear the possibility that a single fast raider might slip in from the Atlantic and wreak havoc on the transport lines before she could be caught. The other possibility was that a mine-layer could break through, and Wemyss was specifically directed to send all merchant ships into Falmouth for a thorough examination. As events turned out, the cruisers were to spend their time almost entirely on trade control, since the Admiralty decided not to send out any ships into the area specifically for the Examination Service.

The battleships of the Channel Fleet were also sent out on patrol. Vice Admiral Burney was ordered to take the Fifth Battle Squadron into the Channel to protect the Newhaven-Boulogne route from a German attack from the North Sea, while Vice Admiral Bethell was sent with the Eighth Battle Squadron to protect the Southampton-Le Havre line and be in a position to support both Burney's ships and the Allied forces to the south. The battleships had no destroyer escort, for the Admiralty was not of the opinion that there was much risk of a submarine attack.

For the time being this estimate was quite correct. Although neither Burney nor Bethell was entirely happy about the position, their reservations did not prohibit either from ordering his ships to stop for protracted periods in broad daylight. The French had every destroyer and torpedo boat they could muster out on patrol, the situation of the French armies being such as to make the French eagerness to see the British troops across the Channel without loss quite understandable. Even in the first days of August, there was at least half a flotilla of British destroyers in the Straits of Dover by day. By night, with the increased opportunities afforded to German raiders to slip through, every available ship was sent out. At this early stage of the war, when morale was at its peak, reaction and fatigue had not yet set in and machinery had not been worn down by overuse, it was easy to muster a 100 percent availability of ships. For nights on end, every destroyer, scout, and gunboat belonging to the Dover Patrol would be operational and at sea. The movement of the British Expeditionary Force was an operation of such importance to both countries and to every man involved that it was accomplished with the utmost cooperation and enthusiasm at every stage. By 11 August a patrol of drifters and trawlers had been organized, and, at this particular stage of war, passage of the Channel by U-boats, or indeed by any German craft, was unlikely to have gone undetected.

Farther to the north, around the area off the Dutch coast known as the "Broad Fourteens," patrolled the old armored cruisers of Force C. They remained by day in this area, intended as heavy cover for the destroyers under Tyrwhitt's command, but by night they moved south and joined the battleships of the Fifth Battle Squadron. On paper, they seemed an admirable support for the flotillas, but being elderly and only just recommissioned, manned by undrilled reservist crews, the protection they could provide was dubious.

To the Harwich Force belonged the first blood of the war, both victims and losses. Tyrwhitt took both flotillas to sea at first light on 5 August. He had long planned a sweep toward Terschelling for the first day of the war, as long as no other orders were sent him, and his decision paid off when the force intercepted a German mine-layer. Tyrwhitt and Keyes had also agreed that it would be useful to combine the sweep with the submarine reconnaissance of Heligoland Bight, and when the force departed Harwich the cruiser *Amethyst* had the submarine E-6 in tow, while the destroyer *Ariel* was allocated E-8. The submarines were quite capable of making the distance, but Keyes considered that the more assistance they could have, the better.

The flotillas sailed separately, Tyrwhitt in *Amethyst* leading out *Fearless* and the First Flotilla. The two forces would be out of visual contact with one another, but within supporting distance. Tyrwhitt intended to stay at sea as long as necessary, but the Third Flotilla would return to Harwich on the 6th to get twenty-four hours in harbor, while the First Flotilla patrolled off the Dutch coast. On 7 August, the flotillas would exchange duties.

At 1015, *Amphion* and the Third Flotilla sighted a steamer ten miles distant, heading east. Captain Cecil Fox sent *Lance* and *Landrail* to investigate, but, as the ship had "every appearance of being one of the Hook of Holland steamers,"[2] the vessels that ran the ferry service of the Great Eastern Railway between Britain and the Netherlands, he was not much interested. But then the *Laurel*, a destroyer out on the western flank of the sweep, signaled:

> Trawler reports that liner has been seen dropping things overboard presumably mines.

Amphion increased speed and headed after the destroyers. The latter soon observed that their quarry was indeed dropping mines overboard even as she fled. It was obvious that this was no British ferry. In fact, it was the German auxiliary mine-layer *Königin Luise*. At a range of 4,400 yards the *Lance* opened fire with her bow 4", the first shot of the naval war.

Königin Luise was an excursion steamer that had been completed in 1912. Of 1,800 tons, with a useful turn of speed, she had run from Hamburg to Heligoland since completion and had long been marked down as suitable for conversion to an auxiliary mine-layer. When the war orders went out, she was immediately requisitioned and put into dock-yard hands. The conversion, however, was hasty and in the twelve hours allotted for the work all that could be done was load aboard 180 mines and their gear and repaint the ship in the colors of the ships of the Great

Eastern Railway Company. The ship was intended to carry two 88mm guns, but these were not installed. All she carried when she put to sea were two 7-pounder pom-poms and a motley collection of rifles. Her crew was a scratch one, made up in the majority by her old crew, with a stiffening of regular personnel and hastily mobilized reservists. Still onboard the *Königin Luise* were most of her merchant fittings, even the windows in her glass-enclosed promenade deck. Late on 4 August, she slipped out of Emden to make her way to the English coast, ordered to lay her mines off Harwich.

The 180 mines she carried were paltry in comparison with the 26,000 mines which some British observers had wildly estimated would be laid in the North Sea in the first few days of the war. In fact the Imperial Navy did have vast stocks of mines and many ships capable of laying them, but all but a few of these were cruisers or destroyers. The Admiralstab was not yet willing to utilize them for such a perilous duty as offensive minelaying. As the few purpose-built mine-layers were occupied in the Baltic, and the conversion of the other auxiliaries could not be completed for at least a few weeks, the *Königin Luise* was all that could be mustered in the North Sea. The other factor militating against an immediate, large-scale mine-laying campaign was that the nights were still too short and the weather too good to permit undetected approach to the British coast.

Despite the fact that the *Königin Luise* was doomed, her mines were to strike a shrewd blow the very next day and amply repay her efforts. Laying had begun at dawn, while the ship moved in toward the English coast. Since *Königin Luise* was continually being enveloped by squalls, her captain had every reason to think that the ship might be able to lay all her mines and escape unscathed. Had it not been for the errant British trawler's observation and report, this might very well have been the case.

Amphion followed the chase north, but not for half an hour did Fox consider that the ship was within effective range. *Lance* and *Landrail* had both been firing with little effect, and it was not until *Amphion* began to score hits at 7,000 yards that the two destroyers also got the range. To the surprise of the *Amphion*'s gunnery officer, the excitement was too much for the guns' crews of the three 4" that were in action, "They started off firing as fast as they could, and it was a good minute before by dint of throwing things at them that I could stop them."[3]

Königin Luise had not long to live. Her pom-poms and handweapons were completely ineffective and she was soon on fire forward and amidships, listing badly after a 4" shell burst on the waterline and blew a hole in her side. To make matters worse, many of the exmerchant-service men began to panic and abandoned ship without orders, and the British were horrified to see German officers firing revolvers at men in the water. By noon, with the German mine-layer lying on her beam-ends, the action was over. Fox ordered his ships to close and pick up survivors. The three collected five officers and seventy men, many of the latter having German-inflicted bullet wounds to add to those caused by the British. In *Amphion* the only available spaces to put the prisoners were the captain's day cabin and a space in the bows, and the prisoners were sent to the latter with the idea that "if we did go up on a mine they might just as well go first." As Captain Fox remarked, "It was little thought at the time how true these words would be."⁴

Once the rescue was complete, the ships turned west again to rejoin the flotilla and continue the sweep, although Fox sent the *Lance* back into Harwich with a defective 4″ gun. The sweep continued until 2100 that night as the flotilla neared Terschelling, but, as nothing short of a few trawlers and merchant ships had been found, Fox ordered the destroyers to turn back for Harwich. He took great care to avoid the area in which the *Königin Luise*'s mines were expected to lie, as well as the submarine patrol which Commodore Keyes had set up off the Outer Gabbard.

At the same time, Tyrwhitt's *Amethyst*, with the *Fearless* and the destroyers of the First Flotilla, came to the planned eastern limit of their sweep as they approached Borkum. From here they would turn south-west and patrol along the Dutch coast for two days until the Third Flotilla came out to relieve them. Before they turned away, however, *Amethyst* and *Ariel* cast off E-6 and E-8, which immediately moved into the Bight to begin the first offensive war patrols of the British submarine service.

Meanwhile, however, though Fox's ships attempted to keep the German mine field to the east, their dead reckoning had gone awry, and the flotilla was in reality seven miles to the north-east of its assumed position—and seven miles happened to be the margin of safety which the British had assumed. As a result, the Third Flotilla ran right over the mines. At 0635 on 6 August, a mine exploded under the fore-bridge of the *Amphion*. The entire forecastle was immediately aflame, and the explosion caused heavy casualties amongst the seamen, who had their mess-decks in the forecastle, and amongst the German prisoners housed in the bow, only one of whom survived this explosion.

The ship was steadily going down by the bows, and, although the destroyer *Linnet* managed to get the *Amphion* in tow, it seemed to Captain Fox that not only had the ship's back been broken—the *Amphion* was now badly hogged and a deep crack ran across the upper deck—but with the fire raging unchecked in the forecastle there was a danger that

HMS *Amphion*

the forward magazine would explode. Fox ordered abandon ship, and it was well that he did so. As he later wrote:

> Scarcely had I left the ship and being about 50 yards away, and whilst I was looking at her to gauge her time, the foremost half of the ship seemed to rise out of the water and break into a mass of flames and smoke, causing a great upheaval in the water and a terrific roar resembling a volcano; masses of material were thrown into the air to a great height, and I personally saw one of the 4-inch guns and a man turning head over heels about 150 feet up; this gun just missed falling on the *Linnet*, much to the relief of her C.O., who saw it coming and thought his number was up.[5]

Fox later expressed the opinion that the explosion was in fact caused by a mine exploding under the magazine. The ship must have traveled forward a considerable distance after the first explosion and the green glow which surrounded the *Amphion* as she blew up indicated that it was the lyddite filling in the high-explosive shells that had gone up and not the propellant charges. This would have been the case had it been a second mine, since the shellrooms were located below the magazines.

Despite *Linnet's* escape from the plunging 4″ gun, she was showered by splinters and one of *Amphion's* bunker-lids struck amidships and pierced a boiler room. Fortunately, she suffered no casualties, but a 4″ shell exploded aboard *Lark* and killed the sole German prisoner to escape *Amphion*, as well as two wounded seamen from the ship. The total casualty list from the affair was 1 officer and 131 men killed, out of a ship's complement of 17 officers and 266 men.

The water was so shallow that the stern of the *Amphion* was still in the air when her bow was on the bottom, but within fifteen minutes of the

HMS *Tiger* on trials

second explosion the ship disappeared. After a search to ensure that no men were still in the water, the progress to Harwich was resumed, the British being considerably chastened by their loss. Only fifteen miles out of Harwich another suspicious steamer was sighted. As she was also in the colors of the Great Eastern Railway Company and was flying a large German ensign, it was too much for the two destroyers sent to investigate her and they opened fire. At this, the remainder of the flotilla, "automatically opened out into a fan and went full speed for her, opening fire at the same time".[6]

Despite the fact that the steamer hastily hauled down the German flag and hoisted the Red Ensign, Captain Fox, by now in the *Llewellyn*, and realizing that the destroyers "were seeing red," had to take his ship in advance of the rest of the flotilla and foul their range before they would cease fire.

It was soon made clear why the steamer, the *St. Petersburg*, had been flying the German ensign. She was conveying the former German Ambassador and his staff from Harwich to the neutral Netherlands, and as such was displaying the flag to indicate her immunity to any German forces. She went unscathed in the hail of shells, but it is recorded that the Germans were greatly impressed by the incident. The German Naval Attaché had earlier been the subject of a minor subterfuge by the ship. Commodore Keyes had arranged with the railway company to have the *St. Petersburg* steer an intricate zigzag as she left Harwich as though the ship was passing through a swept channel between extensive defensive mine fields outside the port.

As far as the British submarines were concerned, neither E-6 nor E-8 saw or did anything of real importance during their short patrols. Both had been ordered to stay in the Bight no more than three days, "and unless they found themselves very well placed for offensive operations they were to return after two days."[7] The outer Bight was clear of major vessels and neither submarine came close enough in to Heligoland to see the German daily patrols. They reported on their return to Harwich, however, that they had sighted and been sighted by large numbers of trawlers and drifters around the Bight. Keyes was moved to conclude that the Germans were using these trawlers as W/T-equipped scouts. He proposed an offensive operation by Tyrwhitt's destroyers against them, but this plan had for the time to be laid aside in the face of other requirements. Since the Germans, were they to become aware of the presence of British submarines in the Bight, would have sent torpedo boats out to hunt them, it is difficult to see on what grounds Keyes was basing his conclusion.

By now it was apparent to the Germans that the British would not be enforcing a close blockade and that even the possibility of raids being made into Heligoland Bight was problematic. While neither the Kaiser, the Admiralstab, nor von Ingenohl were yet prepared to allow a sortie by surface ships, it was decided to send a force of U-boats to sweep north into the North Sea in an effort to find the British blockade line and the Grand Fleet. Ten submarines of the First Flotilla were ordered out on 6 August. They were to proceed, spread at seven-mile intervals, right up the middle of the North Sea until they reached a line between Scapa Flow and Hardanger before turning to reach a line between Scapa Flow and Stavanger, twenty-five miles to the south. Here they were to wait on patrol before returning to Heligoland on 10 August.

The prediction of the Grand Fleet's position was fairly accurate, but the operation was not a success for the Germans. There had been much soul-searching at headquarters over the decision to send the First Flotilla. These were the oldest U-boats in operation, possessed of unreliable engines and renowned for the pall of black smoke they emitted running on the surface by day and the sheets of flame that issued forth at night. They were sent only because they had the most experienced captains, who would stand a much better chance than the raw commanders of the brand-new boats of the Second Flotilla. But small, old, and unhandy, they would be in difficulties if they revealed their position to British ships.

The submarines were instructed to search for the suspected British blockade line. Though the Command had by now accepted that the British were enforcing a distant blockade, they estimated that the patrol area must lie between Buchan Ness and Egersund. It was a fair guess, since the line struck the Norwegian coast at a point where there were few convenient islands or fiords to provide shelter for blockade runners. In making the estimation, however, the Command failed to realize that the British would never use the line because it was simply too vulnerable to German forces issuing out of the Baltic, as well as too near the North Sea bases.

The first indications which the British had that there were submarines in the area came at 1145 on 8 August, when the battleship *Monarch* reported being attacked by a submarine. She, and the *Ajax* and *Audacious*, which had all been detached to undertake gunnery practices, were hastily recalled to the main body, but at 1845 that day both the *Iron Duke* and her next astern, the *Dreadnought*, sighted a periscope. *Iron Duke* attempted to ram, but nothing more was seen of the submarine. As there are no German records of this incident, it seems possible that this was the U-13, which disappeared without trace during the sweep.

The Germans were to suffer another loss, when the light cruiser *Birmingham*, forming part of the cruiser screen disposed thirty miles ahead of the Grand Fleet, sighted a periscope at 0340 on 9 August. She immediately turned to ram and struck the U-boat a glancing blow, forcing it to the surface, astern of the cruiser. *Birmingham* turned back and rammed the hapless U-15 dead amidships, cutting her into halves. The wreckage disappeared in seconds, taking every man of the crew with it. The stoutly built *Birmingham* suffered no more than superficial damage, and she continued with the fleet.

After news of this incident came through, an alarmed Jellicoe suggested to the Admiralty that he withdraw the fleet to the north-west of the Orkneys. He had already ordered every available cruiser and destroyer to clear the North Sea of submarines, but he was of the opinion that the area was no longer safe for heavy ships and that he should keep the Grand Fleet to the west of the Orkneys. Only the need to cover the passage of the Expeditionary Force restrained him from doing this immediately, and the Admiralty's prompt approval must have come as a considerable relief. By 10 August the battleships were clear of the area.

The remaining German submarines, less U-5 which turned back earlier with engine trouble, returned to Heligoland on 11 August. They had seen little and learnt nothing. The Admiralstab still could not be sure where either the Grand Fleet or the blockade line lay. Some valuable war experience had indeed been gained, but to balance against this, two submarines and, more important, their trained crews, had been lost.

Jellicoe, for his part, clung to the notion that the U-boats were either operating from secret Norwegian bases or else had parent ships at sea.

Wireless intercepts ostensibly seemed to support the latter theory, but there was not a grain of truth in it, though this was "a theory which was very generally . . . held in naval circles during the first eighteen months of the war."[8] For the next few days, extensive searches were conducted around the Norwegian coast, while the cruiser *Drake* was sent to search the Faroe Islands for signs of German commerce raiders or submarines. Again, nothing was found, although the scouts from Norway returned with the welcome news that the Norwegians were keeping careful watch on their coasts, and would not permit the Germans to use their waters for any hostile purpose. Jellicoe also ordered that Loch Ewe, on the west coast of Scotland, be prepared for use as a secondary coaling base. This would involve some dislocation, since it required the build-up of coal stocks when the number of colliers allocated to the Grand Fleet was only just sufficient to keep Scapa Flow supplied.

The Fourth Destroyer Flotilla had the embarrassing experience, while on patrol off Norway, of mistaking a shoal of jellyfish for a mine field. The error was only discovered after *Swift* "bumped" one while attempting to extricate herself.

Meanwhile, despite the wanderings of the Grand Fleet, the passage of the Expeditionary Force was proceeding uninterrupted. Though some in the Imperial Navy were keen to attempt a raid on the transport routes, the army, and in particular the Kaiser, was confident of a speedy victory on the western front; so confident indeed that they felt that any measures against the BEF on passage were unnecessary. The "contemptible little army," as Wilhelm derisively labeled it, was tiny on the European scale, but nonetheless the one hundred thousand superbly disciplined troops would help to plug the gaps in the French lines and win the crucial battles of late 1914. The German army's decision had one other factor behind it. The soldiers, not appreciating the bitterness of the naval race, still did not regard Britain as a serious enemy. If France were to surrender, they felt, Britain would be pleased to sue for peace. Furthermore, outright defeat of her troops in the field would be more likely to convince Britain of the futility of the struggle than the wholesale loss of her troops at sea. As the *Staff Monograph* remarked of the German Army Command:

> In their first successful advance they were rather eager than otherwise to settle accounts with the . . . British troops.[9]

The Imperial Navy was taken by surprise by the news from their few active spies left in Britain that the transportation of the BEF was already beginning. They had not expected it to start until 16 August at the very earliest, and combined with their surprise at the institution of the distant blockade, this meant that the atmosphere in the Admiralstab was one of confusion and uncertainty as the prewar plans were hastily revised to meet these contingencies. It was a special shock to the planners, first, that the British would dare transport almost their entire regular army into France while the High Sea Fleet remained intact and while Germany was capable of launching an invasion, and, second, that the British had not sent their ships into the Bight at least during the passage of the BEF, so as to prevent the exit of any German forces. The Emperor gave his permission for the C in C to use torpedo boats, submarines, and mine-layers against the transports—heavy ships were, of course, not to be risked—but neither von Ingenohl nor the Admiralstab thought that anything practicable could be done. With the First Submarine Flotilla out on its sweep, and the bulk of the remaining U-boat force required for the defensive patrols around Heligoland, there were only four submarines available. This number was not large enough to have much chance of success. Similarly, mine laying would be suicidal even if the other auxiliaries could be commissioned in time.

Von Ingenohl did toy with the idea of a massed torpedo-boat attack against the Grand Fleet, but the predicted position of the British ships was at least 150 miles further from Heligoland than the operational range of the torpedo boats. Furthermore, the torpedo boats would have to go without heavy cover as such a movement would be a breach of the Kaiser's restrictions. This would result, in all probability, in the German torpedo boats being cut to pieces by the numerous cruisers and powerful destroyers which the Grand Fleet could dispose. In these first weeks of the war, the Germans were beginning to realize the folly of the careless assumption that the British would attempt a close blockade, and the way which they had tailored their designs, strategies, and tactics around it. The Admiralstab needed pause for thought.

On 8 August, however, four submarines, U-19, U-21, U-22 and U-24, were sent out with instructions to investigate up to and twelve miles past the line drawn between the Terschelling Light Vessel and the Swarte Bank, where the first British patrols were expected to operate. It was hoped that the submarines would encounter heavy ships to the south and south-west, but they were given strict instructions only to proceed in that direction if they could withdraw to safety submerged. As the underwater endurance of the boats was only seventy miles, this was a considerable restriction. The four U-boats, however, saw nothing but patrolling destroyers, several of which they only narrowly avoided. When they returned empty-handed on the 11th, all the information which they could give the Command was that the British appeared to be maintaining a continuous destroyer patrol off the Dutch coast. To add to their uncertainty about the whereabouts of the Grand Fleet, the Admiralstab now had to admit that they not only did not know from what positions the predreadnoughts of the Second and Third Fleets (the Germans were still under the impression that the prewar organization of the Royal Navy held good) were covering the passage of the BEF, but they were unsure whether they were in the south at all. Though the Admiralstab believed that the operation was being heavily guarded, von Ingenohl and his staff suspected that the predreadnoughts had gone north to join the Grand Fleet. Knowing nothing, and with their few offensive weapons to hand having proved to be, for the time, broken reeds, the Germans could do little of importance.

But that very inactivity, as well as the apparent German failure to make any moves whatsoever against the BEF transports, roused suspicions in Britain that the Germans might attempt invasion, or, more likely, a series of raids on the east coast with the small numbers of troops which they were thought to have available. It was now known that the first-line strength of the High Sea Fleet was concentrated in the North Sea ports and the Admiralty could not persuade themselves that the German attack would be limited to the one auxiliary mine-layer and the few submarines that British ships had yet encountered.

By 12 August, the Admiralty wanted the Grand Fleet back in the North Sea, despite the risk of submarines. Jellicoe acquiesced, but insisted that the operation be simply a sweep to ensure that the North Sea was clear of German forces. He did not wish his battleships to linger in the area. He was careful, too, to ensure that Cruiser Force C and Tyrwhitt's flotillas would be available to reinforce the Grand Fleet's escort. The operation was timed to commence as soon as the battleships had coaled and completed essential maintenance. Jellicoe ordered the Grand Fleet to leave Scapa Flow late on the night of 23 August, with the sweep to commence at midnight the next day when the battle squadrons passed through the Fair Island Channel.

Before the sweep began, Jellicoe asked the Admiralty to take over operational control of the flotillas at Harwich. He did not think it possible to exercise command of them from the *Iron Duke*, whether she was at Scapa or at sea. The distances were too great and wireless too primitive for the system to be practicable, and the Admiralty immediately consented to the change, which took effect from 10 August. Despite the First Lord's pleasure at being able to control what clearly would be the front-line forces of the war, it was decided that the best idea would be to amalgamate all the units from Harwich under one command. Rear Admiral A.H. Christian, with his flag in the *Euryalus*, was named in command of this new "Southern Force." As well as Tyrwhitt's destroyers and Keyes's submarines, Cruiser Force C was separated from the Grand Fleet, in order to give the light forces some measure of heavy cover. Christian was not to prove a decisive leader, for Tyrwhitt and Keyes were allowed to continue their operations uninterrupted, and already the two commodores were not only formulating plans for offensive sweeps into Heligoland Bight, but Tyrwhitt had made a good impression at conferences at the Admiralty. Churchill was greatly taken with him on their meeting and Commodore (T) was able to return triumphant to Harwich with the promise that he was to be given the first available, newly completed light cruiser. Oil burning and with a speed of nearly 30 knots, the *Arethusa* would be an enormous improvement over Tyrwhitt's slow and middle-aged *Amethyst*.

While the Grand Fleet came south, Tyrwhitt's destroyers, with the cruisers of Force C in support, were ordered to sweep the area of the North Sea up to a line N 30° W from Terschelling Light. Keyes was also ordered to have his submarine flotilla watching for the Germans. He sent D-2 and D-3 to watch the Ems, and E-7 to watch the Weser.

Despite the fact that the scouts of the Grand Fleet moved as far south as the Horn Reef, which marked the northern point of Heligoland Bight, there was only one warning of a U-boat, a report by the *New Zealand* which proved to be false, and no sightings of surface ships were made. It would have been an opportunity for the Germans to attempt their proposed mass attack by torpedo craft, but the British cruisers swept just too far to the north to be seen by the U-boat patrols and, consequently, the Imperial Navy had no inkling whatever of the presence of the British Battle Fleet so near to Germany. At 0930 on 16 August, the Grand Fleet turned north.

Tyrwhitt found the cupboard equally bare. His destroyers and the armored cruisers remained around Terschelling until noon on the 17th, but by then it was clear that the Germans were not at sea. Accordingly, while Force C moved south-west to the Downs to take up a watching patrol, Commodore (T) took the Third Flotilla into Harwich, leaving the First Flotilla to reestablish the patrol lines on the Broad Fourteens which the Admiralty had ordered for the duration of the BEF's passage.

The submarines had a similarly unsuccessful time. The entrances to the German rivers were found to be heavily patrolled by light craft of every description and though D-2 repeatedly tried to attack an armored cruiser moored off the western entrance to the Ems, the shoals were too much for her. E-5 and D-6 both attacked torpedo boats, but such maneuverable shallow-draught targets were difficult to hit, and these attacks also came to nothing. All E-7 could do was keep out of the way of the German patrols, and it was with relief that the four submarines withdrew late on 17 August. From their reports, however, Keyes was able to deduce that it would be worthwhile putting submarines into the Bight on a permanent rotating patrol. He did remark that he felt that some kind of surface operation should first be attempted against the torpedo boats and numerous suspected W/T-equipped trawler-scouts. It was another move in his campaign to begin offensive sweeps into Heligoland Bight.

The Germans had been well aware of, and considerably alarmed by, the presence of the British submarines. Many of the patrols that had so plagued the four submarines had been sent out specifically to hunt for them, and it was thus not surprising that the British returned to Harwich with an exaggerated idea of the strength of the routine patrols in the Bight. For their part, the Germans had embarked upon a second attempt to find the British blockade line in the north, this time by sending three units of the Second Submarine Flotilla to reconnoiter along the Norwegian coast and to investigate the ports along the British east coast which the Germans suspected were being used as fleet bases. Inclined to favor the Firth of Forth and the Humber, which were indeed the anchorages which the Admiralty had selected for development before the war, the Germans had as yet no idea that the Grand Fleet had been working out of Scapa Flow or that Loch Ewe was just about to come into use.

U-20 and U-21 set out for Norway on 15 August, and passed through the screen of cruisers spread out ahead of the Grand Fleet. Only U-20 saw anything of this, however, and the cruiser and destroyer that she observed were too far away from her to attack. She did see the smoke of the Grand Fleet to the west, but her engines and compass chose that moment to develop defects which forced her captain to abandon his intention of turning west to investigate the Firth of Forth; instead U-20 turned back for Germany. She returned to Heligoland late on 19 August, having spent a total of thirty-four hours submerged during her patrol, which was considered a great feat. U-21 passed very close to both the First Battle Cruiser Squadron and the Second Cruiser Squadron without observing them, and her reconnaissance of Moray Firth, at the head of which was the naval base of Invergordon, came to nothing. There were so many trawlers and drifters in the area, though few of these were in naval employ, that the submarine had continually to submerge. It was not long before U-21's captain decided that it would not be possible to penetrate the Firth in such conditions. Turning south, U-21 sighted four destroyers off May Island at the entrance to the Firth of Forth, but night came down before she could get into position to attack, and eventually she had to return to Heligoland empty-handed, arriving on

21 August. The reports from the two submarines, despite their lack of successes, finally served to convince the Command that the blockade line was much further to the north than they had first estimated.

U-22 had more luck in her reconnaissance of the Humber, for though she found no targets and was several times detected and chased, her captain brought valuable information about the strength and routine of the British patrols in the area, as well as the fact that no mines had been laid around the Humber. This was very valuable information indeed, for it followed that if no mines had been laid off the Humber, then it was unlikely that they would have been laid off any of the other major ports and anchorages on the east coast.

The Germans decided temporarily to abandon long-range offensive submarine operations. They had already lost two U-boats and machinery defects had put several more out of action for weeks. The decision was made instead to begin cruiser operations against the east coast and the British forces before the Channel. The Admiralstab was by now almost certain that all the British heavy ships were in the north and that, consequently, light cruisers could be sent out with little risk or need for heavy support. The first operation decided upon was an attack against the patrols around the Broad Fourteens. The Admiralstab had no idea as yet of the presence of the armored cruisers on the Downs, but they made a shrewd estimate of the strength of the destroyer patrols and guessed that no more than one flotilla could be at sea at a time.

Two of the newest light cruisers, *Stralsund* and *Strassburg*, were selected, along with the submarines U-19 and U-24. The intention was that the two cruisers would move south-west and penetrate the British patrol lines unobserved during the dark hours on the morning of 18 August when they were to turn back at dawn and drive the British destroyers before them. The two U-boats were to position themselves so as to intercept any heavier British ships which might attempt to follow the light cruisers north. A measure of support was to be provided by the cruiser *Kolberg*, which was ordered to station herself off Terschelling, while Hipper was instructed to have his First Scouting Group in the Schillig Roads ready to sail.

The cruisers, under the command of Captain Harder, sailed from Heligoland at 0700 on 17 August. Despite a report that British light cruisers were in the area, the operation continued and the cruisers moved quietly south-west.

The first encounter occurred west of the Smith's Knoll Light, at dawn the next day. The submarines E-5 and E-7, returning on the surface from their patrols off the Weser, were amazed to see a cruiser approaching them from the south-east. Her four funnels suggested to them that the ship was one of the *Cressy* class, but the two submarines were quickly disabused of this notion when the *Strassburg* replied to their challenge by opening fire. Considerably shaken, E-5 and E-7 were nonetheless able to submerge unscathed. The fast-moving German was no target at all, and they were forced to remain underwater until the area was clear and they could resume their journey home.

At 0540, the *Stralsund* was sighted bearing due west by the destroyer *Lizard*. The First Flotilla was further to the east than the Germans had estimated, and their plans to "roll up" the British were thus set at naught. Nevertheless, *Stralsund* turned to engage and within a few minutes the four boats of the Fifth Division were under heavy fire. On receiving the sighting report from *Lizard*, with the subsequent elaboration that the enemy appeared to be a light cruiser of the *Karlsruhe* class, Captain Blunt in the *Fearless* ordered his flotilla to chase north-west. A little after 0600, *Fearless* came into sight of the German and Blunt was alarmed to hear from his lookouts aloft that the cruiser appeared to be, not a light cruiser, but an armored cruiser of the *Yorck* class.

The near identical silhouettes of the two classes made the mistake an understandable one, but it was to have serious consequences. Against a light cruiser with 105mm guns, Blunt could be confident that the 4″ guns and the torpedoes of *Fearless* and his numerous destroyers would give him the advantage. *Yorck*, however, was armed with 210 mm and 150 mm guns. Such heavier metal, with all the advantages of range and height which the German possessed, convinced Blunt that his wisest course would be to turn south and call up help in the hope that stronger forces would be able to come up in time. At 0610, *Fearless* ordered the destroyers to turn south-west while Blunt attempted to make contact with the remainder of the Southern Force.

The effect of Blunt's messages was galvanic. Cruiser Force C was coaling at anchor in the Downs, but Rear Admiral Campbell had the colliers cast off and his squadron moving within twenty minutes. Christian was at The Nore in the *Sapphire*, but he too was very shortly at sea, having transferred to the *Euryalus*. Tyrwhitt was just leaving Harwich with the Third Flotilla to relieve the First on the Broad Fourteens. Hearing the news, his ships immediately worked up speed, joyful at the first real prospect of action since the *Königin Luise*.

Though Harder turned to follow the British south-west, he was not happy with his situation. The only reason that he could find for the British action was that they were trying to lure *Stralsund* onto something heavier; he could not guess at the mistake that had been made and the fact that the British, in their excitement, were transmitting *en clair*, confirmed his suspicions that he was being led into a trap. In this state of

mind, it was natural that the German would expect any further sightings
to be other British warships hunting for the *Stralsund*. And, at 0645,
another sighting was reported—what seemed to be a light cruiser.
Where such a vessel was, more destroyers were likely to be, and reasoning thus, Harder turned *Stralsund* away. In fact, there were no other
British light cruisers in the vicinity, but it is possible that what the
Germans saw was the old torpedo gunboat *Halcyon*, which was conducting mine-sweeping operations in the area. She was just that much larger
than a destroyer to be converted into a light cruiser by fevered imagination.

Seeing the German turn away, Blunt was unsure whether to follow.
He was still not entirely confident of the identity of his opponent, and
now *Goshawk* and *Lizard*, ships of the Fifth Division which had been
closest to the German, submitted that she was not *Yorck*, but a light
cruiser. Blunt was inclined to credit this, for not only had the cruiser
turned away, but there had been no sign of heavy gunfire at any stage,
though several of the destroyers had been well within the effective range
of such weapons. As soon as he had collected all the destroyers about
Fearless, Blunt turned at 0800 to follow *Stralsund*. By now, however, it
was too late. Despite efforts by Tyrwhitt to cut off the German retreat at
Terschelling, the German cruisers got clear away, and they were soon
followed in by the two submarines, neither of which had observed any of
the encounter.

It was a dispiriting episode, especially for Blunt and the First Flotilla.
They were now certain that the German had been only a light cruiser,
and it was difficult to avoid the conclusion that, had the destroyers been
handled better, they could at least have disabled her. Tyrwhitt, too, was
bitterly disappointed, but he and the Admiralty avoided making any
censure, although it was decided to station three submarines around
Smith's Knoll to deal with any further such excursions.

The Germans were not long in launching another operation. Sharing
the British preoccupation with the danger that the enemy might be
using wireless-equipped trawlers as scouts, the Admiralstab had determined on a raid on the British fishing fleet on the Dogger Bank. It was an
age-old convention that civilian fishing vessels should be left to their
trade by the belligerents, but the Germans were convinced that the
British had taken advantage of this traditional immunity to employ
trawlers as scouts. The raid, involving two cruisers and a torpedo-boat
flotilla, was planned to take place as soon as a reconnaissance of the area
to the north and north-west of the Bight could be carried out. A report of
British submarines in the west, however, caused the C in C to cancel the

reconnaissance and go ahead with the raid alone. Keyes sent D-5, E-4, and E-9 into Heligoland Bight on 20 August, and their discovery caused considerable alarm that they might be the forerunners of a British destroyer sweep. However, extensive searches of the Bight on 21 August, failed to uncover any sign of the submarines or of British surface forces.

Thus reassured, von Ingenohl ordered the Dogger Bank operation to begin that very day. The *Strassburg, Rostock*, and the Sixth Torpedo-Boat Flotilla were allocated to carry out the raid, but there was some dispute over the C in C's decision to send only the light cruiser *Mainz* to sea in support. Rear Admiral Hipper considered quite properly that a movement so far into the North Sea should have heavy cover—at the very least the First Scouting Group—but von Ingenohl, with the Kaiser's dictum in the front of his mind, refused to allow the battle cruisers to do anything more than wait in the Schillig Roads with steam up for sea. It was dangerous doctrine, for the Dogger Bank was 150 miles away from Heligoland and if the light cruisers were to make contact with a superior force, most notably the First Battle Cruiser Squadron, they would have little hope of escape.

This "somewhat inglorious venture" resulted in the destruction of eight British trawlers. No wireless installations were found, but this did not stop the Germans, convinced of their theory, from capturing the crews and handling them very roughly. It was their first exercise in total war at sea. The British submarine D-5 made an attack on the force when it was some seventy-five miles from Heligoland, but though she was in a perfect firing position, only some six hundred yards off the bow of *Rostock*, she botched the job. Her two torpedo salvo passed well ahead of the German cruiser. D-5's captain came in for a great deal of criticism on his return to Harwich, for Keyes had specifically ordered that only one torpedo be fired at a time, thus giving the submarine a chance to fire a second if the first had missed. Had D-5 followed this dictum, the range was such that it is probable that, with a revision of calculations, she would have struck the *Rostock* with her second torpedo. It is also possible, however, that the torpedoes ran underneath the German. Keyes noted in his *Memoirs* that the "live" torpedoes were forty pounds heavier than ones with practice warheads; this resulted in their running deeper than their setting.

The next operation which the Admiralstab planned was the real beginning of the much-vaunted mining campaign. Two mine-layers, the purpose-built *Nautilus* and the *Albatross*, were now available and they were to be sent, each accompanied by a cruiser and half flotilla of

torpedo boats, to lay fields off the Humber and Tyne. The intention
behind the field off the Humber was to close the main shipping channel
along the east coast, while the Tyne was selected because the Admiralstab believed it to be a major base for fleet auxiliaries and for major
warships.

Yet again, no heavy support was allowed, Hipper's strong objections
being overruled. The operation was timed to begin on 23 August, but
had to be delayed twenty-four hours because *Mainz*, the cruiser allocated
to accompany *Nautilus*, ran aground. However, at 2000 on the 24th,
Albatross, Stuttgart, and the six boats of the Eleventh Half Flotilla left
Heligoland for the Tyne. *Nautilus, Mainz*, and the six boats of the Third
Half Flotilla, with less distance to go, departed at 0500 the next day.
Both groups had been given instructions to take off the crews and sink
every British trawler that they met, whether wireless equipped or not.

The mine fields, laid around midnight of 25–26 August, went down
without hitch. Each mine-layer carried two hundred mines, and laying
them took little under an hour. *Albatross* set down one field eleven miles
in length, while *Nautilus* laid two, each five miles long. Both groups had
great trouble fixing their positions in the foggy conditions which they
met, and this resulted in the *Albatross* laying her field some thirty miles
to the north-west of the planned position.

The groups returned to Germany late on 26 August. Even as they
moved into the Bight, their fields claimed a first victim. At 2200, the
Danish fishing vessel *Skuli Fogett* sank on the Tyne field, with the loss of
four men. Early on the morning of the 27th, the trawler *City of Belfast*
came into the Humber with the news that she had exploded two mines in
her nets off the port the night before. The Tyne field would claim several
victims in the next few months, but, ironically enough, the loss was
Germany's far more than Great Britain's. The victims were almost one
and all neutrals, and the mines had been laid on a commercial shipping
lane without warning. That she had been the first to resort to such
devices was to lower Germany's credit considerably with the Scandinavian countries. The resultant ill-feeling would greatly ease Britain's task
when the time came to tighten the blockade and impose controls on all
shipping.

The Humber field came close to claiming two very important victims.
Unknown to the Germans, the Humber was now the base of Cruiser
Force K. The commanders at Harwich had jointly informed the Admiralty that the situation with regard to heavy cover for the Southern Force
was extremely unsatisfactory. Were the Germans to make a sortie with
the First Scouting Group against the patrols on the Downs and Broad

Fourteens, it was quite likely that they would be able to annihilate both the destroyer patrols and the antiquated *Cressys* and get back to their anchorages before the Grand Fleet or the First Battle Cruiser Squadron had even reentered the North Sea. It was an incontrovertible argument and the Admiralty was forced, belatedly, to reorganize its dispositions. A force of battle cruisers was allocated to the Humber and Rear Admiral Sir Archibald Gordon Moore was appointed in command. The *Invincible* had only just returned to service, with her turret power system converted to hydraulic after an experimental electrical system had proved unsatisfactory. Beatty was expecting that she would be added to his command, but he had not only to do without her, but also suffer the loss of the *New Zealand* to Cruiser Force K. He was, however, a little mollified by the promise that *Inflexible* and *Indomitable* would join the First Battle Cruiser Squadron as soon as they returned from the Mediterranean. Moore was promised three of the new light cruisers as soon as they were completed and he hoisted his flag at Queenstown, where the *Invincible* had been calibrating her main armament, on 12 August. A week later, *Invincible* and *New Zealand* were in the Humber.

At all events, when the two battle cruisers sailed at 1100 on 27 August for their first offensive sortie, a sortie which was to result in the Battle of the Heligoland Bight, they passed within two miles of *Nautilus*'s first field. The Admiralty sent minesweepers to clear the fields as soon as they had received warning of them, but it was not until the battle cruisers had actually sailed and passed clear of the area that it was realized how small had been their margin of safety.

The discovery of the fields spurred efforts to organize a proper minesweeping service along the entire east coast. It was soon realized that, as long as the position of the German fields was known, it was not necessary to risk extensive losses in sweeping them up. The idea of a "war channel" along the coast was fast growing as trawlers were requisitioned, converted, and allocated to each port.

The Admiralty and many of the coastal patrols were in the throes of "trawler phobia," and considered that fishing vessels had crept into the coast and laid the mines. The breach of convention which the Germans had already committed in laying the mines on commercial shipping lanes perhaps gave some small credibility to this theory, but the expert opinion of the Inspecting Captain of the Minesweepers, Captain T. P. Bonham, was quite correct in that such operations were impossible. Despite this, on 31 August the Admiralty issued a statement denying that any British mines had yet been laid, and saying that:

The mines off the Tyne were laid 30 miles to seaward, not as part of any definite military operation, nor by German ships of war, but by German trawlers, of which a considerable number appear to have been engaged in this work.

In retrospect, the declarations were little more than wishful thinking, but they may be taken as one of the first blows in the long propaganda war that was to rage alongside the "flesh and blood" conflict.

CHAPTER 5

Heligoland Bight

The idea was Keyes's in the first place. With the inconclusive three weeks that had passed, he and Tyrwhitt were thirsting for action. It was not enough to patrol the North Sea outside the Bight in the hope that the Germans would emerge; the Harwich Force would have to go into the Bight and join Keyes's submarines to have any chance of dealing the enemy a blow.

Keyes had discovered from his submarines that large numbers of German torpedo boats were patrolling the Bight during the daylight hours at high speeds—too high for the submarines to attack them. In the late afternoon these vessels were relieved by other torpedo boats which, covered by light cruisers, stood out to sea to patrol before returning at dawn. Most had been observed in an area some forty miles to the north of Heligoland, and Keyes proposed a sweep by light forces from east to west across the Bight. Keyes summed up his thinking in a letter to Arthur Leveson:

> . . . it is not by such incidents (the failure to pursue the *Stralsund*) we shall get the right atmosphere—for ourselves absolute confidence and a certain knowledge that "when the enemy come out we will fall on them and smash them," and, on the other side, "When we go out those damned Englanders will fall on us and smash us. . . ." We must prepare for "The Day" by creating the correct atmosphere on both sides. If that is achieved, the loss of a few light craft would surely be a small price to pay.[1]

Keyes wanted Tyrwhitt's light forces to close the German coast and, at dawn, turn and drive what he hoped would be a confused huddle of the German day and night patrols into the North Sea. Keyes's nine available submarines would be divided into two groups, half to be offshore and occupy the attention of the German torpedo boats before the drive began, thus keeping them away from the coast, the other half to be close inshore where they could intercept any heavy units coming out. To seaward would be positioned heavier units, sufficient to support the Harwich Force against any German light cruisers that might emerge from the inner Bight. Keyes intended that the Grand Fleet would come down from Scapa to support the sweep and he envisaged Goodenough's six light cruisers being in close support while the battle cruisers and battle squadrons patrolled outside the Bight.

The plan relied on two considerations. First, that Tyrwhitt would not meet heavier German metal than his own to seaward of him during the course of the drive, for they would be able to trap him outside the Bight. Second, was that the operation had to be conducted with the utmost speed; a delay would permit warning to get through to the ships in the Jade Bay that were thought to lie at immediate notice for steam. In concept and substance, it was a sound plan with every chance of success—for Keyes and Tyrwhitt had agreed with each other on the need for a powerful covering force, as powerful as could be put together.

While Tyrwhitt went back to sea with the First Flotilla on a routine sweep, Keyes went to the Admiralty on 23 August. Keyes at first followed service procedure. He submitted his plan to the War Staff, as was proper for a relatively junior officer, but he "found the Staff too fully occupied with the daily task to give the matter much attention."[2] Infuriated by this response, and never one prone to circumspection, Keyes sought and received an interview with Churchill.

It was enough. Struck by the proposal, Churchill summoned Tyrwhitt (who had to return posthaste from sea), Prince Louis, Vice Admiral Sir Frederick Hamilton, and Sturdee to a meeting in his offices the following afternoon. Delayed by Tyrwhitt's late arrival, the meeting soon accepted the commodores' proposals, but with some important modifications.

Despite the plea for the involvement of the entire Grand Fleet—and especially the battle cruisers—Sturdee would only approve the use of Cruiser Force C, with the five antiquated *Bacchantes*, and K, with the battle cruisers *Invincible* and *New Zealand*, under Rear Admiral Sir Archibald Moore. The direction of the sweep was also altered; now it would commence close inshore at 0400, when the Harwich Force would begin steaming south for four hours, before altering course at 0800 to the west. Sturdee did not think that the Harwich Force should risk an engagement with both the German night and day patrols and he calculated that by the time the two sides met, the night forces would be in harbor and the stand-by ships at their least prepared, in the expectation of another peaceful day ahead.

The Admiralty made one more alteration to the plan. A vessel had been sighted at anchor off an island at the entrance to the Western Ems and, thinking that this was a German cruiser, the decision was made for three seaplanes from the carrier *Engadine* to attack it. *Engadine* would operate with Admiral Christian's Cruiser Force C until the time for the attack, when she would be detached to carry it out with her own escort, the light cruiser *Sapphire*.

Keyes was sailing on the 26th and the remaining forces on the 27th, to commence the sweep on the morning of Friday, 28 August. Fairly pleased with these plans, Keyes and Tyrwhitt returned to Harwich to make their own dispositions. But, incredibly, Jellicoe was not told until two days afterwards of the results of the meeting. This was an inexcusable oversight on the part of the War Staff, and Sturdee as its chief, for Jellicoe was Tyrwhitt and Keyes's Commander in Chief for all operations such as these. What was worse, when the Admiralty did eventually inform Jellicoe, the message gave no more than the barest outline of the plan, with no precise positions or dates. All the signal said was:

> A destroyer sweep of First and Third Flotillas with submarines suitably placed is in orders for Friday from east to west, commencing between Horn Reef and Heligoland, with battle cruisers in support.[3]

Jellicoe was confused and worried by this bald declaration. He, realizing that there was a grave danger of the light forces and the inadequate support allotted them becoming entangled with vastly superior German forces, soon composed a reply, sent within two hours of receipt of the Admiralty's signal:

> Propose to co-operate in sweep on Friday (28th), moving Grand Fleet Cruisers and Destroyers to suitable positions with Battle Fleet near. Request that I may be given full details of proposed operations by land-wire tonight. I am leaving at 6 a.m. tomorrow.[4]

But once this signal went off, Jellicoe's anxiety and confusion increased still further. He found it difficult to believe that the Admiralty could coolly keep the Commander in Chief in such ignorance. At 1754 he signaled, somewhat plaintively:

> Until I know the plan of operations I am unable to suggest the best method of co-operation, but the breadth of sweep appears to be very great for two flotillas. I could send a third flotilla, holding a fourth in reserve,

and can support by light cruisers. What officers will be in command of operations, and in what ships, so that I can communicate with them? What is the direction of the sweep and [the] northern limits, and what ships take part?[5]

Even these messages did not have the desired effect on the Admiralty which, in the words of the postwar *Staff Monograph*:

. . . seems to have been preoccupied at the time with the prospect of the Germans gaining Calais and Dunkirk and the changes of disposition which this would necessarily require, and possibly they did not wish to see the Grand Fleet involved in operations in the Bight.[6]

Sturdee telegraphed to Jellicoe that "co-operation by battle fleet not required. Battle Cruisers can support if convenient."[7] Having first taken operational control quite improperly out of the C in C's hands originally, Sturdee worsened the confusion by his failure to take responsibility and keep Jellicoe informed at this crucial moment. For, even though Jellicoe acted swiftly, ordering Beatty and Goodenough to sail at 0500 on 27 August, and followed them to sea himself, none knew precisely what was wanted and they were still awaiting the Admiralty's information as to the plans for the sweep. Beatty made a general signal to the Battle Cruiser Force at 0800 which remarked that he imagined

Seventh Cruiser Squadron Cruiser Force C and odds and ends will also take part, but know very little. Shall hope to learn more as we go along.[8]

Keyes and Tyrwhitt had already sailed. Not until 1310 on the 27th did the Admiralty send them any word of the reinforcements and their intentions. There was, it must be admitted, some small excuse for the delay in that the Admiralty had to consult with Beatty and Goodenough as to their intentions, but the light forces should have at least been told at the first opportunity that the heavier ships were at sea. As it was, the delay was so long that the message failed to get through to the destroyers' and light cruisers' inefficient wireless installations. It was to be a near-fatal omission.

All the ships originally involved, including the submarines, had been instructed that the only British ships above destroyer size which would be in the Bight on the 28th were Tyrwhitt's two light cruisers, *Arethusa* and *Fearless*. All other cruisers and heavy ships sighted were to be considered hostile and attacked on sight.

Jellicoe sailed with the Second and Fourth Battle Squadrons at 1745 on the 27th. The First and Third Battle Squadrons were already exercising at sea and the Commander in Chief planned to rendezvous with them at 0700 the next day. Beatty, with his three battle cruisers, determined to join Moore in the *Invincible* and *New Zealand* in a position ninety miles to the north-west of Heligoland. Jellicoe, operating off the Orkneys, would still be too far away to support the operation but, almost by default, his sane measures had restored some chance of success to what had become a dubious venture indeed. It remained, however, for Tyrwhitt and Keyes to be told. The matter was the more urgent since Goodenough's six light cruisers were on a course that would bring them into contact with the Harwich Force by 0800.

That morning, as Tyrwhitt's ships moved into position to begin their sweep, they sighted the indistinct shapes of three of Goodenough's light cruisers. Alarmed, Tyrwhitt made the challenge and, to his relief and surprise, received the correct reply. Confused, Tyrwhitt signaled, "Are you taking part in the operations?" and Goodenough replied, "Yes, I know your courses and will support you. Beatty is behind us."

The Harwich Force began the sweep, steering east-north-east at 20 knots. *Arethusa* was leading, with the Third Flotilla disposed in four divisions of four, two on each beam of the light cruiser, while the *Fearless* and the sixteen destroyers of the Fourth Flotilla were steaming similarly positioned two miles astern of the *Arethusa*. Eight miles further back were the six light cruisers of the First Light Cruiser Squadron. Beatty's five battle cruisers were thirty miles to the west of Tyrwhitt's ships, loitering at their rendezvous as they waited upon events.

On the morning of 28 August 1914, which dawned calm and very misty, the German patrols were particularly weak. The usual outer and inner lines were being maintained, the outer consisting of nine modern torpedo boats of the First Torpedo Flotilla and the inner line, nine minesweepers (converted old torpedo boats) of the Third Minesweeping Division. This was quite in order, but the state of the stand-by cruisers left much to be desired. Of the four vessels in the area of Heligoland, one, *Hela*, was an 1896 museum piece which could barely make 20 knots and would be outgunned by a British L class destroyer. Two of the other three, *Ariadne* and *Frauenlob*, were efficient enough ships, but they were not new and would stand little chance against a British "*Town*." Only the fourth, *Stettin*, could be considered a modern vessel, and she was lying at anchor to the east of Heligoland with steam up in only half her boilers. It would be some time before she could be able to reach her designed speed of 25½ knots. The cruiser *Mainz* was, it is true, lying off the Ems to the south, but all seven of the other light cruisers assigned to the patrol were in Wilhelmshaven or Brunsbuttel. What is more, as the British *Staff Monograph* remarked of the German system:

There were two important points it overlooked; one was an attack by capital ships; the other was the tide flowing quietly seaward over the bar of the outer Jade.[9]

In essence, the patrol forces could not be reinforced by capital ships from inside the bar that morning. The *Monograph* continued:

It was low water on the Bar at 0933, the least depth would then be about 25 feet, and the Bar could not be passed between 0700 and 1200, that is, roughly within 2½ hours of low water.[10]

Captain John Creswell has remarked of the German Command that:

They seem to have shut their eyes to the possibility and merely to have realised vaguely that if it took place their defence line would have to retire under the cover of the fixed defence.[11]

This supposition might have proved correct had the patrols encountered the British *in clear conditions* but the fog that lay over the Bight that morning would bring a very different result.

The first incident of the day occurred at dawn, when the torpedo boat G-194 sighted the periscope of the submarine E-9. G-194 turned to ram but E-9 hurriedly went deep, firing a single torpedo which missed her opponent. The torpedo boat reported this incident to the Scouting Group commanders and the Fifth Torpedo Boat Flotilla and aircraft were ordered out of Heligoland to chase the submarine.

The first surface contact was made just before 0700, when the First Flotilla sighted G-194 to the south-east. *Laurel* and her three sisters in the Fourth Division took up the chase as G-194 fled to the south-east, the ships exchanging scattered and ineffective fire. A few minutes later, when G-194 was able to identify them as British in the haze, she signaled to her consorts and to Rear Admiral Maass in the *Köln*, "G-194 attacked by enemy cruisers. Enemy is in 54°22′N., 7°35′E., steering south." This signal was not itself received by any heavy ships for twenty minutes but G-196, which had picked it up, transmitted at 0706, while she ran down toward the sound of the gunfire, "G-194 is being chased by enemy cruisers. . . ."

As the reports came into his flagship, Hipper was satisfied that his torpedo boats were being attacked only by British light craft and that no British armored ships would dare come into the Bight. He had no suspicion that Beatty was so near, and as a result he ordered merely *Stettin* and *Frauenlob* to "hunt destroyers" while he directed the remainder of the light cruisers not at sea to raise steam. No orders were issued to the heavy ships.

Tyrwhitt was concerned that *Laurel* and her sisters should not become too detached from the rest of the flotilla, but his recall signal was not received, and, as other German vessels were beginning to appear out of the mists, at 0726 he turned his ships to port to follow the Fourth Division.

For by now the other divisions of the flotilla had made contact with the vessels coming out of Heligoland at 21 knots in expectation of a submarine chase. Only G-9, their leader, realized from the first that the gunfire ahead was from a surface action although he continued the run to the north-west until he could be sure that the ships ahead were British. *Laurel* and the other three Ls fired on sight and G-9 immediately hauled the flotilla right around on a course back to Heligoland. Even now, the other boats in the flotilla thought that the shell splashes erupting ahead of G-9 were from his own guns, firing at a submarine and it was only when a division of Ls actually loomed into view that they grasped the situation.

Arethusa and her twelve destroyers were now chasing the German torpedo boats at their maximum speed, and this continued until 0740 when Tyrwhitt altered course to east from east-south-east and came down to 26 knots. The ships were spread out in an elongated line abreast, maneuvering by divisions so as to get their guns to bear. The British fire, though steady, was ineffective in the low visibility and long range. The German torpedo boats later reported that many of the 4″ shells failed to explode. *Arethusa*'s forward 6″ began to get the range, the shell splash creeping closer to the Germans with every salvo.

Fearless and her brood were paralleling the Third Flotilla's movements some four miles to the north-west, in sight of the German units but out of effective range, although one division did briefly fire. To the north-east, *Laurel*'s division were continuing their private chase of G-196 and G-194 as the two raced for the shelter of Heligoland. The four destroyers were, by default, accomplishing the return to the fold that Tyrwhitt had desired as they pursued their south-easterly course.

The German Fifth Flotilla were in serious trouble. Expecting only operations against submarines and worn out by the previous weeks' activities, the engineers in several boats were completely unprepared for such high-speed steaming. In V-I and S-13 the situation was particularly bad, the fires having burnt down in one, and their speeds dropped to 20 knots. While V-I, lagging behind, was smothered in a hail of British fire, G-9 signaled urgently for cruiser support and covering fire from the batteries at Heligoland, which were well within range.

Unfortunately for the Fifth Flotilla, the battleground was still shrouded in mists and, though the batteries strained to see through the murk, they could not discern the British ships and did not open fire. V-I was struck first at 0750, a 4″ shell piercing her upper deck and exploding in the after stoke-hold. It killed one man and wounded two. A few minutes later a second shell struck, under the bridge on the starboard side; this disabled a turbine and wrecked the steering controls.

The inner patrol of minesweepers, meanwhile, had not picked up any of the torpedo boats' enemy reports and they were under the impression that the gunfire was from an unscheduled gunnery practice. D-8 was soon disabused of this notion when she came in sight of the *Arethusa* and the Third Flotilla. They poured a hail of fire into her. Struck by five shells, her captain and first lieutenant dead, seventeen men wounded, and her speed much reduced, she could take little more punishment. Her four sisters were hidden from the British, but there would be little doubt of their fate if they could not get through to Heligoland. Their only hope lay in immediate intervention from the cruiser patrols.

It came. In accordance with Hipper's instructions *Frauenlob* left her anchorage and steered north-north-west, working up speed to 25 knots. *Stettin*'s captain decided that the situation demanded his ship's immediate presence on the scene and he determined to sail without waiting for the remaining boilers to be flashed up. Steaming at less than 20 knots, *Stettin* appeared out of the mists to the east at 0757, the leading British ships sighting her at the same time as they discerned *Frauenlob* coming up from the south-south-east.

The appearance of the German cruisers put a very different complexion on events, and the British forces immediately altered several points to starboard, breaking off their actions with the German light craft. *Arethusa* fired a few salvoes at *Stettin* as she turned south, but the shells went nowhere and *Stettin* was not even aware that she was being fired upon. The duels would fall out between *Fearless* and *Stettin*, and *Frauenlob* and *Arethusa*.

The efficient *Fearless* engaged *Stettin* and soon had her range. By 0805 this had dropped to 7,000 yards and the British cruiser was making good practice. She scored one hit, knocking out *Stettin*'s No. 4 gun on the starboard side and causing several casualties. *Stettin* turned away. Her first duty was done as the embattled torpedo boats were by now under the guns of Heligoland; the minesweepers were, it had to be admitted, still at sea but *Stettin*'s speed had dropped to 15 knots, and her captain decided to withdraw and take the opportunity to raise steam in all boilers. *Fearless*, in accordance with the orders to continue the sweep, did not follow but turned to the south-south-west to follow Commodore (T).

For, as the *Frauenlob* came up from the south-south-east, *Arethusa* had turned to a course of south-south-west to engage her. The German cruiser had the edge over Tyrwhitt's brand new flagship. Despite the

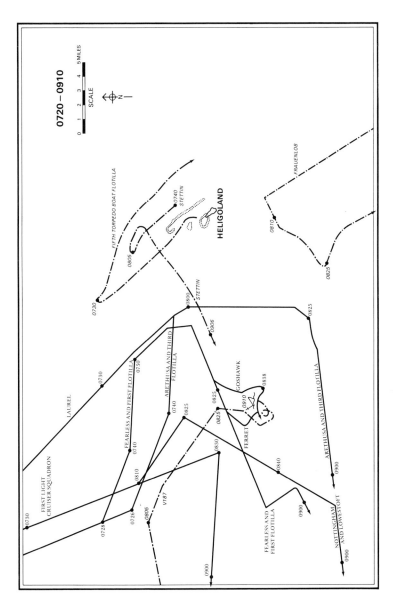

Heligoland Bight Phase 1

support that her flotilla destroyers were giving, the *Arethusa* was soon in difficulty. Two of her port 4" guns jammed. There had been some warning of this in a practice carried out the day before but it had been shaken off as "there was nothing else to do." A third was knocked out of action by a shell which started a major cordite fire, only extinguished by the bravery of the gun captain. Her wireless and searchlights were destroyed and, more important, a shell from the *Frauenlob* penetrated to the main feed tank and the engine room began to flood. This hit would have a cumulative effect disastrous to the cruiser's speed. Tyrwhitt later wrote to his wife:

> . . . I was so surprised that so many projectiles could fall all round one and burst in all directions and yet so few people killed. We lost eleven killed, including poor Westmacott who was killed at my side on the bridge, and about sixteen wounded, all in the first action with the two cruisers. We had fifteen direct hits on the side and waterline and many in board, besides hundreds of shrapnel holes. [12]

Frauenlob had the advantage as the range dropped, but she did not have it all her own way. *Arethusa* scored ten hits, mainly with her forward 6" and there were heavy casualties at the *Frauenlob*'s guns and control positions, although her fighting abilities were not affected. At 0820 *Arethusa* began altering course slowly to starboard and by 0830, she was heading almost due west. She had scored one spectacular, though ineffective, hit under *Frauenlob*'s bridge before she turned to the west but, despite *Arethusa*'s obvious damage, *Frauenlob* would not follow and herself turned away to the east. The patrols had been saved from disaster and *Frauenlob*'s captain wisely decided to leave any revenge on the British to the reinforcements that he knew would soon be coming out. The Ls and *Arethusa* had already unsuccessfully attempted to torpedo his cruiser, and it was obvious that *Frauenlob* would stand no chance in a general melee with the numerous and heavily armed destroyers of the Harwich Force.

With the Harwich Force steering west-south-west at 20 knots, the First Flotilla with divisions in line abreast of the *Fearless*, the Third Flotilla in a very rough line ahead formation about the *Arethusa*, and the *Frauenlob* withdrawing to the south-east to take no further active part in the battle, it seemed for a time, as if the battle were at an end. There were, however, other actors in the wings.

To the north-west, Keyes, with his destroyers, began to get glimpses of two four-funnelled cruisers through gaps in the mist. Still ignorant of the presence of Beatty and Goodenough in the area, Keyes could only think that these vessels must be hostile and he reported their presence as such to Tyrwhitt. But Keyes did not attack, for if they were hostile, they would be able to cut down his two little ships before ever they came within effective torpedo range. And, Keyes reasoned, perhaps they were not hostile. Why, if they could see him, had they not opened fire upon him? Keyes was a man of almost infallible fighting instincts and his urge to caution served both him and Goodenough well that day. For the time being, Commodore (S) was content to shadow.

Eight miles to the north-west Goodenough received Tyrwhitt's action reports and increased to full power, detaching *Nottingham* and *Lowestoft* to assist the Harwich Force. The two turned east, but Captain C.B. Miller, in the *Nottingham*, decided that any action must be further to the south and he accordingly turned in that direction. By doing so, he unwittingly sealed the fate of the German torpedo boat V-187, although the other five torpedo boats in the outer patrol had by 0830 got clear of the British forces and were making for the Jade. It seemed to the Germans as though they had escaped with little damage from the British attack. This was, however, only the beginning of the day.

V-187 had been the central boat in the outer patrol, lying to the south-west of G-194 and G-196. In accordance with orders, she was running to Heligoland, in the hope of evading the British forces in the area. This was not to be. At 0820, *Fearless* and her consorts sighted the lone German some 6,000 yards ahead. Captain Blunt at first detached *Goshawk*'s division to chase but then had sudden doubts as to the identity of the V-187, thinking that she might be Keyes's *Lurcher*. He attempted to recall *Goshawk*, but to Commander Meade it was obvious that the V-187 was hostile, and he ignored the signal and continued the chase.

V-187 at first attempted to run for the Jade to the south-south-east, but the four British destroyers fast began to overhaul her on this course and the torpedo boat's captain turned her to the south-west. Exchanging scattered shots with her pursuers, V-187 began to have some hope of escaping in the mists and the increasing pall of smoke. This hope, however, was soon dispelled when *Nottingham* and *Lowestoft* suddenly came upon the pursuit from the north-west. They immediately opened fire at a range of 4,000 yards. V-187's captain determined upon a bold stroke in a last-ditch attempt to save his ship. It nearly succeeded as V-187 hauled around to the north-east and sped past the *Goshawk* and her consorts. These turned a little late and it seemed for a moment as though V-187 might get away.

There remained, however, the First Flotilla. Its divisions were now well spread out to the north, and they formed a wall through which the unfortunate German torpedo boat could not break. The Third Division opened fire as they came into range and, within a few minutes, V-187 was being smothered by shells from two directions as the Fifth Division turned and came north. All but her after-gun were knocked out of action, the bridge was struck, and the torpedo boat brought to a standstill under the British fire. The forecastle a mass of flames and the whole ship shrouded in smoke, Lieutenant Commander Wallis ordered scuttling charges to be exploded inside the hull as the British destroyers closed around, calling on him to surrender. At 0910, V-187 sank and *Defender* and others of the Third Division stopped their engines and lowered boats to rescue the torpedo boat's survivors. They were soon joined by the Fifth Division, but the operations received a sudden interruption.

Stettin had gained the twenty minutes of peace that she needed to regain full engineering efficiency when the signals began to come in concerning the continuing British attacks on the patrols still at sea. Immediately the cruiser had worked up to full power she turned back to the east. She came upon the scene at 0906, sighting the British destroyers a few minutes before she opened fire. Her captain, Karl Nerger, who was later to distinguish himself as commander of the raider *Wolf*, wrote:

> At 0906 eight destroyers were sighted bunched together. I at once signalled the Admiral commanding the Scouting Forces, "Am in action with flotilla in square 133," turned to port and opened fire at 7200 metres. The first salvo straddled and thereafter many hits were observed. While most of the destroyers scattered, two remained on the spot, apparently badly damaged, but were soon lost to sight in the mist.[13]

The two destroyers "apparently badly damaged" were in fact trying desperately to get their whalers and their crews back on board with the German survivors. *Stettin*'s fire was inaccurate but it was heavy enough to force *Defender* to leave her two whalers and ten of her own crew to shift for themselves as she fled from the German shells. *Stettin* never saw the boats in the water and did not realize that rescue operations had been in progress, contrary to accusations of inhumanity that were leveled afterwards at her captain. *Stettin* scored no serious damage on the destroyers and was herself struck three times, suffering eleven casualties in the brief engagement. *Ferret* fired a torpedo at her which missed, before breaking off the action.

Stettin did not follow. Her wireless had been put out of action and Nerger, with Commander Otto Feldmann, Chief of the Second U-boat Flotilla who was also on board, decided to remain near Heligoland for a half-hour, completing repairs and issuing orders to the few U-boats that were at sea. It was not until 0930 that *Stettin* resumed a cautious advance to the north-east.

Defender's whalers were later picked up by the submarine E-4 which surfaced alongside the boats at 0930 and took aboard the ten Britishers and three Germans, one of each category of officer, petty officer, and rating "as a sample." The remainder were given provisions and compass and the direction of Heligoland but this measure of humanity proved unnecessary, for the Germans were picked up at noon by the minesweepers G-9 and G-11.

To the north, the British forces were being thrown into some confusion by Keyes's repeated reports of enemy cruisers to the east of his position. Goodenough found it difficult to reconcile *Lurcher*'s position signals with the position which he assumed Commodore (S) was in and it may have crossed his mind that this was a case of mistaken identity. At all events he delayed until 0830 before turning to the west, at which time he would almost certainly have turned in the same direction had the sweep met with no opposition at all. *Falmouth* sighted Keyes's two destroyers at 0820 but they went unrecognized. The poor visibility was proving a bane for the operations of both sides, but at this moment it was the worse for the British as the light forces groped about in the murk, trying to establish the true situation. For Goodenough's turn now had the effect of convincing Keyes that the four light cruisers were chasing him and he turned toward the position at whch he thought Moore's two battle cruisers and the five old *Bacchantes* would be waiting. He was, however, still not entirely certain of their identity and, at 0910, he signaled to Tyrwhitt, "Have our light cruisers come to our area?" Because of damage to *Arethusa*'s wireless he received no reply.

Fearless rejoined the crippled *Arethusa* and took up station on her at 0855. They continued a slow movement west-south-west as the *Arethusa* attempted to repair her action damage and waited for the detached divisions to rejoin. The results of the sweep had been only barely satisfactory, although Tyrwhitt was well aware that German cruisers and fresh torpedo boats would soon be emerging. If the Germans did not know of Beatty's presence, and if the British forces could coordinate their activities, then a substantial success might still be expected. Aboard the *Arethusa*, engineers and other personnel worked frantically to make repairs, although the wireless and the feed tank defects were defying all effort expended upon them.

The German light cruisers were moving. The *Hela*, smallest and weakest of those on patrol, was coming down on the scene from her patrol position. By a providence, since the ship could not have lasted five minutes in a general engagement, a signal from *Stettin* reporting that the enemy had withdrawn stopped her and she returned to the northern patrol area and took no further part in the battle. *Ariadne*, too, had emerged as she received the first enemy reports but the gunfire died away as she approached the scene and her captain, fearing that he would only cause confusion by groping about in the fog, decided to return to the ship's previous billet.

Meanwhile, *Köln* and *Strassburg* were emerging from Wilhelmshaven. They passed the Outer Jade Light at 0934 and steered west-north-west. Maass was unsure of what to expect and he did not know whether the action was still in progress, but he was determined to solve the puzzle and despite the lull continued to steam into the Bight, hoping that he might pick off some British stragglers. *Mainz*, for her part, got under-way from the Ems well before 0900 but her progress north was impeded by meeting heavy fog, the same fog which foiled an attempt by a seaplane from Borkum to scout for the cruiser.

The battle cruisers were already raising steam when at 0850 Hipper requested permission of von Ingenohl to send *Moltke* and *Von der Tann* out under Rear Admiral Tapken at the first opportunity. The C in C approved the request but the force could not leave the Jade until at least 1200. Worse still for the Germans, only these two battle cruisers were immediately available. *Blücher* was coaling inside Wilhelmshaven and *Seydlitz*, Hipper's flagship, was suffering from condenser trouble and only her starboard engine was serviceable. For the time being, the Germans would be able to make no reply either to Beatty or to Good-enough's 6"-gunned light cruisers.

The U-boats were not being employed so as to give any chance of success. Those operational did not venture to seaward of Heligoland, for the Germans expected that the British heavy ships, if they came at all, would be rash enough to come right into the inner Bight and up to the mouths of the rivers with the intention of attacking German units as they emerged. Not even the impetuous Beatty had ever considered such a foolhardy idea and, as a result of this muddled thinking, the German submarines were quite wasted.

Forty miles to the north-west of the battlefield, Beatty's five battle cruisers were waiting, with the five armored cruisers further out still. Beatty was determined not to use the *Bacchantes* if possible, since he regarded them as floating death traps, unfit for modern warfare. As the battle cruisers circled about, Beatty was trying to make sense of the confused and conflicting signals that he was receiving. Unable to guess more than that the Harwich Force appeared to be moving west, at 0930 Beatty began heading west-south-west at 20 knots.

At exactly the same moment, the submarine E-6 was attempting to attack Goodenough's light cruisers, mistaking them for Germans of the four-funnelled *Strassburg* class. Her torpedoes missed and she went deep as *Southampton*, naturally under the impression that she had been attacked by a U-boat, came up to ram. Fortunately, *Southampton* went over E-6 and no damage was done.

At 0945, Keyes signaled to Moore in the *Invincible*, "Am being chased by four light cruisers; am leading them in your direction." Both Beatty and Tyrwhitt, the latter's radio having just been restored to service, received this signal. Beatty decided that the best thing to do was to let Keyes lead these "hostile" vessels on and accordingly he reduced speed to 16 knots and recommenced loitering around one position in order that Keyes should find the battle cruisers where he expected them. Tyrwhitt hastily turned his forces back to the east as the last of the detached divisions rejoined the main body. *Arethusa*'s speed was down to 10 knots but Tyrwhitt was determined to aid his friend and, at 0948, he signaled to Goodenough: "Please chase eastward. Commodore(S) is being chased by 4 light cruisers"; a few minutes later he made to Keyes' force, "I am fast coming to your assistance." Tyrwhitt's position was complicated by a side action which occurred when *Stettin*, which had again come out of the inner Bight, suddenly reappeared. *Fearless* attempted to engage her but was thrown into confusion when she had to go astern to avoid one of her own flotilla. Only a few shots had been exchanged when *Stettin* disappeared again. The sweep continued but the confusion of Commodore(S) was now being resolved.

The mist was clearing around *Lurcher* and *Firedrake*, and Keyes was now so certain of the cruisers' identity that he issued the challenge at 0950—and received the correct reply. As he closed Goodenough, Keyes signaled to the battle cruisers:

> Cruisers are our cruisers whose presence in this area I was not informed [*sic*]. [14]

Beatty was well pleased to hear this and, confirmed in his decision to remain just outside the Bight, he signaled at 1000 to

> S.O. 1st Light Cruiser Squadron, and all destroyers, especially *Lurcher*. My position 54deg. 26'N, 6deg 14'E, remaining here. [15]

He was not needed yet.

Meanwhile, *Lurcher* and *Southampton* were communicating. Keyes, at first relieved by his discovery, was now becoming alarmed at the risk posed to the light cruisers by his own submarines. He signaled:

> I was not informed you were coming into this area; you run great risk
> from our submarines. Position of Commander [*sic*] T at 0945 should read
> 45 miles west. Please give me present position. Your unexpected appear-
> ance has upset all our plans. There are submarines off Ems. [16]

This message not unnaturally raised some eyebrows in the *Southampton*,
and Goodenough replied:

> I came under detailed orders. I am astonished that you were not told. I
> have signalled to *Lion* that we should withdraw. *Nottingham* and *Lowestoft*
> are somewhere in the vicinity. [17]

Keyes had neglected the Harwich Force in his relief and surprise at
discovering the cruisers' identity, but Blunt and Tyrwhitt were by now
almost certain that Keyes had been laboring under a misapprehension.
Tyrwhitt asked Blunt, "Is *Firedrake* and *Lurcher* among you?" and,
receiving the reply, "No," he was certain of the mistake. *Fearless* came
alongside at 1017 and for the next twenty minutes the two senior officers
exchanged information by semaphore, the Third Flotilla being sent on
ahead at 10 knots under Commander Arthur Dutton in the *Lookout*. As
the two lay alongside, the engineers of the *Arethusa* completed the
repairs necessary to bring the ship's speed up to 20 knots. By the time
this was done, Tyrwhitt had decided to withdraw. Keyes had obviously
solved his problem, and it was dangerous for the ships to linger so near to
Heligoland while the enemy must be coming out in great strength. At
1039, the movement to the west was resumed and *Arethusa* and her
flotilla worked up to 20 knots while *Fearless* went ahead to rejoin her own
with strict instructions to keep *Arethusa* in sight in case the repairs could
not stand up to the strain and the ship had to reduce speed.

As Goodenough and Keyes were also moving west it seemed yet again
as if the action must have come to a close. This, however, reckoned
without the German reinforcements which were now emerging from the
inner Bight. Three cruisers, *Strassburg, Köln,* and *Mainz* were closing in
on the Harwich Force from different directions.

It would appear that Maass was so keen to pursue the raiders that he
decided against delaying to concentrate his forces. These were sound
enough tactics if, as he thought, the enemy consisted only of a few small
light cruisers and destroyers, but they were to bring disaster when he
came into contact with Goodenough and Beatty. Attacking in piecemeal
fashion, the German cruisers could be dealt with piecemeal.

Strassburg approaching from the south-east came into sight of the
British forces first. It was what Tyrwhitt had been expecting, and he
hurriedly altered course to the south-west to bring *Arethusa*'s reduced
broadside into play. *Fearless*, too, altered to close with *Strassburg*. Cap-

tain Blunt ordered his flotilla to continue to the west but Commander Dutton ignored his instructions and turned back to join the fray. As it was apparent to Tyrwhitt that the *Arethusa* was out-gunned, he ordered the First Flotilla to make a torpedo attack on *Strassburg*. Three divisions joined *Fearless* and began to maneuver into position to launch their torpedoes. Faced with the two cruisers and so many destroyers intent upon making an attack, *Strassburg* turned away into the mist, her commander, Retzmann, unwilling to engage the Harwich Force single-handed. *Fearless* and the destroyers would have followed her but Tyrwhitt was anxious to make as much ground to the west as possible and did not want them embroiled with any heavier ships. He ordered the First Flotilla to rejoin him.

Blunt obeyed and turned his forces to the west but as he did so *Köln* appeared from the south-east. They turned to engage her and Tyrwhitt, mistaking the *Köln* for a *Roon* class armored cruiser, sent two urgent signals in rapid succession to Beatty, "Am attacked by large cruiser. My position 54° N., 7° 13′E.," and "Respectfully request that I may be supported. Am hard pressed." Beatty reacted immediately by instructing Goodenough to detach two of his cruisers, but Goodenough took matters into his own hands and brought his entire squadron down at 25 knots to do what he could. The decision, however, still remained to be made as to what the battle cruisers would do and it would not be an easy one.

Köln could not face the massed ranks of the Harwich Force and she, like *Strassburg*, turned away into the mist. This afforded Tyrwhitt's vessels a temporary respite and they again turned to the west. It does not seem to have occurred to Rear Admiral Maass, even then, and despite his reputation as a tactician, that the important thing for his ships to do was to concentrate before attacking the British.

Once again, *Strassburg* appeared and she resumed her duel with the *Arethusa*. Tyrwhitt wrote:

> We were receiving a very severe and almost accurate fire from this cruiser; salvo after salvo was falling between 10 and 30 yards short, but not a single shell struck; two torpedoes were also fired at us, being well directed, but short.[18]

Strassburg was steering north-west and the ships of the Harwich Force turned west-north-west to open their "A" arcs. At this time, as *Strassburg*'s shells were falling amongst the flotillas, Blunt added his pleas to those of Tyrwhitt, sending to Beatty and Goodenough, "Assistance urgently required. 54° 0′N., 7° 0′E." Beatty considered the requests. His Flag Captain, Chatfield, describes what happened:

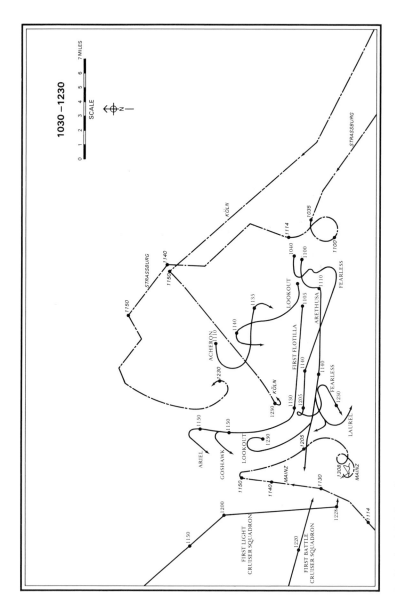

Heligoland Bight Phase 2

The Bight was not a pleasant spot into which to take great ships; it was unknown whether mines had been laid there, submarines were sure to be on patrol, and to move into this area so near to the great German base at Wilhelmshaven was risky. Visibility was low and to be surprised by a superior force of capital ships was not unlikely. They would have had plenty of time to leave harbour since Tyrwhitt's presence had first been known. [Or so Chatfield and the others in the Battle Cruiser Force thought.]

Beatty was not long in making up his mind. He said to me, "What do you think we should do? I ought to go and support Tyrwhitt, but if I lose one of these valuable ships the country will not forgive me."

Unburdened with responsibility, and eager for excitement, I said, "Surely we must go." It was all he needed. . . .[19]

At 1135 Beatty turned his battle squadron to the south-east, increasing speed to 26 knots. Ten minutes later he turned his ships to east-south-east, forming them into line ahead and increasing speed again to 27 knots. He signaled to Captain Blunt, "Am proceeding to your support. . . ."

The action between *Strassburg* and the Harwich Force continued. *Arethusa* and *Fearless* were by now both engaging *Strassburg*, the *Fearless* "most effectively."[20] At 1135 Tyrwhitt ordered a general attack with torpedoes and the First and Second Divisions of the Third Flotilla immediately hauled out to starboard to close the *Strassburg* and fire their torpedoes. The First Division of the First Flotilla turned back and delivered an attack at the same time. Two more divisions of the Third which had been to port of *Arethusa* crossed astern of her in an attempt to approach the *Strassburg* but they failed to get into a firing position and returned to support the cruisers.

Strassburg's captain had feared just such an attack and kept his distance. As the twelve destroyers closed and launched their torpedoes, the cruiser swerved away again, one torpedo being seen to pass to port and another astern. Two torpedoes were fired by *Strassburg* at the *Arethusa* as she was swallowed up into the mist, but they ran short and no British ships were harmed. Again outmatched by the Harwich Force, *Strassburg* kept to her new southerly course, intending to round about and attempt some kind of union with *Mainz* in the south-east. It had been another small victory for Tyrwhitt's forces.

But the units of the First Flotilla still well ahead of the main body were not in such a happy position. At 1130 they sighted *Mainz* moving north ahead of them. The three divisions of destroyers, the Second, Third and Fifth, eleven boats in all, hastily turned into single line ahead

SMS *Mainz*

and paralleled *Mainz*'s course so as to get their broadsides into action and be ready to fire torpedoes.

Both sides were now moving north-north-west and *Mainz* had the better of it, straddling the destroyers repeatedly and receiving no damage in return. The destroyers launched torpedoes, but to no avail and Commander Moir in *Ariel* began to edge over to starboard so as to open the range and lessen the accuracy of the *Mainz*'s fire. By 1145 the action had developed into a chase and it could not be long before *Mainz* disabled one of the British vessels.

Then, at 1150, precisely at the right moment, Goodenough appeared from the north-west. *Mainz* saw the British light cruisers first and hastily reversed course. It was not until a few minutes later that the destroyers, to their great relief, saw what had happened. Immediately the three divisions turned 16 points about, the First positioning itself in the van while the other two fell in astern of the *"Towns"*.

Mainz was fleeing for her life. The *Southampton* opened fire and began scoring hits. *Mainz* was soon in trouble. "Even in the act of turning, the enemy's first salvoes were falling close to us and very soon afterwards we were hit in the battery and the waist. . . ."[21] Disappearing into a bank of mist and cramming on speed for all she was worth, *Mainz* began to leave the *Towns* behind. By 1155 only the flash of the British guns could be seen and, transmitting "Am chased by an enemy armored cruiser," *Mainz* began to have some hope of escaping.

It was not to be. Her run to the south brought her back into the path of the Harwich Force. To the east appeared successively *Fearless*, the First and Second Divisions of the Third Flotilla, and, after a few minutes, *Arethusa* and the other destroyers. *Fearless* immediately opened fire on *Mainz* and scored several hits, damaging *Mainz*'s rudder so that the ship began circling slowly to starboard. The divisions of the Third Flotilla opened out, the First and Second following *Arethusa* to the north-west

HMS *Southampton* in Scapa Flow

while the Third and Fourth turned to the south-west, trying to close *Mainz*.

With three guns soon out of action, her rudder damaged, and fires burning amidships, *Mainz* was quickly reduced to a sorry state but she continued to fight, her gun crews concentrating on the nearby L class destroyers in the Fourth Division. At a range of less than 4,000 yards these ships had turned to fire torpedoes. They were terribly vulnerable and suffered badly.

Laurel led and fired two torpedoes without being struck but, as she turned away, three shells smashed into her. The first exploded in the engine room and did much damage, killing four men. The second struck the forecastle, knocked the forward mount out of action, and killed three. It was the third, however, which did the most damage. This exploded on the mount amidships between the funnels and detonated the "ready use" ammunition, which, being mainly lyddite, went up in one vast concussion. All the gun's crew were killed or wounded and the after-funnel knocked over the side. Shrouded in a pall of smoke and steam, and with her captain lying unconscious, *Laurel* crawled away.

Liberty was next into the hail of fire. She too had fired her torpedoes when a shell struck the bridge, killing the captain and bringing down the mast and searchlight. Her first lieutenant took over and, zigzagging at frequent intervals to throw off *Mainz*'s range takers, *Liberty* continued the action. The third destroyer of the division, *Lysander*, hauled out of line to avoid the damaged *Laurel* and by so doing escaped unscathed but the fourth, *Laertes*, received four hits from *Mainz*'s closely grouped salvoes. One destroyed the center-funnel and a second exploded in No. 2

boiler room and cut off all supplies of feed to the boilers. The ship stopped dead in the water, for the moment completely helpless.

Their work had not been in vain; one torpedo struck the *Mainz*, fired by the destroyer *Lydiard* of the Third Division:

> [The *Mainz*] . . . reared, bent perceptibly from end to end and continued to pitch for a considerable time. The emergency lights went out. Every bit of glass that had remained intact was now shattered, . . . we had nothing left but electric pocket lamps . . . the ship was slowly settling by the bows. . . .[22]

Crippled and with her rudder still jammed to starboard, *Mainz* bore away to the west. She was trapped. Goodenough's light cruisers, coming down at 25 knots, were now less than 6,000 yards from the German, and poured a hail of fire into her. Behind the *Towns* came *Lurcher, Firedrake*, and the Second and Third Divisions of the First Flotilla, adding to the cannonade. To the east were *Fearless* and the battered destroyers of the Third Flotilla's Fourth Division. Circling to the north were *Arethusa* and the other destroyers of the Harwich Force.

The captain of the *Mainz* ordered that the ship be scuttled and abandoned, but this order was not passed and the remaining guns continued to be fought. Stephen King-Hall, in the *Southampton*, wrote:

> We closed down on her, hitting with every salvo. She was a mass of yellow flame and smoke as the lyddite detonated along her length. Her two after funnels melted away and collapsed. Red glows, indicating internal fires, showed through gaping wounds in her sides.[23]

The German official history wrote:

> The state of the *Mainz* at this time was indescribable; she had been hit 200 to 300 times. The W/T office was destroyed, two funnels were down and huge holes had been made in the ship. The ruins of the upper deck were glazed over with green and yellow stuff from bursting shells, which emitted suffocating gas. At the last, only one gun was firing, served by the single survivor of its crew.[24]

When the final round was expended, Goodenough ordered "cease fire" at 1225.

Liverpool, Firedrake, and *Lurcher* closed in to rescue survivors. The latter won the race and, with consummate seamanship, Commander Tomkinson placed the *Lurcher* alongside *Mainz*'s quarter. Though her sea-cocks were open, the ship had not yet taken on a list and there remained time to tranship the bulk of the survivors. Most of the remainder were cut off from the quarterdeck by fires amidships, but

. . . a young officer who had been zealously superintending the removal of the wounded . . . was now standing motionless on the poop. Keyes, anxious to push off before the cruiser capsized and guessing what was perhaps in this young man's mind, shouted to him that he had done splendidly, that there was nothing more he could do, and that he had better jump on board quick; and he held out his hand to help him. But the boy scorned to leave his ship as long as she remained afloat, or to accept the slightest favour from his adversary. Drawing himself up stiffly, he slipped back, saluted, and answered: "Thank you, no."[25]

A few minutes later the ship heeled over to port, hung for about ten minutes and then, at 1310, capsized and sank by the bows. The few left in the water were picked up by *Firedrake* and *Liverpool*, including the young officer who had refused Keyes's offer of rescue, as well as the son of Admiral von Tirpitz.

While Goodenough's forces dealt with the *Mainz*, a new engagement erupted in the west. At 1225 *Köln* and *Strassburg* came into sight to the north. As they bore down, the situation again seemed critical for the Harwich Force. The destroyer divisions were scattered, with three of the Ls badly damaged, *Arethusa*'s speed had dropped again, and it looked to Tyrwhitt as if he would not be able to withdraw without suffering heavy losses. *Fearless* and the destroyers *Goshawk, Lizard*, and *Phoenix* steered boldly to engage the two Germans, even though they were badly out-gunned.

Beatty's timing was perfect. At full speed his battle cruisers appeared out of the mists, passing between the First Light Cruiser Squadron to the south and the *Arethusa* to the north. The two German cruisers could only flee and *Strassburg*, further to the north than her consort, immediately turned away in that direction and was swallowed up by the fog. *Köln* was less fortunate. She delayed too long before running to the north-east, and the seven minutes spent in clear sight of the battle cruisers on the same course were enough to seal her fate. The battle cruisers opened fire, found the range, and began to score hits. Though *Köln* was becoming indistinct in the haze, it appeared as though she had but a few minutes of life. The entry of another German cruiser to the scene, however, won her a momentary reprieve.

The *Ariadne*, older and slower, had been following the *Köln*'s path to the battlefield. Not knowing the weight of the opposition, she had been steering for the sound of the guns, confused as to the progress of events. The only hostile unit that she saw was E-4, and the submarine had immediately dived and made an unsuccessful attack. Just before 1300, *Lion* came into sight on *Ariadne*'s port bow. At a range that was already less than 6,000 yards and was rapidly dropping, *Ariadne* had no chance. She immediately came around 16 points to the south-east in an attempt to escape, but *Lion* had shifted target and opened fire:

> The first [salvo] fell about 330 yards short, but the second pitched so close to our boat that the towering columns of water broke over our forecastle and flooded it.[26]

Lion's next two salvoes struck home and, as the other battle cruisers joined the cannonade, *Ariadne* staggered away, greatly injured. The entire aftercastle was smothered in shell and burst into flames. Forward, shells pierced the armored deck and exploded, wrecking the fire mains, dressing station, and torpedo room. The heat was tremendous as fires broke out all about the ship. Although the hull and machinery were still intact, the magazines had been flooded and the rest of the ship was now one mass of flame and smoke.

Ariadne was no longer a worthwhile target and, at 1310, Beatty altered the battle cruisers' course to port, signaling to all forces in the area to "retire" before he turned to the west at 16 knots at 1315. As the battle cruisers disappeared from sight, the captain of the *Ariadne* decided that the smoke and flames, as well as exploding ready-use ammunition made it too dangerous to continue operations. He mustered the crew on the forecastle, where they began to sing "Deutschland Über Alles."

The cruiser *Danzig* came out of the Jade at 1130 and spent the next hours desperately searching for her own forces, guided, like the others, only by the sound of gunfire. She had finally met *Stettin* when *Ariadne* also appeared and, in answer to the latter's signal "Assistance urgently required," went to her and began rescue operations as the *Ariadne*'s crew abandoned ship.

Meanwhile, the other cruisers were playing a macabre game of "blind man's buff" with Beatty and Goodenough. *Stralsund*, fresh from Wilhemshaven, had also been blundering about in the fog, unable to make contact with her own forces, when at 1306 she sighted the three vessels of the First Light Cruiser Squadron still with Goodenough, moving east-north-east from the sinking *Mainz*. At a range of 8,000 yards, *Stralsund* paralleled the British cruisers' track as they moved to join Beatty. The engagement was brisk and a succession of hits, one of which temporarily knocked out the ship's wireless, convinced *Stralsund*'s captain that it was a futile battle. He turned away again to the south-east and stayed on this course until 1330, when he hoped he would be clear of the British. Goodenough did not pursue. He had received the order to retire and, keen to make contact with Beatty, he was aware that

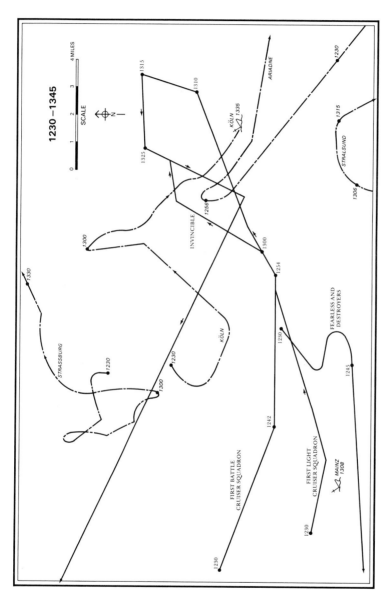

1230 – 1345

SCALE

0 1 2 3 4 MILES

N

STRASSBURG

KÖLN

INVINCIBLE

ARIADNE

KÖLN

STRALSUND

FIRST BATTLE
CRUISER SQUADRON

FIRST LIGHT
CRUISER SQUADRON

FEARLESS AND
DESTROYERS

MAINZ
1308

Heligoland Bight Phase 3

SMS *Ariadne*

he could well be drawn south by *Stralsund* into the arms of superior forces.

Strassburg caught sight of the British cruisers to the south at a range of 8,000 yards at 1308, just after *Stralsund*, but Retzmann did not attempt to get involved and the cruiser began to circle to the north-east, hoping to make contact with the other German light cruisers. At 1330 she sighted Beatty's battle cruisers in clear view to the south-east, at 8,000 yards. Retzmann knew that his one chance was for the four-funnelled *Strassburg* to be mistaken for a *Town*. Accordingly, he held his course. The ploy succeeded, as the British battle cruisers, having just resighted *Köln* were occupied firing at her. At the sight of *Strassburg*, they hesitated and issued the challenge. At the same minute, *Strassburg* was swallowed up in the haze and nothing else could be done. Retzmann, aware of the implications of his encounter, hurriedly sent, "First Battle Cruiser Squadron of the enemy in 117e" before he turned away and began a wide circle to get around to the south. Even as this signal was being received, Hipper, conscious that something was amiss, signaled, "All light cruisers retire on *Moltke* and *Von der Tann*."

It did not save *Köln*. Maass had continued on to the north-east, thinking that the ship had got clear but, too early, *Köln* came around at 1300 to a new course south-east. At 1325, at a range of 4,000 yards,

SMS *Köln*

Köln and *Lion* sighted each other. The battle cruisers immediately altered course to the south-west and opened fire. *Lion's* opening salvoes dealt the deathblow. The 13.5″ high-explosive shells had a catastrophic effect. Within seconds, the steering gear had been wrecked, the engine rooms were useless, and the boilers riddled, one exploding and tearing the side out of the ship. A shell pierced the armored conning tower and killed every man in it and *Köln's* sole survivor later reported that "so many shells were tearing and bursting inside the hull that every moment I expected the ship would go up in the air." She was a useless hulk:

> . . . almost every gun received a direct hit. Many of them had been hurled from their mountings; the armoured shields were pierced and torn. Mutilated bodies lay in heaps amidst a jumble of smashed boats, davits, iron ladders, spars, wireless antennae, ammunition, and shell fragments. The bridge had vanished; each of the three funnels was riddled through and through; shell holes of enormous diameter appeared in the superstructure. . . .[27]

Yet, in spite of the onslaught of the *Lion* and her sisters, *Köln's* guns were able to get away some two hundred rounds at her huge adversaries and these scored five hits on the *Lion*, which, however, did no damage beyond "breaking a few electrical circuits." "One felt the tiny four inch shells spatter against the conning tower, and the pieces 'sizz' over it."[28]

The survivors of the crew mustered on the quarterdeck, gave three cheers, and sang the German "Flag Song" before they were ordered to abandon ship. *Köln* was settling fast, but to speed the end, the last remaining engineer officer set scuttling charges to blow her bottom out. Barely ten minutes after the firing had begun, the unfortunate cruiser disappeared. Beatty ordered his light forces to search the area, but out of a crew of five hundred men, they found only one—Stoker Adolf Neumann.

Beatty's concern now was to get his forces out of this dangerous area with no further damage or losses. He need not have worried. The German light cruisers that had evaded him were still trying to make contact with each other, and it would be almost two hours more before their battle cruisers moved into the outer Bight.

Three cruisers, *Stralsund, Danzig,* and *Kolberg,* the last which had by reason of her slow speed come up to the fray too late, were attempting to save the stricken *Ariadne. Kolberg* was patrolling to the north-west, to give warning should Beatty reappear, while *Stralsund* and *Danzig* took the survivors on board. As the fires died away, it looked as though the *Ariadne* might be saved and her captain began to make plans with his compatriot in *Stralsund* to take her in tow. However, at 1510 she heeled over to port and capsized. German casualties were fifty-nine dead and forty-three wounded.

The *Moltke* and *Von der Tann* came into sight at 1425. Their movements had been restricted by both von Ingenohl, who had signaled, "The large cruisers are not to become engaged with the enemy armoured cruiser squadron," and Hipper, an hour astern in the *Seydlitz,* who had told Tapken to wait for his arrival at 54° 9′N., 7° 5′E. The incoming signals had made it clear that of those cruisers still afloat, only *Ariadne* required any assistance, and Hipper did not want to risk the two battle cruisers in the Bight without *Seydlitz.*

All the German movements were characterized by extreme caution. As Tapken came up to *Ariadne,* he detached the Sixteenth Torpedo Boat Half Flotilla to assist *Kolberg's* patrol but he could do little else save to watch the end of the *Ariadne.* When Hipper came up at 1510, he began a reconnaissance to the north-north-west with *Kolberg, Stralsund,* and *Strassburg* spread out ahead and the three battle cruisers astern. The search for the missing light cruisers was not pressed far because of von Ingenohl's restriction and because Hipper was by now certain that both had been sunk and that the British had rescued all the survivors. It is possible, however, that had the sweep advanced four miles further and come up to the sinking of the *Köln,* they may have found more survivors still in the water.

Joined by *Blücher* at 1600, the First Scouting Group turned for home so as to make the Jade by dark. With the ten torpedo boats of the Eighth Flotilla, minesweepers from Heligoland, and the cruisers *Kolberg, Hela,* and *München,* the night patrols were set and:

at 2003 the *Seydlitz* anchored in Wilhelmshaven Roads and Rear Admiral
Hipper proceeded on board the flagship to make a verbal report.[29]

It was a black day for the Imperial Navy.

The Harwich Force was nursing its cripples home. *Lapwing* attempted
to take *Laertes* in tow but her first wire parted and she was just making
her second attempt when the *Fearless* and the Fifth Division of the First
Flotilla came up to see what they could do. Captain Blunt ordered
Lapwing off and himself took *Fearless* alongside to set up the tow. This
was accomplished in short order and the little force got underway for the
west. Astern came the destroyer *Laurel*. Despite her damage, herculean
efforts by the ship's engine room personnel had managed to bring the
ship's speed up to 10 knots to follow the Harwich Force.

Arethusa, down to 6 knots, gathered the other twenty-three destroyers
about her and was now also heading west again, some eight miles to the
west of *Fearless* and her brood. Beatty and Goodenough continued at
high speed. Beatty, still worried by the possibility of a German counter-
attack, was keen to get Tyrwhitt's ships away from the German coast as
fast as possible.

There were repeated scares as ships believed they could discern
German torpedo boats in the mist, but there was no more activity by the
enemy and, by the time darkness fell, the Harwich Force was well clear
of the Bight and hopeful of getting all its cripples home. *Arethusa*'s
battered and abused machinery gave out, however, and the ship wallowed helplessly as Tyrwhitt waited for the armored cruisers, which
Beatty had ordered in from their patrol position. It would be too difficult
for one of the destroyers to attempt to tow the cruiser, in view of the
darkness and the ship's bulk, and Commodore (T) was very relieved
when the *Bacchantes* loomed up.

Hogue approached the *Arethusa* and her captain, Wilmot Nicholson,
an old friend of Tyrwhitt's, hailed him, "Is that you, Reggie?" As
Tyrwhitt wrote later, "I never was so glad to see him before."[30] *Hogue*
took the *Arethusa* in tow while the other armored cruisers, which had
met with *Fearless*'s more advanced group before sunset, *Cressy* embarking
the wounded and the attached scout *Amethyst* taking *Laurel* in tow, took
ten undamaged destroyers and reestablished the Terschelling patrol with
the three unoccupied armored cruisers under the command of Rear
Admiral Christian.

The other ships went on at 10 knots, *Hogue, Arethusa*, the damaged
destroyers and a small escort heading for Sheerness, while the remainder
returned to Harwich. The next day, Beatty and Goodenough parted

from the Harwich Force and began their journey back to Scapa. A combination of luck, foresight, and courage had ensured that not a single ship had been lost on the operation; it was a considerable success.

As *Hogue* and *Arethusa* neared Sheerness at the end of their progress:

> . . . they were overtaken by a crowded Margate steamer, which passed them quite close and whose passengers evidently concluded that the British cruiser was bringing in a captured German prize. While overtaking the *Arethusa* they stared in silence and some awe at her holed and battered side, but when they came abreast of the *Hogue* they broke into enthusiastic cheering and yelling which they kept up till they were out of hearing. Tyrwhitt signalled to Nicholson, "They evidently think you have a prize in tow," to which his ready witted friend replied, "And so I have, but not the sort they think."[31]

When *Arethusa* came past Sheerness to dock at Chatham, crowds gathered from every direction and the tables were turned as the sight of Tyrwhitt's flagship tore cheer after cheer from the assembled masses. Overnight, the news of the battle had swept Britain, and Tyrwhitt and his men found that they had become heroes, sharing their laurels only with Beatty. The victory went to Britain's head; in the gloom of the retreat in France and the failures at sea elsewhere, it was badly needed. Patriotic postcards, cartoons, and verses were made up, eulogizing Tyrwhitt, but Beatty's image did even better.

Beatty knew little of this as he led the First Battle Cruiser Squadron on a sweep north, while Moore took his two to the Firth of Forth as a refuge until a decision was made on the question of the mining of the Humber. Not until late on 30 August did the First Battle Cruiser Squadron enter Scapa Flow, faced with the wearisome job of coaling before they could relax. Waiting for them there was the battle cruiser *Inflexible*, a long-awaited reinforcement for the squadron.

Twelve hours later, as the Third Battle Squadron left Scapa to begin another of the already tedious succession of sweeps, Jellicoe brought the remainder of the Grand Fleet in for a couple of days of rest. *Iron Duke*'s anchor had barely taken ground before Beatty came on board to make his report.

There was little to be said. Both knew the value of the victory and both knew the risks that Beatty had to take to gain it. Beatty summed up their opinion when he wrote to Arthur Balfour some two years later:

> The end justified the means, but if I had lost a Battle Cruiser I should have been hanged, drawn and quartered. Yet it was necessary to run the risk to save two of our light cruisers and a large force of destroyers which otherwise would most certainly have been lost.[32]

He might well have been disturbed by the risks which he had taken. *Invincible*, for example, was convinced that on two occasions torpedoes had been fired at her by submarines.

Keyes's comments were perhaps the most valid of all. He wrote to Goodenough on 5 September:

> I think an absurd fuss was made over that small affair. . . . It makes me sick and disgusted to think what a complete success it might have been but for, I won't say dual, but—multiple control. We begged for light cruisers to support us and to deal with the Enemy's light cruisers which we knew would come out. Destroyer's short range guns are no match for light cruiser's guns—but were told none were available. If you had only known what we were aiming at, had had an opportunity of discussing it with Tyrwhitt and me, and had been inshore with *Fearless* and *Arethusa* we might have sunk at least 6 cruisers and had a "scoop" indeed. . . .[33]

Jellicoe's confidence in the Admiralty had also been shaken by the inept nature of the planning. Though too-new-a-Commander in Chief to challenge the Admiralty openly, he did protest the lack of consultation and received an assurance that he would, in future, be informed at all times of the plans and intentions of the Admiralty. Goodenough, for his part, was so disturbed by the near loss of *Southampton* and E-4 that he wrote personally to the Second Sea Lord, who was an old friend, to complain about the incompetence of the planning.

Quick to draw lessons out of the results of the battle, Jellicoe laid down the necessity for tighter tactical control at all times—not only the War Staff, but Goodenough, Keyes, and Tyrwhitt came under criticism for letting events get out of hand and failing to maintain an adequate picture of events. Here, again, entered the bugbear of poor communications. Atmospheric conditions were unfavorable on the day of the battle, and several signals failed to get through, but there had been no coherent system of reporting or giving orders. Signals were not sent giving vital information. Frequently, when the commanders had remembered their wireless, they failed to give either their own or the enemy's course, speed, and position. Small wonder that Beatty found it difficult to follow the course of the action from his vantage point outside the Bight, and great wonder that there had not been a major disaster. Jellicoe was now all the more conscious that every ship and all personnel from stokers to flag officers required extensive and exhaustive training.

But the victory was a godsend for Britain, as all had to admit, and Churchill loudly trumpeted when he boarded *Arethusa* at Chatham and "fairly slobbered" over Tyrwhitt. As the *Arethusa* would require at least a month's repair, Churchill extravagantly promised the best and most modern light cruiser he could find to substitute as Commodore (T)'s flagship. Tyrwhitt had cause to regret his mentioning the subject because Churchill was as good as his word and ordered Goodenough to detach the newest and most heavily armed of his light cruisers, the *Lowestoft*. She was not quite what Tyrwhitt had wanted. As he wrote, she was:

> . . . a size larger than the *Arethusa* but slower and rather too big for my job. I shall be glad to get back to A. as it is very unsatisfactory always hunting one's hounds with new horses and new hunt servants. We destroyer folk have ways and customs which are quite unknown to the big ships.[34]

As Goodenough was not pleased with the transaction, it was a valuable object lesson to Tyrwhitt to be wary of talking to politicians, even Churchill. "Their minds just don't work like other people's."

Churchill when he wrote in *The World Crisis* went rather too far:

> Much more important than these material gains was the effect produced upon the morale of the enemy. The Germans knew nothing of our defective Staff work and of the risks we had run. All they saw was that the British did not hesitate to hazard their greatest vessels as well as their light craft in the most daring offensive action and had apparently escaped unscathed. They felt as we should have felt had German destroyers broken into the Solent and their battle cruisers penetrated as far as the Nab. The results of this action were far reaching. Henceforward the weight of British naval prestige lay heavy across all German sea enterprise.[35]

As Captain S. W. Roskill has remarked "The action was certainly not the glorious victory which Churchill among others claimed it to be."[36]

Yet Churchill was all too correct in his statement of the effect on the German Command. Every doubt of the Imperial Navy's ability to face up to this older and heavier opponent had resurfaced. In only one regard, that of the behavior of the personnel of the lost cruisers, had the Imperial Navy any reason to feel satisfied, for that had been exemplary. But in command, tactics, and material, the action had been a signal failure:

> Hipper felt the results of this action very keenly. He repeatedly went into the question of responsibility and could reach no other conclusion than that the system adopted by the naval command dealing as it did in half measures, was to blame.[37]

The Kaiser, still jealous but also nervous of the Royal Navy, was frightened by the loss of the three cruisers and the V-187, and he announced to his naval advisors that the restrictions on the fleet would be tightened. Von Pohl and von Muller acquiesced but it was the occasion for a battle-royal between the Emperor and Admiral von Tirpitz. Massive in his disapproval, Tirpitz would not alter his stand that the High Sea Fleet should be used for what it was—a major and decisive weapon of war. It was the first breach in their long association.

The Kaiser went further, as von Pohl reported to von Ingenohl a few days later:

> After that outpost action, His Majesty feared that the fleet might engage a superior enemy, just as the light cruisers had done. In his anxiety to preserve the fleet, he wished you to wire for his consent before entering a decisive action.[38]

But it was not the Kaiser's tantrums that were the major evil for the Imperial Navy. It was, as Hipper had pointed out, the half-measures, the division of command. Von Ingenohl, himself in an ambiguous position as Commander in Chief, whereby he could be dictated to by the Kaiser, von Pohl, or von Tirpitz, at times interfered with Hipper's plans to a dangerous extent. Hipper, at the beginning of the war, planned to have a battle cruiser on patrol in the Bight but he had been overruled by the Commander in Chief, who agreed to the planned three-tiered patrol system but objected to battle cruisers lying in support. By so doing he left the patrols open to attack by heavy ships at any time, especially when the tide over the Jade Bar was unfavorable.

Tactically, the performance of the light cruisers was poor. Even had Beatty not appeared on the scene, the failure to concentrate before going in to attack Tyrwhitt's forces was inexcusable; several times the British flotillas were able to repel isolated advances by each cruiser. A combination of the light cruisers in the area, followed by a simultaneous attack, would have ensured far greater results and might have saved one or more of the light cruisers lost when Beatty came out of the mist. The bad wireless communications were much to blame here, for the German light forces shared the same problem with the British of a lack of understanding of the medium. They, too, frequently failed to report at critical moments or else left out vital information, and thus contributed to no small extent to the prevailing uncertainty amongst the cruisers and the forces still in Wilhelmshaven. Much had to be done before the position would be satisfactory.

The torpedo boats and cruisers were deficient in offensive powers compared with their opponents. The torpedo boats had been kept too small and with their smaller armament and lower speed, they were vulnerable. The British destroyers were half as large again and threw three times the weight of broadside. In a pitched battle between the two types, there could be only one outcome. The Imperial Navy did not even have the dubious advantage of a heavier torpedo armament. Though their 50 cm torpedo was every bit as good as the British 21", the Royal Navy's destroyers had the edge with their two twin mountings.

The cruisers, too, were underarmed. Although the 10.5 cm was a superb weapon, it did not have the weight of shell required to stop large numbers of destroyers. The *Mainz* had been a case in point. Although her fire had been spirited and accurate, the British destroyers had nonetheless been able to get their torpedoes away before suffering any major damage. What is more, not one of the German cruisers could match a *"Town"* armed with 6 inchers. This was a bitter pill to swallow and many of the gunnery pundits who had advocated the retention of the 10.5 cm would still refuse to accept the fact that the arrival of a hundred pounder shell was far more devastating than that of two thirty-five pounders—and the rate of fire of the 10.5 cm was hardly twice that of the 6".

The Command was at last forced to realise that an adequate defense of the Bight was as much of importance as the protection of the Jade. Unfortunately, von Ingenohl overreacted. The reorganization of the patrols which followed the battle not only included the laying of a mine field off the Norderney Gat, and the allocation of trawlers and roving groups of torpedo boats to replace the "three tier" system, but almost every available U-boat. The absence of the submarines on the 28th had been a major deficiency in the Germany defenses, but it was clear that von Ingenohl was unwise to allocate nearly the entire force for coastal defense. The U-boat officers protested bitterly, but it was several weeks until the Commander in Chief was brought to his senses.

Clearly, confusion reigned in the Command that September. The lack of a coherent war plan was making itself felt. Those who clung to the belief that the British would employ a close blockade against Germany declared that the 28th was the signal for the beginning of British operations. Others still were preoccupied by the Russian threat. The Russian Baltic Fleet was still an unknown quantity, and it was not beyond the bounds of possibility that some simultaneous thrust might be made by the Russians and the British against the High Sea Fleet. Unless reinforced by major units of the High Sea Fleet proper, the German Baltic squadrons were not strong enough to face a properly handled Russian fleet.

Yet these arguments, powerful though they appeared, would not have been enough by themselves to keep the Germans inactive. The major difficulty was that the Command had no intelligence of the British dispositions. Even von Ingenohl, attentive to the Emperor as he was, might have been willing to attack the British forces in the south, had he known their extreme weakness.

The second factor was von Ingenohl's overestimation of the abilities of the British submarines. He believed that any venture into the North Sea by the battle squadrons, even when accompanied by light craft, would result in heavy losses. He was not to be shaken in his belief.

CHAPTER 6

Enter the Submarines

As reports came in of the success of the raid on Heligoland Bight, the Admiralty began to prepare plans for a second sweep into German waters. Churchill was keen to discover whether the Germans had any ships at sea about the Skagerrak and along the coast to the north of the Bight, and he proposed that the Grand Fleet's light cruisers and destroyers, supported by the battle squadrons to the north, sweep the area and destroy whatever was to be found there.

Jellicoe agreed with the proposal. The discovery of the newly laid mine fields off the east coast made him keen on any measure that might end the German mining campaign. He proposed, however, certain modifications to the scheme. The heavy ships and light craft of the Grand Fleet proper would move into position as before, but, at the same time, the Harwich Force, again supported by Cruiser Forces C and K, would come in from the south-east, meeting the Grand Fleet flotillas off the Horns Reef. The two movements were designed to close upon each other like the jaws of a trap with any German ships at sea caught inside.

This operation, fruitless as it would have been—because there was at that time no German activity so far to the north—never took place. On 31 August the Admiralty received information that four German cruisers and six submarines had left the Baltic with the intention of striking across the North Sea to attack any battleships that they met. Jellicoe immediately sent Beatty and the available cruiser squadrons to the Skagerrak while he cruised with the Grand Fleet to the east of the Orkneys in the hope of cutting off these ships, but the report was a false alarm and the British found nothing.

Nevertheless the hope of another operation in the Bight was not dead. Keyes and Tyrwhitt were eagerly pressing for it and opinion in the fleet was largely with them. Even Jellicoe was in favor of such a venture, provided that this time the planning was conducted on a proper basis. Keyes and Tyrwhitt again went up to the Admiralty and laid their plans with Prince Louis, Sturdee, and Churchill. It would be a sweep along the lines originally proposed by Keyes, involving total use of the forces in the theater.

Interrogation of the many prisoners taken on 28 August proved fruitful. They revealed to their questioners that the First Scouting Group would have come out of the Jade as soon as the tide permitted, to support the light cruisers and torpedo boats, and that they might well have been followed out by any of the battle squadrons ready for sea, had the action continued. On 3 September, the Admiralty telegraphed to Jellicoe:

> . . . We must therefore be prepared to meet not only battle cruisers, but perhaps a division of the High Sea Fleet or the whole fleet. You should therefore be in a position with the Grand Fleet to take full advantage of so fortunate a chance. . . .[1]

Almost every available ship in the North Sea would be involved, including the Channel Fleet, which would support the operation from the south and, at the same time, cover the transportation of the Sixth Division to France. The operation was set for 10 September, delayed one day at Jellicoe's request to give his heavy ships a chance for rest after the previous month's rigorous activities. While the Channel Fleet patrolled to the south and the Grand Fleet waited to the north, Beatty's First Battle Cruiser Squadron (reinforced now by the exchange of the *Inflexible* for the faster *New Zealand*) and the other Grand Fleet cruiser squadrons and destroyer flotillas would be spread outside the Bight to the north and north-west. Moore's two battle cruisers and a small escort would be to the east, while Christian was ordered to take the *Bacchantes* close in to the Ems to act as close support for the operations to the south.

Tyrwhitt in the *Lowestoft*, accompanied by the Third Flotilla, would move into the Bight to the west-south-west of Heligoland and begin a sweep to the west at a distance of ten miles from the island before 0400. Further to the south, off the Ems, Blunt was to start his sweep with the First Flotilla at 0500, covered to seaward by the dubious protection of the *Bacchantes*.

Keyes managed to scrape together five submarines for the operation. One, D-8, was to work off the Ems and a second, E-4, to the north of Heligoland, whilst the other three were to conduct a surfaced sweep from west to east in the outer Bight with the commodore's two attached destroyers scouting ahead. Keyes, despite his part in the planning, discovered to his intense chargin that he could not go, for Sturdee had forbidden him to proceed to sea again in a destroyer and his request for a light cruiser had been refused.

The operation got under way on schedule, went as planned and achieved exactly nothing. It was perhaps most unfortunate that the conditions repeated those of the 28th, being warm and still, with the entire Bight shrouded in mists. The intention was defeated by the timing—the sweeps began too early. Under the new system of German patrols, the submarines and torpedo boats did not take up their positions until dawn. By that time the British were well past the patrol lines and were out of sight in the low visibility.

The German Command had indeed some warning of a raid between 8 and 11 September and von Ingenohl persuaded the Admiralstab to recall the *Blücher* and the Fourth Battle Squadron from the Baltic, where they had been detached in order to support operations against the Russians. The problem was largely that von Ingenohl had earlier allowed the battle cruisers to begin urgent repairs to their machinery and this meant that only *Seydlitz* was at all in fighting trim; and even she was limited to 20 knots. Even so, Hipper had his flagship and the two available armored cruisers, *Roon* and *Prinz Adalbert*, lying outside the mine fields at immediate notice for sea, while von Ingenohl kept the rest of the High Sea Fleet at only two-hours notice during the daylight hours.

A single-row field of 689 mines was laid some twenty miles to the west-south-west of Heligoland, stretching fifteen miles to the south-south-west, past the Norderney Lightship. By some miracle the Third Flotilla missed the field, passing just to the north. Had they come any further south, the losses among the destroyers would have been heavy as the mines were set at a depth of little more than eight feet—shallow enough for such light craft to detonate.

One German torpedo boat, S-129, sighted the Third Flotilla as they moved west, but she was not herself observed and there were no other encounters between surface vessels of either side. The only British units which did become involved with the German vessels were the detached submarines E-4 and D-8. The latter spent an uncomfortable seventy minutes dived after she attempted to torpedo U-28. Seeing the torpedo coming, the German hastily submerged and, as the British *Staff Monograph* remarked:

Under the circumstances stalemate was practically inevitable for neither boat knew what to do with the other; and after an hour and a quarter, during which the two boats simultaneously rose and simultaneously dived again, the German retired out of the area.[2]

E-4 made attacks on other U-boats and was similarly unsuccessful. A small and maneuverable submarine makes an extremely difficult target. Although hunted by several German units at intervals during the day, she escaped unscathed.

The Germans received the first real indication that the British were in the Bight when seaplane no. 29 made a dawn reconnaissance over the Ems from Borkum. The aircraft sighted both the *Bacchantes* and the Third Flotilla heading west, but, when its reports reached the Fleet Command, they were unable to discern the British intention. When a further air reconnaissance at 0700 revealed that the Bight was clear of British ships, the mystery deepened. The patrols were alerted and the High Sea Fleet brought to immediate notice for sea, but von Ingenohl would not send out any heavy ships.

The second stage of the operation, Jellicoe's sweep to the north with the cruisers and the battle squadrons, drew a similar blank. Apart from the usual U-boat alarms (the predreadnought *Zealandia* managed to convince herself that she had rammed and sunk a submarine, despite the fact that there were none in the area), no mines, minelayers, or other German surface units were seen.

By dusk on the same day the sweep was over. The Harwich Force and the submarines were withdrawing to their base, Moore was approaching the Humber and Jellicoe had restored the fleet to its cruising formation. Still unhappy about Scapa Flow's lack of antisubmarine defenses, he decided to establish a temporary anchorage at Loch Ewe, on the west coast of Scotland, which he hoped would be out of range of the U-boats. It is hard to escape the impression that Jellicoe intended to stir the hitherto lackadaisical Admiralty into action by this movement—for it was tantamount to admitting that the British had lost control of the North Sea.

For it was only now, at the beginning of September, that the threat posed by the submarines really began to have an effect on British operations. The German Command at last began to employ U-boats on offensive operations against the British patrols and bases. Even before this, however, two incidents occurred which served to convince Jellicoe that his policy of putting the fleet to sea at the first scare had not been enough in vulnerable Scapa Flow.

The system was having a bad effect on both the ships' machinery and their crews, since no real opportunity existed to make repairs or relax and sleep. Breakdowns were mounting and the battle line was becoming attentuated as more and more ships had to be detached for repairs. It was thus the last straw when on 1 September at 1830, *Falmouth* thought that she could see a periscope inside the Flow and opened fire. Every ship in

the Flow hurriedly raised steam and, interrupting all storing, ammuni-
tioning, and coaling, the Grand Fleet moved out into Pentland Firth by
2300. The situation was little short of chaotic as ships fired at repeated
"sightings" and picket-boats plunged to and fro trying to keep the
submarines under. The battle squadrons cleared Scapa leaving behind
the Second Destroyer Flotilla. The destroyers found nothing, but it was a
warning for the Commander in Chief.

On 2 September there was another submarine alarm, this time in the
Firth of Forth. Moore, in the Firth with his two battle cruisers after the
mining of the Humber "did not credit" the report at the time, nor was
there a submarine in the area. The incident, however, highlighted the
weaknesses of the anchorage, there being no nets and only two sets of
batteries to offer any opposition.

Then, on 5 September at 1545, came the first real shock. U-21 was
one of two submarines available for offensive operations and she and her
sister, U-20, were ordered to attempt an attack on the Firth of Forth
because the Admiralstab had received intelligence that the British had
based ships there. U-20 got to below the Forth Bridge but, not knowing
that the battle cruisers lay above it, withdrew on finding nothing. U-21,
however, had just begun her attempt when she sighted a patrolling
cruiser.

It was the *Pathfinder*, a scout and leader of the Eighth Destroyer
Flotilla. U-21 fired a single torpedo at a range of 1,500 yards. The
torpedo struck the forward magazine which blew up, breaking the
cruiser's back. She sank within four minutes, barely ten miles from May
Island. Her flotilla rushed to the scene, thinking that the *Pathfinder* had
been struck by a mine, but when her wounded captain had been picked
up and was able to tell them that it had been a torpedo, the hunt began
and continued until dusk. U-21 nevertheless escaped, having claimed
the first British loss to a submarine of the war.

When the news came through, several new precautions were taken.
Fifteen C class submarines were organized to "search for, stalk, and, if
possible, attack enemy submarines," and Jellicoe decided to recall
Cruiser Force K from Rosyth. All the southern bases were now too
dangerous for such important vessels and he ordered Moore to bring his
two battle cruisers back to rejoin Beatty's squadron.

It was this withdrawal that nearly saved the *Aboukir*, *Hogue*, and *Cressy*
from destruction. Cruiser Force K had been organized with the specific
intention of acting in support of the forces out of Harwich, especially the
patrols mounted by the old armored cruisers. With the removal of the
battle cruisers, these five obsolete vessels were now open to attack by
every sort of modern warship.

Tyrwhitt and Keyes had both been agitating for their withdrawal since the beginning of the war. Keyes wrote to Rear Admiral Arthur Leveson, Director of the Operations Division, on 21 August:

> Think of the tale two or three well-trained German cruisers will tell if they fall in with those *Bacchantes*. How can they be expected to shoot straight or have any confidence in themselves when they know that they are untrained and can't shoot, and may meet a highly trained enemy? Why give the Germans the smallest chance of a cheap victory and an improved morale? . . . For Heaven's sake, take those *Bacchantes* away! . . . I don't say those cruisers will be attacked, but the Germans must know they are about, and if they send out a suitable force, God help them. . . .[3]

To a man, the personnel at Harwich felt that the old cruisers were useless relics which had no place in the North Sea. They were quite correct, but it must be remembered that very few, not even Keyes as Commodore (S), raised the point that the system of patrol which the cruisers employed was a gift to an errant submarine. All concentrated upon the risk of the *Bacchantes* being set upon by armored forces or a massed attack by torpedo boats. The very soubriquet "live bait squadron" had in it the inference that German surface forces would be drawn out to attack the old cruisers. In fact, nothing could have been further from the truth as the Germans did not even know that the patrols existed.

The five armored cruisers at first spent their time over the Broad Fourteens. On several occasions, when the Admiralty had information of German mine-laying activities, they were sent to the Dogger Bank. The most recent occasion had been 12 September, when two of the class were sent to the Swarte Bank to watch for four cruisers suspected to be coming out of Emden, while the remainder stayed with the destroyer patrol on the Broad Fourteens. The decision had been made to keep the divided patrol, for Sturdee decided that German heavy units making for the Channel might well slip past unnoticed by the *Bacchantes* if the latter concentrated solely upon the Broad Fourteens.

At all times the cruisers stayed in their patrol areas, going in only to coal or replenish supplies while the half-flotilla on duty would be relieved every two or three days by another out of Harwich. The joint patrol was supposed to be interrupted only by the withdrawal of all the forces involved for operations such as those of 28 August and 10 September—or at least this was what was intended.

In truth, the patrols by the light forces were spasmodic affairs and this situation could only worsen as the year drew on. The destroyers had several times been forced to run for shelter from heavy weather—and the season of the equinoctial gales had only just begun. The cruisers, it had been intended, would patrol at speeds of 15 knots, zigzagging at the discretion of the senior officer. The former, over the six weeks of operations, proved quite impossible as the ships' aged reciprocating machinery suffered breakdown after breakdown, and the cruisers proved to be voracious "coal eaters" at any speed over 13 knots. As a result, the maximum speed of patrols was 12 knots—and it was more likely to be down to 9. Zigzagging was ignored, principally because there had not yet been a single submarine sighting by any of the cruisers or destroyers. Engine repairs generally kept two of the cruisers in harbor and not one of the five had yet had the opportunity to attain any efficiency by evolutions or practice firings. They were, in short, "paper tigers."

The controversy over the *Bacchantes* came to a head at a conference held aboard the *Iron Duke* in Loch Ewe, on 17 September. Churchill, Sturdee, and Oliver, as Director of the Intelligence Division, left London on the 15th. With them went Tyrwhitt and Keyes, invited to the conference largely at the instigation of the First Lord. On the long trip to Loch Ewe, both the commodores did not hesitate to give Churchill their views on a wide range of naval matters—the two were, in fact, a large part of his "many and various sources of information."

During the conference Keyes and Tyrwhitt raised their objections to the *Bacchantes'* patrol and found Jellicoe in agreement with them. Churchill, who had been "instantly arrested" by the expression "live bait squadron," needed little convincing. Professor Marder, however, records an interesting tale:

> When Keyes (possibly at the *Iron Duke* meeting) remonstrated with Sturdee for keeping the cruisers on that patrol, the C.O.S. replied, with superb conceit: "My dear fellow, you don't know your history. We've always maintained a squadron on the Broad Fourteens."[4]

In any case, the meeting broke up with the resolution that the patrol should be discontinued and the old armored cruisers transferred to other duties. The next day Churchill addressed a memorandum to the First Sea Lord:

> . . . The *Bacchantes* ought not to continue on this beat. The risk to such ships is not justified by any services they can render. The narrow seas, being the nearest point to the enemy, should be kept by a small number of good modern ships.
> The *Bacchantes* should go to the western entrance of the Channel and set Bethell's battleships—and later Wemyss' cruisers—free for convoy and other duties.[5]

It is important to note, as a gauge of the attitude toward submarines then prevalent in the Royal Navy, that at no stage was the threat posed to the old ships by U-boats mentioned. In the available records of all the papers and discussions that went on in the first weeks of war, not one of the critics of the *Bacchantes*, not even the percipient and experienced Keyes, raised the issue. The talk was all of "cruisers" or "mine-layers" or "torpedo boats," and it is most significant that Churchill's memorandum was couched in such terms. Submarines were not yet thought of as an *oceanic* threat; their menace was only perceived when the heavy ships were in exposed anchorages or navigating in confined waters. An attack on the open sea seems to have been incomprehensible to many of the Royal Navy's senior officers.

To give just one example, Captain Robert Johnson of the *Cressy*, although not himself a submariner, had spent three years before the war in command of an active submarine flotilla. If it was possible, after such an exposure to the new weapon, for a man calmly to take his ship out on such patrols—and there is no evidence to hint that he might have been unhappy, nor did he go aboard the flagship to protest—then it is little surprise that the dispositions were so unsatisfactory.

The First Sea Lord agreed with Churchill. He, for much the same reasons as Keyes, had never been happy with the position of the *Bacchantes*, and he readily agreed to their removal from the Broad Fourteens. Sturdee, however, did not. Obsessed by the need to maintain a patrol in the North Sea to watch for a German thrust into the Channel, he persuaded Battenberg that the continual heavy weather proved that the destroyers could not maintain the patrol and that the *Bacchantes* should continue with it until more light cruisers became available. Battenberg gave way to the Chief of the War Staff.

On 19 September, Sturdee ordered Christian to end the Dogger Bank patrol and to concentrate the cruisers on the Broad Fourteens. The weather was foul and the Chief of Staff felt that it was too heavy for destroyers. They would be sent out again, Sturdee decided, when the weather moderated. The four available cruisers, *Euryalus*, *Aboukir*, *Hogue*, and *Cressy*, assembled off the Maass Light Vessel in the early hours of the 20th. The weather was still bad, and there were no British destroyers at sea.

The patrol was soon reduced to three. Rear Admiral Christian's flagship, *Euryalus*, needed coaling and her wireless aerial had been damaged in the gale. Forced to return in the *Euryalus* to Harwich because the seas were too rough to transfer his flag to one of the other ships, Christian handed over command to Captain J. E. Drummond in the *Aboukir*.

This was an unusual occurrence. In fact, Campbell, whose flagship was the *Bacchantes*, was in command of Cruiser Force C and *Euryalus* had only been on patrol to keep the numbers up. Christian, as Commander Southern Force, had other ships to command, and no direct obligation to the cruisers. While he could hardly do anything else on the 20th than he did, he should not have allowed Campbell, nor should the latter have been willing, to remain in harbor while the bulk of the squadron was at sea. Campbell's presence would probably have made little difference to the disaster that was to follow—but he should have been there.

All through the 20th and 21st, the cruisers continued their patrol over the Broad Fourteens, wallowing in the short, steep seas characteristic of the area. The muzzles of the cruisers' broadside 6″ guns dipped underwater as the ships rolled. Christian's signaled instructions were dangerous in their ambiguity and typical of those that had been in force over the six weeks of war. He sent to the squadron:

> When patrolling and squadron is spread it is left to captains to carry out alterations of course to guard against submarine attack. Suspicious vessels should be boarded if weather permits. . . . No destroyers will be out on patrol for the present.[6]

Christian had made no mention of destroyer cover to Drummond in his specific hand-over instructions, and this bald signal was the only mention made of their activities. As a consequence, Drummond did not realize that it was he who was responsible for ordering the destroyers out, if and when the weather eased. It would be fatal.

For, at sunset on the 21st, when the weather began to moderate, Drummond did nothing beyond sending to Harwich, "Still rather rough, but going down." By midnight the wind eased away completely. To the west, however, in Harwich, it still blew and still seemed unsuitable to send the small ships out. Not until 0500 did Tyrwhitt take the *Lowestoft* and eight destroyers of the Third Flotilla out of Harwich. The Court of Enquiry later found that "the weather was [in Tyrwhitt's judgment] not suitable for sending out destroyers at an earlier hour than he did." The nine ships made their course for the Broad Fourteens, but they were four hours too late.

At the same hour that Commodore (T) was leaving Harwich, Lieutenant Commander Otto Weddigen in the submarine U-9 sighted the three armored cruisers steering north-north-east at 10 knots. The German at first believed that they must be the screen of a major fleet, but as soon as he realised that there were no other ships behind, he made preparations to attack. The *Cressy*, *Aboukir*, and *Hogue* were steaming at three-mile intervals on a line of bearing taken two points abaft *Cressy*'s beam. The

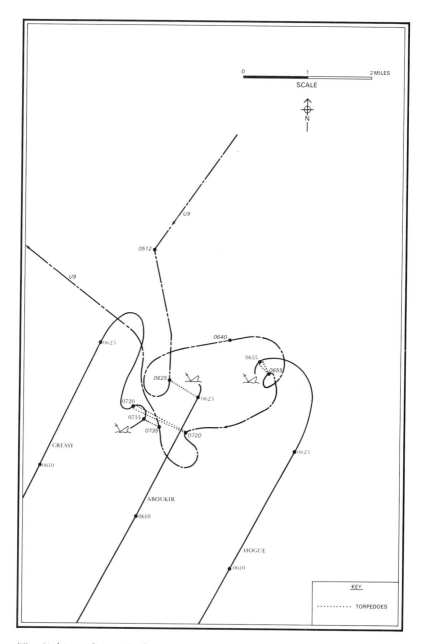

The Sinking of the *Aboukir,* *Hogue,* and *Cressy*

ships were not zigzagging and, as they were still steaming at only 10 knots, Weddigen could not have had a more favorable position for a submerged attack as he approached the *Aboukir*, from fine on her port bow.

U-9 fired one torpedo, which struck the armored cruiser amidships on her port side. The single hit was enough, for heavy flooding caused the ship to take on a twenty degree list to port within minutes of being struck. Boilers and engines crippled, the ship lost way and all that could be done was to load the wounded into the one available boat and fall the ship's company in before abandoning ship. Captain Drummond, at first thinking that the *Aboukir* had been mined, hoisted the mine warning and ordered the other two cruisers to close the ship. Minutes later he realised that it had been a torpedo and ordered them away.

Hogue and *Cressy* kept coming. Captain Wilmot Nicholson in the *Hogue* felt that if he remained on the side away from U-9's original attack, his ship would be safe enough. Losing way to launch her sea boats, *Hogue* came to a stop little more than a mile from the stricken *Aboukir*. Weddigen had, contrary to Nicholson's expectation, brought U-9 around to the east and was now only three hundreds yards off *Hogue's* port beam. He could not miss and, at 0655, even as the *Aboukir* gave a final lurch, heeled over, and sank, two torpedoes struck the *Hogue*. Both hit amidships and flooded the engine-room. With the ship's watertight

SMS U-9

HMS *Audacious* mined and sinking

doors still partially open, there was nothing to stop the ingress of water. One of the cadets who survived the sinking later said:

> I saw *Hogue* slowly turn over on her side, pause for a moment and then disappear under the waves. I didn't feel the slightest bit of suction, but saw large fountains of water coming out of her scuttles, forced up, I suppose, by air being compressed in the compartments below.[7]

By 0705 the second cruiser had gone.

Even with the danger apparent, Captain Johnson in the *Cressy* lingered, the ship having barely steerage way on as she picked up the survivors of the *Hogue*. A periscope was reported and *Cressy* hurriedly got under way at full power in an attempt to ram. In his concern for the men in the water, Johnson did not leave the area, only transmitting signals for help and keeping the guns' crews at the ready as the ship's boats came alongside with men from the *Aboukir* and the *Hogue*.

Captain Johnson's precautions were not enough. U-9 approached and, at 0720, fired two torpedoes, one of which struck *Cressy* forward on the starboard side. The damage was negligible and for a few minutes it seemed as if the cruiser might escape. Weddigen, however, was a determined man and he brought U-9 to within 500 yards before firing a last torpedo. Its impact was enough.

Tyrwhitt received the radio message, *"Aboukir* and *Hogue* sunk," at 0707. Ignorant of the cause of their loss, but

> knowing where they were supposed to be I dashed off at full speed and a few minutes later we received their position from the *Cressy* and part of a signal which ended abruptly and then there was no more. I knew . . . probably what was in store for us, but I could not think of 2100 men drowning without giving them all the assistance in my power.[8]

The nine ships which he had in company arrived at the scene at 1030. The sinkings were seen by several vessels in the area and, despite the danger they thought existed from mines, most, very gallantly, came to the rescue. The Dutch merchantman *Flora* picked up 286 men, but did not wait on the scene as there were many sorely wounded whom she took into Ymuiden. The Dutch government later returned all the survivors to Britain, even though they would have been within their rights to intern them. The Dutch vessel *Titan* and two British trawlers, the *Coriander* and *J.G.C.* were still picking men out of the water when the Harwich ships arrived. Tyrwhitt wrote:

> We first went up to a small English trawler which was loaded with men. They looked just like rows and rows of swallows on telegraph lines, all huddled together to keep themselves warm; they were all naked or nearly so as they had been overboard and were very cold.[9]

Lowestoft and half the destroyers began to tranship the survivors while the remainder steamed around as an antisubmarine patrol. The operation was fraught with difficulty as the seas were still quite heavy and many of the survivors were almost paralyzed with cold. What is more, the process was punctuated by submarine alarms which did little for concentration or morale. These were all false for U-9, having expended all her torpedoes, was already heading north for the Jade and home.

The nine collected 581 men before they could find no more and turned for Harwich. Sixty officers and 777 men were saved, 62 officers and 1,397 men died. What made the tragedy especially poignant was the fact that the ships were manned largely from the Royal Naval Reserve, middle-aged, married men with families to support. Furthermore, in each gunroom there were nine cadets mobilized from the Royal Naval College, Dartmouth. These were among those later nicknamed the "war babies," and most were no more than fifteen. Few survived. Keyes wrote:

> On the night of the 21st September I slept on board the *Maidstone*, and at 2 A.M. my secretary woke me up to give me a letter from the Admiralty which he thought might be important. It was from the Director of Mobilization, saying that he would carry out my suggestion to exchange young men from the depot ships, with the pensioners and reservists in Cruiser Force "C", and asking "how many are available." So that was satisfactory. [But] at about 7 A.M. I was awakened by a signalman, with an intercepted signal from the *Cressy*.[10]

Keyes, "feeling very bloody minded," ordered the First Flotilla to raise steam at once. Since his two destroyers were at sea, he went aboard the *Fearless* to see Captain Blunt and wonder as to the cause of the cruisers' loss. "I could only wait, simply boiling with rage, that my last effort on their behalf had been acted on just too late." As soon as Keyes learnt that it was a submarine, he persuaded Blunt to agree to going out under his command, rang the Admiralty to tell them where he was going, and headed for Terschelling, in an attempt to cut off the escape of the U-boat.

Commodore(S) ordered *Lurcher* and *Firedrake* to join him there. Thirsting for revenge, Keyes persuaded Blunt that the best way to minimize the effect of the cruisers' loss was to raid the German torpedo-boat patrol on the Ems as "a fitting answer and some salve, to the wounded feelings of the country."[11] Keyes signaled to Jellicoe:

> Propose to attack light patrol off Ems River at dawn with First Destroyer Flotilla.[12]

Jellicoe approved the plan, provided Keyes left the area before daylight the next morning, and he moved to organize covering force for the operation. But, at the Admiralty, Sturdee had been enraged by Keyes's cavalier announcement of his intentions,—which were also in contradiction to the direction that the Chief of Staff had given Commodore (S) that he was not to go to sea. At 1900, Keyes was "most peremptorily ordered back to Harwich and told to present myself at the Admiralty." Keyes received a dressing-down but was "eventually forgiven," probably because Sturdee must have known that his own position was very weak and that the blame might well be laid at his door.

The consequences of the sinkings were immediate. *Bacchante* and *Euryalus* were not allowed back into the narrow seas and the instruction went out that armored ships in submarine waters were to zigzag, steaming at least 13 knots. No heavy ship was to be used for boarding at sea in home waters, and any other evolution that required ships to stop was to avoided. Furthermore, as soon as they had examined Nicholson and Drummond, the surviving captains, the Admiralty sent out:

> The serious lesson to learn from the loss of the *Cressy* and *Hogue* is that it must henceforth be recognised by all Commanding Officers that if one ship is torpedoed by submarine or strikes mine, disabled ship must be left to her fate, and other large ships clear out of dangerous area calling up minor vessels to render assistance.[13]

With the advantage of hindsight, Christian wrote to Jellicoe:

> I cannot tell you how much I have felt this tragic disaster which was accompanied by so much loss of life and ships, and feel that you will have no confidence in me now. The sad part of it is that certainly *Cressy* need not have been sacrificed and probably not *Hogue* if they had only dashed up within say a mile to windward, out all boats and away again. . . . A court of enquiry assembles here [Chatham] today on the loss of the cruisers. I am extremely glad of such an opportunity to clear my professional reputation as I feel that nothing I could have done could have averted the disaster. . . .[14]

The court placed general blame on most of the senior officers involved in the affair. Christian's behavior was quite proper, but it was felt that he had erred in countenancing such a vague and unsatisfactory system of command as governed the forces in Harwich. Campbell's absence, on the other hand, was considered quite unsatisfactory:

> Campbell's evidence at the enquiry was extraordinary. He stated that he did not know the object for which the patrol had been formed, had received no instructions, and apparently had issued none himself.[15]

Drummond was criticized for having neither zigzagged nor called for destroyers when the weather moderated, but, as he had been left with no instructions, no real blame was attached to him. In fact, the overall comment concentrated largely upon the Admiralty's part in the affair and, by association, was extremely critical of the First Sea Lord and the Chief of the War Staff.

Despite private acknowledgment that he had erred, Battenberg was not prepared to accept such criticism, and he appended a scathing memorandum to the report. Churchill, who had been conducting his own inquisition of the War Staff to discover precisely why his decision to remove the cruisers had not been carried out, refused to let Battenberg reprove the court for their act of "lese majeste" in attacking the Admiralty. Sturdee, for his part, dived for cover and attached only a vague and unconvincing explanation to the report. Not until both Prince Louis and Sturdee had left the Admiralty was the subject reopened by the Board— and then the junior Sea Lords criticized the actions of Battenberg and the Chief of the War Staff without restraint. Admiral Fisher, still in retirement, was even more abusive when he wrote:

> It was *pure murder* sending those big armoured ships in the North Sea! and H. H. Campbell (like the damned sneak he is)* staying in harbour when he ought to have hoisted his flag in one of the other ships of his Squadron . . . he, Campbell, is the culprit who should have been tried had he been in his proper place. . . .[16]

But it is perhaps the diary entry by Admiral Sir Bertram Ramsay, who was then serving as Flag Lieutenant to Sir Douglas Gamble in the Fourth Battle Squadron, which provides the most revealing indication of the state of mind that had allowed the disaster to come about. Ramsay wrote:

> One ship was sunk by a submarine and the other stupid ships went to her assistance, simply asking to be sunk too. It does seem childish and just shows how utterly without imagination the majority of our senior officers are. About a month ago I remarked at lunch that I supposed it was recognised that if a ship of the Fleet got hit by a submarine, she could expect no assistance from other ships. The Vice Admiral said that I was too bloodthirsty and pessimistic for anything, and why should I always be thinking of the worst side of things?[17]

In the public view it was, ironically enough, Churchill who bore the blame for the disaster, although this was one occasion when his "interfering" tendencies should have been allowed full rein. It was convenient,

---

*Campbell had been an associate of Lord Charles Beresford and King George V and was an old *bete noir* of Fisher's.

however, to blame the obvious muddle upon the mercurial habits of the First Lord. Sturdee and Battenberg went largely unscathed through the hullabaloo.

Euryalus and *Bacchante* were sent on convoy duties to Gibraltar, and Christian and Campbell were ordered to haul down their flags, although both were eventually reemployed. Tyrwhitt and Keyes again became operationally responsible direct to the Commander in Chief, which was a far more satisfactory state of affairs for all concerned. With the Channel Fleet well to the south and Grand Fleet sheltering in Loch Ewe, however, the Harwich Force now had no armored support and the east coast lay wide open to German attack. It was a situation that would have to be rectified.

The Imperial Navy was delighted by U-9's success, and Weddigen received a hero's welcome in Germany. The incident convinced the Imperial Navy as much as the Royal Navy of the potential of the submarine as an offensive weapon. More submarines would henceforth be made available for operations against the British, and, for the first time since the institution of the distant blockade, it appeared to the German Command as if the campaign of attrition might have some chance of success.

Its first effect, ironically, was to blight the operation against the northern patrols which Hipper had been planning for his three battle cruisers. Jellicoe's policy of keeping the Grand Fleet at sea had prevented its execution for fear of the First Scouting Group running into British heavy units. With the news of U-9's success, the sortie was postponed indefinitely. A foray by the two auxiliary mine-layers, *Berlin* and *Kaiser*, was, however, continued. The two ships failed dismally, being unable to get to their planned laying positions off the east coast and Moray Firth, and they soon returned to Germany.

Another submarine thrust was made at the Channel transports, this time by U-18. She attempted an attack on the light cruiser *Attentive*, which was unsuccessful, but the U-boat's very presence was enough to stop the passage across the Channel for twelve hours and cause the Admiralty to place a complete ban on daylight sailings. As the umbilical cord to the western front, the Channel was vulnerable and some means had to be found of combating the U-boat.

Further to the north, the German preoccupation with the Firth of Forth caused the Command to organize a near-continuous patrol of the approaches by two or more U-boats. These had found no targets, but repeated encounters with light forces demonstrated to the British the chronic inability of surface vessels, even destroyers, to deal with submarines. New measures had to be taken.

Jellicoe had already begun them. He continued to keep the Grand Fleet at sea as much as he could, the ships being to the north of the 54th Parallel. Loch Ewe could only be a temporary refuge, and when U-boats were again reported, Jellicoe returned the fleet and all its auxiliaries to Scapa Flow. He pleaded with the Admiralty for destroyers, minesweepers, and antisubmarine vessels of every description, as well as armed merchant cruisers to supplement the Northern Patrol.

Things began to happen:

> An increasing number of British trawlers was being taken up, armed with one or more guns and fitted with the single or the modified sweep, and employed in anti-submarine operations off the coast. Fifteen yachts were already in commission and as many more were being fitted out. About 300 trawlers and drifters and 100 motor boats had been taken up by this date. The payment of rewards to merchantmen and fishing vessels was now authorized for information of enemy submarines and minelayers. [18]

The problem was now basically one of material. The wholesale dismissal of the submarine threat before the war was being paid for in full. While most (though by no means all) in the Royal Navy by now had some comprehension of the problem, there were few tools at hand to deal with it. Before 1914, the problem of defending Scapa Flow, if it were to be used as a fleet anchorage, was solved by allocating predreadnoughts and elderly destroyers to watch the entrances. The answer was the same for the other undefended bases, but, although it was an admirable—and cheap—solution for short-term defense against surface attack, it gave no protection whatsoever against submarines. It would be months before Scapa and the other anchorages were completely secure by means of blockships, nets, and searchlights.

Similarly, little attention had been paid to mine warfare. Were the Germans to launch a major mine-laying campaign against Britain, they could take a heavy toll of the Grand Fleet. Something was being done, but, nonetheless, the Royal Navy should have been fully equipped to deal with the mine threat at the beginning of the war. The prewar conversion of the fourteen elderly torpedo-gunboats into minesweepers had not been enough. And if the mine-sweeping situation was unsatisfactory, that of mine laying was worse.

Matters came to head after Rear Admiral Ballard made the sensible suggestion, following the scare in the Channel caused by U-18, that the U-boats could be prevented from approaching the Channel submerged by the laying of a series of defensive fields across the northern approaches to the Channel.

No mines had yet been laid by Britain, primarily because the War Staff was worried that any mine-laying activity would arouse the enmity of the neutral nations, relations with which were already strained by the blockade. Nevertheless, the transport route to France had to be maintained and permission was given for the operation to begin. Four mine-layers, *Apollo, Andromache, Intrepid,* and *Iphigenia,* were assembled, and the first lay took place on 2 October, further fields going down on the 3rd, 4th, 7th, and 10th of that month.

They were not a success. On the first lay, a mine blew up under the *Intrepid*'s stern, causing much superficial damage and dislocating her mine-rails. *Andromache* was similarly damaged, and on return to harbor, the arming pistols on the mines were hurriedly changed. Moreover, despite the fact that the other operations went off without mishap, within a few weeks the mines began to break their mooring lines and drift down Channel. For months afterwards, the passage across the Channel was a hazardous one, punctuated by rifle shots at passing "drifters."

The mine fields, betrayed by the bad design and poor construction of the British mine, were far more of a liability than an asset. It was not until well into 1915 that any satisfactory mine was produced by the British, and even this would be an almost exact copy of the efficient German contact mine.

The Royal Navy was learning hard the lesson that the creation of the "all big gun" battleship and the furious concentration upon gunnery had not been enough. The preoccupation with material had given only half the answer to begin with, and now, demonstrably, not all the material problems had been dealt with sufficiently. Too often has this been blamed upon Admiral Lord Fisher by critics who denounce his methods and policies as being counterproductive.

But, although some fault might be Fisher's, it must be remembered that he had given up the post of First Sea Lord as far back as 1910. It had been in his administration that the first hesitant steps to deal with the other arms of warfare—such as the conversion of the cruiser mine-layers and the organization of the first antisubmarine patrols—had been taken. The four years since had seen minimal activity. Fisher's successors may have felt that it was better to slow the revolution initiated by him and restore some harmony to the navy, but in doing so they lost precious time which should have been employed in balancing the Royal Navy's strength. Fisher, by his single-minded reformism, gave the navy time to meet the war fully prepared in every arm. His successors, whether by accident or design, lost that time.

The month of October was a grey one for the Grand Fleet as it shifted anchorage again and again in an effort to avoid the U-boats. The northern patrols had begun to attract the attention of the German Command, and it was not long before several U-boats were dispatched to the area. There were many cruisers at sea at this time, for several German liners, such as the *Brandenburg* and the *Prinz Friedrich Wilhelm*, were sheltering in Norwegian ports, and it was feared that a mass breakout might be imminent. As a consequence, every available cruiser was pressed into service to augment Rear Admiral De Chair's Sixth Cruiser Squadron.

On 9 October, the armored cruiser *Antrim* was attacked by U-16 and only escaped being torpedoed by the timely action of her navigating officer. Despite this warning, for *Antrim* had been zigzagging at high speed, the patrols had to be continued. The Canadian divisions were crossing the Atlantic on their way to France, and a successful attack on them would have disastrous consequences. Both Sturdee and Battenberg most feared a sortie by the German battle cruisers, although Jellicoe thought it improbable.

Then, on 15 October, Otto Weddigen in U-9 repeated his earlier success by sinking the cruiser *Hawke* off Aberdeen. Incredibly, only half an hour before the torpedo struck, *Hawke* stopped for fifteen minutes to take on mails from the *Endymion*. The squadron was spread out of sight, and it was not until after U-17's unsuccessful attack on the *Theseus* that the squadron was ordered to withdraw and the loss discovered.

Hawke was struck amidships and capsized and sank within ten minutes. The destroyer leader *Swift* and the Norwegian steamer *Modesta* together picked up seventy-one survivors the next day, but some five hundred men went down with the ship. *Swift* was also in danger, this time from U-17, as she returned to Scapa, but her high speed ensured her safety as the U-boat failed to get into a firing position.

Submarine sightings were coming in from all over the North Sea. Jellicoe was out on a sweep with the battle squadrons to the north of Scotland. Hearing the news of *Hawke*'s loss, he decided that neither Scapa Flow nor Loch Ewe could be considered safe from U-boats. He determined on yet another change of anchorage. The fleet would move in two divisions to Loch na Keal and Lough Swilly. The former was further to the south on the west coast of Scotland than Loch Ewe, while Lough Swilly was on the north coast of Ireland. Jellicoe hoped that these bases would be far enough away from the German ports to ensure the safety of his ships, but, in the words of the *Staff Monograph*:

> Had Jellicoe but known it, in moving his base from Scapa to Lough Swilly and Loch na Keal, he was only exchanging one danger for another. While U-9 was operating on the east side of the Orkneys . . . U-20 . . . was now working up the west coast of Ireland and the Hebrides.[19]

In the twenty-four hours that the submarine took to get around the north of Scotland, U-20 observed almost every part of the movements of the various squadrons of the Grand Fleet as they steamed south. Though she never managed to make an attack, by 20 October U-20 had returned to Germany with the precious information that the Grand Fleet had changed base yet again.

Even as Jellicoe was completing his new dispositions by ordering the various cruiser patrols to move further to the north, the German mining campaign was under way again. Three mine-layers set out on 16 October. Two, the cruiser *Kolberg* and the *Nautilus*, attempted to mine the Firth of Forth, but, because of "nerves," they turned back in the middle of the North Sea after they had seen smoke clouds on the horizon and had intercepted heavy wireless traffic nearby.

The third, the converted liner *Berlin*, had a far more successful sortie. Ordered to mine the southern approaches to the Clyde, she made her way into the Atlantic before turning to begin the attack. The wireless traffic that was picked up convinced *Berlin*'s captain that he would not be able to cross the Irish Sea unobserved and he discovered, too, that the coastal lights which he had been hoping to fix upon were now all either dimmed or extinguished.

Off the Irish Coast, he decided not to attack the Clyde, but lay his mines off Tory Island, to the north-west of Lough Swilly. The captain had no idea of the Grand Fleet's use of the anchorage and he determined upon the site for the field only because it was the nearest convenient shipping lane. On the night of 22–23 October, *Berlin* laid two hundred mines in a long V pattern. Evading nearby patrols, *Berlin* escaped into the Atlantic and rounded Iceland before turning east again. Hopeful of intercepting British merchant traffic to Russia, *Berlin* lingered off the Norwegian coast but found nothing. On 16 November, with coal running low and *Berlin*'s machinery badly in need of repair, her captain took the ship into Trondheim to be interned. On 26 October the first ship struck the mine field. The British merchantmen *Manchester Commerce* sank quickly, and it was not until the 28th that her survivors were brought into Fleetwood with news of the sinking. By this time the Grand Fleet had suffered a heavy loss.

Vice Admiral Warrender had taken the Second Battle Squadron out of Loch na Keal for firing practices at sea to the north of Ireland on 27 October. They had not begun when, at 0805, in the middle of a turn to take the battleships onto the range, *Audacious* struck a mine on her port side aft. *Berlin* had set the mines deep to avoid their being struck by light craft and this device reaped a double reward. The mine exploded precisely where the battleship's underwater protection was least satisfactory. With the ship still turning, the port engine room was flooded within seconds and *Audacious* began to take on a heavy list and settle by the stern. *Audacious* hoisted the submarine warning, her Captain thinking that the ship had been hit by a torpedo, and the other ships sheered away to get out of the danger area.

Captain C. F. Dampier turned the *Audacious* south for Lough Swilly. Though the ship was barely manageable, she could still make 9 knots on her starboard engine and Dampier was hoping that she would be able to cover the twenty-five miles to land and be beached before she sank. While the other battleships got clear, the cruiser *Liverpool*, which had been assisting with the exercise, stood by the crippled *Audacious*. The battleship was steadily broadcasting distress signals and, in response, Jellicoe sent every available destroyer and tug out to assist her. The C in C did not dare yet to send a battleship to tow *Audacious* in, because of the submarine menace, but he ordered several auxiliaries to raise steam and go out to see what they could do. Meanwhile, the White Star liner *Olympic*, under the command of Commodore H. J. Haddock, RNR, arrived on the scene, having also picked up the distress signals of the *Audacious*.

For two hours *Audacious* struggled on, covering fifteen miles as the seas steadily rose. Flooding worsened in the remaining engine room and at 1050 the ship stopped. Dampier feared that the *Audacious* might capsize and he brought her round head to sea to begin taking off personnel. All but 250 were removed in the ship's boats, aided by several from *Liverpool* and *Olympic*. The remainder stayed as a working party, for Captain Dampier thought that there was still a chance that the ship might be saved.

Audacious continued to settle by the stern, but her list did not increase and, at 1330, Commodore Haddock suggested to Dampier that *Olympic* could attempt to tow the battleship. The fleet auxiliaries had not appeared and Dampier readily agreed. The attempt was made half an hour later, the line being passed with great skill by the destroyer *Fury*, but, though Haddock managed to get the two ships moving toward Lough Swilly, the *Audacious* quickly became unmanageable, sheering into the wind and straining the line so much that it parted.

Liverpool and the newly arrived collier *Thornhill* tried in their turn, assisted by the *Fury*, but they too failed. It was rapidly becoming obvious that the ship was doomed, but Dampier and Sir Lewis Bayly, who had arrived in the boarding vessel *Cambria*, did not give up all hope. Jellicoe, who now knew that the *Audacious* had been mined rather than torpedoed, ordered the predreadnought *Exmouth* out to tow *Audacious*, but she had not arrived when Bayly ordered the latter to be abandoned as darkness fell.

The ship sank deeper and deeper and, just as the *Exmouth* came up to the little group, *Audacious* gave a sudden lurch, hung for a moment and capsized. A few seconds later she blew up, scattering debris in every direction and causing the sole casualty of the affair, when a piece of armor plating struck and killed a petty officer who had been watching from the deck of the *Liverpool*, some 800 yards away.

As the ships, including the *Olympic* (which was to be detained for some days for security reasons) returned to Lough Swilly, Jellicoe was facing the repercussions which the loss of the *Audacious* would have on the situation in the North Sea. He was desperately concerned that the Germans should not know of the incident. Although the Grand Fleet still had an advantage in numbers over the High Sea Fleet, the C in C reasoned that the Germans' other advantages had made the balance so delicate that the loss of the *Audacious* tipped it in the enemy's favor.

Truth to tell, Jellicoe was not willing to accept battle with the High Sea Fleet. He considered his own forces to be only half-trained, and he felt that German expertise in the "minor" arms of naval warfare would make the resolution of any battle problematic. The battle line and the heavier guns of the British dreadnoughts were, Jellicoe considered, the only advantage that the Royal Navy possessed and the loss of the *Audacious* was too heavy a blow to be admitted.

Several of the Grand Fleet's dreadnoughts had not been cured of serious machinery trouble brought on by continual high speed steaming. This ailment sadly enough, affected the most valuable 13.5″ gunned super-dreadnoughts—three or four, including Jellicoe's own *Iron Duke*, being out of action at any one time—while the new construction, such as the *Benbow*, the battle cruiser *Tiger*, and the "Turkish" battleships, *Erin* and *Agincourt*, had only just commissioned and were not fit for action. In the words of Professor Marder, it was a "dangerously small margin of superiority" that the Grand Fleet possessed in the last months of 1914.

Jellicoe proposed that the sinking be kept a secret, at least for the time being and the Admiralty agreed. Cabinet too, when consulted, consented, though its reasoning was rather different. The government was now concerned with the effect that the loss might have on opinion in Turkey, the neutrality of which hung in the balance. Furthermore, the situation in France was tense, a final decision on the outcome seeming to rest on the Battle of Ypres, then raging. Censorship was set in motion immediately and, while the news was given out that the ship had been damaged, her crew was quietly distributed around other ships in the Grand Fleet. Even to the end of the war, *Audacious*'s name was retained on all lists of ships' movements and activities.

Although the concealment of the ship's loss was a reasonable enough ploy in the short term, that is for a week or two, it grew ludicrous as time went on. Many of the passengers in the *Olympic* were Americans and it

HMS *Iron Duke* in 1914

was impossible to stop these people talking. Indeed, many had even taken photographs (and one moving film) which clearly showed just how serious the condition of the battleship had been.

It was ten days before the American newspapers began to scent that something had happened and, although it was not until 19 November that the loss of the *Audacious* was accepted in Germany, Britain should have admitted the loss before this. It was not long before every neutral country accepted the sinking of the *Audacious* as fact and the continued silence of the Admiralty only served to convince the world (and many in Britain who had heard of the sinking) that the British government was unreliable—a state of mind that was to have disastrous repercussions after the Battle of Jutland in 1916.

Though the Grand Fleet's dispiriting pilgrimage continued through October, to the south Tyrwhitt and Keyes had not been idle. Their principal concern was cooperation with the army, as the "Race for the Sea" had begun. Now the Allied and German armies had reached stalemate along the length of the western front, both sides were attempting to make a breakthrough by striking along the coast. Dunkirk and Ostend became important ports, for they were the most accessible secure centers to the threatened areas and, since they were nearer Germany, protection of the transports was all the more necessary. All the forces that the British could muster were being prepared for the crossing to the Continent to link up with the embattled Belgian army.

A series of measures was initiated to make the lines of communication more secure for the passage of the army units. Apart from the largely

Battleships of the Grand Fleet

unsuccessful mine laying already described, Tyrwhitt and the commanders along the coast began a new system of patrols to deal with the threat posed by the German submarines and light forces. Keyes made the point, in a memorandum that he had prepared on antisubmarine warfare after the loss of the three armored cruisers, that "the main difficulty of a submarine was to find target ships, and that her opportunities would be few and far between, if regular well-defined patrols were avoided."[20] And from now on they were. Although at least a half flotilla of the Harwich Force was at sea at all times, the ships were allocated areas to patrol and avoided instituting a "beat" system such as the *Cressy* employed. This policy was to reap great reward in the future and certainly paid off in the short term. Destroyers steaming at high speeds were very difficult targets for submarines to attack. This system had just got under way when a second change was made in the transport routes.

The situation in Belgium was deteriorating steadily. The fortress of Antwerp was being encircled by the Germans and the Belgian government decided that it would be best to withdraw the Belgian field army so as to link up with the Allied forces further to the south. While this was a valid military decision, it would leave the Channel ports undefended. The Admiralty, especially the First Lord, considered that a German naval presence in these ports would make the Channel—and thus the lifeline between England and France—untenable. Churchill considered that Antwerp was the key to the situation; in his view it had to be held, at least until the retreating Belgian army had completed its link up with the French and British forces in the field.

After an emergency conference of the Cabinet on 3 October, Churchill volunteered to go and see what he could do in Antwerp. Taking matters into his own hands, he ordered the Royal Naval divisions in from England to assist in the defense of the fortress. The marine brigade was already in France and soon moved up to Antwerp, but the two naval brigades were at Deal and did not arrive until 5 October. Hardly trained, ill-armed, and badly equipped, these six thousand men had little or no experience of war. Captain Richmond was writing with more than a grain of truth when he called them an "untrained rabble."

Although Churchill stiffened the resistence of the Belgians for a few days, the division could not prevent the fall of Antwerp. Churchill was recalled by the Cabinet on 7 October, after his request to stay as a commander in the field had been refused, and Antwerp surrendered two days later. Despite the criticism that was later heaped onto Churchill's head for his behavior in the affair, it cannot be denied that the arrival of a British cabinet minister encouraged the Belgians to hold on, at least for a time, and the naval division's gallant, though disorganized, stand enabled the Allied armies to consolidate some kind of line to the coast.

The casualties among the naval units were, however, very heavy—over 25 percent, including those captured or interned—but the few days respite was crucial.

The part that the navy played in the creation of the new front was considerable. Some twenty-two thousand men in two divisions were promised to aid the Belgian and French armies. The plan had been to land them at Ostend and Dunkirk, but the War Office decided that Zeebrugge would be a better landing site. The Admiralty agreed to the alteration, even though it placed great strain on the transportation arrangements.

Keyes and Tyrwhitt were horrified by the prospect, though determined to do the best they could for the army, because all the mine fields which had been laid had been intended to protect the approaches to Dunkirk and the route from Dover to Zeebrugge lay directly over the first of the fields—which meant, ironically, that it would have to be swept.

The Commodores rose to the occasion, as Tyrwhitt ordered every ship that he could find to mount patrols off the Dutch coast for the three crucial days of the passage, the 6th to the 8th of October. Rough weather made conditions extremely unpleasant and, apart from a few submarine scares, the destroyers and light cruisers saw nothing, spending their time "rolling, rolling, rolling, watchkeeping, sleeping, and at intervals eating something that didn't need cooking" as the navigator of the destroyer *Ferret*, Lieutenant William Tennant, remarked in his diary. But the patrols nonetheless achieved their objective, the divisions got through without loss, and there was no German activity in the Channel.

Keyes's part in the affair was somewhat more pugnacious. He had been afraid that the Germans might attempt to bombard the disembarkation from the sea and, having received the Admiralty's grudging permission, he took his two destroyers and two E class submarines to lie off the port and watch for enemy surface vessels. He himself took *Lurcher* into the port and, stunned by the scale of the harbor facilities that the Belgians had created, stayed at Zeebrugge for two days, watching the troops entrain and taking down details of the harbor. He wrote:

I proposed to destroy the latter (the locks and gates) when Antwerp fell, and we realised that the place must be abandoned to the enemy; but everyone was optimistic in those days, and the army hoped to be using Zeebrugge again before long, so this was not approved. I little thought how invaluable all the information I gathered would be to me three years later.[21]

Keyes left Zeebrugge on 8 October and returned to Harwich on the same day to be greeted with the welcome news that Lieutenant Commander Max Horton in the E-9 had distinguished himself by sinking the torpedo boat S-116 after a very difficult attack on the 6th. Horton described the affair:

> To hit a destroyer always requires maximum luck. She went up beautifully, and when I had a chance of a good look around about five minutes afterwards, all that was to be seen was about fifteen feet of bow sticking up vertically out of the water.[22]

Yet Horton's success, though it provided a useful lift for the navy as a whole, reinforced Keyes's growing conviction that the North Sea was not worth the attentions of the entire Overseas Flotilla. German heavy ships avoided the Bight and von Ingenohl's ban on exercises there continued. Thus, the only targets that the submarines could have were the elusive torpedo boats—and Horton had spent three hours stalking S-116 and himself admitted that he got her in the end only by a stroke of fortune— or the German submarines themselves.

Keyes proposed a "Baltic Enterprise"; that the E class submarines be allowed to go into the Baltic and, basing themselves on a Russian port, harry the Germans in "their own back-yard." The Admiralty at first had some reservations about infringing Danish neutrality, but Keyes was able to still these and, on 14 October, E-1, E-9, and E-11 sailed for the Baltic. The first two made the passage, but E-11 suffered engine defects and was forced to turn back. E-1 and E-9, and the submarines that followed them, were to cause damage to the Germans out of all proportion to their numbers and would more than justify Keyes's high opinion of their value. The amusing thing about the decision was, as Keyes later noted in his *Naval Memoirs*, that

> I learnt later that an hour after I had dispatched my letter to the Commander-in-chief he telegraphed to the Admiralty asking that the question of sending the submarines into the Baltic might receive consideration. I noted in my diary: "A regular case of mental telepathy. I had a most successful day at the Admiralty, and carried my point. Lawrence, Horton and Nasmith will have an opportunity of winning imperishable fame."[23]

The week after the fall of Antwerp was a quiet one, Tyrwhitt concentrating his patrols on the eastern side of the North Sea in an attempt to prevent any German submarines getting through which might use the captured ports as bases. By now, the Harwich Force had been reinforced by the arrival of the light cruisers *Undaunted* and *Aurora*, the former under the command of Captain Fox, who had been captain of the *Amphion* when she was mined. Fox took over command of the Third Flotilla from Tyrwhitt, which made the commodore's overall control of the force a great deal easier. Divisions of the First and Third Flotillas meanwhile alternated on patrol, a division spending two days on patrol, two days off and three more available "as required," concentrating their activities around the Dutch coast.

With the German occupation of the Belgian coast, the decision was made to create a separate Dover Command and reduce the Admiral of Patrols' concern to the east coast. The preservation of the Channel passage was now all the more crucial, with the mass of men and stores pouring into France and the stream of refugees coming back to Britain. The defense of the Channel would be an arduous and difficult duty when the Germans began to operate submarines and torpedo boats out of Zeebrugge and Ostend. Churchill and Battenberg agreed that there was only one man for the job.

The First Lord's Naval Secretary, Rear Admiral the Honourable Horace Hood, was appointed. He had been bursting to get into action, and he came to the task with energy, enthusiasm, and imagination—qualities that would be much needed if he was to make the passage secure. Hood was also given responsibility for any operations in support of the army on the Belgian coast that might be necessary, although the four light cruisers, twenty-four small destroyers, fourteen elderly submarines, and auxiliary patrol vessels that made up his command would need much reinforcement before they would be up to their duties. Hood hoisted his flag on 11 October and immediately began to reorganize the patrols.

As the Germans launched their offensive along the coast, Hood sent three monitors attached to his command to support the Belgians. The German Army had already occupied Zeebrugge and Ostend, but the Belgians were making a stand in front of Nieuport in an attempt to save that town and Dunkirk. Hood's ships were crucial to the outcome. The three, *Humber, Mersey,* and *Severn,* had been river monitors building for Brazil before they were requisitioned for the Royal Navy. Their two 6″ guns and 4.7″ howitzers could lay down a bombardment several miles inland and, almost invulnerable as far as the German army was concerned, they were worth dozens of batteries ashore. A few days later, the battleship *Venerable* was ordered out of Dover to assist the monitors and, though hampered by her great draught, she proved a valuable addition to the force with her 12″ guns.

The battleship was a surprise addition to the Dover Command. Hood had been concerned about the monitors going without support, and sent out large numbers of light craft to escort them, but he had in fact been anticipated by Sturdee. The Chief of Staff at first planned to send the *Queen* and the *Implacable* to Dover, but, mindful of the danger of

Tyrwhitt's forces going without heavy cover, he had diverted them to Harwich and ordered up two more, the *Irresistible* and the *Venerable*. Sturdee instructed Hood that they could be used for the defense of Dunkirk, but that the battleships were precious and should only be used as a last resort. It did not take Hood long to convince himself that the position at Dunkirk was grave enough to justify the risk.

The main reason for Sturdee's diversion of the first two predreadnoughts was the Admiralty's fear that heavy units of the High Sea Fleet would sortie to support a wholesale transfer of torpedo boats and submarines from Germany to the newly acquired Belgian ports. French and British mine-layers were laying offensive mine fields to close off Ostend and Zeebrugge, but there had already been a surface encounter that convinced the Admiralty the Germans were on the move again.

Now that Zeebrugge and Ostend had fallen to the German army, von Ingenohl at last felt able to move against the British forces in the Channel area. Previously, the German C in C refused to allow the torpedo boats to make sorties to the south because he believed that it would have been too easy for the British to close the Dutch coast and cut the German craft off from their bases. Now, however, that the Channel ports stood ready to act as refuges, a sortie would have a much greater chance of success.

Four torpedo boats, S-119, S-115, S-117, and S-118, under the command of Lieutenant Commander August Thiele, were selected to make a mine-laying sortie against the mouth of the Thames. The ships were stripped of all superfluous equipment and each loaded with twelve mines. They left the Ems at 0330 on 17 October, heading for the Downs.

The unfortunate Germans ran straight into the Terschelling patrol at 1340 that afternoon. The patrol had only been relieved some three hours before and the five ships, the cruiser *Undaunted* and the Third Flotilla's First Division, consisting of *Lance, Lennox, Legion*, and *Loyal*, were under the command of Captain Fox. The *Undaunted* sighted smoke bearing north-north-east and, as the British ships closed to investigate, they began to make out the shapes of the four German torpedo boats, steaming in line abreast. On sighting the *Undaunted* and her consorts, Thiele immediately turned his half flotilla sixteen points about and made for home at full speed.

But there could be only one end. The day was bright and calm, and the British ships rapidly began to overhaul their adversaries. The top speed of the torpedo boats when built had only been 26 knots, and they could now make barely 20. At 1405, *Undaunted* opened fire at 8,000 yards, but scored no hits before she stopped firing in order to close the range still further. The Germans were doing their best to evade the

British, laying smoke and zigzagging, while at the same time ditching their mines. By 1500 the range was down to 2,500 yards, and the British destroyers and the *Undaunted* opened fire.

S-115 and S-117 were soon put out of action. *Lennox* and *Lance* reduced S-115 to a sinking condition within minutes of opening fire. They left the torpedo boat to herself, dead in the water and half awash, while the other two destroyers dealt with S-117 in the same fashion before concentrating on the two remaining boats.

S-118 began to suffer badly. On fire, with her machinery damaged and unable to make an effective reply to the British fire with her own popgun four pounders, she turned toward the *Undaunted* in an attempt to make a torpedo attack. Thiele in S-119 followed her, but the two boats were smothered in a hail of fire from the Ls. By 1517, S-118 had sunk and she was followed at 1530, when S-119, ablaze from stem to stern, went under. It took time to sink the other two torpedo boats, crippled and blazing at they were, and it was not until 1630, after the expenditure of dozens of rounds by the British ships, that S-115 finally slipped below the surface. Only thirty-six officers and men were saved, thirty-four by the British forces and two the next day by a neutral fishing vessel, out of the 258 in the crews of the four torpedo boats.

Undaunted and the four destroyers returned in triumph to Harwich. It was a useful little victory and Tyrwhitt was delighted by their success, although he was chagrined at not being present, writing that it was "Just my luck! . . . The very day [Fox] takes on he gets a delightful show!"[24]

Despite thorough interrogation of the prisoners, the British did not happen upon the real reason for the sortie. Although they suspected the Germans' explanation that they had been scouting the area, they did not realise that the torpedo boats had been adapted for mine laying. The Admiralty, however, could not believe that the Germans would not attempt something against Hood's forces, so Tyrwhitt was ordered out to sweep the Broad Fourteens and over to the Dutch coast again, supported by the *Queen* and the *Implacable* in the west.

Despite the Admiralty's belief that a force of German cruisers was operating from Heligoland Bight out to the Broad Fourteens, Tyrwhitt's forces met with no German warships and the only incident of the sweep was the interception of the German "hospital" ship *Ophelia*, whose movements Keyes's submarines had been watching for some time. Tyrwhitt did not believe the explanation that the ship had been sent out to look for survivors of the torpedo boats and sent her into Lowestoft. She was examined by a prize court and condemned in May 1915.

All in all, it had been a successful few days for the British, but the Overseas Submarine Flotilla suffered a heavy blow when E-3 was reported overdue from patrol. Keyes suspected that she had been stalked and sunk by a combination of submarines and seaplanes working together in Heligoland Bight, and this was partially true, for E-3 had been blown in two and sunk with all hands by a torpedo from U-27 off the Ems on the 14th. It was the first time that a submarine had ever been sunk by another submarine and though the British did not know the cause of E-3's loss until well after the war, her sinking rammed home the knowledge of the risks that the submarines were running in their operations.

Now that it had been confirmed that the Germans were not attempting an attack on Hood's coastal force, Keyes and Tyrwhitt began to agitate once more for an offensive operation into Heligoland Bight. Tyrwhitt went up to the Admiralty on 22 October.

> I arrived at 5 P.M. and was at once taken to the Holy of Holy rooms, where Prince Louis, Winston and Sturdee were, and a long discussion followed. I produced my little plan (or rather, Roger Keyes' plan) and got it through right away. . . . Well, they kept me a long time. . . .[25]

In fact, the Admiralty, which was through the Royal Naval Air Service responsible for the aerial defense of London and the Home Counties, had made another plan, but Churchill was willing to include the Commodores' proposals in the scheme as a useful and possibly profitable sideline. The great worry was the use that the Germans might make of their zeppelins and it was decided to attack the zeppelin base at Cuxhaven.

Six seaplanes were to be embarked in the converted cross-Channel steamers *Engadine* and *Riviera*. Tyrwhitt was ordered to escort the two seaplane carriers into the Heligoland Bight and stand by them while the seaplanes were launched, made their raid, and returned. Further to the south, as a diversion, Blunt and the First Flotilla would conduct the sweep off the Ems which Tyrwhitt and Keyes had originally planned. Finally, Rear Admiral Moore, with his two battle cruisers, was ordered to act as heavy support for the attack, patrolling outside the Bight to the north.

The operation was a dismal failure. The sailing of the Harwich Force was delayed by rough weather, and though the flotillas and the two carriers sailed into calm seas early on the 24th, within a few hours heavy rain had set in. It continued to pour all the way across the North Sea and when, at dawn on the 25th, the seaplanes were put into the water and given the order to take off,

> . . . four of the machines failed to rise from the water; one flew 12 miles, but had two engine failures due to the rain, and returned; and the sixth, after slipping its 100 lb bomb, managed to rise and flew 20 miles, but

returned owing to the remote chance of finding the objective and the uselessness of endangering the force for no result.[26]

Captain Blunt's ships sighted no surface vessels and only one aircraft, a seaplane from Borkum, and the single incident to enliven proceedings occurred when the destroyer *Badger* rammed, but did not sink, U-19, one of the submarines that von Ingenohl had dispatched to attack Hood's ships. U-19 managed to get back to Germany, being only slightly injured, but *Badger* had a badly bent bow and had to be detached immediately to return to Harwich. Tyrwhitt was enraged by the entire affair and inclined to blame the aviators for his "having been made a fool of," but when he went up to the Admiralty he "got considerable butter" and found that Churchill only regarded the failure as a temporary setback. Indeed, the First Lord was busy devising better ways of launching the aircraft and he soon roused the Commodore's enthusiasm to such an extent that "we are going to try again and I can't help thinking we shall succeed this time."

Meanwhile, von Ingenohl had again taken fright at the British successes. It was after the sinking of the four torpedo boats that the Germans first began to suspect that their security had been compromised. Although the British had not yet mastered the German codes and the interception of the sortie had been a coincidence, it seemed to the Command as if the size and position of the British force had been so perfect for the task that it had to be deliberate. A ruthless hunt for spies was initiated and found nothing, but, still uneasy, the Admiralstab directed that the arrangements for the transmission of operational orders be tightened considerably. In the meantime, von Ingenohl decided against any further surface raids, but instead ordered five submarines, U-24, U-27, U-30, U-19, and U-28, out to attack Hood's forces on the Belgian coast. They sailed between 22 and 26 October, and, though U-19 was damaged in her encounter with the *Badger* and had to return, by the 23rd the U-boats began to arrive in the Channel. They soon made their presence felt by a series of attacks on ships in the area, and all units but those actually engaged in bombardments were hurriedly sent into harbor.

The U-boats managed to avoid a succession of destroyers and submarines sent out to look for them, but they did not succeed in sinking anything until 26 October, when U-24 torpedoed the steamer *Amiral Ganteaume*, crowded with thousands of Belgian refugees. Forty were killed, and, although the captain, Lieutenant Commander Schneider, had been within his rights because the ship had been under escort and thus not capable of being boarded, it was a false move on Germany's part as the plight of the Belgians was already arousing considerable concern in neutral countries.

Then, on 31 October, the old cruiser *Hermes* was sighted en route to Dover by U-27. *Hermes* was engaged in ferrying aircraft across the Channel to reinforce the RNAS squadrons in France. Though Hood had placed a general ban on large ships crossing the Channel in daylight, her captain apparently considered that *Hermes*'s duties were too important to be so restricted. In any case, the cruiser was zigzagging at 13 knots when the submarine fired a torpedo from a range of 300 yards. *Hermes* turned hard away in an attempt to avoid, but the torpedo struck aft and exploded. *Hermes* lost way and was beginning to settle by the stern when U-27 fired a second torpedo. This too struck and within a few minutes *Hermes* sank. The bulk of the crew were picked up by destroyers and the steamer *Invicta*.

The Admiralty hastily clamped even more restrictions on operations in the Channel and the *Venerable* was ordered home to Sheerness. In daylight hours, "no vessel larger than a destroyer or, in exceptional cases, a scout, was to cross the Channel east of the meridian of Greenwich." In response to his pleas for heavy support, Hood was promised that the antique battleship *Revenge*, which had been resurrected from the Motherbank and adapted for bombardment, would be sent out to him if the need arose. But the Admiralty pointed out that the loss of a battleship would be a grave blow, and they preferred to avoid taking the risk until some practical antisubmarine measures could be devised.

Thus, October in the North Sea closed with the Germans having enjoyed more substantial successes than the British. Much had been learnt and much remained to be learnt. But if the Royal Navy had little reason to be satisfied, at least its "small ships" had been given their head and had managed to achieve something. The German efforts had hitherto been too piecemeal and disjointed. The policy of the preservation of the battle line was an arguable one, but the light forces had been handled badly and, if it could be said that it took the disaster of the loss of the *Aboukir, Hogue* and *Cressy* to alert the Royal Navy to the potential of the submarine, then exactly the same was true of the Imperial Navy. A submarine campaign should have, and could have, been mounted much earlier and would have reaped rich reward. The British system of command was more sound than the German, and this factor was beginning to tell.

It was, however, for the Admiralty and not the various arms of the German Command that the month of October was one of unease, upheaval, and dissension as the strains and setbacks began to prove too much for the administration. Opinion was growing that something was wrong at the Admiralty. It is difficult, more than sixty years later, to comprehend the attitude of the British people at large toward the Royal

Navy. In the hundred years since the end of the Napoleonic Wars, the reality of that struggle—the long years spent on blockade and the frequent invasion scares only punctuated by the glorious successes—had been forgotten and all that was left was an aura of invincibility. Understanding little of the realities of war at sea, most expected that the Royal Navy would have steamed into Heligoland Bight in the first days of the war and annihilated the High Sea Fleet.

Now, months after the start of hostilities, nothing of the sort had happened. Admittedly, some minor successes had been gained, but against the record of the Harwich Force and Keyes's submarines could be set the loss of seven cruisers and the rumored destruction of the *Audacious*. In foreign waters not one of the raider cruisers or those of Admiral von Spee's Asiatic Squadron had been caught. *Emden* was taking a huge toll of shipping, seemingly unchecked, while the *Königsberg* had sunk the old cruiser *Pegasus* at Zanzibar, and *Scharnhorst*, *Gneisenau*, and their consorts had disappeared into the vastness of the Pacific.

What was wrong at the Admiralty? In truth, as far as the dispositions abroad and the loss of the three armored cruisers were concerned, the fault could largely be said to have been Sturdee's. The blame, however, fell on other shoulders—those of Churchill and Battenberg. Churchill was the first to be attacked. Ironically, he had displayed such interest in the working of the navy before the war and spent so much time in the fleet—and with such a blaze of publicity—that now hostilities had begun, popular and service opinion was inclined to credit him with playing an even greater part in the operational side of the Admiralty than he actually did. All the apparent inconsistencies in Admiralty policy were laid at his door, because he was known to be hotheaded and mercurial. "Hated, mistrusted, and feared" by the Conservatives, he was not much liked by his own party, being too brash and self-assertive for many of his older colleagues. He had the same effect upon the admirals at sea, most of whom disliked him intensely. Keyes and Tyrwhitt, who knew more of the true position than most, were his only champions, and even Beatty, Churchill's former Naval Secretary, would have preferred his removal from office. But Churchill had the confidence of two key figures, the Prime Minister, Herbert Asquith, and the Chancellor of the Exchequer, David Lloyd George, and he had too large a personal following in Parliament to be overthrown yet. Prince Louis of Battenberg would be offered up as the scapegoat.

Nonetheless, although the ostensible reason for his departure from the post of First Sea Lord was iniquitous, it cannot in all honesty be said that Battenberg should have remained in office. He had been one of the best "all rounders" in the navy in his day, possessing powers of leadership and imagination rare in his time. An innovative and forward thinker, he had been keen to encourage his juniors and was receptive to their views and ideas. He should have been ideal as First Sea Lord, but by 1914 his powers were failing. Gout was causing him great pain and it seems to have been the case that he was simply not strong enough to exercise continuous control over either Churchill or Sturdee. Unafraid to assume responsibility, as he had done in halting the demobilization in July, he was nonetheless unsuitable as First Sea Lord because he simply could not keep an adequate mental picture of events. It was Sturdee and Churchill who did the work of the war, and it was Battenberg who wrote "concur." It was indeed a tragedy, for Battenberg's mental powers had been enormous and fully fit he could well have made a "second St. Vincent," blessed with both imagination and common sense, two qualities invaluable in war and most necessary when dealing with a First Lord such as Churchill.

Battenberg's German origins finally brought him down. Battenberg had joined the Royal Navy, as he himself frequently pointed out, before a united Germany even existed, the Battenbergs bore no love for the Hohenzollerns, and all his closest male relatives were serving with the British forces. Yet the popular press began to agitate for his removal on the ground that his loyalty was in doubt. It was a scandalous accusation, but rumor began to pile upon rumor that the First Sea Lord had been dealing with the Germans, that he had deliberately engineered the loss of the armored cruisers, and that he had even been imprisoned in the Tower on the orders of the King.[27]

Churchill saw what was in the wind and began to plan Battenberg's removal. Perhaps Churchill's motives were not entirely pure, since it is clear in retrospect that it would have been either his head or Battenberg's, but the First Lord had not for a considerable time been happy with Battenberg's performance. It is possible that the popular clamor acted only as a spur to Churchill. At all events, it was not a hasty decision. A note in the biography of Admiral of the Fleet Sir Henry Oliver is of interest:

> One of his [Oliver's] first jobs was the unwelcome one of taking a letter from Churchill to Prince Louis of Battenberg, the First Sea Lord, asking for his resignation.[28]

Professor Marder remarks, in his work *From Dreadnought to Scapa Flow*, that there was much "evidence that Battenberg was *asked* to resign,"[29] and in fact Churchill discussed the subject with Battenberg on 27 October and saw the King to warn him of the prospect that day. It must have been a painful interview for both Churchill and Battenberg.

They were good friends and had worked well together. Battenberg was in the job which he had wanted all his life, to attain it had been his heart's desire. It was unlikely that he would ever be employed again; there is no place in the active Royal Navy for an ex-First Sea Lord. In great anguish, Battenberg agreed to step aside. It was perhaps the most honorable act of an honorable career. He wrote his formal letter of resignation on 28 October:

> I have lately been driven to the painful conclusion that at this juncture my birth and parentage have the effect of impairing in some respects my usefulness on the Board. In these circumstances I feel it to be my duty, as a loyal subject of His Majesty, to resign the office of First Sea Lord, hoping thereby to facilitate the task of the administration of the great service, to which I have devoted my life, and to ease the burden laid on H.M. Ministers.[30]

Battenberg later wrote to Rear Admiral Hood:

> It was an awful wrench, but I had no choice from the moment it was made clear to me that the Government did not feel themselves strong enough to support me by some public pronouncement.[31]

Sorry as the politicians were for Battenberg, his departure acted as a sop for the rising dissent against the Government, and the Cabinet were relieved to note that it temporarily stilled the Opposition. Nonetheless, although Churchill had already decided upon a new First Sea Lord, and had secured the agreement of the Prime Minister, the question of who was to succeed Battenberg was not yet settled.

CHAPTER 7

The Return of Fisher

As part of his preparations for Battenberg's departure Churchill went to see the King to warn him of the resignation of Prince Louis and inform him that he proposed to nominate Lord Fisher. King George was horrified by the prospect. He had long detested Fisher (who nursed for his part a cordial dislike of the monarch) and mistrusted most of the reforms that the admiral had initiated. During the interview the King searched for alternatives, but Churchill rejected the first three—Admiral Sir Hedworth Meux, Admiral Sir Henry Jackson and Doveton Sturdee— out of hand. The interview broke up with the two still in complete disagreement.

The problem, as Churchill knew quite well and King George was forced to admit, was that the higher ranks of the Flag List were singularly devoid of men with the peculiar mix of talents required to make a good First Sea Lord. Jellicoe could not be spared, Callaghan was too old and could not stand the strain, Jackson was colorless and lacked the energy needed to get the job done, Hedworth Meux lacked the necessary technical expertise. Some of the vice admirals, notably Sir Stanley Colville, might have been a success, but the time had not yet come when the First Lord could reach down into the ranks and raise a junior officer to the supreme professional position in the navy without arousing a storm of dissent in the service and the country as a whole. Beatty's advancement had caused enough trouble. Moreover, Churchill would have been especially vulnerable to such attacks with his record of interference in service affairs. The suspicion would have been voiced that he was installing a cipher in order to gather supreme operational control into his own hands.

The King held out against Fisher's nomination until 29 October, but, with every alternative exhausted, and Churchill and the Prime Minister firm in their resolve, he acquiesced and the appointment was made that day. In spite of some apprehension in the service—for the Fisher–Beresford feud was hardly dead and many of Lord Beresford's supporters now occupied high positions in the navy—there was general rejoicing, save among those such as Rear Admiral Wemyss and Henry Oliver. The latter:

> . . . expressed grave doubts whether Fisher, with his dynamic personality and intolerance, would work in double harness with Churchill who, unlike most First Lords, would expect to be kept well informed and consulted about strategy and dispositions of ships.[1]

Fisher swung rapidly into action. The new broom swept very clean but it cannot be denied that the new appointments he made were largely a great improvement on the old. Even as he joined the Admiralty, the first news came in of the disaster at Coronel on 1 November, when Rear Admiral Sir Christopher Cradock's weak and elderly cruiser squadron was annihilated by von Spee's superbly trained force. Fisher determined upon a bold stroke and detached three battle cruisers from Beatty's force. *Princess Royal* was sent to the West Indies to watch the Panama Canal for von Spee, while *Invincible* and *Inflexible* were prepared for service in the South Atlantic.

Fisher detested Sturdee, who had been Beresford's Chief of Staff in the Channel Fleet, and whom he suspected of having played a major part in organizing the faulty dispositions that brought about the disaster. Because Churchill was unwilling to sack Sturdee, Fisher compromised, saying that, as Sturdee had caused the mess, he should be the one to sort it out. Henry Oliver was appointed as Chief of Staff with the rank of Acting Vice Admiral, while Sturdee was dispatched to the South Atlantic with two battle cruisers to deal with von Spee.

Oliver was a good selection. While was as prone as any in his generation to overcentralize, he had great common sense and possessed the strategic insight so necessary in a Chief of the War Staff. He was also one of the few men alive who could stand up to both Churchill and Fisher. His method was simple; if he could not get either to see his point of view, he would agree with them and then quietly go away and do as he thought best. He was rarely challenged. Admiral of the Fleet Sir Arthur Wilson also joined the Admiralty, as an unpaid assistant. He had at first been offered Sturdee's job, but he refused it because he preferred not to have to take sides between Fisher and Churchill.

In the months ahead, this combination of Churchill, Fisher, and Wilson, aided by Oliver, came to be known as the "Cabal" and effectively constituted the naval staff, largely independent of any outside advice. The remainder of the Board of Admiralty were busy with their administrative and technical duties, and it would have been a brave junior officer who attempted to cross swords over any issue with Churchill or either of the admirals of the fleet.

Rear Admiral Leveson was also originally marked to go. Fisher mistrusted and disliked him for his connections with Beresford and Admiral Sir William May, another *bete noir* of the new First Sea Lord. But Fisher was too busy to bother with Leveson, who in any case was allowed to exercise little authority under the new administration.

It was just as well that the new spirit had entered the Admiralty for, on 3 November, the Royal Navy received yet another setback. This time it struck at the very foundation of the popular image of the fleet as "Britain's sure shield."

On the other side of the North Sea, Hipper had managed at last, on 29 October, to secure permission for a raid on the English coast that would involve the bulk of the High Sea Fleet. The Admiralstab proposed, after the failure of the mine-laying attack on the Firth of Forth, that the emphasis be changed to catch the British off guard by mining sections of the east coast, rather than particular harbors, since the local surveillance and mine-sweeping systems seemed to be too efficient.

Light cruisers were ordered to mine the area off Lowestoft in order to destroy the passing traffic and the fisheries, which the Command thought were particularly active off the coasts of Norfolk and Suffolk in November. As a diversion, Hipper, as he had long recommended, was to bombard the ports on the coast with the First Scouting Group. From the very first, Hipper took a different view from the Admiralstab and insisted that the bombardment of Yarmouth take precedence. It was according to the latter view that the enterprise was carried out. Hipper was a shrewd judge of the worth of the operation in morale effect alone for Germany; it was unfortunate, then, that the German intelligence was incorrect and Yarmouth was not a fortified port.

The role of the First Scouting Group had been outlined only after much argument with von Ingenohl, who did not wish the battle cruisers to expose themselves. The C in C had in fact not agreed to the proposal when he dispatched the telegram to the Kaiser requesting permission for the mine-laying raid, and the telegram merely mentioned that the First Scouting Group would "escort" the mine-layers.

At 1630 on 2 November Hipper led the *Seydlitz, Moltke, Von der*

Tann, and *Blücher* out of the Jade. The First Scouting Group was accompanied only by the light cruiser *Stralsund*, which was to lay the mines, *Strassburg*, *Graudenz*, and *Kolberg*. All the torpedo boats were left behind as the weather was deteriorating and Hipper did not think that they would be able to keep up with the heavy ships. The raiding force was followed out at 1800 by the First and Third Battle Squadrons with a heavy escort. These ships were to go out in support only to the edge of the Bight, with a screen of submarines to seaward of them. Von Ingenohl did not wish to take the risk of going into the North Sea unless it was absolutely necessary.

The British forces around Harwich and Yarmouth were very weak. Since the removal of the surviving armored cruisers, no heavy ships had been allowed into the area other than the old predreadnoughts from Sheerness. These were armed with 12″ guns, but, slow and ill armored, they could have no chance of intercepting any German thrust against the ports to the north. It was the perfect time for a German raid, because all Jellicoe's forces were now so far away that not even the battle cruisers would be able to get into the North Sea and move south in time to make contact.

There were, however, patrols out on the Broad Fourteens and off the east coast. Tyrwhitt had planned to attack German minesweepers that Keyes's submarines had reported off the western Ems. The *Undaunted, Aurora,* and seven destroyers had been selected but, because of the heavy weather, Commodore (T) postponed the operation. Instead, on 2 November he sent the ships out in two divisions, *Aurora* and four destroyers being ordered to hunt the Broad Fourteens for submarines, while Captain F. G. St. John, the new Captain (D) of the Third Flotilla, was to take *Undaunted* and three destroyers to patrol off Terschelling. Ordered to rendezvous at 0800 the next morning, the two groups largely spent their time sinking mines that had broken away from mine fields that now littered the area.

Hipper's force passed unknowing through the British rendezvous at midnight, when the Germans altered course to the west and worked up speed to 18 knots. By this time Captain St. John's force, which had been well to the north-west, turned south and for three hours the courses of the German and British forces converged rapidly. At 0300 *Undaunted* and her three destroyers passed within ten miles of Hipper's battle cruisers, but in the darkness and in their ignorance they missed the Germans completely—and lost a priceless opportunity for a night torpedo attack on the scantily escorted First Scouting Group.

The ships of the Harwich Force passed an uneventful night whilst the Germans steamed steadily towards the coast. Repeatedly the Scouting

Groups came into contact with groups of fishing vessels, but there were so many at sea that night that, despite several efforts by Hipper to avoid them, more and more groups came into sight at frequent intervals. Hipper could not, to his regret, do anything to confirm his suspicions that they were being used by the British to report German movements.

The Germans had to rely upon dead reckoning to determine their position. The North Sea is a notoriously difficult area for navigation, and the Admiralty policy of removing many of the navigation aids and dousing lights was beginning to reap its reward. The Germans became conscious that they could not fix their position within ten miles. Consequently, although *Stralsund*'s captain had been given very definite instructions that he was to begin the lay off Smith's Knoll at 0530, he decided to drop the mines at intervals more than half as much again as had been planned.

It was fortunate that he did so, for at 0630, *Seydlitz* ran almost right over a buoy marked "Smith's Knoll Watch" and the Germans discovered that they were an hour behind in their reckoning. Relying on depth sounding, the Scouting Groups began to work their way south to the Cross Sand light vessel to begin the attack on Yarmouth. From here they would head for the Corton light vessel, laying down the bombardment as they went south.

But Hipper was to be deflected from his purpose by the smallest of adversaries. From the beginning of the war, only six elderly destroyers of the B and C classes, that half of the Seventh Flotilla allocated to Yarmouth, and the antiquated minesweeping gunboat *Halcyon* had been based in the area. Only this force was in the vicinity to stand up to the Germans. Plans were afoot to make Yarmouth into a major escort base, with a full destroyer flotilla and twelve trawlers based on the port, and Captain Wilmot Nicholson, lately of the *Hogue*, had been appointed in charge. Little work had as yet been done. There were no land defenses. Before the war there had been a mobile territorial battery of 6″ guns, of little use for defense against warships, although Keyes had pointed out that their presence technically made Yarmouth a defended port and thus subject to bombardment. They had been removed sometime before, however, in the reorganization of the army for the war in France.

Halcyon sailed from Yarmouth at dawn to search for drifting mines in the swept channel off Smith's Knoll. She was followed out a few minutes later by the first of the three destroyers, the *Lively, Leopard,* and *Success,* which were assigned to the day's offshore patrols. It was a relatively calm but very misty day, and *Halcyon* had only just come up to the Cross Sand light vessel when *Strassburg* and *Graudenz* appeared five miles away and immediately opened fire. Hipper called them back, however, to avoid the danger of mines and ordered *Seydlitz* alone to open fire on the little *Halcyon*. The British minesweeper's fate appeared sealed, but, by a combination of good fortune and great skill, she was to escape unscathed. At the first sight of an enemy vessel since the beginning of the war, the eager gunnery teams of the German heavy ships misunderstood Hipper's order and all four opened fire, their shell splashes smothering the target and rendering spotting impossible.

In the few minutes that it took to sort out the problem, the destroyer *Lively* came up to the fleeing *Halcyon*. The captain of the destroyer, Lieutenant Commander H. T. Baillie-Grohman, handled his ship superbly, laying a smokescreen to hide the *Halcyon*, while he dodged *Lively* in and out of the smoke to draw the German fire onto his own ship.

Hipper soon realized that such an action was a waste of resources and turned the battle cruisers to the east. The operation was already an hour late and the run to the south would soon take the force into mined waters. As they withdrew, the battle cruisers laid down a scattered bombardment on Yarmouth, but the shells had no effect, none getting nearer to the town than the beach. *Lively* and *Leopard*, which had just arrived on the scene, immediately turned to follow the battle cruisers.

Halcyon began to broadcast a general warning of the German presence, but she had been anticipated in this by *Leopard*, senior ship of the destroyers, which signaled at 0720: "Two battle cruisers and two armoured cruisers open fire on *Lively* and myself." The British forces now began to move. By chance, lying in Yarmouth in preparation for a sortie into Heligoland Bight, were the submarines E-10, D-5, and D-3 and, hearing the sound of the guns, they prepared to get under way. Harwich had been alerted by *Leopard*'s signal, but Captain A. K. Waistell, in charge as Keyes's deputy, felt that the submarines would have more of a chance of striking a blow at the German force if they went into the Bight, so he ordered them to sail immediately.

The *Success* had left Yarmouth by now and joined the other destroyers as they followed Hipper's movement to the east. The three "off-duty" destroyers, which had put into Lowestoft for the night, were raising steam but they took too long to play any part in the affair. Tyrwhitt in Harwich was rousing his flotillas and, to seawards, *Aurora* and *Undaunted* and their divisions were alerted and ordered to stand by.

Though *Leopard* and *Halcyon* had together given a clear indication of the position, the Admiralty Staff do not appear to have appreciated the true nature of the raid. As Churchill wrote of the *Halcyon*'s signal in *The World Crisis*:

> What did it mean? It seemed quite certain that German battle cruisers would not be sent to throw their shells at an open town like Yarmouth.

Obviously this was a demonstration to divert the British Fleet from something else that was going to happen—was already perhaps happening. Was it a German raid into the Channel, or a serious attempt by the German Navy to intervene upon the Belgian coast while the land battle was still raging? Was it a descent on the British coast at Sunderland or Blyth? We had no means of deciding. The last thing it seemed possible to believe was that first-class units of the German Fleet would have been sent across the North Sea simply in order to disturb the fisher-folk of Yarmouth.[2]

They took no action for the time being, and for over ninety minutes more the Admiralty played a completely passive role, merely intercepting and noting every signal that was sent out. What is more, for some reason they failed even to inform the operational and local commanders of what had passed, leaving them to their own devices.

Tyrwhitt, on receiving *Halcyon*'s message of the German withdrawal to the east at 0800, immediately realized that the only forces in a position to intercept the Germans before they returned to the Bight were those vessels of the Harwich Force already at sea. Accordingly, he ordered *Undaunted* and *Aurora* to move west and make contact, shadowing the Germans if they could. Meanwhile, as the Germans turned for home, the senior officer of the three small destroyers which had been faithfully shadowing the Scouting Groups wisely decided that his old ships had done all that they could do. He ordered them to turn back for Yarmouth and resume their patrol offshore.

It was not until *Halcyon* got into Lowestoft and the Admiralty received her full report that the War Staff began to act. This was despite the fact that the exact German strength was already known at the Admiralty, from interception of a signal from *Halcyon* to Tyrwhitt giving that information an hour before. At 0955, they started to issue their instructions, summoning Beatty south with all the battle cruisers and ordering the Battle Squadrons to concentrate in Scapa Flow, to sail in the afternoon, while the Channel Fleet was to assemble at Spithead. Jellicoe was still on his way north from the conference at the Admiralty and the orders for the Grand Fleet were sent to Burney, since the Commander in Chief was necessarily ignorant of the situation. By this time, however, Hipper was already more than fifty miles into the North Sea, and contact had been made between his ships and those of the Harwich Force at sea.

Undaunted and her division steamed south-west after Tyrwhitt's orders came through, but when by 0840 they had seen nothing, Captain St. John reversed their course, hoping to cross the track of the returning Germans. For the next hour, at the very limit of visibility, he was repeatedly seen by the Germans, but had only one brief glimpse of them himself. The tracks of the two forces were, however, converging slightly and by 0950 Hipper's four heavy ships came into clear view. Thinking that Hipper would chase his tiny force, he hastily turned his ships away to the north-north-west and then, turning first west, then east, and finally north-north-west again. In an elaborate attempt to shake off the supposed pursuit he finally steamed directly away from the Germans.

But the British forces had only been in sight of the Germans for a matter of seconds before they turned away and Hipper, intent on returning home without loss, did not pursue, altering course further to the north after 1000. The Scouting Groups had been steaming at 22 knots since the *Strassburg* began to lay her mines, but after several hours of this more than one of the ships was beginning to develop defects and, perforce, Hipper reduced their speed to 20 knots.

The brief sighting of the *Undaunted* was the last incident of the raid. Von Ingenohl turned for home before 0800, thinking quite correctly that unless some of Hipper's ships had been disabled, no heavy British forces could get south in time to cut them off. By nightfall both the High Sea Fleet and the Scouting Groups were inside the inner Bight. For the Germans, however, there was one more scene to play in what had been a most unsatisfactory act. Fog shrouded the Bight by the time the fleet got in, and von Ingenohl ordered all his ships to remain in the Schillig Roads until the morning. One unit, the armored cruiser *Yorck*, had developed severe machinery defects, and she received permission to go straight into Wilhelmshaven. In the gloom, she passed to the wrong side of the boom defense vessel which marked the entrance to the swept channel through the defensive mine fields and within minutes had exploded two mines. The cruiser sank with heavy loss of life.

The raid had not been a success for the Imperial Navy. Intercepted mine warnings told them that the *Strassburg*'s field had been discovered—in fact, three unfortunate fishing vessels were sunk by mines within twelve hours—while the bombardment had been a dismal failure, and the breakdown of the fire-control procedure ensured that they had not sunk a single British ship. Hipper came in for a great deal of criticism over his handling of the affair, but the recriminations did not last overlong. It was generally accepted that the incident taught many lessons and pointed clearly as to how future raids should be conducted.

At the same time, the performance of the Royal Navy was by no means flawless. The concentration of the Grand Fleet and the battle cruisers so far to the north meant that the east coast was especially vulnerable to such forays. Some redistribution would have to be made, despite the various admirals' dislike of the anchorages along the coast. It was the problem of the lack of defenses that was the issue yet again. For the cost of a single battleship, fully protected bases could have been established well before the war at the Firth of Forth, the Humber, and Scapa Flow. For the sake of false economy, the matter had been deferred again and again.

Fisher, Churchill, and the War Staff erred badly in their decision to do nothing. Though in the event their failure even to inform the operational commanders of the situation until 0900 was to have no effect on the issue, it was an inexcusable lapse on the part of the War Group and their assistants.

The tactics of the Harwich Force had not been of the best. St. John overreacted to the encounter with the German force; he should have remembered that his ships had the heels of the Germans and that the primary duty of the shadower is to keep his subjects in sight at all times. *Aurora* and her three destroyers had stood too far to the north and crossed well ahead of the Germans. It was only good luck that kept the cruiser away from the mine-strewn track of the Scouting Groups. Indeed, one of her destroyers, the *Lark*, passed right over it. Similarly, *Arethusa* with Tyrwhitt on board only just missed running into the field with an entire flotilla. The movements of the three sections of the Harwich Force that went to sea well demonstrated the difficulties involved in controlling scattered groups of ships. Tyrwhitt had to resort to steaming to the usual rendezvous for the patrols and staying there in order to get them concentrated. It was 1530 before he had all the light cruisers and destroyers together. By this time, of course, Hipper had his ships well into their home waters and was out of reach of the British.

The lack of British submarines in the Bight and off the Ems had been a major deficiency, since the movements of the High Sea Fleet might have provided an opportunity for successful torpedo attacks. As it was, D-5 was struck by a floating mine as she came out of Yarmouth and went down with heavy loss of life. None of the other submarines had, of course, seen anything as they were far too slow to be able to get across the North Sea in time. Keyes's Overseas Flotilla needed sufficient submarines to be able both to maintain a strong patrol in German waters and to support the various sweeps and operations of the Harwich Force. The Baltic venture had been an admirable and worthwhile scheme, but new construction had not yet provided sufficient submarines to make up the numbers. In heavy weather the system broke down very quickly. Keyes could not risk sending his submarines out on patrol if they would return in need of repairs from the effect of the weather. The Overseas Flotilla had no margin for wear and tear.

In the end, however, the greatest failure was that the Admiralty failed to realize the nature of the German sortie as early as they should have. Despite the fact that *Leopard* gave an accurate description of the German force at 0720 and that this was confirmed by *Halcyon*'s description of "four armored ships" sent out by her as a general signal at 0735, not for more than two hours did the Admiralty act as if they wished to make any attempt to deal with the raiders. While it is possible to argue that caution prevailed, the movements of the various forces, which included sailing the Grand Fleet in and out of Scapa Flow in broad daylight, in direct contravention of the policy that Jellicoe had introduced to avoid submarine attacks, would seem to belie this. The staff still had much to learn about the control of ships in war. Preoccupied with the Channel and the struggle for the Channel ports as the Admiralty was, the heavy units should have been put to sea much earlier. If, as Churchill has explained, some major thrust in concert with the raid was expected, then the sailing of the predreadnoughts from The Nore and Dover, as was ordered later in the day, was an extremely dubious move and one contrary to the principle of concentration. On the other hand, if it was felt that the raid was a single event, then the disposition of the old battleships was a reasonable one that prevented the possibility of Hipper turning back and striking at some other part of the coast. All that can be concluded is that the administration had not yet found its feet and sorted out the muddled thinking of the previous months.

On 30 October, Jellicoe dispatched to the Secretary of the Admiralty a letter containing his proposals for the operation of the Grand Fleet. This was a document the contents of which were to have repercussions on the whole war at sea. It has been reproduced in other works, but its importance is such that no history of the Royal Navy in World War I would be complete without it.

>   . . .The Germans have shown that they rely to a very great extent on submarines, mines and torpedoes, and there can be no doubt whatever that they will endeavour to make the fullest use of these weapons in a fleet action, especially since they possess an actual superiority over us in these particular directions.
>
>   3. It, therefore, becomes necessary to consider our own tactical methods in relation to these forms of attack.
>
>   4. In the first place, it is evident that the Germans cannot rely with certainty upon having their full complement of submarines and mine-layers present in a fleet action, unless the battle is fought in waters selected by them and in the southern area of the North Sea. Aircraft, also, could only be brought into action in this locality.
>
>   5. My object will therefore be to fight the fleet action in the Northern portion of the North Sea, which position is incidentally nearer our own

bases, giving our wounded ships a chance of reaching them, whilst it ensures the final destruction or capture of enemy wounded vessels, and greatly handicaps a night destroyer attack before or after a fleet action. The Northern area is also favourable to a concentration of our cruisers and torpedo craft with the battlefleet; such concentration on the part of the enemy being always possible, since he will choose a time for coming out when all his ships are coaled and ready in all respects to fight.

6. Owing to the necessity that exists for keeping our cruisers at sea, it is probable that many will be short of coal when the opportunity for a fleet action arises and that they might be unable to move far to the Southward for this reason.

7. The presence of a large force of cruisers is most necessary, for observation and for screening the battlefleet, so that the latter may be manoeuvred into any desired position behind the cruiser screen. This is a strong additional reason for fighting in the Northern area.

8. Secondly, it is necessary to consider what may be termed the tactics of the actual battlefield. The German submarines, if worked as is expected with the battlefleet, can be used in one of two ways:
(a) With the cruisers, or possibly with destroyers.
(b) With the battlefleet.

In the first case the submarines would probably be led by the cruisers to a position favourable for attacking our battlefleet as it advanced to deploy, and in the second case they might be kept in a position in rear, or to the flank, of the enemy's battlefleet, which would move in the direction required to draw our own Fleet into contact with the submarines.

9. The first move at (a) should be defeated by our own cruisers, provided we have a sufficient number present as they should be able to force the enemy's cruisers to action at a speed which would interfere with submarine tactics.

The cruisers must, however, have destroyers in company to assist in dealing with the submarines, and should be well in advance of the battle fleet; hence the necessity for numbers.

10. The second move at (b) can be countered by judicious handling of our battlefleet, but may, and probably will involve a refusal to comply with the enemy's tactics by moving in the invited direction. If, for instance, the enemy battle fleet were to turn away from an advancing Fleet, I should assume that the intention was to lead us over mines and submarines and should decline to be so drawn.

11. I desire particularly to draw the attention of Their Lordships to this point, since it may be deemed a refusal of battle, and, indeed, might possibly result in failure to bring the enemy to action as soon as is expected and hoped.

12. Such a result would be absolutely repugnant to the feelings of all British Naval Officers and men, but with new and untried methods of warfare new tactics must be devised to meet them.

I feel that such tactics, if not understood, may bring odium upon me, but so long as I have the confidence of Their Lordships I intend to pursue what is, in my considered opinion, the proper course to defeat and annihilate the enemy's battlefleet, without regard to uninstructed opinion or criticism.

13. The situation is a difficult one. It is quite within the bounds of possibility that half our battlefleet might be disabled by under-water attack before the guns opened fire at all, if a false move is made, and I feel that I must constantly bear in mind the great probability of such an attack and be prepared tactically to prevent its success.

14. The safeguard against submarines will consist in moving the battlefleet at very high speed to a flank before deployment takes place or the gun action commences.

This will take us off the ground on which the enemy desires to fight, but it may, of course, result in his refusal to follow me.

If the battlefleets remain within sight of one another, though not near the original area, the limited submerged radius of action and speed of the submarines will prevent the submarines from following without coming to the surface, and I should feel that after an interval of high speed manoeuvring I could safely close.

15. The object of this letter is to place my views before Their Lordships, and to direct their attention to the alterations in pre-conceived ideas of battle tactics which are forced upon us by the anticipated appearance in a fleet action of submarines and minelayers. . . .[3]

Jellicoe may have been a pessimistic and overcautious man, but in sending this letter to the new regime at Whitehall—in spite of his special relationship with Fisher—he displayed considerable moral courage. He knew all too well the popular reaction to the succession of defeats and repulses which the Royal Navy had suffered and that, were the Grand Fleet to meet the High Sea Fleet and fail to destroy it, he would be pilloried, with or without the support of the Admiralty.

Many words have been written and spoken in the long controversy about the correctness of Jellicoe's policy. Where too many of his critics have gone astray is that they have tended to blame him where they should have indicted the whole system and practice of the Royal Navy. Jellicoe was all too correct in his analysis of the situation; *as far as the Grand Fleet was concerned* the German mine and torpedo threat between 1914 and 1916 was too great, and the margin of dreadnought superiority too small, to allow the battle line to be risked. A battle fought to the finish with the High Sea Fleet might well result in a victory for Great Britain, but it would be a Pyrrhic victory, with the Royal Navy bereft of its first line strength. Unless the Grand Fleet could be assured of absolute victory, then it would be better for it to continue its role of guarding the blockade.

But it is true that the other units of the Royal Navy could have been better employed. The problem was that those senior officers who were aggressively minded rarely, if ever, gave proper thought to the risks and difficulties inherent in their plans. Thus, it was all too easy for others to dispose of them by criticism. Notable among this school was Vice Admiral Sir Lewis Bayly, whose proposals to attack the German port with light cruisers and destroyers were, in Tyrwhitt's opinion:

> . . . the equivalent of the death warrant of a very large number of officers and men, besides being impossible and displaying considerable ignorance of the defences of Germany![4]

It was simply true that few officers in the Royal Navy had any conception of the practice of war. Those few who did, such as Keyes and H. W. Richmond, were not senior enough to exercise influence enough to do something about it.

Before Jellicoe could expect a reply to his letter, he was called down for a conference at the Admiralty on 2 November. For the Commander in Chief, it was a complete success, as the various departments were authorized to allot him everything he had asked for, including more than fifty trawlers and armed yachts, an extra flotilla of destroyers for patrol duties, hastening of the work on the harbor defenses, armed boarding steamers, extra minesweepers, and a seaplane carrier. As Fisher wrote to him the next day, ". . . mind like Oliver Twist you '*ask for more*' as soon as you can."[5]

But there would, in the end, be too much of a good thing, as Oliver discovered:

> Fisher wrote private letters to Jellicoe and he replied every day and they were a hell of a nuisance to me; as soon as I got a new sloop to hunt submarines Jellicoe would want it and Fisher would tell me to do it to keep Jellicoe in a good temper.[6]

Neither Churchill nor Fisher questioned Jellicoe's judgment of the position of the Grand Fleet, and, on 7 November, the Secretary of the Board informed the Commander in Chief:

> . . . that they approve your views, as stated therein, and desire to assure you of their full confidence in your contemplated conduct of the Fleet in action.[7]

Fisher, preoccupied with the U-boat threat, went so far as to recommend to Jellicoe that he end his sweeps into the northern part of the North Sea. Jellicoe, who had a more realistic view of the chance that any submarine would have against heavily escorted ships zigzagging at speed, ignored the First Sea Lord and did not alter his policies.

Jellicoe complained bitterly during the course of the meeting about the dangers of unrestricted merchant shipping being allowed into the areas where the fleet operated and the difficulties of policing it without endangering his heavy ships. The same problem had been worrying the staff, who could not rid themselves of the suspicion that the Germans had been using mine-layers disguised as neutral merchant ships. On 2 November, possibly emboldened by Fisher's presence, the Admiralty determined upon a radical stroke. The next day the North Sea was declared a military area, to date from 5 November. From that day onward, "all ships passing through a line drawn from the northern point of the Hebrides, through the Faroe Islands to Iceland (would) do so at their own risk."

Apart from allotted channels within sight of the English coast, and the passage between the mine fields through the Downs for shipping to the Netherlands, the Admiralty now assumed belligerent rights over the entire North Sea. Special exceptions were made for certain shipping companies, but the reaction of the neutral countries would have been very serious had the announcements of the discovery of the *Berlin*'s mine field, which was across the Atlantic shipping lane, and the *Strassburg*'s field off Smith's Knoll not been made almost simultaneously. They added some credibility to the decision, the announcement of which was heavily larded with accusations against the Germans. Within a few weeks protest died.

Even as he was giving Jellicoe all that he wanted, Fisher began to do something about the ship-building yards. Unlike many on both sides, Fisher believed that the war would last for several years and he appreciated that the Royal Navy's strength needed to be augmented in many critical areas. Since the war began, apart from the program of requisitions and conversions and a general hastening of the construction of those ships already on the stocks, only a flotilla of destroyers and twelve submarines had been ordered. The First Sea Lord proposed to alter this situation, beginning with the light craft:

> Lord Fisher hurled himself into the business of new construction with explosive energy. He summoned around him all the naval constructors and ship-building firms in Britain, and, in four or five glorious days, every minute of which was pure delight to him, he presented me with schemes for a far greater construction of submarines, destroyers and small craft than I or any of my advisors had ever deemed possible.[8]

In these few days, the main event of which was a conference on 3 November, two light cruisers, thirty-one destroyers, thirty-three monitors, and vast numbers of smaller craft were ordered—and Fisher gave notice that he intended to more than double these numbers in most areas. He was true to his word; the last months of 1914 and the first of 1915 were punctuated by a stream of further orders. At that conference, too, as a result of Churchill's request on 31 October "to obtain 20 submarines additional to those now ordered in the shortest possible time," Fisher cast about for ways and means of building them. Keyes, one of the First Sea Lord's less favored subordinates, was called up to London to attend the meeting. The Commodore, who was sceptical of Fisher's ability to break the monopoly that Vickers' Shipbuilders held on submarine construction, recorded that:

> He opened the meeting by telling us his intentions as to future submarine construction, and turning to the Superintendent of Contracts, he said that he would make his wife a widow and his house a dunghill, if he brought paper work or red tape into the business; he wanted submarines, not contracts. He meant to have them built in eight months; if he did not get them in eight months he would commit hara-kari. Addison, in an aside which I think Lord Fisher must have heard remarked, "Now we know exactly how long he has to live!." I laughed, and I suppose looked incredulous. It seemed absurd; we had not been able to wring submarines out of Vickers and Chatham Dockyard under two and a half years. He fixed me with a ferocious glare, and said, "If anyone thwarts me, he had better commit hara-kari too."[9]

The conference ended with an order for twenty submarines from British yards, which, if they were not completed within the planned eight months, were at least at sea in half the time taken by their predecessors. And, on the same day, Fisher came to an agreement with Charles M. Schwab, president of the Bethlehem Steel Corporation, for twenty submarines to be built in the United States or Canada. At some $10 million, they were "approximately twice the going rate," but Fisher felt that the return would be worth the expenditure and wrote to Jellicoe, "We have made a wonderful coup (after you left) with someone abroad for very rapid delivery of submarines and small craft and guns and ammunition."[10]

In fact it was Jellicoe who had sent Schwab to Fisher about the construction of submarines. Schwab, on his way to England to secure munitions contracts from the War Office, had been a passenger in the *Olympic* and, chafing over the ship's detention after the sinking of the *Audacious*, asked permission to be allowed to leave immediately for London. Jellicoe gave him that permission, after having him aboard the *Iron Duke* and extracting the promise that he would call at the Admiralty first.

Fisher was prepared to make use of any material that came into his hands. Told by Schwab that the Bethlehem Steel Corporation had been constructing 14″ guns and mountings to arm the German-built Greek battle cruiser *Salamis*, but being unable to deliver them because of the blockade, was prepared to offer the weapons to Britain, the First Sea Lord immediately accepted them and then announced (on Churchill's suggestion) that he intended to have four monitors specially built to take the mountings! Similarly, Fisher knew quite well that the cancellation of the sixth *Queen Elizabeth* and the three R class battleships of the 1914 program must have left several gun barrels and mountings available, as these items were always the first to be started because they required the longest lead time. He knew, too, that the material assembled to build the battleships must also be still inside the yards. Some of the 15″ guns were disposed of by the order of two monitors, but Fisher had other ideas for the remainder.

In these early days of November, the problem of von Spee was occupying the attention of the staff. News of the Battle of Coronel did not reach the Admiralty until the 4th, and the full details were not clear until the 7th. Fisher was furious at the defeat and in no mood to brook opposition, especially as the actions of the staff had violated almost every canon he held dear. At the first minute he had heard the news, he ordered *Invincible* and *Inflexible* to leave the newly created Second Battle Cruiser Squadron and proceed to Devonport to refit for service in the South Atlantic. Demolishing all protest, the First Sea Lord ordered them to sail on 11 November, and sail they did, under Sturdee's command.

Having provided for the South Atlantic, Fisher then turned his attention to the possibility that von Spee might pass through the Panama Canal, join the light cruiser *Karlsruhe*, still believed to be at large (the Admiralty did not hear of her loss by explosion until well into 1915), and harass North Atlantic commerce. Fisher was also preoccupied with the possibility that one of the German battle cruisers would break out into the Atlantic to join them. Terrified of a repetition of Coronel, and acting on his long-held view that "the bigger the armadillo the bigger the digestive smile," Fisher on 10 November ordered *Princess Royal* to be detached from the First Battle Cruiser Squadron, to proceed to join the cruiser *Suffolk* in the western North Atlantic.

The order strained relations between Jellicoe, Beatty, and the Admiralty. Jellicoe took advantage of a gale to delay *Princess Royal*'s departure and signaled to the First Sea Lord: "Is *Princess Royal* to go? . . . Strongly urge *New Zealand* instead."[11] Even from Jellicoe, this was too much for Fisher in his present mood and he replied: "*Princess Royal* should have proceeded at once on Admiralty orders. . . ."[12] The Commander in

Chief was forced to obey, but he would not remain silent and replied: "I am quite certain that the Germans, if they send battle cruisers into the Atlantic Ocean, will not send one, but all."[13]

The Commander in Chief had reason to feel dismayed by Fisher's dictatorial behavior, especially since, as he wrote to the First Sea Lord, "In your letter of 7/11 you say: 'I'm sure you'll AT ONCE telegraph to me personally in cypher *if you want anything* or *wish anything altered* or *doubt the wisdom of any orders you get.*"[14] Despite the Admiralty's assertion on the 13th that "since war began you have gained two Dreadnoughts on balance, and will have by 20th, 27 superior units to 20," the position was not nearly as rosy as this.[15] Jellicoe had little or no knowledge of the state of the Germans, but of his "27 superior units," the number included, as he signaled, "three ships, two of which have never fired a gun, and the third is only partially trained."[16]

The super-dreadnoughts were having trouble with their condensers, the ex-Turkish *Agincourt* was considered an odd number of dubious value, and *Benbow* and *Emperor of India* had only been commissioned in the previous few weeks, while *Erin* was also not properly worked up. The main battle line was thus only just superior to that of the Germans. What is more, as Jellicoe pointed out, the recent detachment of the Third Battle Squadron to reinforce the Channel Fleet against a German attack on the Channel had been approved on the dubious understanding that the *King Edward VII*s would be able to reinforce the Grand Fleet if necessary. Jellicoe had not himself believed that they could do it, but he had thought before that the Grand Fleet was strong enough to bear the loss.

It was not so now. The situation was especially critical as far as the battle cruisers were concerned. The detachment of the *Invincible* and the *Inflexible* reduced the number of ships under Beatty's command from six to four. To compensate, Fisher ordered the *Tiger* to cut short her firings at Berehaven and join the Battle Cruiser Squadron posthaste. The *Tiger* was of little value until she was fully worked up, but her presence would, Fisher thought, at least balance that of the hybrid armored cruiser *Blücher*.

Although Beatty's three older 13.5″ gunned ships and the *New Zealand* could be considered superior (if barely so) to Hipper's four battle cruisers—including the newly completed *Derfflinger*, which was thought to carry 35 cm guns—the removal of the efficient *Princess Royal* would make a great difference, especially, as Beatty wrote to Fisher, ". . .the *Tiger* is not yet fit to fight. Three out of her four dynamoes are out of action for an indefinite period, and her training is impeded by bad weather, which might continue for many weeks at this time of year, and at present she is quite unprepared and inefficient."[17] As Jellicoe pointed out, "she would simply be a present for the Germans."[18]

Churchill's complaint of Jellicoe—that "he always credited them [the Germans] with several ships more than we now know they had, or were then likely to have"[19]—may have been true on other occasions, but it was quite unfair at this time. What had really annoyed Jellicoe in the affair was that *"Princess Royal*'s coal expenditure for the distance is not far from *double* that of *New Zealand."*[20] Fisher had to concede this point when he wrote on 16 November, "I'm distressed above measure that you should have been harried in any way by Admiralty action. Certainly I would have sent *New Zealand* had I known all you tell me. . . . It wont [sic] happen again. Just then I was sore pressed. . . ."[21]

Several measures were taken by the Admiralty to compensate in some part for the three battle cruisers' extended detachment. *Indomitable* was recalled from the Mediterranean to join Beatty, although it would be some weeks before she could arrive. Jellicoe's pleas for more cruisers were in part answered when the decision was taken to begin recalling the modern armored cruisers which had hitherto spent their war in the Mediterranean. *Warrior* and *Black Prince* were ordered to return immediately. They would be useful, but they could not make up for the battle cruisers. The Third Battle Squadron was also moved again. The Admiralty felt that Scapa Flow was too far north to prevent further raids on the east coast and they suggested that the "Wobbly Eight," as the Third Battle Squadron was known, be based upon Rosyth, within supporting distance of the Grand Fleet and also capable of covering the coast. Jellicoe at first demurred, complaining that they would be too far away from the fleet to allow them to be supported by cruisers and destroyers. He suggested that they go to Cromarty, the base of the Fourth Destroyer Flotilla and only 100 miles from Scapa. Churchill and Fisher overruled him and the ships were sent to Rosyth. They telegraphed:

> The coast has been so denuded of destroyers for the sake of strengthening the force with you (amounting now to 71 destroyers), that there is only a skeleton force of patrol vessels available on the East Coast. . . . In these circumstances, we are reluctantly compelled to decide on the *King Edwards* and the 3rd Cruiser Squadron going to Rosyth and you should detach half a flotilla of the 71 destroyers at Scapa Flow, to act with them. . . .[22]

The tone seemed stronger than it was, for on the next day, the 17th, they ordered the Senior Officer in the Mediterranean to send a half flotilla home, "as soon as possible." But, for all the compensation, it remains true that at this point in the war, the Grand Fleet was at its weakest in relation to the High Sea Fleet, so weak that a good case can be made that the High Sea Fleet would have had the advantage in battle. It will be seen what use the Imperial Navy made of this opportunity.

November was the occasion for the War Office to become preoccupied with the threat of a German invasion on the east coast. It is difficult to say precisely how this concern came about, for, as the *Staff Monograph* comments:

> . . . the War Office . . . in the first months of the war had looked upon invasion as so remote a possibility that they had pressed for the despatch of more divisions to France than the Cabinet was disposed to allow.[23]

It is possible that the War Office's new respect for the mobility and efficiency of the German army may have been combined with a sudden realization of the importance and potential of seaborne attacks as a result of the loss of the Belgian ports.

The Admiralty did not believe that an invasion was possible because of the tremendous difficulties involved with the transportation of 250,000 troops (the number which the army believed that the Germans would have available), their equipment, and supplies, even apart from the fact that seasoned British divisions could readily be returned from France. It had to be admitted, however, that the naval arrangements were insufficient to stop a surprise attack by a German invasion force. Coastal submarines had been held to be the answer before the war, but, as Keyes reported, he "had an insufficient force of submarines to meet invasion in every possible locality."[24] Nor were the depleted destroyer patrols in any better position, while Admiral Burney, commanding the Channel Fleet, reported that he could not possibly move his force up to the east coast within twenty-four hours, the time that the Germans would need to effect an uninterrupted landing. Jellicoe, in a memorandum on the subject, pointed out that it was now impossible to keep a watch on the Germans because of the dangers that any scouts off the German coast would face from U-boats.

Jellicoe suggested that an "antiinvasion" force of 300,000 men be created, while predreadnoughts should be stationed at each of the major ports on the east coast. He further suggested that preparations be made to destroy all facilities at any port that might be threatened by invasion; such a measure would prevent the Germans gaining control of an all-weather disembarkation point, although Fisher and Wilson pointed out that the danger existed that the demolitions could be triggered off by overzealous personnel were the Germans even to attempt a simple bombardment.

The problem was partially solved by the movement of the Third Battle Squadron to Rosyth, but the forces on the east coast were also reinforced by the arrival of more old *Majestic* class battleships, as well as a number of cruisers and gunboats.

In fact, the entire invasion threat was a false alarm. It might have been possible for the Germans to have landed two or three divisions, though no more, in a surprise attack on the east coast, but they would have been devoid of artillery and cavalry support and would either have been cut to pieces onshore or doomed to a man had a reembarkation been attempted. Considerable material damage might have been caused, but the German losses would have been terrible since it is unlikely that a single transport or warship in any covering force provided would have escaped the combination of the Grand Fleet coming south out of Cromarty, Rosyth, and Scapa Flow and the Channel Fleet and Harwich Force moving north. In any case, the Imperial Navy never considered the possibility, since a serious attempt to land an army in England would have necessitated a showdown between the High Sea Fleet and the vastly superior *combined* British fleets—which would have only one conclusion.

At the beginning of November the British added a priceless intelligence weapon to their armory. Without fanfare, and with the knowledge of no more than a handful of the most senior officers, the British had obtained copies of two out of three of the major German codes and were shortly to secure the third.

The merchant, U-boat, small ships, and zeppelin code—HVB (*Handelsverkehrbuch*)—was captured on 11 August 1914 when the RAN took possession of the German steamer *Hobart* in Port Phillip Bay. Already in use by the Australians in the hunt for von Spee, a copy arrived in London in late October.

In the same month the cruiser *Theseus* returned to Scapa Flow from Russia carrying a copy of the major unit code, the SKM (*Signalbuch der Kaiserlichen Marine*). This came from the cruiser *Magdeburg*, which went ashore on Odensholm Island at the entrance of the Gulf of Finland on 26 August and became a total loss. By great good fortune the Russian units which examined the wreck found three copies of the SKM, together with material of lesser importance.

The third and final code, VB (*Verkehrsbuch*) came into the Admiralty in late November. A fishing vessel working the Broad Fourteens, scene of the destruction of the German mine-laying torpedo boats on 17 October, brought up in her nets a chest containing cipher material. This included VB; a most important find for the war effort at large, because VB was the code employed between Berlin and its embassies and consulates, as well as by detached warships in foreign waters.

Consequently, the British possessed the key to all levels of German maritime radio communications. In terms of naval operations in home waters HVB was the most significant capture. In Patrick Beesly's words:

> . . . a mass of seemingly routine and unimportant messages disclosed information of great value . . . it was often the HVB signals which gave warning of the sorties of the Hoch See Flotte.[25]

In the first days of the war Henry Oliver foresaw the need for a cryptographic analysis organization and enlisted the services of the brilliant Sir Alfred Ewing, Director of Naval Education. Although the first recruits were paymasters and teachers from Osborne and Dartmouth, Oliver was shrewd enough to realize that Ewing would be the best man to approach Oxford and Cambridge and obtain from the universities reliable men who were not only fluent in German but capable of dealing with the mathematical intricacies of cryptography. Ewing succeeded in enlisting a wealth of talent. If the men of Room 40 Old Building lacked experience of ciphers and cryptography, they would soon make it up by application and hard work.

They possessed, however, a serious fault. Room 40 lacked personnel with naval experience sufficient to be able to analyze deciphered messages for their operational content. This was a crippling defect, for the means by which information of importance is obtained from cryptographic analysis is for the deciphering organization to build up such an extensive knowledge of the enemy's procedures and routines that any transmission out of the ordinary is immediately apparent. This naturally calls for a body of trained experts with access to all traffic and a deep knowledge of naval operations.

No such body was created in 1914. The fault lay primarily with Oliver who, in his passion for secrecy, insisted that the War Group be the sole repository of all deciphered material. When he became Chief of the War Staff, Oliver continued to dominate Room 40, excluding the Intelligence Division and its new Director, W. R. Hall, almost entirely. Although Hall was given access to Room 40's material, he was not, as he should have been, its controller. This situation was not rectified until 1917.

Since Churchill and Fisher were principally occupied with higher matters of organization and administration, Oliver and Wilson were thus almost the sole analysts of information. These two senior officers, overworked as they were, could not possibly cope with the mass of material that was deciphered. Inevitably, they made mistakes.

In his own insistence on security, Churchill compounded the error in his directives of 8 and 29 November by restricting the decrypts to the

War Group, the Director of Operations, and the Director of the Intelligence Division. As to officers outside the Admiralty, only Jellicoe and Madden, Beatty, Keyes, Tyrwhitt, and Hood at Dover were aware of Room 40's activities and they were permitted access only to such material as the Admiralty saw fit. Seeing the enormous tactical advantages inherent in being able to decipher the High Sea Fleet's transmissions at sea, Jellicoe asked for a copy of the SKM for the Grant Fleet. Apparently at Oliver's behest, this request was refused.

Churchill's desire for secrecy was understandable, although it is worthy of note that as early as October 1914 it was apparently common knowledge in the Grand Fleet that *Theseus* had brought south a codebook from the *Magdeburg*.[26] Nevertheless, at no point was there any system by which comprehensive and meticulous analysis could be effected, and this deficiency robbed the intercepts of much of their value.

A step was taken in the right direction with the appointment of Commander H. W. W. Hope to Room 40 as liaison officer, but Oliver's peculiar organization prevented him from doing much of substance, although his instincts were sound and his knowledge of German procedures formidable.[27]

The first signals intercepted and translated were of little operational value but, on 5 November, Room 40 deciphered several messages announcing the departure of U-boats to attack the forces off the Belgian coast. From this day on, the Imperial Navy would rarely be able to embark on any operation without being compromised by its wireless traffic.

November in the Channel was a month of uncertain and largely inconclusive activity by both sides. The German Command sent the submarines, U-29 and U-12, referred to in the intercept, to the Channel to deal with Hood's bombardment forces, which had been proving a thorn in the side of the German armies on the coast. To forestall this move, for the Admiralty's intelligence was that the submarines would not be in the area until at least 12 November, Hood was ordered to withdraw all but the smallest gun-vessels to form an antiinvasion flotilla at Sheerness, while the *Revenge* remained at Dover as a reserve for the "last eventuality" on the Belgian coast.

The transport sailings across the Channel were hastily reorganized and ships forbidden to sail except at night, and, if possible, under escort. The British forces in the area were very weak, amounting only to Hood's ships, some elderly torpedo gunboats and six destroyers out of Portsmouth; the bulk of operations had to be conducted by the French forces.

Tyrwhitt ordered *Fearless* and a half flotilla to sail in an attempt to find any submarines that might be passing down the Dutch coast. He sent *Undaunted, Aurora*, and seven L class destroyers out two days later to reinforce the patrol, but, although they must have come very close to intercepting the Germans, no one saw anything in the heavy fog that spread over the Broad Fourteens and Terschelling on the evening of 6 November. Commodore (T) then came out of Harwich on the 7th and joined *Fearless*'s half flotilla to patrol Terschelling while he sent the *Fearless* and the other light cruisers and destroyers back into Harwich for a few days rest.

Then, on the 9th, Tyrwhitt received a signal which delighted him. Room 40 had intercepted a German message which they decoded to read that a torpedo boat flotilla would be patrolling off the Gabbard for thirty-six hours from the evening of the 10th. Units were rushed into the area but, after three days' wait in steadily worsening weather, the light forces were ordered back to Harwich by the Admiralty. The cryptographers in Room 40 were not infallible. The signal group that represented "Heligoland" in a routine order to the patrol flotilla at the island had been misread as "Gabbard." The frequency of this sort of mistake would lessen rapidly as Room 40's personnel became used to the routines and procedures of the Imperial Navy, but it was a bitterly disappointing experience for the Harwich Force and hardly calculated to raise the credit of the cryptographers in the eyes of either Tyrwhitt or the staff.

The two submarines had relatively limited success, only U-12 claiming a victim when she sank the torpedo gunboat *Niger* in the Downs on 11 November. The torpedo gunboat had been employed on examination duties but, as her machinery was too elderly and unreliable for continuous steaming, she spent most of her time riding at anchor with steam up, and it was thus that U-12 found her. The submarine fired a single torpedo from 2,000 yards away and the *Niger*'s captain saw the track and attempted to get the ship under way, but to no avail. The torpedo struck amidships, sinking the gunboat within twenty minutes. The really ominous note of the patrol was not U-12's destruction of the *Niger*, but the fact that the submarine went into Zeebrugge and spent a number of days there before she returned to Germany.

Submarine scares were to plague Jellicoe for the next few weeks, causing exercise programs to be disrupted, placing a heavy burden on the already overworked destroyers, and again throwing doubt on the security of the bases. The scares were largely imaginary, despite the fact that daily reports of U-boats off the coast began to pour in even as the Grand Fleet came into Scapa Flow. Typical of this sort of report, Keyes described the origin of a scare that caused him to be roused out to defend The Nore:

> At daylight I motored round the coast interviewing all the people who claimed to have seen submarines. Five more were sighted by natives while

I was in the neighbourhood; one had been seen to chase, at a speed of quite 20 knots, one of the destroyers which had been sent to hunt for the enemy! The supposed submarines were flights of wild geese or other wild fowl skimming the surface. A wild-goose chase indeed![28]

The German Command had sent only submarine U-22, which escaped gunboats off Scapa. Ironically, the Germans, who by now knew of the use of Loch Ewe as an anchorage, had ordered U-22 to investigate it, and that was precisely where the submarine went, despite sighting at various times cruisers operating around the Flow.

On 20 November, light nets were laid at the entrances to the anchorage and twenty trawlers arrived to take over harbor defense duties. With this protection, admittedly makeshift, Jellicoe could at last begin to allow his heavy ships enough time in harbor to do essential maintenance and give the engineering personnel some relaxation. This advance immediately proved a great benefit, as the incidence of machinery troubles became steadily less and less.

The Commander in Chief was nevertheless preoccupied by the relative weakness of the Grand Fleet. He had no high opinion of British security and feared that the detachment of the three battle cruisers would become known to the German Command. If there was ever a "golden moment" for the High Sea Fleet to come out and seek battle, it was now. Within months the battle cruisers would have returned, the new battleships worked up to full efficiency, and the first of the 15″ gunned battleships have joined. Within a year the Grand Fleet's strength would be overwhelming, but, for the rest of 1914, Jellicoe knew, the outcome of any engagement would be doubtful if it took place on German terms, rather than those of his own choosing.

In fact, he did not need to worry about the detachment of the battle cruisers. The general round-up of known spies at the beginning of the war had destroyed the German network, and though there were still many at large with access to the dockyards and ports, they had little or no way of communicating with Germany.

The Admiralty, however, and the Commander in Chief were apprehensive of the least signs of German activity. Early on the 17th, Room 40 deciphered a signal from Hipper ordering three half flotillas of torpedo boats to assemble off Heligoland the next day. It was in fact merely a signal ordering a heavier patrol, since Hipper was worried about the possibility of a repetition of the 28 August action, but Oliver warned Jellicoe and placed the Channel Fleet and the vessels assigned for coast defense on immediate notice for sea. Jellicoe sent Beatty and all the cruisers to patrol off the Shetlands, while the battle squadrons prepared to sail. Oliver, and others at the Admiralty, believed from the volume of intercepted wireless traffic that the Germans would strike south, while Jellicoe was concerned with the possibility that the German battle cruisers might attempt to break out into the North Atlantic. Consequently, there were no heavy ships in the North Sea that day. Tyrwhitt was ordered to take *Aurora* and *Undaunted* in to scout the Bight, and he obeyed with alacrity. The two ships spent several hours in the area, but saw nothing, not even patrolling German flotillas.

It was a false alarm, but the Admiralty's attention was soon caught by another matter. It was argued by many that, while it was now unwise for the Grant Fleet to accept battle with the High Sea Fleet, a properly set trap, with a lure sufficient to entice out the entire German battle line, could ensure that the British fought at their maximum advantage. The key to the situation, and the factor that would ensure Jellicoe's cooperation, was that the German submarine activity in the north and in the Channel seemed to indicate that there would be few U-boats in the North Sea for the next few days. Thus, the Grand Fleet would be able to venture south with little or no risk.

The "bait" would be a second attack on the zeppelin sheds at Cuxhaven. Jellicoe had not been impressed by the results of the previous raid and did not think that the aircraft were reliable enough to be used, but the Admiralty had intelligence that the German ships were massing in the Jade and Jellicoe was overruled.

Tyrwhitt was to lead the "coat trailing" operation, with the Harwich Force assigned to escort the seaplane carriers *Engadine* and *Riviera*. These carried three seaplanes each, which would be launched against Cuxhaven while Tyrwhitt's ships "made their presence known." Jellicoe would bring his ships down to within 110 miles of Heligoland, while, 40 miles nearer, Beatty would lie with his battle cruisers and cruisers. In close support, only 40 miles from the island, would be the Second Cruiser Squadron and two light cruisers.

The operation against the High Sea Fleet could, the Admiralty decided, be combined with one further to the south. The dangers from submarines using Zeebrugge had been causing great concern, most especially because of the threat posed to the transport lines across the Channel. Some way was being sought by which the port could be neutralized.

The problem was that Zeebrugge was already well defended and it would be an extremely difficult and costly operation to block the port. A bombardment by heavy ships seemed the only answer, and this was decided upon. The four *Duncan* class battleships which had been attached to the Third Battle Squadron were now based on Dover as an antiinvasion force, and their Rear Admiral, Stuart Nicholson, was ordered to take two, with a half flotilla of the Harwich Force and eight minesweepers from Lowestoft, to bombard the port. The principal objective of the attack was to destroy the locks to the inner harbors, thereby preventing the passage of the U-boats.

The bombardment took place on the 23rd, and despite considerable difficulties with minesweeping, and several submarine warnings, the *Russell* and the *Exmouth* fired more than four hundred rounds before Nicholson broke off the action. The attack had little effect: the locks and pumping stations remained largely undamaged, despite lurid reports from Holland "of extreme destruction at Zeebrugge and submarines reduced to scrap-iron." It was now obvious that the massive installations at Zeebrugge were hardly vulnerable to bombardment from the sea. As a consequence, Rear Admiral Nicholson recommended against any further such operations.

Further to the north, the simultaneous attack on Cuxhaven proved equally abortive. Tyrwhitt's forces left Harwich at 0500 on 23 November, the operation having been delayed a day by the need to complete repairs to the *Arethusa*, with the *Engadine* and the *Riviera* escorted by the three light cruisers and eight destroyers of the L class.

The weather had been very stormy, but was easing when the Harwich Force sailed and Tyrwhitt was confident that the seaplanes would be able to make the attack. However, four hours out he received a signal from the Admiralty ordering the seaplane carriers back. Room 40 had deciphered signals indicating that a force of German armored cruisers would be at sea off Heligoland, lying directly in the path of the seaplane carriers. This obviously made the seaplane raid impossible. In fact, it was only *Derfflinger* completing her work-up with a small escort, but the Admiralty feared that the First Scouting Group might all be out and, consequently, the recall was issued to *Engadine* and *Riviera*.

Tyrwhitt sent them back with the destroyers, keeping only the three light cruisers. In the early morning darkness, however, *Lennox* became detached from her sisters and wound up back with the cruisers, "like a lost pup looking for companionship." Jellicoe, informed of the abandonment of the seaplane attack, now altered his plans. Tyrwhitt was ordered to reconnoiter within fifteen miles of Heligoland, and, if he made contact with any German ships, was to draw them on to the Second Cruiser Squadron, which would in turn draw them to the battle cruisers and onto the main body of the Grand Fleet.

The venture into the Bight began early on 24 November, preceded by confusion on the lines of the 28 August action, when Tyrwhitt discovered at 0715 that he had been chasing the two light cruisers attached to the Second Cruiser Squadron for half an hour, mistaking them for *Strassburg* class cruisers.

Tyrwhitt's ships spent the morning in the Bight, but saw nothing, apart from a few torpedo boats and a submarine lying under the guns of Heligoland. As Commodore (T) wrote:

> . . . we reconnoitred Heligoland [and the garrison] got very excited. They fired a lot of stuff (Black Marias) at us but no one of them came within miles of us. . . . We pirouetted about for an hour admiring the view of Heligoland and as no one appeared anxious to come out after us I retired.[29]

Von Ingenohl knew from the wireless traffic that had been intercepted that the British were out in force, but, fearing a submarine attack on his heavy ships, he merely directed that the torpedo boat flotillas be reinforced, ordering them to keep well clear of the enemy. The lone submarine in the Bight, U-5, was too far to the north to affect the issue and, though seen, she could not get into an attack position. Two seaplanes and an airship were ordered out to investigate, but only one came near the British ships. This aircraft dropped five hand bombs over the *Liverpool*, "but they missed. I wish she had come my way, as I was dying to try my aerial guns, but she was never in range."[30]

As the units of the Grand Fleet and the Harwich Force withdrew, there was a scare that the German torpedo boats might be coming out after them to attempt a night torpedo attack. Von Ingenohl, who had in fact been considering a sortie by light craft, canceled it when news came that the cruisers had withdrawn, for he was still ignorant of the presence of the Grand Fleet only 110 miles away.

By the 25th, Tyrwhitt was back in harbor and, as he wrote, was "furious" at the decision of the Admiralty to recall the carriers:

> They waited until I was well in the danger zone and then told me by wireless that a large force was patrolling in the area I was going to operate in. I had then to do a sort of disappearing trick with about half my force without making signals, etc.—a very difficult operation on a pitch-black night.[31]

Room 40 had again made a serious mistake in the deciphering of the signal, and yet again this resulted in considerable disruption to operations. It was, of course, inevitable that the system had to go through such teething troubles, but it would have been better had the Admiralty refrained from interfering with the commanders at sea.

When the Grand Fleet returned to Scapa Flow on the 27th, it was greeted with the welcome news that a U-boat, U-18, had been sunk and her crew captured. What gave Jellicoe pause for thought was the fact that the submarine had managed to penetrate the Flow and nearly managed to escape after she found the anchorage empty of heavy ships. By sheer misfortune, she ran aground off Hoxa Sound, got off, was then rammed by a trawler, and finally almost broken in half on the Pentland Skerries before her captain ordered the submarine to be scuttled.

The attempt was part of a massive effort involving five submarines against the Shetlands and Scapa Flow. The others made attempts to get into the anchorage, but failed and, with the weather steadily worsening, the four survivors turned for home. Battered and exhausted by their northern patrol in that "inclement time of year," they took the direct line between Scapa and the Ems, and so missed the Grand Fleet, which Jellicoe wisely kept to the eastern side of the North Sea, hugging the Norwegian coast before his ships turned west.

The last days of November marked a lull in operations for the Grand Fleet and other forces of the Royal Navy, but two unfortunate incidents occurred. D-2, under the command of Lieutenant Commander C. G. W. Head after the loss of her previous captain over the side, was one of two submarines ordered into Heligoland Bight on the 26th to investigate suspected German activity. The other submarine, E-15, found nothing and withdrew on the 29th in the teeth of a heavy gale. D-2 disappeared without trace. As the *Staff Monograph* wrote:

> The Admiralty assumed that she had been sunk in the Heligoland Bight; but the Germans know nothing of the circumstances of her loss, and it is all too probable that she struck one of the drifting mines with which the North Sea was dotted. She was the first of the Harwich submarines to be lost without trace, and in her commander the Service lost a brilliant officer.[32]

But another, heavier, loss had already been suffered. The Channel Fleet was lying at its moorings at Sheerness on the morning of 26 November, when the predreadnought *Bulwark* blew up. Vice Admiral K. G. B. Dewar, then serving as the Commander of the *Prince of Wales*, was:

> . . . shaving in my cabin just before 8 a.m. when the scuttle flew open with a bang and a terrific explosion shook the ship. The possibility of a Zeppelin attack flashed through my mind, but on reaching the upper deck I saw an enormous column of smoke mounting slowly towards the sky and spreading a tragic fog over the *Prince of Wales*. Flaming debris was rattling on the upper deck. . . .[33]

There were only a dozen badly injured survivors out of a crew of some 750.

An immediate investigation discovered that the temperature in the ammunition passages often "rose to as much as 142 degrees in the conditions then obtaining." Accidental ignition of any loose cordite would have been enough to explode the shells stowed in the passages, and this seemed sufficient explanation for the ship's loss. Despite hasty revision of ammunition procedures and arrangements, the Royal Navy was to be plagued by a succession of such disasters, notably the loss of the armored cruiser *Natal* in 1915 and the battleship *Vanguard* in 1917. While the quality of the cordite was admittedly poor and the propellant liable to become unstable under certain conditions, there remains to this day the possibility that the destruction of one or more of the three ships may have been due to sabotage.

In fact, the loss of the elderly predreadnought meant little on the material scale, since the Fifth Battle Squadron to which she had belonged still had eleven units, and the Grand Fleet was cheered on the same day by the arrival of the *Warrior* and the *Black Prince* from the Mediterranean. They and the older *Leviathan* were formed into the First Cruiser Squadron and Rear Admiral Moore, whose previous command had been reduced to one ship by the detachment of the *Invincible* and the *Inflexible*, was transferred to the *Leviathan* from the *New Zealand* to command them.

The cruiser forces were undergoing a reorganization. The destruction of the *Emden* and the blockade of the *Königsberg* in the Rufijii River meant that the need for patrols in the Indian Ocean had ended and the Admiralty was also hopeful that Sturdee's battle cruisers would be able to eliminate von Spee before very long. It was not to be disappointed, and, with the elimination of the other raiders, this meant that the cruisers on foreign stations could return home to reinforce the Grand Fleet. To give just one example, the powerful armored cruiser *Minotaur* had already been ordered home from the Far East to join the Seventh Cruiser Squadron.

Admiral De Chair's elderly cruisers of the Tenth Cruiser Squadron were to be paid off. Antiquated and unreliable to begin with, they suffered greatly in the harsh northern waters, the more so as winter began. They spent most of their time sheltering from the weather and attempting to repair defects. De Chair had already sent three to the south for major refits, and he informed Jellicoe and the Admiralty that similar treatment could not be long delayed for the remainder. Conversely, the few armed merchant cruisers already in commission had proved themselves to be seaworthy and reliable patrol vessels, able to keep the seas in almost all weathers. The new patrol system would eventually consist of twenty-four armed merchant cruisers and slightly smaller and slower

boarding vessels, manned largely by the crews of the *Edgars*, sup-
plemented where necessary by reservists. De Chair was to remain in
command. By 20 November, the withdrawal of the old cruisers had
commenced, and, on 3 December, the last ship, *Crescent*, arrived in the
Clyde to pay off. (The cruisers of the *Edgar* class were in time refitted and
put back into service, though most were sent to the more kindly waters
of the Mediterranean.)

On 5 December, Tyrwhitt was informed that it had been decided,
because of the responsibilities he bore, to advance him from Commodore
Second Class to Commodore First Class. It seemed, on surface, a reasonable decision, since Tyrwhitt's command was expanding all the time and
the appointment would free him from having to worry about the
minutiae of running his own ship and leave him to deal with the
Harwich Force as a whole, but the matter was not quite so simple.

In fact, Lord Fisher, who had conceived a great admiration for
Tyrwhitt, meant the appointment as much as a slight upon Keyes. The
one-sided feud had its origins in a misunderstanding, for Fisher always
tended to confuse Keyes with another "Keys" who had been Lord Charles
Beresford's secretary and, having written several anti-Fisher articles, was
anathema to the First Sea Lord. Fisher had several times been disabused
of this notion by those on his staff who were friends of Keyes, but he had
somehow never managed to rid himself of the idea. This, coupled with
his conviction that the submarine service stagnated after his departure
from the Admiralty in 1910, and that this was largely the fault of the
Supervising Commodores, meant that Keyes was a marked man.

Matters were not much improved by the exchange at the conference
on 2 November, and Fisher soon began his campaign by importing
Captain S. S. Hall, an old associate in submarine development, to take
over from Keyes. Much to Fisher's rage, however, the First Lord would
not permit the change. Churchill apparently managed to calm the old
man down, for, on 8 November, Fisher wrote to Keyes, saying:

> *On no* account imagine that I have any designs on you. If I had any such
> designs you would certainly have been told—but, like many other
> things, I have not yet mastered on what basis our submarines harm the
> enemy more than themselves![34]

Keyes replied:

> . . . I must confess that I thought your advent would mean my eclipse,
> but like others who may have had personal misgivings, I was glad because
> I felt it meant that—"we shan't be long"—in making war, which is the
> only thing that matters—besides, if I am translated to another sphere, I
> shall only regard it as Kismet and trust to my luck to give me opportuni-

ties of engaging the enemy and proving that you were right in promoting me nine years ago.[35]

This was just the sort of thing that Fisher delighted to hear, and the exchange had the effect of placing their relations temporarily on the most amicable level. But it was not to last. By the end of November, Fisher was again intent on Keyes's removal. It was thus that Tyrwhitt's appointment came as a heavy blow, for Keyes, who was four years Tyrwhitt's senior on the Captain's List, remained a Commodore Second Class. Although their relative seniority on the list meant that Keyes was still the senior and would reach Flag Rank far earlier, it was an obvious slight to Keyes and could only mean that the Admiralty considered Tyrwhitt to be in charge of all operations from Harwich. The friendship between Keyes and Tyrwhitt suffered severely. They had an argument, and Tyrwhitt was "horribly hurt at [Keyes's] attitude."[36] It took some days to patch things up. Tyrwhitt was not overpleased with his appointment. It took him some time to get used to not being in command of his own ship, and it is hard to escape the impression that he would have been happier to remain a Commodore Second Class. It, however, did have the clear benefit for him that his position at Harwich was now much stronger, since a Commodore First Class was in all but name a Rear Admiral, and Tyrwhitt was now all the more difficult to "crowd out" of the job.

CHAPTER 8

The Scarborough Raid

The first days of December were quiet, apart from the now regular submarine alarms, and work on the protection of the anchorages proceeded steadily. The principal difficulties impeding progress were the lack of a coordinate system of command in certain areas and a shortage of enthusiasm for the projects in the south. Mass reappointments by Jellicoe, however, and the whirlwind entry of Lord Fisher had galvanized activity. The Commander in Chief considered that the fleet would have enough completely secure anchorages for all its needs by the end of the year. This would be an enormous relief for him, since the strain of ordering the fleet's movements without any certainty of its safety in harbor had been a great burden.

Despite this relief, Jellicoe still believed that the situation was very dangerous, for he was convinced that the German Command must be already aware of the absence of at least *Invincible* and *Inflexible* and would, in consequence, be planning a raid on the east coast. He pinpointed 8 December as the date. On that day there would be no moon and the tides would be favorable for a German night sortie. He proposed sending the battle cruisers south to cut off the German retreat, while the Grand Fleet remained in the north to support. The Admiralty, which was gaining increasing confidence in the work of Room 40, told him that there were no signs of any German activity and that it would be unnecessary to risk the battle cruisers in mine-infested waters. Jellicoe took the hint and canceled the operation, merely sending the First Battle Squadron to sea for exercises around the Shetlands.

The Germans were planning another raid on the east coast, but were not yet beyond the stage of discussion. Hipper had been making continuous proposals for new ventures against the British, proposals which von Ingenohl equally steadily rejected. Hipper then became interested in making an attack on shipping in the Skagerrak to draw out the Grand Fleet, but von Ingenohl, who now knew that British ships had been detached to hunt down von Spee, began to incline more toward another bombardment of a defended port.

The problem, as von Ingenohl saw it, was the very uncertainty of the German position. There was no precise knowledge of which ships the British had detached, one or two battle cruisers being the most quoted figures, while the absence of the *Princess Royal* was not even considered. Furthermore, the Command was still preoccupied with the weakness of German security. Von Ingenohl was concerned that any operation might be compromised to the British from its very inception. Finally, the weather made submarine reconnaisance of the projected target areas on the east coast almost impossible. The dispositions and strength of the British were, in fact, one large question mark.

In mid-November, von Ingenohl determined upon a raid against the ports of Hartlepool and Scarborough, to take place as soon as he could obtain the Emperor's consent. Flushed with the victory at Coronel, Wilhelm was willing to agree to almost anything and the planning began. The Admiralstab, however, ordained that every ship in the First Scouting Group must be available for the operation. This decision immediately meant that the raid would have to be delayed until mid-December because the *Von der Tann*, which had been suffering serious machinery troubles, would not be out of dockyard hands until then.

As the planning went ahead, some mention was made in the High Sea Fleet of the possibility that the wireless codes had been broken, but, as Hipper's biographer wrote:

> It cannot, however, be denied that on the whole such questions were not treated very seriously. We trusted the rising patriotism and common sense of the people, and under the influence of popular opinion made war on genuine or alleged spies, but did not tackle the fundamental evil, neglecting constantly to make sure that espionage should find no material to work on.[1]

Von Ingenohl again began to waver over the operation, but his resolve was stiffened when the news came through of the near annihilation of von Spee's force at the Battle of the Falkland Islands on 8 December. At one stroke the British had restored their lost prestige. Von Ingenohl realized that a swift counterstroke was necessary to convince the world that the German Navy had not become impotent. He would take the entire High Sea Fleet to sea, even as far as the Dogger Bank. This decision he kept from the Kaiser as such a movement would certainly risk a major fleet action with the British. The final factor was that it was now certain that at least two British battle cruisers were out of the North Sea. Von Ingenohl decided to act before they could return.

Precautions were taken; at Vice Admiral Reinhard Scheer's suggestion, the oldest predreadnoughts were kept in the Baltic so as to obviate the need for an attention-arousing movement through the Kiel Canal. As soon as the weather moderated, U-27 was sent out to report on the target areas, and she returned with the welcome news—confirmed by a second reconnaissance—that the defenses were weak and mine fields nonexistent. Yet despite all these arrangements, wireless traffic continued in liberal fashion as the raid moved to its execution.

It was enough for Room 40 to deduce the major part of what was to happen. The Admiralty had been waiting for this, as it informed Jellicoe on the 11th:

> . . .They can never again have such a good opportunity for successful offensive operations as at present, and you will no doubt consider how best to conserve and prepare your forces in the interval, so as to have the maximum number possible always ready and fresh. For the present the patrols to prevent contraband passing are of small importance.[2]

But the cryptographers did not predict the operation in its entirety. The signals picked up gave an adequate picture of the movements of the forces assigned to Hipper and their strength, but they did not mention the fact that the entire High Sea Fleet would be following the Scouting Groups out and onto the Dogger Bank. It was a vital omission.

The Admiralty was convinced that only detachments of the Grand Fleet would be necessary to entrap and destroy Hipper's ships. Consequently, it ordered Jellicoe to detail off Beatty, out of Rosyth; Vice Admiral Warrender, with six battleships of the Second Battle Squadron and eight destroyers of the Fourth Flotilla, out of Cromarty; and Tyrwhitt from the south to be involved. They were ordered to be in position on the morning of the 16th, so as to be able to cut the Germans off from their bases when they began their withdrawal. This would mean that the Germans would be able to bombard Hartlepool and Scarborough almost unopposed, but the Admiralty was prepared to exchange this damage for the destruction of the Scouting Groups.

Jellicoe was unhappy about the division of his battle squadrons and, as events were to prove, he was quite correct in his surmise. Despite the fact that the other battle squadrons would not have been necessary to deal with the German battle cruisers, the Grand Fleet's ascendancy depended upon its concentration. Warrender's six battleships were precisely the sort of force that the Germans dreamt of being able to isolate and destroy and thereby attain the superiority in numbers they so fervently desired. The Admiralty's dispositions were giving them that chance.

At 2000, on 15 December, Hipper sailed from the Jade. The First Scouting Group was at full strength, with the *Seydlitz, Derfflinger, Moltke, Von der Tann*, and *Blücher* all present. They were escorted by four light cruisers of the Second Scouting Group and two flotillas of the best torpedo boats. One of the light cruisers, the *Kolberg*, was to lay a mine field in conjunction with the battle cruisers' bombardment, and she had 100 mines embarked for the purpose. Von Ingenohl followed his subordinate out in the afternoon, and, after the three battle squadrons and their attendant light craft had assembled, he set course for the eastern edge of the Dogger Bank, where he planned to hold the High Sea Fleet at daylight the next morning. The position was still too far to the east to properly support the bombardment and withdrawal, but von Ingenohl did not dare risk the imperial wrath by venturing any further to the west.

Warrender sailed from Scapa at 0530 on the same day, his ships suffering badly in the "race" in Pentland Firth as they cleared the Orkneys. Beatty sailed at 0600, the destroyers of the Fourth Flotilla following independently because of heavy seas. Warrender and Beatty met off the Moray Firth at 1100, and, by 1500 all Pakenham's cruisers and the destroyers were in sight, which meant that the rendezvous was complete.

The orders for the force were for the ships to be in a position 54° 10′N, 3°E at 0730 the next morning, ready to cut Hipper off. In fact, this rendezvous was a bare thirty miles to the south of the dawn position which von Ingenohl planned to take up—54° 40′N, 3°E. Warrender himself was unconvinced that the raid would be against Hartlepool or Scarborough. He signaled to Beatty that he considered that it could just as easily be against Harwich or the Humber. Meanwhile, he disposed his forces for the night.

Tyrwhitt had been detailed off by the Admiralty to watch Hipper's movements. He sailed at 1400 on the 15th, with four light cruisers and two flotillas of destroyers. He was ordered to be off Yarmouth at daylight, with selected destroyers spread out on observation lines further to the north and south. Warrender, who had only seven destroyers in company, was concerned with the threat posed by German torpedo craft, and he had requested the Admiralty that Tyrwhitt be ordered to join him. This had been refused, and Commodore (T)'s orders were confirmed before he sailed. Keyes, too, was ordered out, with eight submarines. These were sent out to Terschelling, followed by the *Lurcher* and the *Firedrake*, with the intention that they all be in position by late on the 16th to cut off the German retreat.

The Germans had sailed in calm, if murky, weather, taking a wide northward sweep past Heligoland as they moved out into the North Sea. The weather worsened as the day drew on, and the force began to pick up British wireless activity. This raised the possibility that they had already been seen and reported, either by a submarine or by spy-trawlers (for many fishing vessels had already been passed) but Hipper decided to keep going. At 1700, the Scouting Groups passed the Dogger Bank and set a course of west-south-west at 15 knots, heading almost directly for Warrender. Hipper crossed ahead of the British forces at 0015 the next morning, passing only fifteen miles away from Beatty, and ten miles from Goodenough's light cruisers, which were spread to the west. In the gloom and rough seas, neither force discovered the presence of the other, despite the activities of the torpedo boat S-33. This vessel became separated from her consorts and called up *Strassburg*, asking, "Have lost touch; course please." The cruiser immediately replied, "Stop wireless" and an enraged Hipper complained when he heard of the incident:

> Doesn't the ship know where we're heading for? Can't they get into touch again at daylight? The fools will give us away yet![3]

But no British unit picked up the exchange. S-33 turned back for Germany, her captain deciding that it would be impossible to regain contact. Then, at 0400, the torpedo boat ran almost straight into four of Warrender's destroyers on the Dogger Bank. S-33 hastily turned to starboard to parallel their track, in the hope of being mistaken for one of them. Despite the fact that the distance was down to two hundred yards, the ruse succeeded. S-33 was able to slip away into the night, signaling to the Scouting Group, "Four destroyers 54° 55′N, 2° 15′E." The signal was picked up in both *Seydlitz* and *Strassburg*, and it added yet another difficulty to the problem Hipper had now to solve.

The weather was steadily getting worse, one torpedo boat had already been sent back, and Hipper did not think that the small craft could continue into the teeth of a rising gale. Now from S-33 came the news that there were British forces behind the Scouting Groups. It was the fact that von Ingenohl was at sea that finally prompted Hipper to continue the operation, but he decided too, that in view of S-33's report, he would not risk sending the torpedo boats back to cross the North Sea unaccompanied, but keep them with the heavy ships.

The High Sea Fleet, however, was not to remain on the Dogger Bank. The four destroyers which S-33 had encountered, led by the *Lynx*, were steaming south-east ten miles to the eastwards of Warrender's battleships at 0515, followed at some distance by the other three destroyers of Warrender's force. At that moment they sighted V-155 on their port bow. The High Sea Fleet was steaming west-north-west with the three battle squadrons in line ahead; five light cruisers to starboard; the light cruiser *Rostock* and the Fifth and Seventh Flotillas to port; the Second and Eighth Flotillas astern; and the armored cruisers, *Roon* and *Prinz Heinrich*, the light cruiser *Hamburg*, and the Sixth Flotilla ahead.

V-155 had been detached from the Sixth Flotilla by the *Roon* to investigate a Dutch merchant ship when she sighted the British destroyers. Both sides were confused as to the other's identity and issued the challenge. It was not until 0525 that they opened fire, signaling the presence of the enemy to their superiors as they did so. Despite the British superiority in numbers and firepower, it was they who suffered in the engagement with V-155.

The divisional leader, *Lynx*, was hit twice by shells, which caused flooding in the magazine forward, pierced an oil tank, and jammed her helm to port. As *Lynx* went involuntarily hard over and turned sixteen points, the others followed her around, and V-155 put a shell into *Ambuscade*, which caused a bad fire forward, before she turned away to the north-east.

The British destroyers were in some confusion, since *Ambuscade* hauled out of line to the west, and *Lynx* and *Unity* to the south-east as the other four destroyers came around to a south-south-west course. The light cruiser *Hamburg* and her two attached torpedo boats had turned to the north-west as soon as they received V-155's enemy report and, at 0553, the former sighted and challenged the destroyer *Hardy*, which was leading the other three undamaged destroyers south-south-west. *Hardy* and *Shark* opened fire at 800 yards, while the German cruiser illuminated them with searchlights. In another confused, close-range action, *Hamburg* concentrated upon the *Hardy* and, although she suffered some damage herself, the cruiser quickly reduced *Hardy* to a shambles. The British destroyer suffered seventeen casualties, had her steering gear and forward 4″ wrecked, and was on fire amidships when *Hamburg* turned away to the east to avoid torpedoes. To the surprise of the British, she did not reappear.

It was now 0603, and the sky was steadily lightening. The seven British destroyers were in a sorry state, scattered in three groups and with several of their number badly damaged. The *Ambuscade* was struggling north-west to get clear of the action, while *Unity* and *Lynx* were still to the west of the other destroyers, although they were steering the same course as they moved south-south-west. *Hardy* had hauled out of line also, sheering to port as she struggled to repair her steering gear. The destroyers had not yet lost any of their number, but they were in no condition to fight another engagement against more powerful forces.

Despite the fact that the situation was in favor of the Germans, it did not seem thus to their Commander in Chief. Von Ingenohl's thinking put a very different complexion on the matter. He had earlier received S-33's report of four destroyers, and had, because of the fact that the position was so far to the east, found it very difficult to understand. He was, however, desperately concerned by the possibility of a massed torpedo attack by the Grand Fleet flotillas. Despite the fact that dawn was little more than two hours away, when V-155's report of destroyers to the west came in at 0520, von Ingenohl's fears increased.

Incredibly, he ordered the fleet to turn away to a south-easterly course. It was a completely mistaken decision. At the moment that the C in C determined upon the retreat, Warrender's and Beatty's ships were barely ten miles to the south-south-west of the armored cruiser *Prinz Heinrich*, deployed on the port wing of the High Sea Fleet. Von Ingenohl, with the imperial dictum preying on his mind, was convinced that the destroyers to the west and north-west were the screen of the entire Grand Fleet. The reality was otherwise:

> Here at last were the conditions for which the Germans had been striving since the beginning of the war. A few miles away on the port bow of the High Sea Fleet, isolated and several hours steaming from home, was the most powerful homogenous battle squadron of the Grand Fleet, the destruction of which would at one blow have completed the process of attrition and placed the British and German fleets on a precisely even footing as regards numerical strength.[4]

Perhaps von Ingenohl was keeping "strictly to the letter of the general order of operations," but never again would such an opportunity to redress the balance present itself to the Imperial Navy.

The turn was executed at 0542, and, as the battle squadrons wheeled around to the south-east, the cruisers and torpedo boats followed suit, falling in behind the main body as they did so. The armored cruiser *Roon* and her escorts of the Eleventh Half Flotilla, which had all been directly ahead of the battle squadrons, thus at first turned toward the north-east to assume their positions in the new formation. At 0616, the *Roon* came into sight of the *Lynx* and *Unity*, now heading south-south-east. Confused as to their identity, *Roon* challenged. Commander Parry in the *Lynx* remembered the signal which V-155 had used in their previous encounter with the Germans and replied with four white and five green lights. To the destroyers "this appeared to satisfy the enemy and he disappeared to the eastward," but the captain of the *Roon* was actually so worried about the risk of a torpedo attack that he decided to turn away, to prevent a torpedo attack, before he opened fire. As a consequence, "by the time that the *Roon* was able safely to turn towards the *Lynx* and *Unity*, the latter were so far off that it was useless to proceed in chase."[5] The armored cruiser and her consorts now turned south-east to follow the High Sea Fleet, while Commander Parry, who had likewise lost the *Roon* in the gloom, decided to continue on his previous course until full daylight.

Further to the north, the *Hardy* had managed to make repairs to her steering gear, and, at 0620, Commander Loftus Jones in *Shark* ordered the four destroyers to follow him, a few minutes later altering course south-south-east to parallel Warrender's track. For the time they could see nothing, since Warrender's ships were more than twenty miles away, but Jones decided to keep to the course in the hope of sighting the Germans again.

To the south-east, Warrender and Beatty were wondering what was afoot. Yet again, the system of reporting had broken down. Although as early as 0540, *Lynx* had informed them that she was chasing German torpedo boats, all the succeeding signals received in the heavy ships lacked either course, position, or both. As a consequence, though Warrender had been largely able to piece together the course of events, he was in the dark as to precisely where the engagements had taken place. Since it was clear, however, that the large ship sighted had been of cruiser size, which meant that the German units could be either alone or part of a group as large as the High Sea Fleet, Warrender decided to continue for the morning rendezvous. If German ships were to the north-east, then it would be better for the British to let them get as far west as possible before the Second Battle Squadron turned to the north and cut them off from their bases. By 0710, Goodenough was in sight and, a few minutes later, Beatty and the two other commanders turned their squadrons in toward Warrender in preparation for taking up their daylight positions.

At 0650, Jones's destroyers sighted smoke to the south-east. Jones turned his division in that direction to investigate. At 0659 they were able to make out the shapes of five torpedo boats—*Roon's* half flotilla. The British destroyers immediately worked up to full speed and, at 0708, at a range of four thousand yards, they opened fire on the Germans. The visibility was still poor and it was not for some minutes that Jones realized that a large cruiser was steaming behind the torpedo boats. Jones correctly surmised that this could only be the *Roon*, and, sheering off to the north-east, he signaled to Beatty:

> My position is lat 54° 22′N., long 3° 20′; am keeping in touch with large cruiser *Roon* and five destroyers steaming east. . . .

It was a good report, but, in the confusion of the night, *Shark* had lost her position and the estimation given in the signal put her a good fifteen miles further to the south than she actually was—and made Warrender think that the Germans were only fifteen miles away from his 0730 position. There was also confusion at the other end. *Shark* had difficulty getting off the signal because of German jamming, but it was finally sent at 0725. The battleships received it, as did the *New Zealand*, which had been told off as the destroyer wave guard for the battle cruisers. However, *New Zealand* failed to pass the signal to *Lion*, which left Beatty for the moment in ignorance of the encounter.

At the time he received the signal, Warrender's battleships were steaming east, while Beatty's battle cruisers were moving north to cross behind them and take up their screening position. As it happened, it appeared to Warrender as though Beatty was steaming toward the position that *Shark* had given, and it was not until 0736 that Warrender realized something was amiss and signaled, "Have you received messages from *Lynx*?", but *Lion* did not receive this signal. When Beatty wheeled the battle cruisers to take up their screen position and so turned directly away from the enemy, Warrender was certain. At 0755 he signaled, "Are you going after *Roon?*"

Beatty was astonished by this message and replied, "Have heard nothing of *Roon*. . . ." Warrender then passed on the signals that had been received. Just as *Lion* was taking these in, *New Zealand*, after a delay of nearly half an hour, finally chose to relay the *Lynx*'s signals also. Immediately Beatty turned the battle cruisers sixteen points to starboard and worked up speed to 22 knots. Ordering Goodenough to spread his light cruisers along a line to the north, and Pakenham to remain with his three armored cruisers and screen Warrender to the west, Beatty headed for the position given by the *Shark*.

Jones was continuing to shadow *Roon* and the torpedo boats as they moved to the east at a speed of 20 knots, closing the armored cruiser at 0740, when a patch of mist lowered visibility still further. When, ten minutes later, the mist cleared suddenly, Jones discovered that he was faced with not one, but three cruisers, *Roon* having been joined by the *Stuttgart* and *Hamburg*. With the range closing rapidly, Jones hastily turned his division around to the west and worked up speed to 30 knots to get clear of the Germans, signaling to Beatty as he did so, "I am being chased to westward by light cruisers; my position lat 54° 34′N., long 3° 48′E." His position was still a misestimate, since it put the *Shark* at least ten miles further to the south-south-east than she actually was. The British destroyers rapidly began to draw away from their pursuers, in spite of the fact that the battered *Hardy*'s speed soon dropped to 26 knots. So quickly did they get out of range that, at 0802, *Roon* ordered the other two cruisers to break off the chase and turn south-east to follow the rest of the fleet. This was to be the last engagement of the affair involving the High Sea Fleet, for submarine reports from several ships in the main body now finally convinced von Ingenohl to withdraw without delay. By the end of the day the precious battle squadrons would be safe within Heligoland Bight.

Jones did not realize that he was no longer being chased; he thought, rather, that the Germans had turned south-east to open their "A" arcs and he moved to parallel their course. In the haze, not one of the British destroyers realized that the Germans had withdrawn, and they continued their course. This confusion did have the advantage, however, that the four destroyers were now approaching Beatty and Goodenough rapidly, so fast as to largely wipe out the positional discrepancy caused by *Shark*'s error. At 0850 *Shark* caught sight of Goodenough's light cruisers.

But Warrender, Beatty, and Goodenough were no longer concerned with the pursuit of the *Roon*. Between 0841 and 0900 reports began to trickle in of the bombardment of the east coast. At 0850, still concerned for the Humber, Warrender turned the Second Battle Squadron north-north-west, but Beatty realized immediately that Scarborough had been the enemy's main objective and, at 0900, he ordered "Course west-north-west." A few minutes later Warrender came to the same conclusion, although for the time being he continued to head north-north-west in order to let Beatty and Goodenough get ahead of the Second Battle Squadron. Commander Loftus Jones caused momentary confusion when he signaled to Beatty, after his destroyers had come up to the main force, "Am being chased by light cruisers." Beatty assumed that Goodenough, at least, must be able to see the enemy and signaled to the Commodore to engage them, but Goodenough, whose northern horizon was empty, held his course. If, as the commanders estimated, the Germans had bombarded Scarborough an hour before, then it would not be long before they would be in sight.

The hours before dawn were anxious ones for Hipper. After his decision that the entire force would continue to the coast, the weather steadily worsened. At 0600, Commander Retzmann, scouting ahead with the *Strassburg* and the Ninth Flotilla, reported that he had sighted neither the coast, nor any lights and that, with the heavy sea and wind, the torpedo boats could not keep their course. Hipper immediately decided on a change of plan and, at 0632, he ordered all the torpedo boats and all the light cruisers, except *Kolberg*, to turn back and make for the 0600 rendezvous of the High Sea Fleet. At 0640, Hipper was sure of his position off the coast, and the First Scouting Group divided into two. The *Von der Tann, Derfflinger,* and *Kolberg,* under Rear Admiral Tapken were to head south for Scarborough and Whitby, while Hipper took *Seydlitz, Moltke,* and *Blücher* north-north-west to bombard Hartlepool.

SMS *Seydlitz*

SMS *Kolberg*

The patrols that morning at Hartlepool were weak, for only four destroyers of the *River* class were at sea. Despite the Admiralty's instructions that all vessels be at sea before dawn in the period of alert, the weather in the previous two days had been so bad that Ballard, the Admiral of Patrols, had instructed his captains not to go to sea unless specially required but remain in harbor with steam up. Consequently, the Senior Officer at Hartlepool, Captain A. C. Bruce, had sent out only the destroyers and kept his two light cruisers, *Patrol* and *Forward*, and the specially assigned submarine C-9 in the anchorage. It was the latter's absence that was to be most crucial, for as Keyes later wrote:

> . . .it was deplorable that the submarine which was stationed at Hartlepool, solely to meet the situation which arose, should have been in harbour, in a position from which she could not dive to attack. . . .[6]

At 0745 *Seydlitz* was challenged by the port war signal station, and ten minutes later the destroyers *Doon, Waveney, Test,* and *Moy* sighted the Germans to the south-east at a range of nine thousand yards. Lieutenant Commander H. M. Fraser in *Doon* led his destroyers to investigate. The three battle cruisers immediately opened fire with their main and secondary armaments and, amidst a hail of shell, all the destroyers but *Doon* turned away to the north. The latter attempted to launch a torpedo, but at five thousand yards the range was still too much and the German fire too heavy for the attack to have any chance of success. Fraser turned *Doon* away, the destroyer riddled with splinters and with eleven casualties in her crew.

At 0803 the bombardment began at a range of two miles. *Blücher* circled to the south while *Seydlitz* and *Moltke* steamed up and down on a line to the north-east of the town. The fire was devastating, although far more damage was done to civilians than to any military installations. Eighty-six were killed and 424 wounded during the half-hour attack, but the 6″ guns in the batteries at Hartlepool were able to make some reply when they struck *Blücher* four times, damaging a 21 cm turret, knocking two 88 mm guns out of action, and causing eleven casualties. Both *Seydlitz* and *Moltke* were also hit, the former three times and the latter once, but their damage was minimal. The accuracy of both sides' fire was hampered by a very heavy mist, although it may be said to have favored the British more because it sheltered their ships from the consequences of the inept patrol arrangements.

Patrol and C-9 were under way immediately, but they had little luck. C-9 dived to avoid the battle cruisers' fire and in doing so she grounded on the bar at the entrance to the harbor. *Patrol* made a brave thrust against the battle cruisers, and might, in the mist and confusion, have been able to do some damage. As she passed the entrance of the harbor, however, she was struck by three heavy shells, which so damaged the ship that Captain Bruce was forced to ground her to make temporary repairs. She was out of action for the remainder of the engagement, as was C-9. The latter took so long to extricate herself from the shoal that by the time she was clear the Germans had disappeared, and C-9 could do little more than make a token search before reentering harbor. *Forward*, for her part, was not able to raise steam in time and when she too finally emerged, it was to discover that Hipper had turned away to the south-east to rejoin the southern group.

The bombardment of Scarborough and Whitby went entirely un-opposed. The three ships in Tapken's force came up to the coast from the north-east of Whitby, and ran south to Scarborough, before they opened fire. Both ports were undefended and had no warships based on them, so the battle cruisers were able to proceed with their attack uninterrupted. At 0806, they opened fire at a range of less than one thousand yards with their secondary armaments. At 0816, the two heavy ships reversed course, heading north to attack Whitby. When this first stage of their bombardment ceased at 0835, they had killed eighteen and wounded ninety-nine civilians and had damaged more than two hundred build-ings. *Kolberg* continued south, and at 0814 began to lay her mines, from close to the coast to some ten miles out. Twenty seven minutes later, the task was completed. The British war channel blocked, *Kolberg* turned north-north-east to rejoin the First Scouting Group.

Von der Tann and *Derfflinger* began their second bombardment at 0906. It lasted but seven minutes, and, though the German battle cruisers had fired nearly two hundred shells into the town, and caused severe structural damage before they turned away to the north, there were happily only five casualties. By 0930, the First Scouting Group and the *Kolberg* were reunited, and Hipper was shaping a course for Germany, signaling to von Ingenohl:

> Operation completed. Battle cruisers and *Kolberg* 54° 42′N., 0° 30′W. Course south-south-east, 23 knots.

The Admiralty was making its arrangements to meet the situation. From 0818, it began to intercept signals from the ships off Hartlepool. By 0840, from messages from both Scarborough and Hartlepool, it was obvious that the expected attack on the east coast was under way and that it involved at least two, and probably four, heavy ships.

In rapid succession, orders were sent out to Warrender and Tyrwhitt to join and search for the bombarding forces. The Third Battle Squadron was ordered out of Rosyth to join Warrender, but Jellicoe, who had also been ordered to sea and already had his ships at short notice for steam, ordered Bradford to bring his squadrons to a rendezvous with the Grand Fleet off Berwick. Jellicoe was concerned with the possibility that the Germans might strike to the north and he was determined to have the Grand Fleet concentrated to prevent it.

As Warrender and Beatty turned west, Tyrwhitt led his forces out from the shallows off Yarmouth behind which they had been sheltering. As soon as they got into the open sea on their way to Scarborough, the Commodore realized that his destroyers could not take being pushed into the teeth of a gale, and he accordingly ordered them home. Retaining only the light cruisers, Tyrwhitt pressed on, but instead of the ordered speed of 25 knots, the cruisers could barely make 15 as they battered into the short, steep sea. The weather damage began to mount.

Warrender's problem was not, in the poor weather conditions, an easy one. Jellicoe had earlier declared that the ships of the Grand Fleet were not to pass west of a line drawn north-east/south-west off the east coast, because of the existence of the German mine fields. Although the Vice Admiral was now steering for Scarborough, he realized that the Germans could emerge from any point along a hundred mile stretch of the forbidden area. To find Hipper, he would have at least to send in the light cruisers. Therefore, as the First Light Cruiser Squadron and the Third Cruiser Squadron deployed in front of the heavy ships, Warrender signaled, "Light cruisers must go in through minefield to locate enemy." This, perhaps not unnaturally, caused "some excitement"

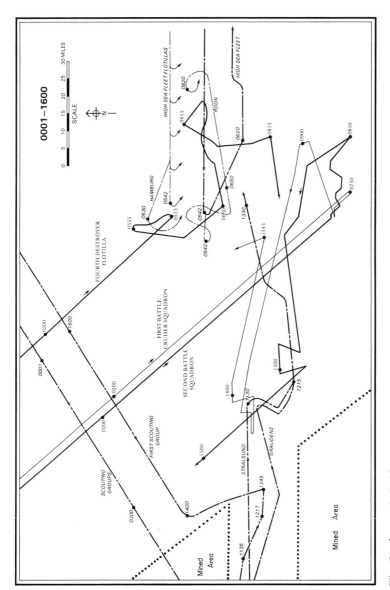

The Scarborough Raid

aboard the *Southampton*, and a few minutes later a doubtful Warrender signaled to the Admiralty, "Is it safe to go straight across mine fields?"

At the same time, aboard the *Iron Duke*, Jellicoe had been studying the charts and one thing was abundantly clear to him which Warrender had missed. Although Jellicoe had, as Commander in Chief, bidden his ships not in normal circumstances to go west of the line described, the actual danger areas from the German minefields did not stretch the entire length of the coast; there was a gap almost exactly due east of Whitby and Scarborough. At 1004, Jellicoe signaled to Warrender and Beatty,

> Gap in minefield between parallel lat 54° 40N., and 54° 20', and [W] as far as 20'E. long. Enemy will in all probability come out there.

Jellicoe's intuition was completely correct, all Hipper's ships emerged from almost precisely the middle of the gap. But avoiding mines had taken little of Hipper's concern. His intention was to gain as much easterly ground as possible to link up with the High Sea Fleet at the rendezvous, before they turned south-east for home. Had he steamed straight for Germany, his ships would have passed at least twenty miles to the south of the British and so avoided making any contact at all.

By 1025, the British forces had largely taken up formation. Warrender was steaming west, with Pakenham's three armored cruisers to the south-south-west, and, ten miles to the north, Beatty and Goodenough were about to turn west also, with the light cruisers spread on a line abeam at two mile intervals. The battle cruisers, in close order, were following *Southampton*, the southernmost ship of the line, while to the north the remaining operational destroyers attached themselves to the *Falmouth*.

Conversely, the Second Scouting Group and the torpedo boat flotillas had suffered badly as they made their way east. With the seas on their quarter, the German ships had moved so much that several torpedo boats rolled their masts out. With ready-use ammunition and other gear being carried away as the ships broached-to, one by one each cruiser had to order her attendant half flotilla to turn into the wind to connect their auxiliary bow rudders. Despite the senior officer's decision, when signal traffic from British ships to the east was intercepted, to order each group to proceed independently at maximum speed, progress had been erratic, and Hipper, with his four more weatherly battle cruisers, was beginning to catch up his light craft.

Until 1100, the visibility had been good for the North Sea in winter, but by late morning squalls were beginning to set in, and the visibility became patchy, frequently dropping to less than two miles. The light cruisers were forced to close in on each other to maintain visual communication, and even then *Nottingham* and *Birmingham* lost touch and caused much confusion when the *Nottingham* resighted her consort suddenly and reported her as an enemy. This problem was only just being sorted out, when, at 1125, *Southampton* sighted other, real enemies.

Barely three miles ahead of the *Southampton*, and steaming straight toward her, were the *Stralsund* and her attendant torpedo boats of the Second Half Flotilla. Turning hard to starboard to clear his gunsights from the spray, Goodenough ordered the other light cruisers to concentrate on *Southampton* and signaled to Beatty, "Am engaging a cruiser and destroyers." At the same time, *Stralsund* sighted *Southampton* and herself hastily turned hard to starboard. Both cruisers then opened fire, but in the heavy seas, their shooting was wild and they scored no hits. *Birmingham* soon came up to the *Southampton*. When he sighted the second British cruiser, *Stralsund*'s captain, Harder, ordered the torpedo boats to lay a smokescreen. *Strassburg* and *Graudenz* were fast nearing *Stralsund* because of the latter's turn to the south and, as they approached, they and their half flotillas turned to follow suit.

While *Nottingham* and *Falmouth* turned to the south-west to support Goodenough, the Commodore realized that there were two more light cruisers and even more torpedo boats behind the *Stralsund*, but he failed to report this information to Beatty. As had happened before, this failure in communication triggered off a series of errors that was to have a critical effect on the outcome of the affair.

Further to the east, Beatty was still under the impression that *Southampton* and *Birmingham* were engaging only one light cruiser. He was preoccupied by the need to make contact with Hipper, and, on the information that he had to hand, the German battle cruisers could be anywhere within a wide semicircle to the north, south, or west. Had Goodenough now informed him of the discovery of the other light cruisers and torpedo boats, it would have been obvious to Beatty that his scouts had encountered the entire Second Scouting Group, and that the First Scouting Group—Hipper's battle cruisers and the *Kolberg*—must logically be some distance astern, to the west. To find and engage Hipper would then have been a relatively simple matter.

But Goodenough did not report the other Germans. To the northwest, Beatty sighted *Falmouth* and *Nottingham* going down to support the *Southampton* and the *Birmingham*, and the Vice Admiral, conscious of the necessity to keep as much area under observation as possible for the first sign of the heavy ships, and thinking that Goodenough had more than enough strength to deal with the *Stralsund*, made a searchlight signal to the two light cruisers, "Resume your position for lookout duties. Take station ahead five miles." It was here that another error crept in. When Seymour, Beatty's Flag Lieutenant, worded up the signal, he did not address it specifically to the *Falmouth* and the *Nottingham*, but to the light cruiser squadron as a whole.

Astern of *Southampton, Birmingham* saw the signal and passed it to the flagship, as did the *Nottingham*. Goodenough now made his second mistake. Despite the fact that he still had not reported the presence of the other German ships, and that it should have been obvious to him that this information would have changed radically whatever picture Beatty had of the tactical situation, the Commodore at 1155 turned his ships sixteen points about to return to the *Lion*. In doing so, the light cruisers broke off their engagement, since the battle cruisers were now well away to the north-north-east. Goodenough later justified his decision by pointing out that when he turned away the Germans were steering due south, directly for the Second Battle Squadron and the Third Cruiser Squadron. Despite this, however, it was a bad mistake, especially in view of the fact that the visibility was still worsening, frequently dropping to less than half a mile when the ships were enveloped in squalls.

As his cruisers headed away amidst the heavy seas, Goodenough temporarily resighted *Stralsund* to the south. She had become separated from her sisters, and the British now mistook her to be yet another German cruiser. At this, Goodenough finally made another report, "Enemy's cruisers bearing south by east," but Beatty had only just received this message when, to his astonishment, he realized that *Southampton* was making for the *Lion*, apparently out of contact with the enemy. At 1212, the Vice Admiral signaled, understandably tartly, "What have you done with enemy light cruisers?" Goodenough replied, "They disappeared south when I received your signal to resume station." An acid exchange followed.

BEATTY: "Engage the enemy."

GOODENOUGH: "There is no enemy in sight now."

BEATTY: "When and where was the enemy last seen? When you sight enemy, engage him. Signal to resume previous station was made to *Nottingham. I cannot understand why, under any circumstances, you did not pursue enemy.*" [Author's italics] Strong words indeed for an operational signal.

While the British engaged in their recriminations, Captain Harder's cruisers and destroyers were drawing away to the south-east. They were fast approaching Warrender and, at 1210, *Stralsund* caught sight of the Second Battle Squadron through a gap in the mists. Harder hastily turned his ships to the east and flashed the recognition signal which he had seen the British use, in an attempt to deceive the battleships. Vice Admiral Warrender did not at first see the Germans, but, only a few hundred yards away, the second division of the squadron, under Rear Admiral Arbuthnot in the *Orion*, had a clear view. *Orion* reported, "Enemy in sight," to *King George V*, but did nothing else. Her captain, F. C. Dreyer, one of the most highly regarded gunnery experts of the day, was frantic with impatience, and, ordering the main armament guns to be laid on the leading light cruiser, begged for permission to open fire. But Arbuthnot was adamant, and replied, "No, not until the Vice Admiral signals 'open fire'."[7]

Warrender did not order "open fire" when he sighted the Germans himself a few minutes later, rather he ordered Pakenham to take his three armored cruisers and chase, while he informed Beatty of what had been seen. Dreyer later wrote of Arbuthnot:

He never spoke to me about it afterwards, but I am certain from his silence that he was mortified to realise that he had been too punctilious. If we had fired, the other five battleships would have done so too. . . . One of the German cruisers challenged the *Orion* by flashing 'B.O.X.' at us with a searchlight. He would have had a thick ear for that, if we had fired![8]

The battleships should indeed have opened fire, but despite Dreyer's later declaration that "our golden moment had been missed," it was only twenty minutes before the German ships, which had been hauling rapidly away from the Third Cruiser Squadron, disappeared into yet another squall and were not seen again. British gunnery in 1914 was not adapted to firing at small, rapidly moving vessels in heavy seas and poor visibility.

What was more critical to the outcome of the engagement was the effect that Warrender's signal had upon Beatty's movements. At 1205, the battle cruisers had turned east. It had been Beatty's intention to head for the entrance to the gap between the mine fields, and, at 1230, to turn south to begin patrolling the passage along a north-south line. Had he remained in this area, he would almost certainly have sighted Hipper at around 1300.

The First Scouting Group was steaming almost due east, when, at 1139, Hipper received from *Stralsund*:

Main body of enemy's fleet 54° 30′N., 2° 16′E. Am being chased SW by S.

He immediately turned the battle cruisers south-east and then south-

south-east at 23 knots. The series of signals which Hipper received from his light cruisers was confusing in the extreme, as the three variously reported the enemy's course as being, "south-west by south," "east," and "west". Then, at 1213, came the signal from the *Stralsund*, "Five enemy battleships in 54° 15'N., 2° 7'E." Despite his confusion, it was now apparent to Hipper that these ships were at least twenty miles to the south of those reported earlier and that he was now faced by not one but two separate battle squadrons. At 1217, he altered course to east by south and held on, "though he had every expectation of being outnumbered." By this time, the German battle cruisers were steaming down the middle of the gap—and straight toward the patrol line which Beatty had intended to take up.

But the British were to miss this opportunity. As soon as Beatty received Warrender's signal, he turned his battle cruisers back to the east. At 1240, Beatty received, "Enemy's course east—no battle cruisers seen yet," and at 1257, Warrender sent, "Second Battle Squadron have resumed original position."

Warrender failed in this signal to inform Beatty that he had lost contact with the German cruisers and torpedo boats, but the latter realized that this must be the case. It was evident to him now that Hipper must have been well astern of his light forces and would thus be still to the west. To Beatty's mind, it was obvious that Hipper would turn and steam to the north, avoiding the Dogger Bank and the battleships that had been seen and reported there. This was, in fact, precisely what Hipper had done. Knowing that at least two battle squadrons were to the east of him, and that he would have to risk encountering one or both to support the Second Scouting Group and the flotillas, his relief must have been immense when, at 1244, he received from *Stralsund*, "Enemy is out of sight." This meant, of course, that Hipper could now leave Harder to get home. Only a minute later he turned the battle cruisers north, hoping to clear the danger area as fast as possible, while at the same time he signaled, "Are you in danger?" At 1305 the flagship received a bald, but cheering "No" from *Stralsund*. With his light forces clear of the enemy and steering east-north-east, his battle cruisers continued north. In the prevailing poor visibility Hipper could begin to hope that his ships would escape. When he turned at 1245, his battle cruisers had been little more than twelve miles away from the First Battle Cruiser Squadron.

At 1315, Beatty turned north, and nine minutes later, Warrender, who had by now come to the southern end of the patrol area, decided that Hipper's ships must have evaded him in the mist and he too turned north.

But curiously, Room 40 now began to issue to the Admiralty a stream of signals, within an hour of their original transmission. The first of these was one Hipper had sent to von Ingenohl at 1215, giving his position and course; the translation was sent out to the ships at sea at 1325. For the next few hours, Beatty and Warrender tried to interpret the German movements. The problem was that it took between ninety minutes and two hours for the British ships to receive the information, and this delay was too much to do little more than confuse the tactical picture.

The first signal caused Beatty, who was doubtful of its validity but had nothing else to go on, to turn east at 1355 and so lose whatever chance that still remained to catch the First Scouting Group. Warrender decided to continue north, conscious that if the Germans had crossed the Dogger Bank from the position given, they would then have been well to the east of his ships and out of reach. At all events, by doing so he came closest to Hipper, for the *Kolberg*, which had been lagging behind the battle cruisers, badly damaged, with her decks and superstructure swept almost clean by the head seas into which she had been ploughing, sighted funnel smoke just after the battle cruisers had turned north-east. With the sea now on her beam, *Kolberg* was able to work up speed rapidly and rejoin the First Scouting Group, leaving the smoke behind. Neither Pakenham's battle cruisers nor Warrender's battleships saw anything of the Germans.

Another intercepted signal, this time from the High Sea Fleet's flagship, *Friedrich der Grosse*, to the *Stralsund*, at last gave the Admiralty to understand that the High Sea Fleet was or had been at sea, and they hastily warned Warrender not to go too far to the east. Yet another signal gave Hipper's position when he turned north-east at 1245, and when this signal was finally sent to Warrender and Beatty at 1450, and taken in by them, it was obvious that they had missed Hipper. At 1547, Warrender ordered Beatty to "Relinquish chase—rejoin me tomorrow."

But at the Admiralty, the "Cabal," though bitterly disappointed, were not prepared to accept the failure. They remembered Tyrwhitt, still plunging north-north-east with his light cruisers and signaled to Warrender: "Twenty destroyers of First and Third Flotillas are waiting off Gorleston. If you think it advisable you may direct Commodore (T) to take them to vicinity of Heligoland to attack enemy ships returning in dark hours." It would have been a vain and troublesome effort, as the flotillas could not possibly have got across the North Sea in time and both Warrender and Jellicoe, who had intercepted the signal, opposed it. Warrender replied: "Certainly not advisable, as there is a strong NW wind and nasty sea." Jellicoe simply signaled to the latter: "It's too late."

By sunset all British forces were moving north and Jellicoe now ordered Tyrwhitt to join the Grand Fleet at a rendezvous with the Third Battle Squadron at dawn the next day. There remained for the British only one more chance that they might be able to inflict any damage on the Germans, and it was now Keyes upon whom Churchill had his remaining hopes pinned (though Fisher was somewhat less sanguine as to Commodore (S)'s prospects of success).

Keyes had been anxiously awaiting events from his position on the Terschelling line, when, at 1034, *Lurcher* intercepted a signal from the battleship *Monarch* to the destroyer *Ambuscade*, warning the latter that the Germans were off Scarborough. The Commodore's reaction was prompt, for he immediately dispatched *Firedrake* to get within wireless range of the submarine tender *Adamant*, which was lying at Harwich with a telephone link to the Admiralty. The *Firedrake* was instructed to inform the command that Keyes was gathering his submarines and would await instructions. Meanwhile, he took *Lurcher* and began to steam up and down the patrol line, attempting to collect his submarines. In the low visibility it was a difficult job, especially as the weather had been so bad on the passage out that several submarines became separated from the main body and hardly knew their position within thirty miles. Keyes wrote:

> I had a most trying day endeavouring to collect the submarines; in the visibility prevailing, they had to dive the moment they sighted a vessel, if they wished to remain unseen, and once submerged, it was very difficult to get them on to the surface again in the absence of sound signalling, which we did not possess in those days; and by dusk I had only succeeded in finding four.[9]

At 1410 the Admiralty signaled "High Sea Fleet is at sea, and at 12.30 p.m. was in lat. 54° 38′N., long. 5° 55′E. They may return after dawn tomorrow, so proceed to Heligoland and intercept them. They probably pass five miles west of Heligoland, steering south for Weser Light." By the time that this signal arrived, Keyes had still only managed to gather four submarines, the French *Archimède*, E-10, E-11, and E-15. These he dispatched to Heligoland, but, faced with the Admiralty's signal, Keyes was uncertain as to what to do.

The Admiralty made one critical error in the message, their estimate of the High Sea Fleet's movements was exactly twelve hours too slow. Von Ingenohl would actually have the battle squadrons in the Jade by 2100 that night. Keyes naturally thought that they would still be at sea at dawn the next day and that there was thus still enough time for him to muster the other submarines—assuming that he could find them—and send them in to the Bight. He toyed with the idea of taking his two destroyers into the area that night, but, knowing little or nothing of the movements of the other British forces and ignorant of the state of the weather on the other side of the North Sea, he assumed that Tyrwhitt must be following the High Sea Fleet with his cruisers and destroyers, ready to make a night torpedo attack. Keyes knew that his appearance without warning could cause untold and even fatal confusion, and, having been accused of "bush-thwacking[*sic*]" even by Churchill, he could not risk further criticism. Finally, Keyes remembered his duty as a submarine commander; if the Germans were to be still at sea by the next morning, it was clearly his job to attempt to reassemble the missing four and send them into the Bight, where they would have more chance of attacking the Germans than his destroyers ever would. Keyes was forced to abandon the project.

Although already too late to intercept von Ingenohl, Keyes would have had the opportunity to attack Hipper, whose battered forces were steaming back to Germany in scattered groups, had the Admiralty's next signal been passed correctly. For, at 2012, they sent:

> We think Heligoland and Amrun lights will be lit when ships are going in. Your destroyers might get a chance to attack about 2.0 A.M., or later, on the line given you.

This signal should have got to Keyes within the hour. But it was not until after 0120 that an enraged Commodore (S) held the signal in his hand—more than five hours after first being sent out.

The problem with operating from a destroyer, as Keyes had earlier discovered, was that the "D" or destroyer wavelength had a range of no more than fifty miles. Now, while *Lurcher* and *Firedrake* could only transmit on this wavelength, which was the reason for Keyes's earlier detachment of the latter to act as a relay, they could receive messages at long distance on the "S" or ship wavelength. Keyes had made the specific request to the Admiralty that it pass all messages via the *Adamant*, which would then transmit them on the "S" band. But this message was instead relayed via Ipswich to the destroyer depot ship *Woolwich*, and this vessel spent three hours trying to raise Keyes on the "D" band—which was obviously impossible. Not until 2238 did the Admiralty learn that the message had not been sent, and not until 0023 was it sent out again. Keyes had good cause to feel annoyed.

For at 2000, having found no more submarines and received no new orders, Keyes reluctantly turned away for the rendezvous which had been arranged previous to leaving harbor for any submarine that had not been able to make contact. Not until he was a good two hundred miles away from Heligoland did he receive the signal, and, as he later wrote in his *Naval Memoirs*, "Words fail me even now, after more than nineteen years, to express my feelings when I received this belated message."[10] The submarines had little better luck. Hipper, with great difficulty, managed to enter the Jade in the darkness through the unwatched eastern passage and he was not seen by any of the four. Ironically, E-11, under Lieutenant Commander Martin Dunbar-Nasmith, did get one more chance at the Germans. The First Battle Squadron had the night before been sent into the Elbe and von Ingenohl ordered them to move at dawn to the Jade. E-11 observed the movement and Nasmith launched one torpedo at the battleship *Posen* at four hundred yards range, but it ran too deep and passed under the battleship's keel. Nasmith tried again at another, but this battleship saw E-11's periscope and turned to ram. Nasmith dived E-11 so hurriedly that he lost control of her and she shot to the surface, broaching-to before her crew could get her back under control. At this, the Germans scattered and ran into the estuaries, and despite yet another attack by Nasmith, this time on the last ship of the squadron, she too eluded him and E-11 was forced to return to Harwich empty-handed.

Of the other submarines, the French *Archimède*, a steam-driven submarine, had her funnel bent in the heavy seas and had to crawl across the Bight and into the North Sea on the surface with most of the crew "incessantly baling out the water which surged through the funnel aperture at every plunge."[11] She survived the experience, however, and arrived at Harwich late on the 19th, followed at intervals by the other three submarines, which were the last ships to return from the operation. The *Staff Monograph* rather maliciously understated the attitude of *Archimède*'s captain when it reported that he "was considerably impressed by the weather and conditions of winter service in the Bight."[12]

Jellicoe wrote to Fisher on 18 December, telling him how "intensely unhappy" he was about the whole affair and how the "business required explanation." The affair certainly did, for it seemed that the British forces had repeatedly been offered the opportunity to make contact with the Scouting Groups and had as repeatedly missed their chance. The commanders at sea returned to harbor to face a veritable inquisition by Jellicoe and the Admiralty.

Beatty escaped without censure. His actions had been quite proper and he had exercised continuous good judgment, the validity of which had been set at naught by his Flag Lieutenant's error, the failure of Goodenough, and the poor information that he had received. Jellicoe summed up the official opinion when he penciled, on the 18th, "There *never* was such bad luck."[13] Fisher replied, "How unkind was the heavenly mist!"[14] Indeed, as more information came to light, there were times in the action when it appeared to the analysts that it was Beatty who was exercizing overall command, not Warrender.

There was what must have been a painful interview between the deeply disappointed Beatty and a mortified Goodenough. Despite the signal error, and, as Jellicoe later noted, "Beatty [is] very severe on Goodenough but forgets that it was his own badly worded signal to the cruisers that led to the German being out of touch," Commodore Goodenough's actions were inexcusable.[15] Beatty wrote:

> . . . time after time I have impressed upon Goodenough the necessity of always using his own initiative and discretion—that my orders are expressions of intentions and that they are *not* to be obeyed too literally. The Man on the Spot is the only one who can judge certain situations.[16]

Beatty and his staff commander Reginald Plunkett had an exchange on the subject after the latter submitted a paper summarizing the lessons of 16 December. In it he wrote:

> I earnestly submit that it would be of value if some of these lessons could be impressed on Flag Officers, Commodores and Commanding Officers who may be detached. Also the urgent importance of *using initiative* so as not always to "wait for instructions" when in doubt, and not always to be tied by the letter of an order when it is obviously unsuitable.

Beatty commented waspishly:

> Quite agree but [it is] so obvious that if they do not understand [?] them they are not fit to command and should be removed.
>
> It is too late to begin to impress obvious truths such as this on flag officers at this stage who no doubt think that they already comprehend their duties—I might remind you that criticism without holding responsibilities is the easiest of all duties, if it is a duty.[17]

Jellicoe explained to Fisher:

> It was a most unfortunate error. Had the Commodore disobeyed the signal, it is possible that an action between the light cruisers might have resulted in bringing the battle cruisers to action. The Commodore had reported the presence of the first light cruiser and destroyers and knew that the V.A. was aware of their being in sight; there is therefore every justification for his obeying the signal from this point of view, but he had *not* reported the sighting of the three other cruisers and in my opinion, he should certainly have disobeyed the signal on this account, and kept touch with them until he had informed the V.A.[18]

In short, Goodenough had been, as Fisher succinctly remarked, "a fool." Despite all the criticism, however, he retained his command.

Fisher wanted the Commodore relieved, but Churchill would not hear of it, and neither Jellicoe nor Beatty really desired a change. Beatty's reaction was especially interesting. He had been grievously disappointed in Goodenough, so far as to name a possible relief (Lionel Halsey, then captain of the *New Zealand*), but as Plunkett wrote after Beatty's death of the interview with Goodenough, "He [Beatty] patiently explained his views, but, as he said afterwards, 'I never blamed him, and we parted friends.'"[19]

Beatty made the point to Jellicoe and the Admiralty that Goodenough would either have to be relieved—and quickly—or else the matter be closed without delay. Goodenough was acutely conscious of his mistake and further recrimination would only serve to break his spirit and damage his judgment. Jellicoe concurred, and, despite Fisher's fury, Goodenough retained his command. In this case, the mercy shown by the Admiralty and the senior commanders paid good dividends. Goodenough's activities at the Battle of the Dogger Bank and at Jutland were to be models of aggressive scouting and concise reporting. And, as Plunkett wrote, "Generosity such as this not only set a fine example but also helped to create around him a band of brothers."[20]

Warrender also survived in his command, despite the fact that his performance had been only mediocre. He was an adequate and loyal squadron admiral, but he should never have been entrusted with an independent command. Admittedly he had been poorly served by several of his subordinates and by the Admiralty's information service, but, as Fisher commented, "A. K. Wilson says that very few Admirals from his experience have the 'mooring board mind!' They steer for where the enemy is, not where he will be."[21] Although hampered by the heavy weather (which Jellicoe seemed inclined to count as the principal reason for the lack of success) and lack of destroyers, Warrender still failed to make a proper use of even the three armored cruisers of Pakenham's squadron which were accompanying him. The First Sea Lord, for one, took a dim view of Warrender's leadership when he wrote, ". . . and Warrander . . . covering so little space when he ought to have spread like a fan."[22] Certainly, although it would have been dubious doctrine for Warrender to have scattered his battleships, the Third Cruiser Squadron had been given little or no opportunity to act as a proper scouting force. Separated, they might have been vulnerable to Hipper's battle cruisers, being both slower and weaker, but Warrender should have been prepared to accept the risk. In the event, Jellicoe was to have him relieved by the end of 1915 on the ground that his health was deteriorating. Warrender was aged very rapidly by the war; he was already rather deaf, and by this stage he may not have been completely fit. A remark in a letter from Lieutenant Stephen King-Hall to his father, Admiral Sir George King-Hall, written on 14 February 1915, would appear to be talking of Warrender:

> If what you say about Sir What's-his-name is true, everyone thoroughly agrees in the mess. He is defined as follows: "He never spoke in peace because he was deaf; everyone thought he must be thinking a lot. When War came, everyone said, good gracious, what on earth *was* he doing the whole time?"[23]

One of the two principal villains in the piece had been the very outlook of many of the senior officers. If two officers with such reputations of aggressiveness and eagerness for responsibility as Commodore Goodenough and Rear Admiral Arbuthnot could act as they did, one breaking off the action by the authority of a signal that had been patently made without critical information and the other failing to open fire without the direction of his senior officer under conditions in which that officer might very well not be able to see the enemy and where contact might be lost at any minute, then something was very wrong. Senior officers, with a few exceptions, seemed to share a common misunderstanding of the qualities needed for war, and indeed, the very traditions that the Royal Navy had always espoused.

The second villain was the Royal Navy's communications system. Goodenough's error had its roots in the ambiguity of the signal made up by Beatty's ill-qualified flag-lieutenant, Ralph Seymour (it was not the last signaling mistake the latter was to make that would have serious consequences). In this case, however, visual signaling was not the principal worry. There had been serious errors in wireless procedure at several points. Admittedly, wireless was only just out of its infancy, but many signal officers apparently possessed a congenital inability to draft a sighting report and maintain an adequate flow of information to authority. A sighting report should contain several clear, and simple, points: (1) own course, speed, and position; (2) enemy's numbers and composition; (3) enemy's course, speed, and relative position; (4) own intentions. Yet, despite the simplicity and obvious nature of the reports, very few commanders, junior or senior, appeared to understand what was needed. The series of signals from the destroyer *Lynx* to the *Lion* during the first encounter before dawn is typical. First: "Am chasing enemy's destroyers in north-west direction"; then: "Am being chased by enemy's cruiser; am steering south-south-west"; which was followed, nearly an hour later, by: "Have reason to believe one destroyer sunk. *Ambuscade* damaged, *Unity* standing by her." It was only *Lion*'s interception of signals passing between the destroyers that enabled Beatty to have some idea of the action that was taking place. Of course, it was dark and confused, and in the heat of action it was easy to be preoccupied with matters in hand, but the destroyers should have kept in mind that they were employed at this stage of the battle primarily as lookouts and only secondarily as "destroyers." This lesson was not, unfortunately, rammed home after the Scarborough Raid, and the Grand Fleet flotillas were to continue on their ignorant way, with dire results in the night actions of the Battle of Jutland.

The Admiralty's communications, too, were in need of modification. There had been the glaring error in the case of the last signal to Keyes, when in spite of all his requests and his insistence on the need for the special treatment of messages to the *Firedrake* and *Lurcher*, the last, even if forlorn, chance to deal a decisive blow at the raiders was wasted by the delay involved in using the "customary channels." The messages from Room 40 were also taking too long to get to the commanders at sea, because they had to pass through the hands of the War Staff and the waiting "Cabal" for discussion before the decision was made to pass them on. Fisher's criticism that Vice Admiral Warrender failed to interpret those signals he had received in the correct fashion was valid, but Warrender's task would have been greatly eased had he either been sent the signals an hour earlier, or the Admiralty had attached their appreciation of the signal to the transmission—either of which would have been practicable. The organization was still in its teething stage, but there were nonetheless inherent faults that were to manifest themselves again when the failure to pass on the message giving the key to the High Sea Fleet's course on the night of Jutland occurred and lost the British the chance of a total victory. Speed and accuracy are essential in communications; the systems employed by the Royal Navy in 1914 possessed neither.

There were other repercussions from the raid. The Admiral of Patrols, G. A. Ballard, and the Senior Naval Officer at Hartlepool received a sharp reprimand from Fisher over the failure to have C-9 at sea. Ballard was now marked down by Fisher as one to go and Oliver, who "had a poor opinion" of Ballard, set about taking "away bits of his command at the north and south ends until there was nothing left."[24] Captain Bruce escaped anything more than censure by reason of his gallant conduct. Oddly, it was Keyes who came in for most of the blame about the C-9. All Fisher's apprehensions about the state of the submarine service erupted yet again, and Ballard had a stormy interview with him on the subject on 19 December. As the latter reported it to Keyes, with more than a hint that Fisher held Commodore (S) to be as much to blame for the incident as the Admiral of Patrols, the First Sea Lord's tirade included such gems as "submarines didn't require a harbor as they could always lie quite comfortably on the bottom", and that twelve submarines, working without any support, "should make it impossible for a German ship to show herself anywhere from St Abb to Harwich." Ballard was quite justified when he remarked that "as far as the service is concerned the sooner somebody makes clear to him what submarines can do and cannot do the better."[25] Churchill again had to calm the First Sea Lord's antipathy to Keyes and he wrote to Fisher on 21 December, saying:

> Keyes is a brilliant officer, with more knowledge of and feeling for *war* than almost any naval officer I have met. I think the work and efficiency of our submarines are wonderful.[26]

There was one major change in the dispositions of the Grand Fleet. Fisher had been agitating to bring the entire fleet south, an agitation in which he had been joined more recently by Beatty. The defenses at Rosyth had been completed and there was space inside the anchorage above the Forth Bridge for Beatty's forces, as well as the ships of the Third Battle Squadron and the Third Cruiser Squadron which were already based there.

On 21 December, the First Battle Cruiser Squadron and the First Light Cruiser Squadron left Cromarty for Rosyth, arriving there late the same day. The Firth of Forth became the battle cruisers' base for the remainder of the war. In fact, in all but name—and this was soon to be corrected—Beatty now possessed an independent command. Though Beatty was junior to Vice Admiral Bradford, the latter received specific instructions from the Admiralty not to interfere with any ships under Beatty's command. To Jellicoe, Fisher, and Churchill, Beatty was a trusted subordinate, who was capable of holding responsibility far beyond his rank. In essence, the battle cruisers became a separate fleet, on a par with the Channel Fleet, subordinate to Jellicoe but largely independent of the Grand Fleet itself, when they were renamed the Battle Cruiser Force. The First Light Cruiser Squadron and the First Destroyer Flotilla were now permanent parts of the force. In the aftermath of the raid, Beatty also received one more reinforcement to his command. The battle cruiser *Indomitable*, which had been refitting in the south after her return from the Mediterranean, was hastily ordered to join at Rosyth, after proceeding west about Scotland. Her arrival brought the battle cruisers' strength up to five—a number that Beatty considered was the minimum he needed to operate with confidence against the German Scouting Groups.

Apart from the shift of the battle cruisers' base, there was no other change in the arrangements and the Admiralty stood firm in its policy of concentrating the Grand Fleet in the north, despite a popular furor in the wake of the bombardments. The realization that the Germans could apparently attack ports on the east coast and cause massive damage came as a considerable shock to many Britons. As Professor Marder wrote:

> The Admiralty had, after all, led the public to believe that the German Fleet would not dare to venture beyond the Bight. The query used by the coroner at the Scarborough inquest was picked up and repeated everywhere: "Where was the Navy?"[27]

But the Admiralty managed to survive the controversy. The general press stood by the Government's naval policy and students of naval strategy hastened to point out the dangers inherent in a division of the Grand Fleet merely to protect the east coast. Although much of the good effect of the success at the Falkland Islands was lost, the complaints eventually died away, despite the fact that in the Admiralty:

> . . . we could not say a word in explanation. We had to bear in silence the censures of our countrymen. We could never admit for fear of compromising our secret information where our squadrons were, or how near the German raiding cruisers had been to their destruction.[28]

However, if the British public were unhappy with the Admiralty and the admirals at sea, there was little satisfaction in Germany either. The personnel of the Scouting Groups had been enraged by the High Sea Fleet's pusillanimous withdrawal and the captains of the force, the staff, and Hipper himself were deeply disappointed by von Ingenohl's action and the stunning success that had been missed. Hipper's biographer wrote:

> . . . Hipper's disappointment at the premature breaking off of the enterprise by the German Main Fleet was unreservedly shared by the majority of the officer corps. Admiral Behncke, the Deputy Chief of the Admiralstab in Berlin, expressed this opinion which was strongly held in most quarters. He wrote from Main Headquarters, "The Commander-in-Chief interprets the qualifying explanations of the operations order as a rigid guide and feels himself so bound by it that there remains little hope of vigorous exploitation of favourable opportunities."[29]

Von Ingenohl also came in for harsh criticism from the Emperor, on the ground that he had on this occasion been too careful with the High Sea Fleet and had missed exactly the opportunity that the fleet needed to establish its ascendancy in the North Sea.

But in the event, the restrictions were not lifted and von Ingenohl continued as Commander in Chief. A more flexible and imaginative man, such as Scheer, might have been able to persuade the Emperor to rescind his instructions or else find some way of circumventing them. Von Ingenohl, who might have been a competent Commander in Chief had he been given a free hand, was not a subtle man. Confronted with the mammoth problems as he was, his only answer was to stick closely to the letter of his unrealistic orders, and, in such a situation as the North Sea in 1914, this policy was quite as bad as doing nothing at all.

CHAPTER 9

The Old Year Endeth

In mid-December Keyes and Tyrwhitt were at last given permission to go ahead with the long-delayed "Plan Y," a repetition of the attack on the zeppelin sheds at Cuxhaven. The first air attacks on Britain were beginning, and the threat was giving cause for concern both in the Admiralty and at large in Britain. Although the methods needed to defeat the zeppelins were obvious—a coordinated searchlight and gun battery system around the main cities, together with fighter aircraft armed with incendiary bullets—these things were not yet to be had. While Britain lay open to attack for the next few months, clearly the only way of dealing with the airships was to attack them at their bases. Fisher and Churchill were both keen on the project, although Oliver complained bitterly that by mid-December he was fed up with the idea because it was always being canceled as more important "flaps" arose.

The two commodores were directed to proceed on 18 December, but a report that the German fleet might again be coming out caused the Admiralty to delay the attack until Christmas Day, "much to the chagrin and alarm of Mrs. Tyrwhitt."[1] The force, consisting of the *Arethusa* and the *Undaunted*, with six destroyers and the seaplane carriers *Engadine, Riviera*, and *Empress*, sailed for Heligoland Bight at 0500 on Christmas Eve.

It was only a small force, since Tyrwhitt believed that it would be easier for a limited number of ships to penetrate the Bight undiscovered than for the entire Harwich Force. It was arranged, however, that *Fearless* and a half flotilla of destroyers would follow at a distance and enter the Bight to join Tyrwhitt after the seaplanes had been recovered. Keyes sent ten submarines into the area for the day, stationing some around the launching and recovering positions and the remainder closer inshore to intercept the High Sea Fleet if it emerged. Jellicoe would be at sea with the Grand Fleet, but, despite the relative weakness of Commodore (T)'s force, he would not bring his heavy ships south unless it was clear that the Germans were out in strength.

As Tyrwhitt's ships sailed, the weather seemed perfect for the aircraft raid of the next day. It was bitterly cold, but the sea was very calm. The high visibility and slight breeze held not a hint of fog. At 1000, *Fearless* led her half flotilla out. The good conditions still held.

> A lighter note was provided by the fact that since the ships had sailed under sealed orders and "with utmost despatch" some stewards who had been landed after breakfast to obtain extras for Christmas Day could not get back on board in time and were seen on the quay frantically waving turkeys and geese and ingredients for other Christmas fare.[2]

The seaplane carriers and their escorts crossed the North Sea without incident. At 0430 on Christmas Day, when Tyrwhitt's ships were some thirty-five miles north-west of Heligoland, they passed four vessels trawling with their lights up. Tyrwhitt decided to ignore them but a few minutes after they had dropped out of sight *Arethusa* intercepted German wireless traffic from a small ship's installation—apparently from the direction of the four trawlers.

The "telefunken" was not from any trawler, but from the patrolling submarine U-6. Within half an hour the ether was filled with wireless traffic from Heligoland, the British realizing that much of it was prefixed by the recognizable group for "urgent." Still three hours from the launching position, Tyrwhitt was debating whether to continue. If the ships went on, they would run the risk of being cut off from the North Sea and from escape before the seaplanes could be recovered. The seaplane carriers were not fast enough to outrun the German light cruisers. If these ships were at sea already—on patrol in the inner Bight, as the British thought was still the practice—there would be ample time for them to intercept the Harwich Force. But Tyrwhitt decided to go on. At that

> juncture a dim light appeared above the horizon almost dead ahead and rose slowly swelling and growing brighter the while. It was in fact the planet Venus rising, much magnified by a low fog that lay over the land, and for a time all those on *Arethusa*'s bridge took it for a fire balloon or a Zeppelin with some strange kind of searchlight. Then the Navigating Officer, Lieutenant Watson, said to Tyrwhitt: "Do you know that it is Christmas Day and that light bears due east?" "It then dawned on me," said Tyrwhitt afterwards, "that this was the Star in the East. From that moment I had no doubts or fears. I firmly believe the Almighty arranged for that star to act in this peculiar manner."[3]

The plan was for the force to steer between the set rendezvous points, which were at intervals of just under twenty miles. Moving from what had been position II, Tyrwhitt led his ships west until, at about 0810, they turned south-east at position III. It was along this leg that the British ships first sighted German forces.

The zeppelin L-6, alerted by U-6's warnings, had been criss-crossing the northern half of the Bight in search of the British before her captain decided to turn south-east and examine the central Bight outside Heligoland. His search was rewarded when he came upon Tyrwhitt's ships just after they had turned south from rendezvous IV. The Harwich Force, having sighted L-6 some time before, were waiting apprehensively to see just what the much-vaunted zeppelins could do.

Lagging behind the main force, unable to keep up speed because of trouble with her condensers, was the seaplane carrier *Empress*. She was an attractive target, isolated from her more heavily armed escorts. L-6 make straight for her, beginning the first real air-sea action in history. The zeppelin came in from directly astern, presenting a very difficult target to riflemen, the only antiaircraft defense the *Empress* possessed. The two cruisers, from three miles ahead, attempted to cover her with their special weapons, but they had to check fire at frequent intervals to avoid the risk of hitting the *Empress* as well. Despite these disadvantages, the *Empress*'s captain, Lieutenant F. W. Bowhill, soon discovered that the airship could not put her bows through the wind when altering course, but had rather to wear right around. He took immediate advantage of this:

> My method of defence was to watch (the Zeppelin) carefully as she manoeuvred into position directly overhead. I then went hard over. I could see her rudders put over to follow me, I put my helm over the other way. . . .[4]

By turning away eight points each time the zeppelin came over her, *Empress* was able to avoid the bombs that were dropped, although there were several near misses, one falling within twenty feet. When L-6 finally drew away, her bomb racks empty and her buoyancy decreasing, the *Empress* was again attacked, this time by two seaplanes from Borkum. They dropped hand bombs, which fell close alongside but did no damage.

Indeed, Tyrwhitt's ships that day led charmed lives. The Germans had been expecting an attack on the Bight, but it was not an air raid that they awaited. A project of Churchill's to create a squadron of dummy dreadnoughts had come to German ears in a much garbled form. The Admiralstab was now daily expecting an attempt to block all the major

German ports in the North Sea by means of some two hundred merchant steamers, escorted by the Channel Fleet and a vast number of destroyers. Fresh mine fields were laid to the south-west of Heligoland, and each day flotillas were sent out to scout as far out as Horns Reef, while great use was made of the zeppelins to keep observation on the entire Bight.

This routine had been followed for most of December, but, late on Christmas Eve, the Admiralstab received information that a British attack could be expected the next day. What saved Tyrwhitt's weak forces was that the German Command expected the penetration to involve British forces on a massive scale, too massive to permit the use of the battle squadrons, or risk a repetition of the disaster of 28 August by sending only the Scouting Groups out. Consequently, only U-boats and zeppelins were allowed into the Bight. The submarines had been sent to Borkum and to the Amrum Bank. It was from this latter position that U-6 made contact with the Harwich Force. The two available airships, L-5 and L-6, cruised to the west and north respectively. It would take more than their reports to convince von Ingenohl and the Admiralstab that Tyrwhitt's ships were not the vanguard of a much larger British force.

U-6 turned to follow the Harwich Force, trying to launch a torpedo attack, as well as to ascertain the exact strength of the British. The latter steamed south-east until, half an hour before dawn, the three seaplane carriers hove to and each hoisted its three seaplanes into the water, while the escort circled about. Despite the perfect conditions, two of the aircraft failed to take off. Thus, only seven made their way south-east toward Cuxhaven. The time taken to hoist the disabled aircraft inboard gave U-6 a chance to come up to the force, but, at 0820, Tyrwhitt turned his ships west toward the recovery position, foiling the U-6 just as she moved into a firing position.

There was then a respite from air attacks for an hour as the Harwich Force steered for the position where they planned to collect the seaplanes. Arriving at the spot at 0930, there was nothing to be seen. Tyrwhitt ordered his ships to spread out along a broad front and search to the south. A few minutes later, *Fearless* and her half flotilla joined Commodore (T) and were spread to the west, extending the search line to six miles. For nearly an hour the force continued south but found only two seaplanes. Keyes in the *Lurcher* had reported that he had picked up the crew of a third, but Tyrwhitt realized that the other four had been out for half an hour over their endurance and had to be considered lost. The search was confused by the appearance of the L-5 and more German seaplanes from Borkum. By now *Empress* had closed up with the rest of the force, but the German aircraft still made for her and the other seaplane carriers.

In the action that followed, the German seaplanes and airship again proved ineffective. No hits were made with bombs, and L-5 had the greatest difficulty in even making an accurate approach on Tyrwhitt's rapidly zigzagging ships. The seaplanes did a little better, spattering one of the light cruisers with splinters, but their tiny hand bombs could have effect only against personnel in exposed positions. As for the British, the relevant *Monograph* wrote:

> The air attacks to which he had been subjected convinced the Commodore that, given ordinary searoom, our ships had nothing to fear from either seaplanes or Zeppelins, an opinion apparently shared by his ships' companies who, with much merriment, looked upon their attacks chiefly as fine opportunities for letting fly with any weapon that chanced to be handy.[5]

As Tyrwhitt himself declared, "Zeppelins are not to be thought of as regards ships. Stupid great things, but very beautiful. It seemed a pity to shoot at them."[6] As the last attack died away, Commodore (T) signaled, "I wish all ships a Merry Christmas." At 1100, having reconnoitered right down into the Norderney Gat and not having found the four remaining seaplanes, Tyrwhitt sadly ordered his ships to return to Harwich, which they did without further interference.

Keyes's submarines were to see the most action that day and, happily, E-11 under Lieutenant Commander Martin Nasmith was able to rescue the crews of three of the four missing aircraft. E-11 had been off Norderney when seaplane no. 120 recognized her and landed close alongside, reporting that she had run out of fuel. E-11 attempted to tow the seaplane to the rendezvous, but just as the two got under way their progress was rudely interrupted by the sudden appearance of the zeppelin, L-5, as well as two more of the errant seaplanes, nos. 814 and 815, both of which had run out of fuel.

To add to Nasmith's worries, a submarine now appeared on the surface, heading directly toward his little group. In fact D-10, well out of her position, had seen the seaplanes land and was coming up to see if she could help. Thinking her a U-boat, and with L-5 barely a mile away and losing height rapidly, Nasmith hastily collected the crews of the seaplanes and machinegunned the floats before he dived, which was just as L-5 dropped two bombs onto the submarine. They were both near misses and E-11 managed to slip away to Harwich without further trouble. D-10, however, had a narrow escape. She had dived as L-5 approached, but her captain, Lieutenant Commander R. C. Halahan brought her back to the surface to check whether the seaplanes had sunk a little too early. He found L-5 directly above—at a height of barely fifty feet! Halahan resubmerged hastily amidst a hail of machinegun fire as

L-5 turned her Maxims onto D-10. Fortunately, the submarine suffered no damage and she, too, turned away for Harwich.

During the day, the other submarines criss-crossed the mine fields, which Tyrwhitt himself had, unknowing, only narrowly avoided. E-10, mistaking *Lurcher* for a German torpedo boat, was on the point of firing when her captain recognized the destroyer as Keyes's flagship. D-7 was spotted by L-5, fresh from her encounter with E-11 and D-10, and the zeppelin forced the submarine under and waited overhead while she tried to slip away. It was sixteen hours before D-7 was able to shake the airship off. She finally made Harwich just as she was being given up for lost. Despite the trouble caused by the zeppelins and the danger from mines, however, all Keyes's submarines returned from the Bight. In fact not a man had been lost in the operation, for it was discovered a few days later that the crew of the seventh and last aircraft had been picked up by a Dutch trawler and would be returned by the Netherlands as "ship-wrecked mariners," without being interned.

Again the German defensive scheme had failed. Von Ingenohl and the Admiralstab had been so preoccupied with the risk that the Harwich Force might be followed in by the Grand Fleet and that vast numbers of submarines might be waiting at the entrances to the estuaries to attack the heavy vessels as they emerged, that they had refused to allow out any of the High Sea Fleet's surface ships. As there were only two submarines on patrol—von Ingenohl later admitted that the number was clearly insufficient in view of the warning that had been received—and no time for any others to reach Tyrwhitt before he left the Bight, the reply had thus been left up to the zeppelins and seaplanes. This too had obviously not been enough, in spite of the fact that the airships cheerfully reported that they had sunk at least two submarines and damaged a seaplane carrier.

Von Ingenohl's inactivity had a further depressing effect on the fleet. The Scouting Group commanders had pleaded to be allowed into the Bight, but, despite their proposal to take out every torpedo-boat flotilla with them, they were refused. Apart from agreeing to send out all available submarines to Borkum when the next such warning came, von Ingenohl would not consider any alteration to his plans. Dissatisfaction among the senior officers of the fleet reached new heights as influential captains and flag officers began to discuss the possibility of having a new Commander in Chief appointed. The lack of confidence in von Inge-nohl's command was such that it would take a major success for the dissent to be stilled, and that success would have to be brought about very soon.

Although the British were relieved and delighted to discover the zeppelins were not the menace to ships at sea that had been feared, the raid had not been entirely satisfactory. Jellicoe's covering force had seen little and, despite several submarine alarms, pursued its sweep in peace. However, when late on the 26th, in bad weather and very poor visibility, the Grand Fleet went into Scapa, there was a serious collision between the super-dreadnoughts *Monarch* and *Conqueror*. Though neither was in any danger of sinking, both had been badly damaged and had to be sent after temporary repairs to dockyards in the south for major refits. It was a heavy blow to the British, for at a stroke two of the best ships in the battle line had been put out of action. Had the incident occurred a month, or even two weeks earlier, the position of the Grand Fleet relative to the High Sea Fleet would indeed have been precarious, but Jellicoe was able to reflect that all of four battleships of the *Iron Duke* class and the two ex-Turkish ships were now efficient units. Furthermore, his cruiser strength had been vastly increased—a Second Light Cruiser Squadron of four ships was constituted on 28 December—and that, if the detached battle cruisers had not yet rejoined Beatty, they were at least on their way home. Despite the many defects that were cropping up under war conditions, the fleet was a much more efficient unit than it had been in August.

While the Commander in Chief was considering his position in the north, the Admiralty was analyzing the raid from the reports of the air crews as they were brought in. As far as the destruction of any zeppelins was concerned, the venture was a complete failure, but it had been invaluable experience, and, as Tyrwhitt reported to his wife of the Cabal:

> They are awfully pleased with the raid and most complimentary. Couldn't be nicer! I was really surprised at everybody's pleasure and delight. They want more and I expect they will get it before long.[7]

Of the seven seaplanes which had taken off, only one got to the sheds, and because they had been mistakenly briefed that the base was seven miles further to the south, the crew failed to recognize them and contented themselves with dropping their bombs on some antiaircraft batteries. Another dropped its bombs on several large sheds on the island of Langeoog, thinking that they were for aircraft, while another dropped a bomb on a passing U-boat before a fractured fuel pump forced her down. Of the remainder, only two achieved anything of importance. No. 811 bombed the light cruiser *Graudenz* and achieved one near miss, but no. 136 had the most interesting career. With her engine misfiring, she had turned back and passed low over the Schillig Roads, causing considerable anxiety to the units anchored there. They opened up with machineguns and rifles. Despite the aircraft taking several hits, the pilot, Flight Commander C. F. Kilner, and the observer, Lieutenant Erskine Childers, RNVR, of *Riddle of the Sands* fame, were able to bring back much valuable information on the German arrangements. Childers was an expert on the area, having spent many summers sailing about the estuaries. He was able to pinpoint positions almost exactly by eye alone. His report was convincing proof of the value aircraft possessed in gathering information, though it had to be admitted that in this case the author's name was a considerable help. Plans for further raids were already in hand.

On 17 December, Sir Lewis Bayly and Sir Cecil Burney exchanged commands. There were several reasons for this rather unusual event. In the first place, neither admiral had been entirely happy in his previous job. Bayly did not like having to be second to Jellicoe. A restless, ambitious, and sometimes arrogant man, he chafed for active employment. Command of the First Battle Squadron had given him little outlet for his energies, consisting as it did largely of administrative and subordinate tactical duties. In conference, he was the first to propose large-scale attacks on the German coast and ports, and he had bombarded the C in C and the Admiralty with his proposals.

Burney, on the other hand, was not a man cut out by design or intent to be an independent leader. He was a good and efficient administrator, and a reliable and loyal subordinate. The C in C was delighted with the prospect of having Burney as his second. Bayly must have been an uncomfortable man to work with. It may well have been that he thought he knew better than the C in C in many matters—and made it obvious that he did. At all events, when the possibility of a change was raised, Jellicoe accepted it eagerly.

In fact, the transfer largely stemmed from the attitude Burney had to the employment of the Channel Fleet. He did not approve of the dispositions the Admiralty had made and considered that, were the Germans to make a large-scale attack with torpedo boats and submarines against his predreadnoughts, the Channel Fleet's position would be untenable. The only real destroyer support assigned him was Tyrwhitt's Harwich Force, and events soon proved that even this was problematic. Consequently, on several occasions Burney had been loath to take his ships out into the Channel or the southern part of the North Sea. He fell out with the First Sea Lord over this, for Fisher did not hesitate to label such conduct as pusillanimous.

Matters came to a head in early December. At that time, the Admiralty began to espouse a more aggressive policy of attacks on the Belgian and German bases and fortifications. The attack on Zeebrugge, for all its lack of results, had been the first evidence of this change of thinking.

Since Jellicoe refused point-blank to allow the use of any of the heavy ships of the Grand Fleet, the only units available were the predreadnoughts of the Fifth and Sixth Battle Squadrons—Burney's Channel Fleet. The exchange was thus inevitable and was heartily welcomed by all concerned, although the two commodores at Harwich were more doubtful. It seemed as if the first venture would be an attempt to capture the island of Borkum. Both Tyrwhitt and Keyes had already clashed with Bayly over the latter's conception of the risks involved in making such an attack.

Bayly seems to have had the Borkum project in mind when he hoisted his flag in the predreadnought *Lord Nelson*. He had some support in the Cabal, with Churchill wholly for the idea, and A. K. Wilson somewhat less so, but neither Oliver nor Fisher was happy about the scheme. It was unusual that matters had got so far, for, as Oliver complained:

> Churchill wanted to land troops at Borkum Island and capture it. Emden was to be captured at the same time—both impossible to hold if captured as we had not the land forces. Fisher wanted to send the Grand Fleet into the Baltic and convey a Russian Army from Petrograd to land and take Berlin. . . . Wilson wanted to bombard Heligoland . . . and land and capture it; our old ships with their short 12″ guns would have stood little chance against the modern guns of shore batteries. If captured, every time supplies were required would involve a major operation for the Grand Fleet in the minefields, and the island was within gun range of the mainland. I hated all these projects but had to be careful what I said. The saving clause was that two of the three were always violently opposed to the plan of the third under discussion.[8]

At the same time, Fisher's "Baltic Project" was only embryonic. The First Sea Lord would not present his scheme in its entirety until well into 1915. For the moment, it was the plans of Churchill and Wilson, who had made a temporary alliance, that looked to become policy. Events, however, overtook their schemes.

When Bayly arrived in the Channel Fleet, he was annoyed to discover the poor state of the old battleships' gunnery. With few destroyers and fewer cruisers, Burney had not felt able to send the predreadnoughts out for exercises. While he had attempted to set up a range around Sheerness, the distances involved did not permit this. As a result, most of the Sixth Battle Squadron and all of the Fifth Battle Squadron had hardly fired their guns since the war began. Bayly first proposed that he exercise the ships by conducting a preliminary bombardment of Borkum, but, wisely, this was not approved as the venture would have required the support of the entire Grand Fleet. The ships' gunnery efficiency was obviously dubious, and there would be no way of telling how well they had shot. The War Staff considered quite rightly that the Channel Fleet would have to be fully worked up before they would allow Bayly to bring it into the North Sea.

Instead, Bayly was ordered to take the Fifth Battle Squadron from Sheerness to Portland. From this base, the War Staff considered, he could exercise the battleships without risk from submarines. In exchange for the Fifth, the Sixth Battle Squadron, then lying at Portland, would be sent to Sheerness. In order to give these latter ships a chance to exercise, the movement was to be delayed until 30 December.

The submarine situation throughout December had been quiet. There had been no firm reports of U-boats for several weeks. But there were U-boats in the area and one, U-24, was at sea when Bayly took his battleships out of The Nore. U-24 should have been seen by the patrols, but continuous heavy weather and recurrent machinery defects had sapped the strength of Rear Admiral Hood's destroyer force. The Channel had been divided into eight areas, each with a destroyer stationed in it day and night, but rarely could all eight be manned at once. The destroyer crews' initial enthusiasm was being worn down by the monotonous routine, lack of rest in harbor, and the ever-present cold and damp. The French submarine and destroyer patrols on the other side of the Channel were in a similar state.

U-24 arrived in the Straits of Dover at dusk on 28 December. In the heavy weather of the next few days, she was able to elude all the Allied patrols while she waited for a major target. Meanwhile, Bayly was preparing to move. There had been no submarine warnings for the Channel, and Bayly "who had a slight contempt for the submarine" did not think that an escort would be necessary. At the Admiralty's insistence, however, he agreed to have six destroyers for the passage from The Nore up to Folkestone. On the 29th, Bayly ordered Tyrwhitt to make the necessary arrangements. Folkestone was the furthest normal western limit of German submarine penetration, and Bayly must have been confident that his ships were safe to passage unaccompanied past this point. It is important to keep in mind, when considering Bayly's failure to order an escort for the rest of his journey and exercises, that the Admiralty itself only ordered an escort for the Sixth Battle Squadron from Folkestone to The Nore—and not before.

Whatever may be said of his plans, Bayly's actions over the three days that he had the Channel Fleet at sea indicate what can only be described, after the events of September, as a complete disregard for the submarine menace. The Fifth Battle Squadron sailed from Sheerness at 1000 on 30 December, into calm seas. Bayly had eight battleships and two light cruisers in company and they were deployed in single line ahead, Bayly in the *Lord Nelson* leading the battleships, with the cruisers fallen in astern. The six destroyers from Harwich were spread ahead of the force, with three forward of either beam, for the time that they stayed with Fifth Battle Squadron. Bayly informed the Admiralty before he sailed that the force would be steaming at 15 knots, but, for no apparent reason, on leaving harbor he ordered a speed of only 8 knots, and at no time did Bayly order any zigzagging. Thus it was that the battleships came down Channel. Two hours later, the Sixth Battle Squadron passed on its way to The Nore, and, once through the Straits of Dover, Bayly dismissed the destroyers and began his tactical exercises.

By dawn on the 31st, the force was thirteen miles south of Portland Bill. With the weather showing signs of worsening, the battleships began to prepare for heavy seas. All that day, Bayly exercised his command, as they steamed to a position south of Start Point and then reversed course back up the Channel. Even these tactical exercises were conducted in slow time, for the greatest speed that the Vice Admiral ever ordered was 12 knots. As dusk fell, Bayly decided to turn down Channel. By this time there was a strong southerly sea running, but he wanted to be outside Portland at dawn, and it was not yet rough enough to prevent the squadron steaming in formation.

It might have been better for the British had the weather been foul, or at least that the very heavy seas that came up after 0100 had risen earlier. The conditions were ideal for a night torpedo attack. The sea was choppy, and a swell was running, but it was not yet enough to drive any small craft into shelter. A fresh breeze was blowing, there was a full moon, and the night was cloudy but clear, with a visibility of some three miles. The battleships were still in line ahead, at intervals of only two cables, and were steaming at only 10 knots. *Topaze* and *Diamond* were a mile behind. The Channel Fleet, in short, presented a target that was a submariner's dream.

U-24 was in the western Channel. The submarine had sighted both the Fifth and the Sixth Battle Squadron on the previous day, the former as it left Portland on the 30th, and the latter as it passed early on New Year's Eve. She had spent four hours attempting a submerged attack as Bayly conducted his exercises, but failed. Her captain, Lieutenant Commander Schneider, gave up at last and withdrew to recharge the submarine's batteries.

When Schneider had last seen the Fifth Battle Squadron, the ships were steering east, apparently for Portsmouth, and he had given up hope of making an attack. When the charge was completed, Schneider turned U-24 for Start Point, running on the surface. At 0008, on the morning of New Year's Day, he sighted three large ships on his starboard beam.

Recognizing them as battleships, he turned U-24 and fired one torpedo at the third, the *Queen*. The angle was unfavorable and the torpedo missed astern. Schneider now saw the other five battleships, which had become separated from the leaders, and he turned toward them. Crossing astern of the last in the line, he turned again and fired two torpedoes at her. One struck. Schneider's victim was the predreadnought *Formidable*. The torpedo exploded amidships, under the forward funnel. When he realized that his ship had been badly damaged, *Formidable*'s captain, A. N. Loxley, hauled her out of line and turned her head to wind. The old battleship was soon in a bad way. Her engine-room flooded rapidly, and all steam and power went as she took on a heavy list to starboard. The seas were rising rapidly as, with great difficulty, the ship's boats were got out and launched. Loxley did not think that the ship could be saved and ordered the stokers and engine-room personnel up from below. In the surf around the ship one of the cutters capsized, smashing against the side, and several other boats were damaged. The *Formidable*'s remaining personnel began to heave wooden mess tables and other gear over the side to support men in the water.

In the darkness, only *London* of the battleships had seen *Formidable* leave the line and she reported this fact to Bayly, not knowing the reason why. The two light cruisers had seen the incident, however, and *Topaze* immediately closed the stricken *Formidable* and began to pick up survivors. A passing liner was hailed and asked to assist, but she refused and continued on her way. *Diamond*, which had been standing off, due to the U-boat danger, now closed the battleship and began to join in the rescue operations. As she did, at 0310, U-24 fired another torpedo into the *Formidable*. Schneider, following the battleship's progress at periscope depth, had decided that she was not sinking fast enough. The torpedo struck the battleship amidships on her port side. The flooding immediately brought her back to an even keel, although she was settling fast. Satisfied with his work, Schneider took U-24 away to the southeast. *Topaze* had seen the periscope, but since there were so many men in the water and *Diamond* was foul of the range, she dared not open fire.

At 0300, just as he turned the Squadron east-north-east to head for Portland, Bayly received the signal from *Topaze* reporting the nature of the damage to the *Formidable* and the progress of operations. With the strict Admiralty instructions as to submarines, Bayly could do little with his own ships and had to content himself with ordering out light craft. As he ordered 18 knots, the predreadnoughts' maximum operational speed, Bayly could see clearly the *Formidable*'s distress signals to the east. Ordering *Diamond* and *Topaze* to continue to stand by the stricken ship, he turned the squadron now north-north-east in an

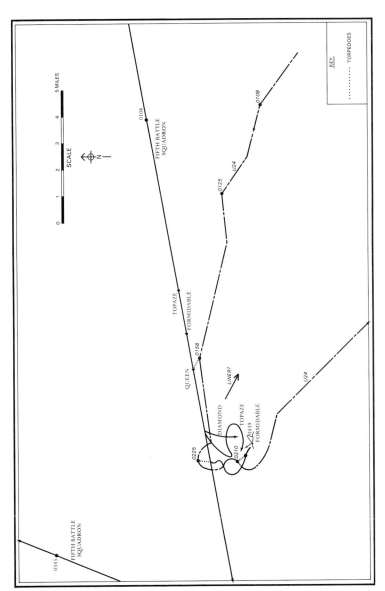

The Sinking of the *Formidable*

HMS *Formidable*

attempt to get well clear of the area. All thought of the exercises forgotten, Bayly's purpose was now to get the remaining battleships into harbor without loss.

The seas were steadily becoming rougher across the Channel. *Diamond* and *Topaze* became almost unmanageable as they slowed to rescue men from the water. The torpedo boats and other craft sent out from Portland and Devonport found the going so hard that they were forced to turn back and run for shelter. At 0439, the *Formidable* closed matters by quietly going under bow first. The two light cruisers stayed on the scene until daylight and did the best they could, but many of the boats in the water had been capsized or crushed, and men could not long survive in a mid-winter Channel storm.

By 0900, it was clear that no more could have survived and *Diamond* and *Topaze* reluctantly turned for Portland, carrying altogether only 114 men out of *Formidable*'s complement of 780. Four destroyers were sent out from Portsmouth by the Commander in Chief, Sir Hedworth Meux, at the request of the Admiralty, but only the *Savage* found anything and this was but five bodies. Yet there were more survivors. The *Formidable*'s launch, though badly holed, managed to get away from the ship, but had been lost in the darkness before she could make either of the cruisers. The 73 men aboard her were picked up at noon by the Brixham sailing trawler *Provident*, having survived more than twelve hours in the heaviest seas in living memory. One other boat, the ship's pinnace, also stayed afloat and close to midnight put into Lyme Regis with 6 of the 55 men aboard dead of exposure and 3 dying. Out of the 780 men, only 233 had survived. Captain Loxley and most of his crew went down with the ship.

U-24 made Zeebrugge on 3 January, to find that Germany was ringing with her exploit. The announcement of the loss of the *Formidable* was the first clear admission that Britain had made that the policy of attrition was having any effect, however small, on the battle line. The success had a considerable tonic effect both on Germany and the Imperial Navy. In Britain, conversely, the news came as a heavy blow. The loss of the *Audacious* was already rumored, that of *Bulwark* and the numerous cruisers known, the sinking of the *Formidable* came hard upon the failure to stop the raid on Scarborough. Yet again, popular opinion was doubtful over the state of the Royal Navy and the Board of Admiralty which controlled it.

The Admiralty's reaction to the disaster was swift. Destroyers were hastily sent out to convey into harbor the various battleships on passage around the British Isles. No heavy ship was allowed out to sea without a strong escort and the brand-new 15″ gun battleship *Queen Elizabeth* was sent down to Gibraltar so as to be able to conduct her gunnery firings in a safe area. It is worth noting, however, that the Admiralty's response was not quite complete. The battleship *Commonwealth* had been sent westabout from the Third Battle Squadron to refit at Chatham. Unescorted, she was into the Channel and off the Start exactly twenty-four hours after the sinking of the *Formidable*. Had U-24 remained on station, she might well have been able to claim *Commonwealth* with her last two torpedoes, for it was not until well into the afternoon of the 2nd that the battleship was met by any destroyers.

Bayly came in for a good deal of criticism. His initial defense was that the Admiralty had given him no warning that submarines could be found so far to the west, that they had made no protest when he informed them that he intended to dismiss his escort off Folkestone, and that they had indeed made precisely the same arrangements for the *Duncans*, which sailed unescorted from Portland until they were met by four destroyers, again off Folkestone. And, as Captain C. E. Le Mesurier, commanding the *Cornwallis*, remarked to Commander Dewar of the *Prince of Wales*:

The Admiralty gave Admiral Bayly written orders to moor targets off Portland and to practise the fifth battle squadron at bombarding a buoyed area with two ships anchored in the vicinity for marking purposes. On the face of that they had the impertinence to ask him if he did not know the Channel was infested with submarines, to which Bayly replied that if it were so, why was he not informed.[9]

Despite the Admiralty's definite measure of culpability, the real point was that Bayly had failed to exercise even simple common sense. As Fisher wrote to Oliver and Churchill of Bayly's first explanation:

> It is pressing to send following telegram to Admiral Bayly, "Remain at your present anchorage at Portland pending further orders," for the reason that his letter indicates no sense on his part of the dangers of submarine attack and of necessary precautions, and until this telegram is sent we may have another calamity put upon us by a pig-headed officer, for it must have been patent to every officer and man in his squadron that to steam at slow speed in close order on a moonlit night on a steady course in the vicinity of the Start was to make his Squadron an easy target [Dewar noted that "the lack of ordinary precautions struck me at the time."]. . . . There's not a word in his letter exculpating himself or to indicate that he won't do it again, hence this telegram should be sent to him, pending the further action on his report of the disaster.[10]

Bayly might have been retained in command had he not been so obviously convinced of his own rectitude. Even Churchill began to insist on his removal, writing to Jellicoe that the Vice Admiral had "outraged every principle of prudence and good seamanship without the slightest military object."[11] Bayly was relieved of his command by telegram on 16 January. The Admiralty's view was summed up when they wrote to him on 11 January, that his behavior:

> . . . was marked by a want of prudence and good seamanship in the avoidance of un-necessary risks inexplicable in an officer holding high and responsible command.[12]

Bayly was to take but half a page to describe the incident in his autobiography, remarking that he "asked for a court-martial, but was refused—I have never known why. It sounds like a fairy story . . . and presumably was done to encourage other admirals."[13]

Bayly was quite right, but Churchill decided to let him down lightly by sending him to replace Sir Alexander Bethell, the new C in C of the Channel Fleet, as president of the Royal Naval College, Greenwich. To the end of his days Bayly continued to protest that he had done nothing wrong. Jellicoe, oddly enough, had some sympathy with Bayly. He wrote to Bethell on 22 January, noting that he was "much surprised at the Admiralty action, which seems to me unwise. The constant slights are a great pity and tend to disorganization. Here I suffer terribly from them."[14]

With Bayly's undignified exit, the ambitious projects to make use of the predreadnoughts died a sudden, if only temporary, death. Bethell was a much quieter and less aggressive man than his unfortunate predecessor, although Fisher always held him in high regard. Not only was the fire-eating Bayly out of favor, but even the obstinate A. K. Wilson seems at this time to have faced the realization that the submarine had utterly changed warfare at sea and that battleships could not be sent into enemy waters without the risk of considerable losses. For the next month he was noticeably silent on the subject of ventures with the predreadnoughts against the German islands. The Admiralty Board as a whole had actually taken fright, though for rather different reasons. The loss raised many of the old doubts about Churchill's administration and the First Lord had his hands full both inside and outside the Parliament. Fisher, on the other hand, was now going through a stage of submarine-phobia worse than any Jellicoe ever suffered. On 4 January, he wrote to the C in C:

> In the meantime, the one great naval policy is to conserve our ships and not recklessly send them out as food for German submarines! Personally, in your place, not one single vessel of my Fleet should ever go outside Scapa Flow! Not one, not even a little one! But I don't wish to fetter your discretion, but sure as fate you'll lose another *Audacious* if you do send your ships out![15]

The more prudent Jellicoe, who realized what an effect prolonged inactivity in dreary Scapa Flow would have on the efficiency and morale of the Grand Fleet, paid him little attention and continued his sweeps in the north. One thing was clear, however. With the land war in France already bogged down and apparently no way of applying fresh pressure on the Germans in the North Sea with any chance of success, it would not be long before the Admiralty, willing or unwilling, would have to look for some fresh theater of operations.

CHAPTER 10

The First
Offensive Mine Field

As the New Year dawned, the War Group was searching for some means of scoring a success without having to involve heavy forces. They returned to the vexed question of mine laying in German waters. The initial moral objections had gone, since the Germans now planted fields in British waters without warning as a matter of course. But there was still a considerable division over the nature of mine warfare and how best the few mine-layers could be employed. The "strategic" school, concentrated in the Admiralty, argued that the Bight should be heavily and continuously mined, but this body of thought was violently opposed by the "tactical" school. These, led by Jellicoe and Keyes, pointed out that the old, slow mine-layers would be death traps in German waters and that the British mines were of such poor quality that they would break their moorings within days, betraying the location of any field immediately. They argued that the waters of the Bight should be kept clear of mine fields because they would limit the operations of British submarines and light forces as much as they did the Germans. Keyes had visions of concentrating his submarines round the habitual routes of the Germans into the North Sea the next time a raid was mounted. A mine field laid across the passages would cause the High Sea Fleet to change its movements and force Keyes to spread his submarines over every entrance to German ports and rivers to be sure of catching it. Jellicoe, for his part, wanted to use properly equipped fast mine-layers across the German line of retreat when next the High Sea Fleet ventured out. Such utilization would minimize the poor quality of the British mines, since they would have no time either to break away or drag. (Some of the mines from the early fields in the Channel had been found to have dragged their moorings fifteen miles in a month.)

Oliver was keen on the prospect of a mine-laying raid* and his view prevailed in the War Group, the other members of which may have welcomed the proposals as a last and welcome, if unglamorous, alternative to the admission that a purely defensive strategy was the only solution. Keyes's argument was accepted as valid to some degree, and the decision was made to mine the area around the Amrum Bank, to the north of the Bight. The High Sea Fleet did not normally use this passage, since it was not on a direct line between its ports and the British coast, but submarines, and merchantmen coming down the Jutland coast from the Atlantic to avoid the British patrols did. Oliver considered that interference with these activities would be worth the risks—especially as information was now coming through that the blockade was not as successful as had been hoped and that the German seaborne trade was reviving.

Oliver presented an interesting bait with his proposal, one that was certainly to prove attractive to Commodore (T). Since the mine fields, whether they claimed any victims or not, would soon reveal their position to the Germans when the first "drifters" broke their moorings, it stood to reason that the Germans would send out minesweepers to deal with them, possibly accompanied by covering forces of greater or lesser strength and that this would be the perfect opportunity for Tyrwhitt to make another sweep into Heligoland Bight with the Harwich Force.

On 5 January, Oliver issued the orders for the first phase of his plan, the mine-laying raid, which was designated Operation OQ. Escorted by Harwich Force destroyers, four of the elderly *Apollo* class mine-layers, including the *Naiad* as senior ship, the *Apollo, Iphigenia*, and *Latona*, were to sail from The Nore at daylight on 7 January. The destroyers were assigned only as an antisubmarine escort until the *Aurora* and *Undaunted* met the mine-layers outside Harwich at dusk on the same day. The two light cruisers would convoy the mine-layers to a point thirty miles to the west of the Amrum Bank, where the light cruisers would wait in case their support was required until the mine-layers returned. Tyrwhitt was not to go, because the *Arethusa* was undergoing repairs, and Wilmot Nicholson in the *Aurora* was to be senior officer.

The day before the ships sailed was calm and the mine-layers and destroyers left Sheerness in relatively high visibility and smooth seas. As is so often the case with such weather in a North Sea winter, a fog

---

*Oliver, as Naval Assistant to Fisher, had been responsible for the original conversion of the *Apollo* class to mine-layers in 1909, when the First Sea Lord would have had them scrapped.

descended that was so thick that the mine-layers' senior officer, Captain M. H. Cobbe, had to order his ships and their escorts to anchor for two hours. They were under way again at 1145 and, at 1600, met the *Aurora* and *Undaunted*, which had been similarly delayed. The operation very nearly did not proceed beyond this stage as the Admiralty had by now learnt of the fog and telegraphed to Tyrwhitt to order Nicholson and Cobbe to delay proceedings for twenty-four hours. Tyrwhitt, who knew that the cruisers and mine-layers had met and were on their way, did nothing of the sort, despite the fact that he fretted somewhat because "it was the first sizeable operation that had taken place without his presence," and told the Admiralty so.[1] They did not dispute the point and replied that night, "Let Plan continue."[2]

The operation went as planned, despite the fact that the mine-layers found that the "mine-catchers" fitted to their bows tended to break adrift, with resultant chaos. The mines were laid on the night of the 8th. There were, fortunately for the elderly mine-layers, no German patrols out on the Amrum Bank that night and conditions were perfect for their operation. The mine-layers were hidden by frequent heavy rain squalls and choppy seas, and they completed their lays without interruption and withdrew to the west to rejoin *Aurora* and *Undaunted*.

The force returned to harbor on 10 January, and Cobbe and his crews received the well-merited appreciation of the Admiralty. The old *Apollos* were floating death traps as far as offensive operations in the North Sea were concerned, and Oliver fully realized this. On the same day as the *Apollos* returned, he ordered the requisitioning of three new, 23-knot cross-Channel ferries, *Princess Margaret, Biarritz*, and *Princess Irene*. Denny Brothers at Dumbarton were ordered to do the conversion, and within three months these three ships were in commission, adding (or rather, creating) a fast-laying capability of nearly two thousand mines altogether.

On 11 January, the plan was drawn up for the attack on the German minesweepers and designated OR. Tyrwhitt was to take two cruisers and sixteen destroyers into the Bight, and dividing these latter into two divisions, have them fall simultaneously upon the Germans from the north and south at dawn on the 13th, while the cruisers waited to the west as support. The Admiralty made one strict provision with which Tyrwhitt could not disagree. If the weather was so bad that the destroyers would not be able to run away from any German light cruisers encountered, then the operation was to be canceled.

Commodore (T) had barely taken his ships out of harbor when he realized that the seas were too heavy. Bitterly disappointed, he ordered the force to turn back. It was not, in spite of Tyrwhitt's frustration, an entirely gloomy homecoming for him, because already Keyes was immersed in plans for yet another seaplane raid, this time on the Emden zeppelin sheds, or, if the weather continued bad, a "simple" probe of the German patrols around Heligoland.

The Amrum Bank minefield had effects that were unlooked for by the Admiralty. As well as arresting much of the merchant traffic to and from the north, it upset preparations for a second raid on the east coast. Emboldened by the success against Hartlepool and Scarborough, there had been general agreement in the Admiralstab and among the fleet staff that the venture should be repeated. Hipper was particularly enthusiastic and von Ingenohl agreed to bring the entire High Sea Fleet out as a covering force and, for a change, keep it within supporting distance of the Scouting Groups.

The target for the new raid was to be the Humber, and the main objective the laying of a mine field outside the anchorage, for the Germans now believed that there were at least six heavy ships based there. The attack was to take place at dawn on 13 January. The discovery of the mine field altered all this. Von Ingenohl was terrified by the possibility that the High Sea Fleet might be cut off from its bases, and he was inclined to believe that the Amrum field was the beginning of some deep British scheme to seal off the Bight. At all events, the Commander in Chief refused to take the battle squadrons into the North Sea until the passage over the Amrum Bank was clear.

To sweep the field would take at least ten days, more if the weather were bad, but the operation would have been delayed to include the entire fleet, had it not been for the resurfacing of an old preoccupation of the Germans—the possibility that the British might attempt to block the entrances to the various rivers. Vastly exaggerated reports of the dummy warships that had been fitting out at Belfast were now pouring into the Admiralstab from its agents. A considerable body of opinion believed that the laying of the mine field was the signal that the raid was imminent. As a consequence, von Ingenohl's decision was confirmed; the heavy ships were to be retained in home waters to deal with the attack.

This did not mean that the light forces had to stay in harbor as well and, on 14 January, Hipper was able to detach Captain Harder of the *Stralsund* to take his ship and her sister, the *Strassburg*, to lay the field outside the Humber. Accompanied by the Fourth Torpedo Boat Flotilla, they sailed at 1600 and emerged from the Bight into a heavy head sea. The torpedo boats suffered badly:

> . . . seas washed over them, preventing both observation and signalling; boats, ventilators, and weather screens were carried away, bridges driven

in, gunsights bent, and ammunition washed overboard. In some boats the fires in the forward boiler-rooms were put out; and V-25 and V-26 collided in the dark. . . .[3]

Their commander eventually ordered them to turn back, knowing that the small torpedo boats could never keep up with the more weatherly light cruisers.

The weather moderated enough to let the *Strassburg* lay her 120 mines and the rest of the operation passed off without trouble, *Stralsund* and *Strassburg* getting into Wilhelmshaven after dusk that night. In fact, since the mine field, which had been laid well to the south of the Humber near the Indefatigable Banks, was well away from any swept channels, it was of little use, and although it soon claimed an unfortunate trawler, the mines remained otherwise undiscovered for six months.

Hipper was relieved to see the two light cruisers return. The doctrine of sending such ships into enemy waters without any heavy support was a dangerous one, all the more so since the cruiser strength had been grievously depleted by the losses since August. Any further raids should, he believed, have the support of the First Scouting Group, if not the entire fleet. The battle cruisers would at least be able to fight anything from which they could not run, which was more than could be said for two detached light cruisers.

Keyes and Tyrwhitt soon had the plan for a new seaplane raid in shape which, after several consultations at the Admiralty with the War Group, was set for the first fine weather. Plan Z1, as it came to be called, was somewhat more sophisticated than the earlier ventures. Keyes this time intended to keep two submarines with each of his destroyers, setting the remainder along the various entrances to the German anchorages. Commodore (S) hoped that this time events would not run away from him, as had happened all too often in the previous months.

Tyrwhitt decided on one major change in his dispositions. Keeping all three carriers and their escorts together was cumbersome and could possibly prove vulnerable, in the event of repeated air or submarine attacks. In Plan Z1 each carrier would operate independently, escorted by a division of destroyers as it launched, awaited, and recovered its aircraft. Seven miles to the east, to take the brunt of any attack, would be stationed three light cruisers and a fourth division of destroyers.

Admirable as the arrangements were, all depended upon the seas within the Heligoland Bight being calm and, in the dismal weather of mid-January, there seemed little possibility of this. On 14 January, when the two had barely got back to Harwich from a previous session, Keyes and Tyrwhitt were recalled to the Admiralty. In the discussions that followed, Plan Z1 was postponed. Yet again, they had only just returned to their ships when word came that they were wanted back at Whitehall. Tyrwhitt, who was very tired and might be excused for venting some spleen over such peripatetic activities, complained bitterly that he thought "they must have all gone off their onions."[4]

The recall was justified, for Room 40 now had indication from intercepted wireless traffic that the Germans were concerned by the possibility of a British attack on their ports, and that they were taking defensive precautions. The conclusion that the Admiralty drew, quite reasonably, was that the Heligoland Bight would be thick with German torpedo boat patrols. Tyrwhitt was ordered to make a sweep north-east from Borkum, to the Horns Reef, to gather up the patrols which were believed to concentrate along that line. Specific arrangements were made to ensure that Tyrwhitt's forces would not become too scattered, while Keyes was ordered to send three submarines to lie off Heligoland and the Ems. As a covering force, Beatty was ordered out of Rosyth with his Battle Cruiser Force, to lie outside the Bight until the Harwich Force had withdrawn.

Tyrwhitt sailed from Harwich at 1430 on 18 January, straight into a blizzard. Conditions in the Bight had been predicted clear, but this was not the case when the Harwich Force arrived at the start of their sweep at 0630 on the 20th, and all that was seen amongst the snowstorms and choppy seas was a single seaplane. Beatty ordered a general withdrawal at 1000, and the disappointed British forces turned for home.

The sortie had been a distinct failure, save to confirm that the Germans did not allow patrols out as a matter of course. No material success had been achieved, while, on the debit side, two destroyers of the Harwich Force had suffered damage in accidents during the return, and, on the 21st, Keyes discovered to his grief that E-10 was missing without trace. Even the usual morale boost from venturing into German waters was absent, for the weather had been so poor as to make the entire sortie a sodden misery for all the crews.

The morning of the 20th had found only seven U-boats at sea around the Bight, although air reconnaisance was sent up in the morning. The submarines at first saw nothing, but the seaplane observed by the Harwich Force immediately turned back for its base with the report that at least one hundred ships were inside the Bight. The pilot had been too eager; had he waited for a few more minutes to make a precise count, he would have realized that there were far fewer ships than that, as well as the fact that there were no heavy ships among them.

To the south-west, U-8 and U-35 had both sighted Beatty's ships and were making desperate efforts to raise the signal stations on wireless to pass on this information. It was only the report of the seaplane that von

Ingenohl received, and, on the strength of this, at 1000 he alerted all the coast defenses, ordered the High Sea Fleet to raise steam, and recalled all surface units at sea in the Inner Bight. He sent out more seaplanes and submarines, but when the reports of the aircraft came in, it became obvious that the British had withdrawn and that the entire sortie had been intended as some kind of raid on isolated units in the outer Bight. Von Ingenohl did entertain some hopes that the seven U-boats at sea might have been able to achieve something, but these were dashed when only six returned, with the unenviable score of one merchant ship, and—as U-22 had to confess—U-7 from Flanders, which had been mistaken for an enemy submarine. U-31 was never heard of again.

Although the weather seemed set foul, both antagonists appreciated that some new move was needed to restore morale and confidence. The Germans, for the time, seemed content to wait until a clear and protracted lull in the heavy weather had set in, but Tyrwhitt and Keyes were already pushing for permission to go ahead with another raid on the zeppelin sheds at the first opportunity. A plan against Cuxhaven had been devised and this and the one against the Emden base had received the new code names Z1 and Z2 respectively. On 21 January, Tyrwhitt began to think that the weather might clear. If it did, he could go ahead. The raids were all the more important now because, in the past few days, the zeppelins had made their first substantial attacks on England, and there was little that could be done to stop them. Despite the enthusiasm at the Admiralty and in the Harwich Force for the project, yet again the venture was to be overtaken by events. The Germans were on the move.

CHAPTER 11

The Battle of the Dogger Bank

The Germans were becoming increasingly worried by the apparently infallible means which the British possessed of detecting their operations and intentions. While they did not identify the true reason, there were two schools of thought in the High Command and the fleet. One held that Berlin and the naval dockyards were rife with spies and that the British had penetrated even to the highest levels. Repeated witch hunts discovered little of importance but their lack of result did little to discourage the proponents of the theory.

The second body of opinion was largely to be found in the High Sea Fleet and won special favor with von Ingenohl's Chief of Staff, Vice Admiral Eckermann. He and the commanders at sea, especially Hipper, could not rid themselves of the thought that some of the many fishing vessels that littered the North Sea might be wireless-equipped observation vessels with instructions to report any movements observed to the Admiralty. Such vessels would, of course, be masquerading as neutrals under the Dutch flag. It was indeed true that every time the Germans had been to sea they passed some vessels apparently fishing and to link them with the British habit of being uncomfortably prompt in reply to any sortie was not unreasonable, although incorrect.

Eckermann, Hipper, their staffs, and the senior officers of the Scouting Groups agreed that if such spy ships did exist they would be concentrated upon the Dogger Bank. Midway between the Continent and Great Britain, this shallow patch was not only the best fishing ground in the North Sea, but also straddled the direct route between the Jade and the east coast; a route which Hipper's ships had taken to bombard the English ports. A wireless message from the Dogger Bank and a prompt response by the Battle Cruiser Force would, the Germans felt, enable it to be in position by the time the First Scouting Group began its withdrawal. Furthermore, the German intelligence was that British scouting craft might also be on the bank, without the support of their own heavy units, in which case the Scouting Groups were being offered the perfect opportunity to avenge the debacle of Heligoland Bight.

The intentions of the High Sea Fleet in this regard had largely been frustrated by heavy weather. Emboldened by his earlier successes, Hipper proposed and had accepted a raid on the Firth of Forth by mine-laying cruisers that would be combined with an attack on the British forces on the Dogger Bank. The operations would be covered by the First Scouting Group, supported by the High Sea Fleet itself. Success in both missions would neutralize the Battle Cruiser Force and the British information gatherers at one blow. Continuous bad weather had prevented, however, the execution of the raid and the Germans had resigned themselves to an idle New Year.

Then, quite suddenly, on 22 January the weather cleared, promising calm days for at least a space. Hipper and Eckermann felt that the opportunity could not be wasted. They persuaded von Ingenohl to allow the use of the First Scouting Group. The moment was not an auspicious one for the Imperial Navy since much of its frontline strength was unavailable. The Third Battle Squadron, which consisted of the new and powerful battleships of the *König* class, was conducting exercises and firings in the Baltic. It was their first chance to do so since the ships had commissioned, and the practice was badly needed. The Scouting Groups were also well under strength. Von Ingenohl had seized the chance afforded by the lull to send *Von der Tann* for a much needed refit. She could not be operational for at least two weeks. Several of the light cruisers were also refitting and the torpedo boat strength was well under the normal, because winter conditions were hard on the small ships and inexperience had several times caused unnecessary damage.

Nevertheless, Hipper and Eckermann continued with their plan for a raid on the Dogger Bank. They intended it would follow the pattern of the earlier sorties against England, Hipper using the Scouting Groups to perform the required task while the High Sea Fleet remained in the east of the North Sea, covering the retreat. Hipper pointed out that the sortie would remove a very dangerous threat, since it seemed to him quite possible that it would not be long before fishing vessels in British employment graduated from acting as observation platforms to dropping floating mines or even torpedoes in the path of German forces.

To the criticism that his ships stood a good chance of being cut off by the British, Hipper replied that he intended to turn at the slightest suspicion of their presence. Nevertheless, the plan was flawed in both conception and execution. Von Ingenohl was unwilling to take the operational battle squadrons to sea. The Kaiser had been unhappy at the risks taken with his heavy ships in the past few months and reaffirmed his objections to their employment outside German waters in no uncertain terms. To von Ingenohl's mind, a sweep in the North Sea would be inviting trouble. He would not take the battle squadrons out of the Jade.

The Scouting Groups were another matter. The C in C agreed to their employment without support. He did not believe that the High Sea Fleet could possibly be required in the course of what would be a twenty-four hour operation. He also made the point that he felt that any sign of the battleships preparing to proceed to sea would somehow bring the raid to the notice of the British and prejudice the chances of success of the operation.

Somewhat unhappy at the prospect of going without the support of the battle fleet, Hipper was nonetheless pleased by the opportunity for action when von Ingenohl finally gave him a verbal order to "reconnoitre the Dogger Bank." This was confirmed at 1000 on the 23rd when the Commander in Chief sent a signal in cipher:

> To *Seydlitz*, for Senior officer of the Scouting Vessels. 1st and 2nd Scouting Groups, Senior Officer of torpedo boats and two flotillas chosen by Senior Officer of Scouting Vessels to reconnoitre the Dogger Bank. Proceed to sea this evening after dark, return after dark the following evening.

On the other side of the North Sea, the listening British wireless stations intercepted the signal and passed it to Room 40.

In gathering his forces, Hipper made one error that was to have disastrous consequences; he yielded to persuasion and included the armored cruiser *Blücher* in the First Scouting Group. A hybrid, with no correspondent in the Royal Navy, she should never have been taken. Weakly armed and armored, and a good 3 knots slower than the other ships of the First Scouting Group, she destroyed the homogeneity of Hipper's unit. The force was now not only too weak to stand up to the British battle cruisers, but too slow to escape them in a chase. In spite of the limited objective of the raid and the short distance to the target, many were uneasy over her inclusion in the force. This was not the first time that she had come on such a mission but it seemed to tempt fate to continue the habit—how long would such a freak last in an engagement between dreadnoughts?

Hipper's ships left the Jade at 1745 on 23 January, intending to return twenty-four hours later. There was a little apprehension amongst the more thoughtful officers as to how successful British intelligence might have been on this occasion, but, in the words of Hipper's biographer:

> No one on board had any idea that the plan was known to the enemy and that every movement and disposition was followed . . . as accurately as if the British themselves were directing them.[1]

The German force steamed out past Heligoland and into the North Sea.

The British, for their part, watched the clearing weather and wondered what it might portend. The bulk of the Grand Fleet was at its anchorages, save for the light forces out of Harwich. Just as German plans had been delayed by the succession of gales, so had the British schemes for attacking the zeppelin sheds. On 22 January, Tyrwhitt and Keyes asked for and received permission to proceed with Plan Z1, which would employ almost every unit under their command.

Commodore (S) sailed at 1300 on 23 January, escorting eight submarines with his two destroyers, *Lurcher* and *Firedrake*. A few minutes later he was recalled, but the difficulties of communicating with the submarines and the confusion that inevitably surrounds countermanded orders meant that Keyes did not return to Harwich until 1600.

The Admiralty had been well roused. The day started out in a quiet manner with Fisher in bed with a cold, too ill to take any active part in affairs. Churchill, who was never an early riser, went across to the First Sea Lord's residence after 1000 and had a long discussion. Churchill wrote:

> It was nearly noon when I regained my room in the Admiralty. I had hardly sat down when the door opened quickly and in marched Sir Arthur Wilson unannounced. He looked at me intently and there was a glow in his eyes. Behind him came Oliver with charts and compasses. "First Lord, those fellows are coming out again." "When?" "Tonight. We have just got time to get Beatty there."[2]

The important signals, to Tyrwhitt, the recall of Keyes, and that to Beatty were sent off in quick succession. At noon was sent to Tyrwhitt and Keyes:

> Negative Plan Z. All your destroyers and light cruisers will be wanted tonight. Negative sending destroyers to Sheerness for escort.[3]

Twenty-five minutes later the Admiralty ordered Beatty to:

> Get ready to sail at once with all battle cruisers and light cruisers and sea-going destroyers. Further orders follow.[4]

Filson Young in the *Lion* recorded that the ships at Rosyth had not been expecting this:

> Saturday, January 23rd, found us with the impression that nothing would ever happen again and that we were fixed in the Firth of Forth forever.[5]

The heavy ships began raising steam immediately in anticipation of the amplified orders promised by the Admiralty. They had little time to wait before the Admiralty made the dispositions. In Fisher's absence, Sir Arthur Wilson and Oliver were making the decisions:

> There was . . . just time for Beatty and Tyrwhitt to join forces at daylight near the Dogger Bank. Wilson and Oliver had already drawn on the chart, with what afterwards proved to be almost exact accuracy, the probable line of the enemy's course. They stepped it out with the compasses hour by hour, at what they guessed would be the German speed, till it reached our coasts. They then drew from Harwich the intercepting lines of Beatty and of Tyrwhitt. The intention was that the British forces should meet and be united at daybreak at some point about ten miles, or half an hour behind the enemy after he had passed westward and consequently be *between* him and his home.[6]

The calculations had not been, however, quite as simple as that. Oliver takes up the story:

> Knowing a little about the German mentality from many talks with Rotter, I was pretty sure a German Admiral would steer N45W and not merely to the north westwards and I laid off his course accordingly and fixed a rendezvous on it. Wilson wanted a rendezvous about thirty miles to south of mine but our battle cruisers had hardly time to reach it owing to a minefield off the Northumberland coast. I knew it was hopeless to argue and we had no time to spare, so I agreed and he went away and I telegraphed my rendezvous to Beatty and Tyrwhitt and they met the Germans and each other there next morning.[7]

Jellicoe was alerted by telegram and ordered to ready his ships for sailing. It might be mentioned at this time that the Admiralty made the greatest possible use of the secure telegraph since it was quite obvious that two could play at the game of intercepting and decoding wireless messages. They informed Keyes of the situation and ordered him to:

> Proceed with *Lurcher, Firedrake* and our submarines in the direction of Borkum Riff, but do not get out of wireless touch and await any orders you might receive.[8]

The other orders were issued apace. The Admiralty plan was simple. Beatty and Tyrwhitt were to rendezvous at dawn on the 24th at the

Dogger Bank on a position 55° 13′N, 3° 12′E, with the hope that they would be in contact with the German force to the west at that time. Vice Admiral Bradford, with the Third Battle Squadron and Rear Admiral W. C. Pakenham's three armored cruisers of the Third Cruiser Squadron would rendezvous at 55° 35′N, 2° 0′E, and "be prepared to intercept enemy if they are headed off by our battle cruisers and attempt to escape north."[9] Jellicoe was to be even further to the north, cruising with the Grand Fleet against the event that the German battle squadrons were at sea. Keyes was to attempt to act against any German units entering or leaving the Jade. Fearful that his four submarines might not be enough, the Admiralty ordered him to send four more to close off every possible exit but, as these could not possibly be in position before the morning of the 25th, they were to play no part in the events that followed.

The dispositions were admirable, but they were flawed in that only three of the four sides of the trap were secure. The British could only trust to luck to ensure the closure of the most important fourth—the east.

The ships at Rosyth were the first to move:

> . . . there was no doubt about it this time. There was a frantic commotion at the slipway where the steam boats were waiting and much panic on the part of individual officers lest their respective boats should depart without them. In half an hour the pier was empty and the boats were being hoisted in aboard the battle cruisers.[10]

The *New Zealand* carried a distinguished visitor, Prince Louis of Battenberg. A guest of his son Prince George for a few days in harbor, Prince Louis was eager to go with the battle cruisers but insisted he be put ashore. Sir Archibald Moore and Captain Halsey pleaded with him to stay but Battenberg felt that he could not remain lest it mean trouble for someone in the aftermath.[11]

They sailed at 1800, working up to 18 knots as the force pushed down the length of the Firth. At 2030 Bradford's "Wobbly Eight" (down to seven with the absence of the *Commonwealth*) weighed and made for their rendezvous. As it happened, Oliver's concern for the suspected mine field around St Abb's Head came to naught. The Chief of the War Staff thought, in planning the movement, that Beatty would have his ships assume a cruising speed of 20 knots. At 18 knots, Beatty did no such thing, though it is difficult to discover precisely why. Steaming at high power for long periods placed enormous strain upon the stokers and engine-room personnel, but as all the battle cruisers were capable of making 20 knots with ease and the duration of the entire operation could only be a few days, it may well have been that Beatty was being overly solicitous of his men. As it was, Oliver came in for a great deal of abuse from the Battle Cruiser Force.[12] The telegram sent by the Admiralty had made mention only of the rendezvous and the time and not of the assumptions under which they had been planned. In proceeding at 18 knots, a corner had to be cut and the battle cruisers ended up going directly over the danger area which Oliver had been so anxious for them to avoid.

The First, Second and Fourth Battle Squadrons sailed from Scapa between 1830 and 2030 in independent formations. A wholesale exit of the Grand Fleet was difficult enough from the Flow even under ideal conditions, and Jellicoe felt that it would be wiser to make the concentration in the morning, at 0930, in a position 150 miles north-north-west of the battle cruisers 0730 rendezvous. To avoid the suspected mine fields, Jellicoe determined to keep his forces well to the east.

Tyrwhitt sailed at 1730, intending to round the North Hinder Light Ship and steer for the rendezvous. He had intended to keep all his ships together but a sudden fog developed as he was taking *Arethusa* and the "M" class destroyers out of Harwich. The fog delayed the sailing of the other Harwich Force vessels and Tyrwhitt decided to press on ahead, leaving *Aurora*, *Undaunted*, and the two other destroyer flotillas to press on as best they could. They eventually sailed some forty minutes late.

As the ships moved towards their meeting places, spirits rose amongst the British. Although their personnel were as ignorant as their enemies as to the source of the Admiralty's knowledge, they had a growing appreciation of its value. The whole fleet was at sea, there had to be some reason for it:

> . . . we were confident on this occasion, in a way we had never been before, that we should meet the enemy on the morrow. No one had any doubts about it and there was an air of suppressed excitement which was very exhilarating.[13]

In the Scouting Groups, the atmosphere was also one of confidence. The Germans were happy about the ships they manned, but there was always the risk that the British might be preparing a trap. There were no illusions as to the fate of the First Scouting Group if it came into contact with the Grand Fleet. Hipper was fully conscious of the risk created by von Ingenohl's decision not to take the High Sea Fleet to sea as a covering force.

While the long winter night drew to its close the various forces were moving to their conjunction. Hipper was steering toward the British coast with his heavy ships in line ahead and the destroyer flotillas disposed ahead of them. The light cruisers *Stralsund* and *Graudenz* were in the van, a few miles in front of the main force and *Kolberg* and *Rostock* were steaming ten miles out, just forward of either beam. Hipper and his staff were apprehensive about the future. They already suspected that something was amiss with their intelligence, and the weather gave ample indication of a day of clear and calm. There was no chance that rain and mists would hide the Scouting Groups as they had done during the Scarborough raid.

Beatty, meanwhile, was steering south-south-east with his five battle cruisers to make the rendezvous with Tyrwhitt. It was in his mind that the Germans, if out, would be found in a position to the west of his units, in which case they would be caught with a superior force between themselves and their base.

Tyrwhitt was moving north with the Harwich Force. *Arethusa* and the seven M class destroyers were still ahead of the rest of the force after the delay caused by fog out of Harwich. At 0630 Beatty signaled his intentions to Tyrwhitt, asking that he dispose his light forces to the west of the battle cruisers, Goodenough's light cruisers being to the east. In later years Tyrwhitt was to lament the time of rendezvous that the Admiralty had ordained. Had the whole force been earlier, he felt, then the Germans would have passed to the west and been isolated. On the other hand, had all the British units been delayed a little longer, Hipper might well have run right into Beatty's arms, and any chase would have been at much shorter ranges.

At 0705, as the first glimmerings of dawn appeared on the horizon, *Aurora* sighted the *Kolberg* and four torpedo boats four miles to the east. In the gloom it appeared to Captain Nicholson that the three-funnelled cruiser might well be the *Arethusa* with the Ms. He delayed a few minutes to issue the challenge. *Kolberg* noted down the code and flashed a single letter in reply before opening fire. She immediately signaled the presence of enemy light forces to Hipper. As was to be expected with German gunnery, her opening salvoes were very accurate, and she soon scored three hits on *Aurora* which caused minor damage. The British cruiser took somewhat longer to settle down but hit *Kolberg* twice. The first shell struck below the waterline and the second under the bridge. Structural damage was not severe but two ratings were killed and the captain of the *Kolberg*, realizing the weight of metal he was facing, turned away to the north-east at 0725.

To both commanders the position was still ambiguous. Beatty had no more than a vague idea of what the German main force, if any, bore, and Hipper thought he was only facing light forces. Unable in the gloom of twilight to discern the situation he turned his battle cruisers toward the *Kolberg*—although his suspicions forced him to proceed with caution.

Beatty in *Lion* saw the gun flashes to the south and immediately turned his forces in that direction, ordering Goodenough and the light cruisers to do the same. *Aurora* followed the first rule of the scout and signaled a report to the flagship, but it was unhelpful in the extreme, being only: "Am in action with German Fleet."

The pretension of this statement caused some amusement in the flagship but it gave little or no useful information to Beatty. He ordered Tyrwhitt in the *Arethusa* to take position three miles ahead of the *Lion* with his seven destroyers and continued the run to the south. *Undaunted* and *Aurora* altered course to the north-east with their flotillas to parallel the movement of the *Kolberg*.

At 0730 Goodenough made simultaneous sightings of cruisers to the south and east. Visibility was rapidly increasing to about ten miles, and the Germans to the east were silhouetted against the dawn. Goodenough challenged both forces. Receiving the response only from *Aurora* and the Harwich Force to the south, he began to haul around to the south-east to pursue *Stralsund* and *Graudenz*. *Aurora* had by now sighted the German battle cruisers, assisted by the vast pall of smoke that they were sending up, and she communicated this fact to the *Southampton*.

Goodenough signaled Beatty that the enemy force had been sighted and appeared to be steaming toward the north. To David Beatty it seemed as if his golden moment were at hand. He continued to head for the south while his battle cruisers worked up to full speed. If the two forces continued their relative courses and speeds for a few more minutes, then the Germans would inevitably be cut off. If, on the other hand, the Germans ran for home and forced a stern chase, British possession of the lee gauge in the prevailing north-easterly wind would ensure that Beatty's battle cruisers had the enormous advantage of visibility unimpeded by their own funnel smoke. As Beatty and his staff awaited events on the signal bridge of the *Lion*, the euphoria in the British ships on that clear winter dawn rose to tremendous heights. It was the first real chance their crews had had at the Germans since the war began. They were determined not to miss it.

On his bridge in the *Seydlitz*, Hipper was becoming deeply worried by the situation. Both *Kolberg* and *Stralsund* had reported seeing smoke clouds—infallible indication of the presence of heavy units—in different positions and as *Stralsund* pressed home her reconnaissance she reported sighting eight heavy ships to the north-north-west. Hipper and his staff were in an agony of indecision. They knew from intelligence reports that Beatty had no more than five battle cruisers under his command. Yet the amount of intercepted British wireless traffic indicated that numerous units were at sea. If these ships were one of the battle squadrons—where was Beatty?

Hipper knew the weakness of his force and the dangers of being drawn into a trap. Every minute that his ships steamed to the north-west increased this risk. *Kolberg's* meeting with light forces and her report of smoke to the west-south-west meant that he could already be cut off. Brave though he was, Hipper had no intention of having his ships cut to pieces. He ordered his force to turn around to the south-east, "in order to get a view of the whole situation" as he would declare in his report. [14] At the same time as his battle cruisers were altering in succession onto the new course he recalled the detached light cruisers and torpedo boats to the main body. In the event of a stern chase, it was important that they not be strung out astern of the First Scouting Group. Their lack of protection would render them appallingly vulnerable to the British ships' heavy guns. Any ship disabled would have to be left behind. All this was sound reasoning on Hipper's part, but it was unfortunate for Germany that he did not think to apply it to the *Blücher* and reverse the steaming order for his heavy ships.

Hipper signaled to the Commander in Chief the information, sketchy as it was, that he had been able to gather:

> My position 54° 57′N. Lat., 3° 30′E. Long. Course South East Speed 20 k. Have sighted eight large ships, one light cruiser and twelve destroyers. [15]

Von Ingenohl received the signal at 0750 and ordered the various squadrons and flotillas of the fleet to commence raising steam. He attached no particular note of urgency to this direction as he felt that the battle cruisers' line of escape to the Bight was clear. Once steam was raised, the High Sea Fleet was ordered to assemble in Schillig Roads, but it would be at least three hours before this could be completed. Hipper's forces were quite alone.

The situation was beginning to clear for all concerned. A flow of signals was coming into the *Lion* from the detached units. At 0735 *Aurora*, *Undaunted*, and their destroyers altered course to the east to follow the German cruisers, the First Scouting Group being just in sight on the horizon. *Southampton* and the other cruisers of her squadron had wheeled to the east-south-east and were in line with the Harwich Force vessels, the whole being spread out on a rough north-south line. *Arethusa* was to the west of these ships, working up speed on a southeasterly course, heading to the south of where Tyrwhitt surmised the German battle cruisers to be.

As Beatty gained a grasp of the situation, he began to increase the speed of his battle cruisers still further. At 0743 he turned his ships to the south-east and then, refining his estimation of the position of the Germans, turned them, successively, at 0747 to the south-south-east and at 0751 to east-south-east as the German battle cruisers appeared temporarily to be heading north-east in the midst of their wheel. When the German movements seemed clearer, Beatty turned further to the east, waiting for the precise resolution of the Germans' course.

Both sides' scouting units were moving into some kind of battle order. The German ships had a fairly clear-cut defensive position to resolve, but the British problem was extremely complex. They had to position themselves so that they did not mask their own heavy ships' fire or confuse the engagement with their funnel smoke. They had to be able to repel any possible torpedo attacks. They had themselves to be ready to undertake a torpedo attack if so ordered. Finally, they had to also remember their duties as scouts and collectors of information. In view of the small advantage they held in speed, the decisions had to be made without hesitation.

Commodore Goodenough determined to place his four light cruisers on the port quarter of the German force where, because of the wind, he would have a clear view and be in a favorable tactical position. Accordingly, at 0753 he ordered his squadron to turn together to the north-east, followed at 0756 by a turn to the south-east. A minute later he refined this to south-south-east, a course which put him a comfortable 17,000 yards to the north-west of the *Blücher*.

By 0750 Beatty had Hipper's battle cruisers in sight to the east at what he estimated was a range of 20,000 yards. The pall of smoke between the German ships and his own force made precise identification difficult, although the accuracy of the earlier reports from Goodenough helped greatly. For his part, as his ships commenced their run to the south-east, Hipper began to discern the five clouds of smoke that marked the path of the British battle cruisers. He now saw that he was only facing one force instead of the two reported, and this afforded him considerable relief. It was patent to the German staff, too, that as the British battle cruisers were logically the out-runners of the Grand Fleet it was unlikely that any other British force was now interposed between the Scouting Groups and Wilhelmshaven.

Giving Hipper, von Egidy, and Raeder some food for thought was the nature of their meeting with the British forces. The Harwich Force and Beatty's Battle Cruiser Squadrons had clearly been in the process of a rendezvous. It seemed disturbingly more than coincidental that such a meeting should be timed for dawn directly on the intended position of the Scouting Groups at the same time. It was a matter to be left until harbor was raised, but the implications were alarming.

The ships of the Harwich Force were taking up positions to port and ahead of the battle cruisers, trying to attain the most favorable positions possible. *Aurora* and *Undaunted* were still abreast of each other, about 7,000 yards apart, with their flotillas strung out astern. *Arethusa* was moving to a position nearly ahead of the *Lion* with the M class destroyers accompanying her. Tyrwhitt, however, gave the Tenth Flotilla commander in *Meteor* a free hand in view of his destroyers' far superior speed.

At 0807 Hipper began a sharp turn to port, in a northerly direction, to permit the last of his laboring torpedo boats and light cruisers to assume their stations around his heavy ships. On observing this movement Goodenough hastily turned his squadron east to prevent their closing the distance and coming under German fire. He informed Beatty and the Commander in Chief, but he did not turn his ships any further to the north as he realized the nature of the movement and did not think that the Germans would hold their new course for long.

He was proved correct as within a few minutes Hipper had hauled round to the south-south-east in an effort to gain as much southing ground as possible before Beatty's ships could get in range. The British battle cruisers' speed was steadily rising. Beatty, confident in his engineers, ordered 25 knots at 0816 and then, at 0823, 26 knots. Although some of his staff were more than a little dubious as to the practicality of these orders—*Indomitable* was thought to be capable of no more than 25 knots at the maximum—Beatty believed that it would give the engineering staff and stokers something to aim at. Indeed, the enthusiasm spread to all quarters, especially when it became obvious that the two older ships were keeping up with the leaders.

The range to the German ships was now dropping slowly. At 0814 the range from the *Lion* to the *Blücher* was estimated at twenty-five thousand yards, only three thousand more than the maximum effective range of the 13.5″ gun. At 0816 Beatty ordered his battle cruisers to form on a line of bearing seven points abaft *Lion*'s beam on her port quarter. The measure had the dual purpose of facilitating visual signals and clearing the battle cruisers' arcs of fire. The chase was now beginning to settle down as the run to the south-east began. Hipper's hopes of escaping scot-free dimmed as the British ships loomed larger on the horizon. With the *Blücher* attached, the First Scouting Group could not exceed 23 knots and, as Hipper later described it in his report:

> The pace at which the enemy was closing in was quite unexpected. The enemy battle cruisers must have been doing 26 knots. They were emitting extraordinarily dense smoke clouds.[16]

For the next half hour both sides could only settle down to wait. Muffled in greatcoats and scarves, admirals, staffs, and commanding officers stood on windswept compass platforms, watching and waiting.

Dawn on the 24th had found Commodore Keyes's little force well to the south of Beatty and Tyrwhitt. Commodore (S) determined, on his own initiative, to alter the dispositions dictated by the Admiralty. He detached only E-11, which was to patrol the entrance of the swept channel at Norderney Gat.

Keyes, realizing from all the signal traffic that *Lurcher* was intercepting that a major engagement was under way, attempted to place his ships across the German line of retreat. He was not to receive any official word of the battle in progress until at 1055 the Admiralty made a tardy signal:

> Send submarines to Heligoland Bight. High Sea Fleet are coming out.
> Our battle cruisers are chasing German battle cruisers at 9.23 A.M., Lat.
> 54° 39′N., Long. 4° 16′E. Very important.[17]

The few hours lost by the return to Harwich came into fatal play. Keyes could not leave the three submarines behind as they were his major offensive weapon. An unsupported attack by the destroyers on the German main force would be suicidal and useless. The E class submarines were the largest and most efficient in the Royal Navy, but their utmost surface speed was only 15 knots and this was just not enough.

Beatty's light forces were nearer the enemy than he and had a clearer view of proceedings. *Arethusa* signaled at 0817 that Hipper's torpedo boats were stationed on the First Scouting Group's starboard bow—knowledge of their whereabouts being vital to Beatty if he was to maintain the pursuit with any degree of security. At 0823, Goodenough, remembering his duty as a scout not only for the Battle Cruiser Force but for the Grand Fleet as well, signaled to the Commander in Chief:

> Position Latitude 55° 02′ north, Longitude 4° 04′ east. Enemy in sight consisting of four battle cruisers, steering between east and south-east.[18]

This was the kind of information that Jellicoe so desperately wanted, the kind of information few of his subordinates remembered to send their Commander in Chief.

Hipper ended his southerly movement as the British ships began to get dangerously close and hauled around to the south-east. When this movement became apparent to Beatty at 0830 he ordered his ships to steer south-east themselves. At 0834 he ordered 27 knots—more than the *New Zealand*'s designed speed.

The distance Hipper had gained to the south put the Harwich Force close behind and to the north of the *Blücher*. *Aurora* and the M class destroyers were steadily closing her, and Hipper considered momentarily the possibility of ordering his light forces to drop back and attack them. He was forced to reject the idea as it would have been difficult for his cruisers and impossible for most of his torpedo boats to catch up again with the First Scouting Group. *Blücher* would have to rely for the time being on her own secondary armament.

Hipper's signals in this period were few and far between. Because the speed of the slowest dictated the speed of the squadron, he was not able to urge his ships on further. His dispositions made, he could only wait on events. If he was to initiate a melee, it would be far better to do this in Heligoland Bight when he hoped Beatty would have outrun his supporting units and the positions would be precisely reversed with the British turning to flee and having their stragglers picked off, one by one.

A minute after his order for 27 knots, Beatty signaled to Jellicoe:

> Enemy sighted is of class denoted, four battle cruisers, four light cruisers, destroyers number unknown, bearing south 61° east, 11 miles. My position is Lat. 54° 51′N. Long. 3° 37½′E. Course south 40° east 26 knots. [19]

Meteor and her six sisters approached too close to *Blücher*. She opened fire on them at a range of seven thousand yards and although *Blücher* scored no hits, Beatty must have been aware of the futility of a stern attack by torpedo craft on undamaged heavy ships at this speed. He signaled the Ms to take station astern. Obediently, the three cruisers and the destroyers of the Tenth Flotilla turned south-west to close the *Lion*.

Hipper signaled:

> My position 0830, 54° 50′N, 3° 55′E. Course SE, speed 21 knots. Seven enemy light cruisers [*sic*] and twenty six destroyers are following me. Intend not to attack until Inner Bight is reached. [20]

The range was slowly but steadily dropping. Beatty had by now ordered 28 knots, more than *Indomitable* and *New Zealand* could possibly reach. Gaps began to open between the three "Splendid Cats" and the two of Moore's squadron; *Indomitable* herself began to fall away from *New Zealand*.

At 0852 the rangefinder on the gunnery control platform of the *Lion* reported to the gunnery officer, Lieutenant Commander Geoffrey Longhurst, that the range was down to twenty-two thousand yards, which was the maximum range of the 13.5″ gun. The small size of the British prismatic rangefinders meant, however, that accuracy dropped off sharply after fifteen thousand yards and disappeared after twenty thousand. Salvo firing with such information alone would be almost certain waste of shell. Longhurst reported the range to Captain Chatfield, and a sighting shot was ordered. Amidships one gun of "Q" turret elevated and fired the first shot in the first engagement between dreadnoughts. The shell fell short.

At 0854 Beatty signaled 29 knots and, a minute later, "Well Done, *Indomitable*." The effort being made in the engine- and stoke-rooms of the British battle cruisers was incredible. Vice Admiral B. B. Schofield, who was serving as a midshipman in the *Indomitable*, writes of the battle cruiser at full power:

> Anyone brought up in the oil fuel age can have no idea of the physical effort required of the stokers of a coal-fired ship steaming at high speed. With the fans supplying air to the boilers whirring at full speed the furnaces devoured coal just about as fast as a man could feed them. Black, begrimed and sweating men working in the bunkers in the ship's side dug the coal out and loaded it into skids which were then dragged along the steel deck and emptied on to the floorplates in front of each boiler in turn. No hygenic or sterilised suits for these men. If the ship rolled or pitched there was always a risk that a loaded skid might take charge with resultant danger to life and limb. Looking down from the iron catwalk above, the scene had all the appearance of one from Dante's *Inferno*, "For flames I saw and wailings smote mine ears." Watching the pressure gauges for any fall in the steam pressure, the Chief Stoker walked to and fro encouraging his men. Now and then the telegraph from the engineroom would clang and the finger on the dial move round to the section marked "MORE STEAM." The Chief would press the reply gong with an oath. "What do the bastards think we're doing," he would exclaim, "Come on boys, shake it up, get going," and the sweating men would redouble their efforts, throw open the furnace doors and shovel still more coal into the blazing inferno.[21]

The firing of "deliberate" shots continued for some minutes as the shell splashes crept toward their targets. At 0900 *Tiger* joined in, firing her own sighting shots at the *Blücher*. By 0905, *Lion* had the *Blücher*'s range and Beatty signaled: "Open fire and engage the enemy."

Lion and *Tiger* at once began to fire full salvoes of armor-piercing shells; the guns belching forth every three-quarters of a minute. *Princess Royal*, a thousand yards behind, now began her own series of sighting shots to establish the range on *Blücher*. Further back still, the *New Zealand* and *Indomitable* remained silent, for their 12" main armaments could not hope to span the range.

Hipper made another signal, distinguished by its brevity:

> Am in action with 1st battle cruiser squadron, 109 7 (145 miles WNW of Heligoland). Course south-east-¼-south.[22]

In the Jade, von Ingenohl noted the signal and continued his leisurely preparations, but further to the north of Hipper it was taken in by another unit. The zeppelin L-5 was flying a routine patrol in the North Sea when the message came through. Her commander, Lieutenant

Commander Klaus Hirsch, immediately turned the airship south to see what he could do.

At 0911 the Germans opened fire at what they estimated was twenty thousand yards. For their gunners, firing was abominably difficult because

> in view of the enemy's position astern, the view of the enemy from the fire control was very much hampered and partially blinded as the result of the dense smoke.[23]

As far as the gunnery of both sides was concerned, it was still very much a process of "learn as you go." The Battle Cruiser Force had more than an inkling of what long-range gunnery was all about, but to the Germans the ranges employed came as a complete surprise. Their estimation of British gunnery went up considerably, so much so that they came to believe that Beatty was trying to maintain the maximum ranges for his own advantage.

It appeared to the observers in the *Lion* that at this time she made her first hits on the *Blücher*. This seems to have been the case, although the hit was on the quarterdeck and did not affect the fighting ability of the ship. It is important, however, to take the observers' estimates of hits with caution, in spite of Filson Young's words:

> There was no mistaking the difference between the bright, sharp stab of white flame that marked the firing of the enemy's guns and this dull, glowing and fading glare which signified the bursting of one of our own shells.[24]

This clear distinction was not the case, and there was often confusion between the firing of salvoes and shells striking home.

To prevent Hipper attempting to redress the balance by ordering a torpedo attack, at 0920 Beatty ordered the ships of the Harwich Force to take station ahead: "Proceed at your utmost speed." In obedience to Tyrwhitt's orders, *Aurora* had taken up station to starboard, *Arethusa* and *Undaunted* to port of her, with their flotillas astern and the M class destroyers ahead and to starboard. Although this would put some of the older ships into difficulties, Beatty at least had the comfort of knowing he had the *Arethusa*s and Commander the Honourable Herbert Meade's seven ships as outriders, whatever the speed of his battle cruisers.

As the range began to drop still further, *Lion* shifted her fire to *Moltke* at a range of 17,200 yards, but not before observing another hit on the *Blücher*. *Seydlitz* and *Derfflinger* were also starting to become visible to the fire-control positions. In her turn, *Lion* was being straddled by German salvoes "on both sides of us and quite close, so that the spray from them drenched our decks." *Lion* was to be the principal target for the First

Scouting Group throughout the engagement, not only in observance of the dictum that the destruction of the head rendered the body harmless but because the Germans were finding the lesser range of their weapons an infuriating limitation. At about this time *Blücher* struck *Lion* on "A" turret with a 21 cm shell. This did not pierce the armor, but the concussion was severe and the left gun was knocked out of action for two hours. Two wing compartments had already been flooded by detonations below water level.

At 0933 Beatty altered course to east-south-east and, at 0935, he signaled: "Engage the corresponding ship in the enemy's line." *New Zealand*'s improved shells and her slight margin of speed had put her in range of the *Blücher* but *Indomitable* was still well behind and Chatfield took this into account when he suggested the target allocation to Beatty. Each ship was to engage her opposite number; *Lion* was to take *Seydlitz*, *Tiger* the *Moltke*, *Princess Royal* the *Derfflinger*, and *New Zealand* the *Blücher*. Inexperience took charge in the *Tiger*. In spite of the fact that she was equipped with director firing, *Tiger* had been shooting very badly, and nerves and disappointment may have contributed to Captain Henry Pelly's mistake. He chose to engage *Seydlitz* and leave *Moltke* alone. He based his decision upon one of the *Grand Fleet Battle Orders* which read that when the enemy's ships were in lesser number than the British, the two leading British ships were to engage the first German and the process was to be continued down the line until numbers were equalized and the latter ships in line were engaging each other on a one-for-one basis. Were all five of the battle cruisers in action this would have been correct procedure but *Indomitable* was quite obviously not firing, as Pelly should have realized. The mistake was aggravated by the fact that *Tiger*'s gunnery officer, Lieutenant Commander Evan Bruce-Gardyne, took the shell splashes that marked the fall of *Lion*'s salvoes as *Tiger*'s. Within three minutes Commodore Goodenough signaled to *Lion* and *Tiger* from his vantage point in the north, "Salvoes of three, apparently from *Tiger*, falling consistently over." Although *Lion* certainly took this signal in, there is some doubt as to whether *Tiger* did so. It was not logged in the ship, and it does not seem as if Bruce-Gardyne ordered a range decrease at that time. Yet *Tiger* did score one hit—a 13.5″ shell struck the forecastle of *Seydlitz* and caused minor damage. By a fluke, the corrections ordered from *Lion*'s salvoes resulted in *Tiger* getting *Seydlitz*'s range at least temporarily and apparently quite unconsciously. It would be some time yet before *Tiger* had the measure of *Seydlitz*.

Unfortunately for the British, *Tiger*'s error resulted in the *Moltke* going unengaged and able to concentrate undisturbed upon the two leading British battle cruisers. *Moltke*'s efficiency at gunnery would ensure that she made the most of the opportunity.

In every heavy ship in the battle, senior officers were finding their conning towers of no use to them in action. Chatfield of the *Lion* gives his view:

> . . . to the conning tower I had to go. . . . It was situated immediately behind B turret, noisy and wet from spray and from steaming at high speed through the vast columns of water, which somehow incredibly forced its way through the lens threads of my Ross binoculars. Edwards, the navigating commander, put on an oilskin.[25]

The situation was as bad in other positions. Prince George of Battenberg, "A" turret officer of the *New Zealand*, wrote:

> By this time my range-finder was useless; I was soaked through to the skin by the spray coming in through the slit in my hood, hitting me in the face and then trickling down outside and inside my clothes, and I was frozen by the wind which came in with the spray. My eyes were extremely sore, and I was blinking all the time.[26]

By 0943 the range from *Lion* to *Seydlitz* was under seventeen thousand yards, and *Lion* was straddling *Seydlitz* with every salvo. *Princess Royal* was engaging *Derfflinger* and *New Zealand* was working on *Blücher*.

Hipper was now becoming increasingly concerned by the state of his weakest heavy unit. *Blücher* had neither the armor nor the armament to stand up to even the oldest British battle cruiser. She was beginning to show signs of damage. But the first crippling blow would be to *Seydlitz*. The flagship had already been struck by one heavy shell, which had caused little damage, when a 13.5" armor-piercing shell from the *Lion* struck her aft. In Admiral Scheer's words:

> The . . . shell had a terrible effect. It pierced right through the upper deck in the ship's stern and through the barbette armour of the near (that is: after) turret, where it exploded. All parts of the stern, the officers' quarters, mess, etc., that were near where the explosion took place were totally wrecked. In the reloading chamber, where the shell penetrated, part of the charge in readiness for loading was set on fire. The flames rose high up into the turret and down into the munition chamber, and thence through a connecting door usually kept shut, by which the men from the munition chamber tried to escape into the fore turret. The flames thus made their way through to the other munition chamber, and thence again up to the second turret, and from this cause the entire gun crews of both turrets perished almost instantly. The flames rose as high as a house above the turrets.[27]

Filson Young in the fore-top of the *Lion*: " Well do I remember seeing those flames and wondering what kind of horrors they signified."[28]

Seydlitz was now in great danger. Nearly 14,000 pounds of propellant charges had already gone up and were the flash to penetrate to the magazines they would explode, break the back of the battle cruiser, and send her to the bottom within seconds. She was saved by three men. In spite of suffocating gases and intense heat, Lieutenant Commander Hagedom, Chief Artificer Hering, and Gunner's Mate Muller worked their way to the flooding valves for the magazines. They turned the valves and admitted six hundred tons of water to flood the magazines. *Seydlitz* was saved. Her after turrets were useless, but her speed was unimpaired. In spite of the impact, her engines, boilers, and shafts were still sound, a tribute to the robustness of German design. Although down by the stern, the *Seydlitz* had no list and her stability was hardly affected.

All this time, Rear Admiral Hipper had stood impassive, the only indication to his staff that he was under any strain being his chain-smoking. Captain von Egidy's reaction had been to order rapid salvoes so as to do the most damage to the enemy before the ship was lost, and *Seydlitz* was now firing faster than she had ever done before, with right and left gun salvoes every thirty seconds. Hipper realized that the damage to the *Seydlitz* dramatically altered the balance in favor of the British, since one of his three battle cruisers had now lost at a stroke half her fighting power. He signaled von Ingenohl for help; another hit of that kind and the Scouting Groups would be lost. Not for the first time that day did Hipper regret the total absence of any covering force.

Von Ingenohl received the signal at 1000. At last some note of urgency entered into the activities of the High Sea Fleet. Within ten minutes, the order to sail went out. It was too late. Getting the fleet out through the channels and into the Bight would take at least two hours. Von Ingenohl could not possibly be in a position to support Hipper, even if the battle continued its course, until 1430. Hipper would have to depend upon his own resources.

The German torpedo boats were giving Hipper cause for anxiety. Disposed on the starboard bow of the First Scouting Group, abreast and ahead of the light cruisers, the old and slow vessels of the Fifteenth Half Flotilla were experiencing difficulties in maintaining this position, even with the relatively calm seas and the restriction on the speed of the battle cruisers. They began to drop astern and crossed over from starboard to port behind the battle cruisers, the movement of several of the boats being somewhat erratic as they passed the battle cruisers, desperately trying not to foul the heavy ships' range.

Beatty, for his part, could not be sure what they were doing. The movements visible seemed to lack the cohesion of a torpedo attack but it was quite possible, in view of the fact that less than four thousand yards lay between the German force and the track which his battle cruisers intended to take, that the German torpedo boats were attempting to drop floating mines across his path. The warning of the Admiralty rang recent in his ears. Beatty began to haul his force around to the south-east to increase the parallel displacement between the two forces and prevent the apparent German maneuver.

The British battle cruisers were beginning to separate beyond the distance for mutual support. At this stage of the action *Lion* was probably making 28 knots, somewhat less than the 28½ that Beatty was to give in his report and definitely not the 29½ that triumphant engineers later estimated. *Tiger* was keeping up well, a feat possibly due to the fact that Beatty's fleet engineer, Captain C. G. Taylor, was accommodated aboard and had devoted much of his time to the new ship. All three of the other battle cruisers, however, including *Princess Royal*, had dropped well astern.* At 0952 Beatty therefore signaled a reduction in speed to 24 knots. This measure was intended to have the dual merit of enabling his battle cruisers to close up and permitting the slower units of the Harwich Force to regain a forward position for defense against attack by torpedo craft.

At the same time, still unable to ascertain *Tiger*'s fall of shot, Captain Pelly directed his gunnery officer to shift target to *Blücher* whose much closer position would probably enable even the raw *Tiger* to obtain hits. In the circumstances, it was probably the wisest decision, although the problem of *Moltke* remained unsolved.

When the full extent of the damage to *Seydlitz* became known, and bearing in mind the increasing vulnerability of the *Blücher*, Hipper bore away to the east-north-east in an attempt to confuse the British gunnery in the pall of smoke which hung over the force. Hipper was also becoming nervous of the First Light Cruiser Squadron, which seemed to him to be slowly closing the distance, perhaps with a view to isolating the *Blücher*. A feint in their direction, would, Hipper knew, soon force the *Towns* away. Sixteen thousand yards to the north, Goodenough saw the maneuver and wisely believing that, as far as any duel with battle cruisers was concerned, discretion was the better part of valour, turned his light cruisers to the north. He maintained that course until he was quite sure what Hipper intended. When he had increased the range to twenty thousand yards beyond both the main and secondary armaments of the First Scouting Group, Goodenough brought his ships back to a south-easterly course and returned to his watch. The turn away was only

---

*It seems that *Princess Royal* had not been docked after her return from the West Indies and that she had in consequence a very foul bottom.

just in time, for *Blücher* had opened a heavy and accurate fire with her 15 cm secondary armament.

With the guns of the *Moltke* and the *Seydlitz* concentrated upon her, the *Lion* began to suffer. At 1001 she was struck by a shell from *Moltke*. This pierced *Lion*'s side-armor and flooded the engineer's workshop, passing through the 4″ magazine trunk. It did not explode but the flooding had serious consequences. The water reached the main switchboard and short-circuited two of the ship's three dynamos. The loss of power disabled the control circuits for the secondary armament and the after fire-control, and the ingress of water caused *Lion* to take on a list to port. In spite of the damage, however, she maintained her speed and place in the line.

As the movements of the two battle cruiser forces were carried out, the leading ships temporarily lost contact. The leading German ships were themselves indistinct in the mass of smoke that continued to obstruct their own view of the British vessels. On the British side, *Lion* and *Princess Royal* were both forced to check fire at frequent intervals because of the poor visibility. In such conditions, the Germans had the advantage of stereoscopic rangefinders, which enabled them to take an accurate range from only indistinct targets. The unfortunate *Blücher* was, however, in spite of her move to the north, still in clear sight of her antagonists. Both *New Zealand* and *Tiger* began to straddle her. She was not yet crippled, but she had little hope of survival.

To Beatty, all the signs were that Hipper was turning to the north to leave the vast mass of accumulated smoke between his ships and the British, hiding them from each other and facilitating a torpedo attack. At 1010 Beatty ordered the Harwich Force to "attack enemy des-

SMS *Blücher*

troyers." This signal had no immediate consequences as Hipper's light craft were not attempting to drop back and all Beatty's destroyers and light cruisers were already straining their utmost to catch up with and pass the battle cruisers. As the *Princess Royal* and *New Zealand* had regained their positions he also ordered speed 26 knots and to prevent the range opening any further he altered course to the east-south-east.

Seydlitz now had only *Moltke* in line astern of her, *Derfflinger* and *Blücher* being strung out to the north. Hipper began to regain his former course. The British battle cruisers had not followed him north as he had hoped and, as a result, his position was relatively worse, the wedge being inserted further between his ships and the safety of the Bight.

As the battle began to settle down once more, it was discovered that *Lion* had lost the range completely and was firing over by more than two thousand yards. This was yet another lesson in the intricacies of long-range firing. The elevation was stepped down and *Lion* began to get the range and straddle *Seydlitz* once more.

From the mists in the north appeared the zeppelin L-5, drifting toward the embattled forces as the crew watched the spectacle below them. Lieutenant Commander Hirsch turned his ship on a reciprocal course to that of the First Scouting Group and cruised down the battle cruisers' unengaged side. Not unnaturally, the First Light Cruiser Squadron were concerned by the vision of L-5 looming overhead, and they opened fire with the few antiaircraft weapons the cruisers possessed. Their fire was surprisingly accurate and an alarmed Hirsch forced L-5 up into the protection of the clouds and out of range of the British guns. Ignoring the great scouting powers of the airship he commanded, Hirsche determined to remain to the north-east of the action and keep an eye out for any forces coming down on the battle cruisers from that direction. It appears to have quite escaped the commander that he could have performed a much more useful function scouting over the whole area around the battle and keeping Hipper informed of all movements.

Lion suffered damage at 1018. Two 28 cm shells from the *Seydlitz* struck her. In the fore-top:

> . . . we thought she had been torpedoed, and the mast, to which the fore-top was secured, rocked and waved like a tree in a storm, and the ship seemed to be shaking herself to bits. We looked at one another and prepared to alight from our small cage into whatever part of the sea destiny might send us, but nothing happened, and the old *Lion* seemed to pick herself up and go on again.[29]

One shell struck forward on the waterline, penetrated the armor belt and exploded in a wing compartment abreast the torpedo body space.

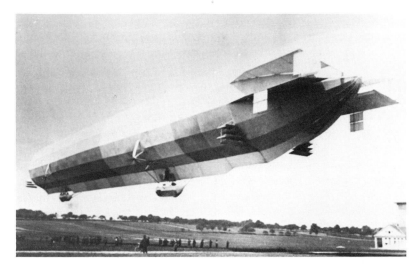

The zeppelin L-6

Within a few minutes extensive flooding up to the main deck had occurred. The capstan compartment was among those flooded. A splinter pierced the exhaust pipe from the capstan engine, permitting salt water to pass into the secondary condenser. Within hours the resultant salt contamination of the boilers would stop the ship.

The second shell struck below the waterline and drove in two 6″ armor plates, shattering the backing. Several coal bunkers forward were flooded and the inner and outer bottoms were bulged in over a large area.

Blücher was dropping behind. Her fighting capacity was still largely unimpaired, in spite of the heavy fire she was under, but she was well away from even the *Derfflinger*. Hipper did not attempt to recall his ships into a tight formation for the time being. Given the British system of gunnery, it was far better for the four ships to be well spread and steering erratic courses.

Beatty himself was becoming anxious. The action had been in progress for nearly ninety minutes and although the severity of the damage to *Seydlitz* was guessed, no decisive blow had been struck. Every mile to the south-east worsened his tactical position and improved Hipper's. At 1027, Beatty signaled:

> Form on a compass line of bearing NNW and proceed at your utmost speed.

The signal system was breaking down. Never before had such a strain been placed on visual signaling; the opportunity for such a test had simply never before occurred. In the first place, the battle cruisers were steaming at between 24 and 29 knots. Filson Young in the fore-top of the *Lion* recorded that the force of the wind made standing almost impossible. The wind caused the signal flags to stream dead astern, and thus they were extremely difficult to read. Beatty realized this when he ordered his ships to form on a line of bearing, but seven points abaft the beam could only give marginal inprovement.

Second, the visibility between the battle cruisers was not good. Not only were the funnels emitting masses of thick black smoke but the ships were enveloped by cordite fumes as they fired repeated salvoes from their main armament. The bridge of the *Lion* was only visible from the fore-top at irregular intervals and the position was no better as regards the next astern—especially as the cordite smoke was swept directly back onto the signal bridges. Furthermore, the exposed positions of each ship were continually swept by spray and splinters. Even the redoubtable Beatty was forced to return temporarily to the armored conning tower during a particularly bad period. It is hardly surprising that errors crept in.

Tiger and *Princess Royal* received the signal and repeated it correctly. *New Zealand* and *Indomitable* did not. Both mistook "form line of bearing" for "course." *Indomitable* did not even see the second half of the signal, although luckily it was of little importance to her. The Second Battle Cruiser Squadron was thus thrown into some confusion. Sir Archibald Moore and Captain Halsey in the *New Zealand* were mystified. What on earth did Beatty want with a course to the north-north-west? They knew something had to be wrong. When *Lion* hauled down her pennants as the executive signal, Moore determined to hold his course. He was confirmed in his decision by the fact that *Lion* did not alter course at all. Light finally dawned when *Princess Royal* and *Tiger* were seen to have sheered out of the previous formation, and Moore quietly followed suit. Unlike peacetime maneuvers, there had been no time to question the signals. In such a matter, subordinates had to exercise their common sense and initiative.

In the *Indomitable*, Captain Francis Kennedy was doing just that. It was quite plain to him that some mistake had been made in the transmission of the signal, but he was not sure whether Beatty intended a northerly movement to close the Germans regardless of the dangers posed by their torpedo craft—a move that would have been well in keeping with the Admiral's popular character. When the executive was made, Kennedy hauled out of formation and bore away nearly due east. It was, in its own small way, a useful decision, since it cut the distance between *Indomitable* and the German units and made her that much more valuable to Beatty. Kennedy was well aware of the risks involved but the value of his ship's broadside as an addition to the engagement would be enormous. He stood on even when the realization of what Beatty had wanted came to him—*Indomitable* was not masking any of her consorts' fire, and she was well within supporting distance.

On his own bridge Beatty appreciated Kennedy's move. In spite of the fact that the German torpedo boats were moving dangerously close to his planned track he signaled, at 1035, "Turn together 1 point to port." All ships received the signal except the *Indomitable* but as she had already anticipated the move it did not matter—this time. Beatty was conscious that the crisis of the battle was at hand.

Derfflinger received the third and last hit scored upon the German battle cruisers proper. It struck at 1040, nearly an hour after the last two. In the event the shell failed to penetrate the *Derfflinger*'s armor and burst outside.

For the *Blücher* it was the beginning of the end. Two shells struck amidships. They pierced her thin-armored deck and crashed through two decks to explode in the amidships ammunition gangways. The explosion set fire to the "ready use" cordite that lay stacked all around. The flash penetrated to her two 21 cm wing turrets on the port side. it wrecked both and killed every man inside them. The concussion also had a serious effect on the ship's machinery. All her engines were either temporarily or permanently disabled and her steering gear jammed out of action. She began to sheer right away to port as other shells struck, one landing forward which started yet another fire and knocked "Anna" turret out. *Blücher* sent to Hipper: "All engines out of action." It was the signal that he and his staff had been dreading. They were being forced to the decision as to whether they should turn back in support or continue the run to the south-east and leave the unfortunate ship to her fate.

The British, it seemed, had finally cracked the German nut. Beatty moved to sort out the "loose ends," and he ordered *Indomitable* to deal with "the enemy breaking away to the north," thus allotting *Blücher* exactly the opposition that was required—decisive, but not excessive. At 1045 Beatty again signaled a turn together one point to port. At 1047 he threw all caution to the winds as *Lion* made to the other battle cruisers: "Close the enemy as rapidly as possible consistent with keeping all guns bearing." Beatty was determined to hound Hipper's ships to destruction, and he was confident that he was moving in for the kill.

Two things, however, told against him. In the first place, none of the other battle cruisers correctly received the signal. *Princess Royal*, *New Zealand*, and *Indomitable* did not even see it, while *Tiger* only got, "Close the enemy." In the short term the failure was of little importance because the course already being steered was near the optimum possible. In the long term, however, it was a disaster. Had Sir Archibald Moore received this signal he would have had a much clearer picture of Beatty's intentions, even through the confusion that was to ensue.

For all was not well with the *Lion*. She was losing speed. So much so, in fact, that the *Tiger* was by now abreast of *Lion* and any successive turn to port that Beatty may have had in mind would be impossible. The feed water contamination was beginning to tell, and *Lion* was struck again and again. A 28 cm shell burst against the armor of "A" barbette. This caused a small fire in "A" turret lobby and, although this was extinguished with little difficulty, in the confusion a message was sent to the bridge that there was grave danger of a magazine explosion. The order was passed to flood the magazine, and there were two feet of water in the compartment before the alarm was realized to be false and flooding stopped.

Between 1049 and 1051 *Lion* was hit repeatedly. The effect was catastrophic. A shell burst on the armor belt amidships and forced a nine-inch plate two feet inward. The port feed tank was opened up and this overflowed into the reserve feed tanks. Only the fact that the valves to the port engine-room were shut saved that compartment from immediate and serious flooding. The port engine had to be stopped, and the ship's speed was reduced to 15 knots.

Although the port engine-room was temporarily safe, flooding in lower and surrounding compartments increased the ship's list to 10 degrees. This had the disastrous effect of shorting the single remaining dynamo. All light and power gone, the ship was in a sorry state, with 3,000 tons of water on board, "A" turret and the main fire-control out of action, and all but two signal halliards shot away.[30]

Tiger shot ahead of the flagship and headed after the Germans, but she, too, began to suffer. She received three hits in rapid succession. The first struck the roof of "Q" turret and caused substantial damage. It did not quite pierce the armor, but the turret's left gun was disabled, two men were killed, and several wounded. A second shell exploded in the forward superstructure, destroying the intelligence office and signal distribution station and killing eight men, including Beatty's very efficient fleet engineer, Captain Taylor. The third shell struck amidships between the funnels. This exploded amongst the boat stowage, setting fire to the boats and igniting the petrol tank which was a fuel store for the motor boats. The mass of flammable material caused the flames to shoot funnel high in one vast blaze. *Tiger* looked like a torch, the entire ship past the bridge being hidden in a mass of smoke and flame. Although the ship's fighting abilities were unaffected, to the observers in the *Moltke* it appeared that the blaze must be *Tiger*'s funeral pyre, and they jubilantly claimed her sunk. But aided by the fact that little remained to burn, the battle cruiser's repair parties had the fire under control within a quarter of an hour. The damage done, however, was not just to the ship and her personnel. Beatty wrote in his *Report of Proceedings*:

> At 10.54 a.m. submarines were reported on the starboard bow and I personally observed the wash of a periscope, 2 points on our starboard bow (1059). I immediately (1102) signalled "Turn 8 points to port together."

Of all Beatty's decisions at the Battle of the Dogger Bank this was to be the most controversial. It was not just because of the dubious tactical thinking employed, which will be dealt with later, but the nature of the signal. Captain Pelly, in *Tiger*, wrote afterward:

> . . . the *Lion* hoisted the signal "Alter course 8 points to port." Whilst this signal was still flying I observed the flagship developing a big list. She was evidently badly damaged. She began to drop back and from then onward took no further part in the action.
>
> *Tiger* steered to pass between her and the enemy, and the German's fire was concentrated on her. For nearly five minutes this alter course signal remained flying and giving us all plenty of time to comment on it.
>
> I remember asking my navigating officer if he could explain the meaning of it, for to my mind it seemed to mean breaking off the action. He replied: "I have no idea, unless the *Lion* has better knowledge of minefields about than we have."[31]

The confusion was as great upon the bridge of the *Lion*. It would seem that Beatty not only made the sighting himself but ordered the turn away as an instantaneous reaction *without* giving the reason why. Plunkett, astonished by the order, recorded that his first reaction was to say, "Good heavens, Sir, surely you're not going to break off the engagement?"[32]

What made the signal fatal was that it was hoisted without the submarine warning. This is to some extent excused by the fact that only two signal halliards remained, but Beatty should have given thought to the confusion that the bald signal must inevitably cause. It should have been the submarine warning first and only *then* the turn signal.

As his battle cruisers thundered off, Beatty was quick to attempt to regain control of the situation, and it was in this attempt that the final confusion set in. Beatty first ordered "Course North-East" to be hoisted in order to bring the battle cruisers back to the pursuit. By themselves, the "Compass" pennant and the letter flag "B" meant just what was intended—"Course North-East." For Beatty, however, this was not enough. Time was slipping away, and the quarry was escaping to the east. He ordered Seymour to find a signal to direct his ships to engage the German main body. Lieutenant Commander Seymour, consulting his signal book, discovered that no such direction seemed to exist. The nearest he could come to Beatty's intention was: "Attack the rear of the enemy." Beatty agreed he should hoist this, and it was here that the ambiguity appeared. The signals were hoisted nearly simultaneously on the two halliards left—which happened to be adjacent. When *Lion* hoisted "Compass B" on one, and "A F" on the other, what was intended as "Course North East. Attack the enemy's rear" became "Attack the rear of the enemy, bearing north east." The accumulation of missed signals, scares, and snap decisions now brought disaster upon the British.

Not one of Beatty's captains, and still less Sir Archibald Moore, was quite sure what the Vice Admiral had intended by his series of signals. What had he meant by his eight-point turn? What was meant by the "enemy's rear"? Moore could not be sure what was wanted. In the *New Zealand* he must have reflected on the anomaly between the Vice Admiral's character and his predefined intentions, and his apparent actions. It was not like Beatty to give up the chase while there was still a chance of total victory, yet, what else could be the meaning of his last two signals? The tragedy of the decision Moore reached in the few minutes given to him to make up his mind lay in the missing signal halliards of the *Lion*. Had the flagship been untouched in this particular area or had even *all* the halliards been shot away, then matters would have turned out very differently.

But Beatty was hoist with his own petard. The image of near-infallibility which had been created, of the man who was always right, misled Moore in no mean fashion. The Vice Admiral, Moore reasoned, must have some good purpose in his mind. What was the enemy's rear? *Blücher*. What did *Blücher* bear? North-east. What did the signal read? "Attack the rear of the enemy bearing North East." But there was still one chance; were the *Tiger* to steer for the German main force, Moore would follow. All, however, was not well with the *Tiger*. The shell that destroyed the intelligence office had other effects. The blast went up through the conning tower and the gun-control tower above it and "rattled us all in the conning tower very considerably." Captain Pelly found that most of his communications were severed by the explosion. He was also under the impression that the director and the main gunnery controls were out of action. "So there was a good deal of chaos and eventually I decided more or less to complete the turn which appeared to be in accordance with the other ships' movements."[33]

Tiger's movements meant that *Princess Royal* had to follow suit or be run down. Osmond de B. Brock raged helpless on the compass platform of his ship. The keen student of war guessed that something was amiss, but he was hemmed in inside the line and a turn toward the First Scouting Group, such as Nelson had made at St. Vincent, would have made *Princess Royal* immediately vulnerable to twice her weight of metal and all the torpedoes that Hipper's light craft possessed. Such a venture would have been foolhardy rather than daring.*

The Vice Admiral and his staff found it difficult to comprehend what was happening before their eyes. When Beatty realized what was going on he tried once more to restore sanity to proceedings. The Flag Commander, Reginald Plunkett, said to Beatty: "What we need now is Nelson's signal, 'Engage the enemy more closely.' " Struck by the suggestion, Beatty replied, "Yes, certainly. Hoist it." Again Seymour went through the signal book and discovered that the signal no longer existed. He hoisted instead, "Keep nearer the enemy," but this weaker and less specific command had no effect. By 1105 *Blücher* bore less than eight thousand yards to the east and Moore had worked the battle cruisers into some kind of line; the massacre would soon begin.

Hipper and his officers were as mystified as the British by what was going on. Hipper could only think that they had suffered even more damage than he had hoped. As he watched the battle cruisers move toward *Blücher*, Hipper turned toward his staff and proposed a move to the south-west to support the stricken ship. As a preliminary the three heavy ships were turned to the new course and the light craft ordered to prepare for a torpedo attack; within a few minutes this latter direction had been canceled as Hipper wanted to keep his ships together. The British, it seemed, were getting another chance.

It was not to be. Hipper's advisors were against the move to a man. Von Egidy informed his admiral in no uncertain terms that the *Seydlitz* was not fit for battle and had barely 200 rounds of 28 cm ammunition

---

*A tantalizing story of what O. de B. Brock might have said comes from Tyrwhitt who, in the course of a letter to Roger Keyes, written from his flagship, *Centaur*, on 29 December 1916, said: "I heard of another one which was made at the Dogger Bank fight & want to find out if it was really made. It was from O. de B. Brock to Moore. 'What the hell are we waiting for.' " As there is no other evidence of such an incident, the story must be considered apocryphal. Nonetheless, it is worth mentioning as an indication of the passions that were to be aroused in the navy by Moore's failure to pursue.

left on board. It was Raeder who suggested, tentatively, that Hipper
might be overcome by sentiment in bringing his three ships back into
action with the four hardly touched British ships. At the sound of this
voice in his ear, Hipper pulled himself together, ordered the course to be
brought back around to the south-east and "dismissed any further
thought of supporting the *Blücher*."

The return to a course of south-east soon put the German ships out of
range of their opponents and *Seydlitz* ceased fire at 1114. As they drew
away from the battlefield all eyes were on *Blücher* which, at Hipper's last
sight, "was still firing vigorously with all guns." A young officer who
was serving as a supernumerary in the G-9 describes this stage of the
action:

> At twelve o'clock (1100 GMT) the *Blücher* began to fall astern in the
> centre of large numbers of splashes. She was returning the fire very
> vigorously, apparently on both sides. The idea of sending the flotillas to
> the attack was given up, in my opinion because they had quickly lost their
> advanced position. Moreover, their attack, having regard to the wide
> intervals between the British ships, could only have been against a single
> ship, and at the same time the ships would merely have run under the
> guns of enemy light cruisers and destroyers. The breaking off of the
> forward movement caused by the turn of the battle cruisers was of great
> assistance to individual ships which had been unable to stay the pace and
> gave them an opportunity to join up again. At 1115 the *Blücher* was
> enveloped in one huge column of steam and water. Still firing, she was
> lost to sight.[34]

Blücher was trapped. Tyrwhitt closed *Lion* to see what could be done
and was ordered by Beatty to detach a force to form a screen for *Lion*.
Commodore (T) left *Undaunted*, *Aurora*, and all their destroyers save
Lookout's division to stay with *Lion*. The seven M class destroyers had
gone on ahead and, with the three L's working their way to the north to
support the First Light Cruiser Squadron, it seemed to be simply a
matter of administering the coup de grace. These arrangements made,
Tyrwhitt took *Arethusa* off to the east to be in on the kill.

Lion, now escorted by the two cruisers and twenty-five destroyers,
turned north and began to head for home. Beatty, longing to regain
control of events, called the destroyer *Attack*, under the command of
Lieutenant Commander C. V. Callaghan, alongside at 1120. In spite of
skillful seamanship on the part of the destroyer's captain, the process of
shifting his flag occupied Beatty for another precious twenty minutes.
Attack did not get under way to follow *Princess Royal* until about 1140,
Beatty being sped on his way by a cheerful stoker, on the upper deck for a
breather, who clapped him on the back and roared, "Well done, David."
Seymour wrote to his mother after the battle, saying:

The men came up from below to see the Admiral leave, and the sight of him seemed to send them off their heads.

It really was a remarkable scene as the *Lion* was one huge grandstand of cheering men, but she looked rather a sad sight heeled over to port with a good many holes in her side.[35]

Blücher was still fighting valiantly. She had assumed a heavy list to port and only a fraction of her armament was left in action. So effective had her fire been, however, that at 1105 Commodore Goodenough's cruisers were forced to execute a hurried turn away together to the north-east to throw *Blücher* off. It was a tribute to the ship's company and their training that even when their ship was so badly damaged as this they were able to straddle fast-moving light cruisers at over twelve thousand yards range. It was not until the distance had opened to sixteen thousand yards that Goodenough felt confident enough to bring the ships back to their former course.

At 1120 Commander Meade led the *Meteor* and three other M class destroyers in to attack the *Blücher* with torpedoes. The cruiser still had some sting left, for *Meteor* was struck by a heavy shell in the forward boiler room. The explosion killed four stokers and disabled the destroyer. She and her division, however, managed to get off their torpedoes, scoring what they estimated were five hits. These destroyed most of what was left of *Blücher*'s capacity as a fighting unit, but she nonetheless managed to launch a torpedo at the *Arethusa*, which was engaging the German with her forward 6" gun. The torpedo missed and *Arethusa* closed still further to twenty-five hundred yards: "very dashing and rather risky considering the *Blücher* was still firing."[36] The armored cruiser did not, however, have much longer. Her last guns began to fall silent and the list to port increased.

The account later written by the officer who interviewed the *Blücher*'s survivors, though in parts overdramatized, has the merit of giving a vivid impression of what the conditions were in the ship:

> . . . the shells came thick and fast with a terrible droning hum . . . when the range shortened . . . their trajectory flattened and they tore holes in the ship's sides and raked her decks. They penetrated the decks. They bore their way even to the stoke-hold. The coal in the bunkers was set on fire. Since the bunkers were half empty the fire burned merrily. In the engine room a shell licked up the oil and sprayed it around in flames of blue and green, scarring its victims and blazing where it fell.
>
> The terrific air pressure resulting from explosion in a confined space left a deep impression on the minds of the men of the *Blücher*. The air, it would seem, roars through every opening and tears its way through every weak spot. . . . As one poor wretch was passing through a trap-door a shell burst near him. He was exactly half way through. The trap door

closed with a terrific snap . . . men were picked up by that terrible *luftdruck* . . . and tossed to a horrible death amidst the machinery.

The decks presented a tangled mass of scrap iron. In one casemate, the only one as they thought, undestroyed, two men continued to serve their gun. They fired it as the ship listed, adapting the elevation to the new situation. . . .[37]

Arethusa launched two torpedoes and both struck—one under the fore turret and one under the engine-room. All lights and power failed, although even now a few guns spoke.

At 1145 Tyrwhitt signaled to Moore, "Enemy has struck." It was obvious that the *Blücher* could do no more damage as the *Arethusa* closed in. "She was in a pitiable condition—all her upper works wrecked, and fires could be seen raging through enormous shot holes in her side."[38] Men were emerging from below all over the ship and on her starboard side and net shelves some three hundred clustered. They raised a defiant cheer as *Arethusa* closed to within one hundred yards to begin rescue operations. Then the *Blücher* herself took a hand. As she wallowed in the swell, her list to port was steadily increasing. Quite suddenly *Blücher* gave a heave and turned turtle. She floated bottom up for a few minutes and sank. When the *Arethusa* and the destroyers began to pick up the survivors one note of high comedy sounded. *Arethusa* herself picked up 11 officers and 110 ratings. As one sailor was being hauled over the side by a rather stout stoker called Clark, he looked up at his rescuer and said, "Hallo Nobby, fancy meeting you here." The two had been next-door neighbors in prewar Hull.

But they were in a real war after all. Thinking only to ascertain precisely what was going on, Hirsch had taken L-5 in the direction of the sinking. Hirsch kept his ship high and would have been probably little noticed had it not been for one of the most tragic and futile incidents of the entire sea war. An errant German seaplane from Borkum suddenly appeared and flew over the stopped British ships, raining hand-bombs down on them. The pilot and observer must have mistaken the *Blücher* for a British ship because of her tripod mast, unique to the ship in the German navy. The seaplane could be little more than nuisance value but the same could not be said of the zeppelin, and heads were craned anxiously at the droning shape above.

The Germans had no idea of the stir they were causing. One of L-5's officers saw:

> . . . a tremendous picture, although we could hear almost nothing of the thunder of the guns, because of the noise of our engines. The *Blücher* was left behind as our forces steamed off and she was unable to follow. The four English battle cruisers fired at her together. She replied for as long as

she could, until she was completely shrouded in smoke and apparently on fire. At 1207 she heeled over and capsized. We then observed the enemy's withdrawal, and followed our forces as rearguard. You can imagine how distressing it was for me to watch the *Blücher* capsize, and be helpless to do anything but observe and report. We didn't drop bombs on the English ships. We had no chance because the clouds were at 1,300 feet. If we had dared fly over them at this altitude, we would have been shot down.[39]

It did not seem so to the ships below and Goodenough, who had also brought his ships into the area, ordered an immediate withdrawal. Tyrwhitt's *Arethusa* had engaged the seaplane and, keeping in mind the Nelsonic prayer for "humanity after victory," the Commodore kept the rescue going as long as possible. As a consequence, all but a few survivors were picked up before the Harwich Force turned for home. The real tragedy lay in the fact that the only casualties which the bombing claimed were Germans in the water. At the end, out of a complement of at least 1,026—and at least 1,200 were actually on board, the balance being made up from temporary drafts from *Von der Tann*—only 234 survived.

Content while the action was in progress to follow the movements of the *Tiger*, Moore began to bestir himself when Tyrwhitt signaled: "Enemy has struck." Most of the battle cruisers had ceased fire immediately on receipt of Tyrwhitt's signal, and Moore was faced with the problem of whether to withdraw or resume the pursuit of Hipper. The German battle cruisers were already nearly 30,000 yards away. It would take at least two or three hours to get back into range, by which time, Moore calculated, the force would be dangerously near to Heligoland. He was also influenced by the signal from the Admiralty to Roger Keyes which the *New Zealand* had intercepted, "Send submarines to Heligoland Bight. High Sea Fleet are coming out." In spite of the fact that Room 40 had been able to crack the coded postscript, its significance had been missed by the Admiralty although knowledge of the Jade River and a glance at the tide tables would have shown that, for the time being, the German declaration was impossible. What was worse, the *New Zealand*'s signal staff somehow transposed the sender and recipient of the signal. Moore was told that it was Commodore (S) who had sent the crucial "High Sea Fleet coming out." Keyes would only have sent such a message had he actually observed that himself. Admiralty reports could still be taken with a grain of salt; information from the man on the spot could not. What had been intended as information thus had the force of holy writ. The last real chance of the chase continuing crumbled away, for Moore now thought that the High Sea Fleet must be at least two hours further advanced than it actually was.

Moore fully realized that there was no immediate danger from any German surface forces; on the other hand, three hours further to the south-east. . . .He was also becoming worried over the fate of the *Lion*. The battle cruisers had last seen her rapidly losing way with a heavy list to port and, since then, there had been no signals from or word of her at all. Moore resolved to withdraw and at 1152 he signaled: "Form single line ahead in sequence of 4, 3, 2, 5 (*New Zealand, Princess Royal, Tiger, Indomitable*) course west."

At 1200, Rear Admiral Moore informed the Admiralty: "My position Lat. 54° 19′N, 5° 15′E. Course NNW. Speed 20 knots. Commodore (S) reports High Sea Fleet coming out. Am retiring."

At the same time Goodenough, realizing that operations against the *Blücher* were finished, signaled: "Lost touch with the enemy. What are your course and speed?" In reply, Moore sent at 1205: "Retire north-west."

Beatty in the *Attack* came up to the force at noon. There was no time for recriminations or explanations, and he immediately ordered the battle cruisers to turn sixteen points about to the south-east. Callaghan brought *Attack* alongside the *Princess Royal* and by 1227 Beatty had hoisted his flag in the latter.

Given time to think, Beatty too now realized that the chase was hopeless. The German ships were by now so far away that there would be no overtaking them before the German coast, especially as they had, without the *Blücher*, been able to work up to their squadron speed of 25 knots, thus making the differential almost nonexistent. The news was still that the High Sea Fleet was coming out and although Jellicoe was moving down from the north-west, Beatty's battle cruisers were in no state to tangle with the German battle line. Furthermore, Beatty had the crippled *Lion* to consider, together with the fact that submarines were thought to infest the area. "Expecting to meet the High Seas [*sic*] Fleet . . . [he] . . . was filled with anxiety as to the possibilities that might ensue. . . ."[40] At 1245, Beatty ordered the battle cruisers to steer west-south-west to close the *Lion*.

Jellicoe now knew that the battle cruisers' engagement was over. The Grand Fleet had worked up to 19 knots and was steering south, and Jellicoe decided to continue the movement. He did not think that von Ingenohl was at sea but he did not feel that it was worth the risk to leave the Battle Cruiser Force and Vice Admiral Bradford's squadrons unsupported. Bradford, for his part, continued to steam south-east toward Heligoland with the Third Cruiser Squadron disposed ahead.

On the other side of the North Sea, the Scouting Groups continued on their way unmolested to the Norderney Gat. Hipper pondered on the possibility of sending his light craft back for a torpedo attack at night but the small torpedo boats were growing desperately short of fuel and their crews were very tired. The High Sea Fleet flotillas were not far enough into the North Sea to do the job and the vessels out on forward patrol were old and few in number. Hipper was thus forced to abandon the idea of such an attack though his disappointment was somewhat mitigated by a series of coincident (though incorrect) reports from the *Moltke* and the L-5 of the loss of the *Tiger*. *Moltke* had thought the huge fire amidships would detonate the magazines. This prediction was reinforced when, in response to a query from Hipper as to the number of enemy battle cruisers, L-5 signaled, "Four." The fact was that the zeppelin had not seen the *Lion* drop out, while the battle cruisers had, and the observers in the ships naturally thought that L-5 was including her in the total; thus the mistake.

The First and Second Scouting Groups went into the Jade River late on the night of the 24th. They anchored there, waiting until the morning when *Seydlitz*, *Derfflinger*, and *Kolberg*—the three ships which had suffered damage in the action—left for Wilhelmshaven. *Derfflinger* and *Kolberg* were able to berth in Wilhelmshaven harbor on Monday morning, *Kolberg* going into dry dock for repair of her underwater damage. *Seydlitz* had to pump out the 600 tons of water in her after-magazines before her draught was reduced enough for her to get into the locks. Hipper had landed at Wilhelmshaven to give his verbal report to the Commander in Chief, and his flagship did not arrive until the late afternoon, when she, too, went straight into dock.

By 1800 Keyes was to the west of Heligoland, E-7 and E-4 had just been detached to take up patrol stations to the south of Heligoland and at the mouth of the Weser river, respectively. At 1830 E-11 assumed her billet to the north of Heligoland. Thinking that Tyrwhitt's light forces would be following the Germans into the Bight, harrying them as they retreated, Keyes at first intended to remain in the area of the Norderney Gat, but when he learnt from intercepted signals that all the destroyers and light cruisers were occupied in escorting the *Lion* home, he made a sweep to the north of Heligoland, hoping that he might find the Germans there. He did not and by 1900 he had decided to come round to a south-westerly course, with the intention of making contact with any German units coming in or out of the various channels.

He was too late. Von Ingenohl had brought the High Sea Fleet out of the Jade River and into the North Sea before Keyes could span the entrances to Wilhelmshaven. After the rendezvous with Hipper, the Battle Squadrons left the North Sea through Norderney Gat at dusk. By the time that Keyes had turned and sped down to the western corner of the German triangle, they were through and into the channels to Wilhelmshaven. Once into the Jade River, there was nothing even Keyes could do to them. It had been his faint hope that the German heavy forces might have been delayed by cripples but he knew by midnight that this hope was vain and that Hipper and von Ingenohl had escaped. He stayed in the vicinity of the Ems for a few more hours before turning his two destroyers home for Harwich. Unlike the submarines, it would be foolhardy for them to linger in an area frequented by strong German patrols.

The submarines, even E-11, saw "nothing but trawlers" as they patrolled on the surface during the dark hours. E-11 herself only arrived at Norderney Gat at 1830 and this itself was just too late. The primitive nature of night fighting and submerged attacks in darkness would have made any attempt against the Germans problematic, even had the High Sea Fleet not passed through the Gat before sunset. At noon the next day, E-8 sighted three flotillas of torpedo boats moving out to sea from the south of Heligoland, and she attacked them without result when they returned before dusk. At sunset on 26 January, the submarines turned for home and were in Harwich twenty-four hours later.

Lion's very efficient executive officer, Commander "Carlo" Fountaine, had all the damage-control procedures well under way. Collision mats were placed and suspect bulkheads shored up, the ingress of water being largely arrested. The engine-room, however, gave cause for concern. The only thing preventing the wholesale flooding of the huge port engine-room compartment was a badly crushed 12-inch diameter, ¼-inch thick copper suction pipe. The port engine was completely out of action, and Engineer Commander E. C. Green soon realized that the contamination of the feed water was such that all the boilers and thus the starboard engine would have to be shut down. For only a few more hours could *Lion* make even 10 knots.

Beatty now had as his primary mission the safe arrival of the *Lion* in Britain. A strong destroyer screen was disposed around her and the battle cruisers and the First Light Cruiser Squadron was detailed to act as a mobile covering force. *Antrim*, *Argyll*, and *Devonshire* made contact with Beatty at 1345. Bradford, though senior, obeyed his orders not to interfere with Beatty. He recalled the Third Cruiser Squadron and turned his whole force to the north-north-west to conform with Beatty's course at a distance of twenty-five miles. He did, however, place the Second Light Cruiser Squadron under Beatty's orders to assist in screening the *Lion*.

At 1530 Jellicoe met Bradford and ordered his ships to join company with the Grand Fleet as it continued its sweep to the south. An hour later, at a position 54°N, 4°E, he came into sight of Beatty and, in his turn, hauled his force around to the same course. He detached the cruiser *Galatea* and seventeen destroyers of the Second Flotilla and the *Caroline* and the eighteen of the Fourth Flotilla to further strengthen the screen around *Lion*. Jellicoe had just received an urgent signal from the Admiralty, sent at 1545:

> Germans are preparing a night attack by destroyers, but the two flotillas which were out with their battle cruisers last night have not enough fuel to take part. Our destroyers should protect damaged ships.

A night attack by German destroyers was an eminently plausible risk, especially if the German flotillas had put to sea before the battle. Destruction of the *Lion* would more than balance the loss of the *Blücher* and would be a prize well worth seeking by the highly trained torpedo boats of the High Sea Fleet.

Britain could not afford the possibility of the victory being further sullied. The Grand Fleet, with Beatty's force directly between it and the German coast, was stripped of its light craft and *Lion* and the crippled *Meteor* now had an escort of four battle cruisers, thirteen light cruisers, and sixty-seven destroyers—most of the Royal Navy's front-line strength in these types.

At 1500 Commander Green informed Chatfield that the engines were unlikely to remain operational during the night. Beatty decided to have *Lion* taken in tow. In view of *Indomitable*'s low speed and the reputation of her captain as a seaman, Beatty ordered her to do the job. The operation was a ticklish one at the best of times, but the condition of the *Lion* made it nearly impossible. Although Green had managed to reduce the list somewhat by counterflooding various tanks and trimming the bunkers, the ship was virtually helpless as both her capstans were out of action. One had been blown away by the heavy shell hit on the forecastle and the other was disabled by a fractured steampipe.

Beatty returned to the *Lion* to examine the damage and watch the passing of the tow. The entire operation took nearly two hours, all being done by hand in the *Lion*. A 5½ inch wire hawser was first passed and successfully secured, but, in the delicate operation of getting under way, the wire parted when the strain of *Lion*'s 33,000 tons of inert steel came on too quickly. On the second attempt, a 6½ inch hawser was passed over and this held under the strain. By nightfall the ships were working up to 10 knots.

Aware of the vulnerability of his charges to underwater attack, Tyrwhitt signaled to his forces: "Keep a good look-out for submarines at dawn. If seen, shoot and ram them regardless of your neighbors."

The night passed quietly as some measure of internal order was restored to the *Lion*:

> . . . the silence of the ship was the strangest element of all . . . the echo of voices through the long steel alleyways, the strange gurgling of water where no water should be. Most of us had headaches, all of us had black faces, torn clothes and jangled nerves. The ship was as cold as ice. . . . The sickbay was a mass of blood and dirt, feebly lighted by oil lamps. . . .[41]

At dawn on the 25th, Jellicoe detached Bradford's predreadnoughts and the Third Cruiser Squadron to return to their base at Rosyth. Any threat of a surface attack by heavy ships had now disappeared and Jellicoe determined to take his battle squadrons on a sweep to the north before going into Scapa Flow. All through that day Beatty's ships crept across the North Sea, the destroyers maintaining a close watch for U-boats.

Just after midnight they finally arrived off May Island, at the entrance to the Firth of Forth. *Indomitable* transferred the tow to waiting tugs from the Tyne and Beatty detached the ships additional to his command, the Second Cruiser Squadron and the Second Flotilla proceeding to Scapa, and the Fourth to Cromarty. As the transfer was made, Beatty came onboard, accompanied by Commodore Tyrwhitt, and remained on the bridge for the passage up the Firth from Inchkeith to Rosyth. In the early hours of the morning of 27 January 1915, the *Lion* was brought to anchor below the Forth Bridge.

CHAPTER 12

The Aftermath

The German toll in the Dogger Bank action was as high as that of the battles of the Falkland Islands and 28 August, and it had a similarly depressing effect upon the morale of the High Sea Fleet. With those who went down in the *Blücher*, her crew increased with men from the *Von der Tann*, and the huge casualty list from the *Seydlitz*, the First Scouting Group had suffered almost a thousand killed, with about three hundred more wounded or taken prisoner.[1]

The material damage was less dramatic. *Kolberg* and *Derfflinger* took but a few weeks to repair. Although the battle cruiser was struck by at least three shells, the German official history declared that only one hit had been scored. This curious anomaly was caused not by any overt desire to deceive but an overrigorous definition of the word *hit*. Despite the fact that the concussion opened up the underwater hull, the two shells, which had exploded close alongside, were not included because they did not actually strike *Derfflinger*. Another restriction to the total came from the German habit of not mentioning shells which did not pass through plating of 20 mm or greater thickness.[2] The eyewitness testimony of Seaman Richard Stumpf that *Derfflinger* was struck on her superstructure aft therefore cannot be ignored.[3] Despite all this, however, and the problems which realigning the shaft caused, *Derfflinger* was back in service by 17 February.

Seydlitz took far longer to repair. She had to have a large section of her forecastle and her entire after-battery rebuilt and the process was not complete until 1 April. During that time, her tenancy of the floating dock at Wilhelmshaven caused considerable disruption to the High Sea Fleet's program of refits. Even the Kaiser came down to Wilhelmshaven on 4 February, to inspect the damage and see for himself the results of the first engagement between dreadnoughts.

As far as gunnery was concerned, the First Scouting Group had some reason to feel satisfied. In spite of extremely difficult conditions, with all the disadvantages of the weather gauge and the vast amount of funnel smoke about, they had at least crippled the *Lion* and, they thought, sunk the *Tiger*. The scoring rate, taken in comparison with the British hits on *Derfflinger*, *Seydlitz*, and the long-range successes against *Blücher*, must have been far greater than that of their opponents. There were, however, two points of concern. First, as the captain of the *Seydlitz* reported:

> During the two hours action the ammunition in the two turrets in which fire was maintained continuously was shot away, all but 65 and 25 rounds respectively. The average time between the salvoes was 42.3 seconds. In this connection it is to be noted that the rapidity of fire cannot be accelerated further if the guns are to hold their target. The consumption of ammunition surpassed anything that had been previously anticipated. New ships will have to be provided with greatly increased space for ammunition stowage.[4]

The second matter was that the Imperial Navy had been even more astray than the British in its calculation of the need for long-range gunnery. There may have been some hint of the Dreyer-Pollen controversy raging in the Royal Navy, perhaps because some British gunnery officers had been less circumspect than they should, but the warning had not been heeded. The Germans had been content to regard the absolute maximum fighting range as eighteen thousand meters. The results of the battle forced a hasty revision of thinking.

Not that the results would be wholly to the good. Again, the German tendency to be satisfied with the less than ultimate made its entry. The German 28 cm and 30.5 cm guns, though excellent weapons, simply did not have the potential that the British 13.5″ and 15″ possessed. The 28 cm and 30.5 cm were, with the technology of the time, at the limit of their development. They were medium-range artillery, and superbly efficient as such, but their value fell off sharply when the range passed over nineteen thousand or twenty thousand meters. The British had recognized this very early, as far back as 1908, when they made the jump from 12″ 45-caliber guns to those of 50 caliber. The conversion had been made in the interests of increased range, but the results had been such as to force the British to take further steps up the ladder to the 13.5″ and 15″. The 12″ gun was not accurate at very long ranges; what is more, the high muzzle energies involved in impelling the shell such a distance soon wore down the barrel and reduced the accuracy still further by destroying the integrity of the rifling and introducing wobble.

A program of 38 cm armed battleships was in hand, but the Germans, already impressed by the efficacy of the 13.5″, were now faced with the dismal prospect of further 13.5″ gunned ships and at least ten vessels with 15″ joining the British fleet within the next two years, while they could muster no more than three or four at the end of that time. No more gun mountings for barrels were available. For the time being, the Germans would have to do the best that they could with their 28 cm and 30.5 cm weapons, and while it would be a superb effort, it could only be second best. The Germans had not used their talents wisely.

The matter of the near-loss of the *Seydlitz* was swiftly dealt with. Antiflash precautions were drastically improved, and passage between the turrets made far more difficult. Finally, the amounts of "ready use" ammunition and propellant charges prepositioned in the lobbies and passages were drastically reduced. Taken together these measures completely solved the problem and, although several of the battle cruisers suffered similar hits at Jutland, there was never any real danger of the ships being lost. The improvements were, of course, applied to the battleships and armored cruisers as well.

The brief duel between the *Arethusa* and the *Kolberg* came as final indication to the Imperial Navy that the 10.5 cm gun was inadequate. A two-stage rearmament program was instituted and applied to all the more modern light cruisers. By the end of 1915 all had had their bow and stern weapons replaced by single 15 cm guns fore and aft. This development paralleled the earlier British light cruisers, but as soon as enough of the heavier guns became available, the cruisers had all their 10.5 cms removed, receiving instead a homogeneous armament of seven 15 cm guns.

The dockyards at Wilhelmshaven and Kiel were put under considerable strain, for these were not the only refits. The armored cruiser *Yorck* had capsized and sunk after striking mines in the Jade Bay and this incident cast doubts on the stability of many of the heavy ships of the fleet, necessitating their withdrawal from service for extensive alterations. The poor performance and inadequate endurance of the torpedo boats at the Dogger Bank forced a revision of certain aspects of their boiler-firing. Finally, one more lengthy piece of work remained to be done on the heavy ships, though it could be largely performed by the ships themselves; this was the revision of the fire-control arrangements for long-range actions. All these modifications meant that the High Sea Fleet would not be able to emerge in strength until at least the spring.

Hipper's conclusions to his report of proceedings were concise:

1. Damage to the English Fleet is again possible.
2. All enterprises must be so arranged that timely support is assured

to the advanced forces. This may involve at any time the development of a fleet action. This action must not, if possible, be brought on in easterly winds. The systematic disposition of a line of submarines to attack before or during the battle should first be organized.

3. Only completely efficient ships should take part in the battle. All ships other than the most modern must, in view of the tremendous effectiveness of modern artillery, fall an easy prey to the enemy.

4. The flotillas must present in full force at every operation.

5. With regard to calibre and speed, it is necessary always in naval construction to keep to the outside limit. Otherwise one is at a disadvantage from the outset. The effect even of angle shots, and at extreme range, can be of decisive importance.[5]

The Scouting Forces fully realized every mistake made in the course of the operation, both by themselves and the Fleet Command. The battle squadrons should have been at sea as a covering force. The battle cruisers could have fallen back on them and converted retreat into triumph. The Scouting Forces also had rammed home to them the necessity of selecting their moment of greatest strength to move against Britain. They could afford to pick their time, unlike the Royal Navy, which had to be continually at the ready. The First Scouting Group, Hipper and his subordinates knew, should never have sailed without the *Von der Tann*.

It had been folly to include the *Blücher* in the sortie and madness, in spite of her gunnery prowess, to place her last in the line. The light forces were too few and too weak. In numbers alone they were so outmatched by the British that an assault on the latter's battle cruisers could very easily have resulted in a massacre of the German torpedo boats. The Schichau-built vessels of the Fifteenth Half Flotilla should not have gone with the force. With their coal-burning reciprocating engines they could not keep up, nor could they keep their funnels clear of the smoke that had done so much to impede the heavy ships' gunnery. Had an attack been launched by the Harwich Force their popgun four pounders and their old-model torpedoes would have been far more of a liability than an asset. One clear advantage in numbers that the High Sea Fleet did have over the Grand Fleet was in modern light craft but this superiority had not be properly utilized. The use of submarines had also been inadequate. Proper planning before the raid might have meant that there were enough around the Dogger Bank to seal the fate of the crippled *Lion*.

Hipper himself had been particularly struck by the speed of advance of the British ships, and he felt somewhat bitter at the German failure to match such speeds in their own ships. It took Jutland for him to realize that the British might perhaps have paid too high a price for the extra knot or two they had built into their ships at the expense of armor and subdivision.

There remained, however, the problem of the command itself. There were fears in the Scouting Groups that Hipper himself might be made a scapegoat for the loss of the *Blücher*, but von Ingenohl approved his actions and reported the fact to the Kaiser. Hipper had fought an extremely skillful battle, save for the fact that he would have been wiser to turn his ships together when he decided to withdraw; had he done so the battle cruisers would have been behind and *Blücher* out of the way ahead.

Once he had received official approval, Hipper thought no more about the ramifications of the affair, beyond expressing a vague dissatisfaction with the High Command to his staff. Hipper was very much a "simple seaman," a fine leader of ships and men and a competent tactician but he was in no way a political animal and never attempted to be. The same, however, could not be said either of his staff or his senior captains. They were the cream of the Imperial Navy, the most brilliant, ambitious, and generally the best-connected officers in the service. They had no hesitation in placing blame squarely where they felt it should lie.

The Kaiser, of course, could not be faulted. Once the "All Highest" had issued a directive there was no gain-saying it, at least at this stage of the war. The Commander in Chief, however, could be criticized. If he had followed what were only the half-policies of the Kaiser, he had attempted to execute them with only half-measures. The niggling losses at sea, the Heligoland Bight action, the failure to trap the squadrons of Beatty and Warrender after the Scarborough Raid, and now the Battle of the Dogger Bank made Admiral von Ingenohl a figure of public ridicule. In the streets of Kiel and Wilhelmshaven housewives jeered at him from their doors and little children followed him, singing derisively: "Lieb Vaterland magst ruhig sein, Die Flotte schlaft im Hafen ein" (Rest in peace, dear Fatherland, For the fleet is sleeping in port).

The campaign against von Ingenohl was ruthless. The "palace revolutionaries," led principally by Captain von Levetzow of the *Moltke* and Hipper's own Flag-Captain, von Egidy, intrigued at court, among senior army and navy officers, in Berlin, and with the Chancellor. They wanted the defeat of the Royal Navy and they knew perfectly well that von Ingenohl's dispositions could lead only to a disaster for the High Sea Fleet—the destruction of the Scouting Groups in precisely such a fashion as the Germans planned to isolate a squadron of the Grand Fleet.

Captain Zenker of the *Von der Tann*, all the more irate because he knew that the presence of his ship in the line might have made all the difference, wrote to Admiral Hugo von Pohl, Chief of the Admiralstab:

The blame for such an unfavourable result lies with the C-in-C. His belief that the English Fleet was coaling in Scapa Flow is not a valid justification for making no provision for an encounter with stronger enemy forces. Our previous advances to the English east coast have had such an effect on English public opinion that it should have been expected that strong forces would be in the North Sea. Also from previous experience, it should have been no surprise to find that the enemy had warning of our sortie. Such lack of foresight and prudence is all the more astonishing and regrettable because the C-in-C has already been excused for the defeat on 28 August; and in the two operations against the English east coast only luck enabled him to avoid painful consequences. The only way to avoid further disasters from such obstinate inflexibility is to change the C-in-C.[6]

But the change in German policy did not result merely from the efforts of the battle cruiser captains. The Admiralstab, von Pohl's department,

reviewed the whole conduct of the war since the High Sea Fleet had been in Admiral von Ingenohl's hands and came to the conclusion that he had not realised the truth that dissipation of forces is always disastrous, particularly for the weaker side.[7]

Von Ingenohl had attempted to play the game both ways and had failed. He was perhaps unfortunate in that the Battle of the Dogger Bank came as confirmation of the growing belief in Germany that changes had to be made. The intention of German policy had been to employ all naval forces against the Royal Navy in home waters with the aim of wearing down the Grand Fleet's strength to a point where it was weak enough for the High Sea Fleet to inflict defeat in a single decisive action. This policy had been a signal failure.

The only major successes of the mining campaign had been the destruction of the super-dreadnought *Audacious* and the light cruiser *Amphion*. In every other respect mining had become a two-edged weapon. For the mine fields to be any success at all they had to be laid without warning. As the British generally had good notice of the position of any new mines by interception of German wireless traffic, it thus followed that the first to stumble onto the fields were neutrals. This did not endear Germany to the neutral powers such as Holland, Norway, and Sweden who used the North Sea. As a result, they acquiesced to the British decision to declare the North Sea a war zone and to channel merchant shipping into several declared routes. This, of course, made it easy to search the neutral merchantmen for contraband and was of immense disadvantage to Germany.

The submarines had not been as successful as had been hoped against major warships. It soon developed that warships zigzagging at high speed with a proper escort were relatively immune. Of the battleships, only *Formidable* had yet fallen victim, and she only because of inept handling by the Vice Admiral Commanding. The submarines in the North Sea, it seemed, were largely wasting their time. That this was so is largely to the credit of Jellicoe, who never forgot the menace of the submarine and never neglected to take adequate precautions.

Germany's position at sea was deteriorating rapidly by the end of 1914 and on 27 December the Kaiser had asked Admiral von Pohl for suggestions as to the ways and means needed to rectify the situation. Captain Zenker was asked by the Chief of the Admiralstab to prepare such a document. He was not long in completing it and minced no words in his conclusions. In the course of assessment he wrote:

> The detrimental effect of our mining operations on enemy trade has not been sufficient to cause the British to try and block the German Bight in order to catch our commerce destroyers as they come out. The two cruiser attacks on the English coast resulted in no appreciable gain of a purely military nature, and in spite of their great political effect they have caused no change in the naval strategy of the enemy.
>
> The methods hitherto adopted, i.e., submarines and mining operations and occasional attacks on the English coast, will, in all probability, prove still less effective in the future, and will result in great losses to us.[8]

Zenker strongly advocated bringing about a general engagement with the Grand Fleet. He pointed out, in probably the first enunciation of three-dimensional naval warfare, that, with the proper tactical employment of ocean-going submarines, aircraft, and airships, the High Sea Fleet was fully the equal of the Grand Fleet as a whole and overwhelmingly stronger than any detachment. He stressed the importance of concentration—a point that would be strongly reinforced by the results of the Dogger Bank action.

As a consequence of all this, Zenker proposed that the High Sea Fleet be given a free hand to engage the British wherever and whenever it seemed fit. The document received von Pohl's support on the most important points, although he paid little attention to von Zenker's enthusiasm for employing aircraft and submarines with the fleet. Von Pohl went to the Kaiser and proposed that the restrictions be lifted and the High Sea Fleet become fully operational. The Kaiser hedged, preferring not to commit himself outright. He replied:

> Yes. But it must not be lost sight of that the main portion of the High Sea Fleet must be preserved as far as possible as a political instrument in the hand of the All-Highest War Lord. Advances on a large scale into enemy waters must be reported beforehand to His Majesty.[9]

Rebuffed in this fashion, for von Pohl considered that the note amounted to an outright refusal, the Admiralstab began to consider the possibility of a submarine campaign against British trade. The success and stringency of the British blockade preyed upon von Pohl's mind, and he reasoned that a reply had to be made. He did not feel that the neutrals could object overmuch because he believed that, in the first place, they had compromised their neutrality by acquiescing to the Royal Navy's arrangements and that, second:

> . . . if we declare the blockade 14 days before the date fixed for its commencement and issue a general warning to neutral shipping regarding the dangers of proceeding within British waters, we shall deprive neutral countries of all good grounds of complaint. The Belgian imports can be assumed by vessels from America taking the route round the North of Scotland. [10]

The political advisors opposed von Pohl because of the risks involved in dragging neutrals into the war, but even they were forced to agree that, in view of the effectiveness of the British blockade, Germany should "adopt those measures of warfare best adapted to bring hostilities to a speedy end." The point told. It was becoming clear to the Kaiser and those in authority that the defeat of Britain was the key to winning the entire war, and they were forced to accept the proposition. In the event, on 9 January, the Kaiser issued a decision that indicated the division between the politicians and the military. He decided against the submarine blockade, for the time being, but he gave his permission for the submarines to be prepared for work against commerce.

The Dogger Bank forced a drastic review of the situation. Badly frightened by the results of the battle, the Kaiser was more loath than ever to risk his precious dreadnoughts, but he was aware that the navy could not remain completely passive. Von Pohl, now resigned to the inactivity of the fleet, combined with the generals (who had received exaggerated reports of the troops and equipment arriving in France by sea) to convince the Kaiser that some decisive move was needed. On 4 February 1915, above von Pohl's signature, appeared the declaration:

> 1. The waters around Great Britain and Ireland, including the entire English Channel, are hereby declared a military area. From February 18 every hostile merchant ship found in these waters will be destroyed, even if it is not always possible to avoid thereby the dangers which threaten the crews and passengers.
>
> 2. Neutral ships also incur danger in the military area, because in view of the misuse of neutral flags ordered by the British Government on January 31 and the accidents of naval warfare, it cannot always be avoided

that attacks intended to be made on enemy ships may also involve neutral ships.

3. Traffic northwards around the Shetland Isles, in the east part of the North Sea, and a strip of at least 30 sea miles in breadth along the coast of Holland, is not endangered.[11]

The campaign eventually failed, for the effect on neutral opinion was too much for the politicians to cope with.

In the meantime, however, von Pohl took advantage of the considerable feeling against von Ingenohl to obtain his removal from the High Sea Fleet. To the horror of the officers who had also been pressing for von Ingenohl's replacement, his successor was not the aggressive Vice Admiral Reinhard Scheer, but von Pohl himself. Zenker and his colleagues had overplayed their hand, as the Kaiser refused to consider anyone so avowedly in favor of the active employment of the High Sea Fleet as Scheer. The Kaiser was determined upon von Pohl.

What the officers of the Imperial Navy also wanted, and failed to obtain, was a naval supreme commander. They had little objection to the Kaiser dictating general policy but felt that some appointee with the powers of a First Sea Lord was required. Despite his faults, von Tirpitz remained the obvious man for such a job, but the Kaiser had begun to distrust the Grand Admiral, and Chancellor von Bethmann-Hollwegg and Admiral von Muller were determined to prevent him assuming the supreme role. Hope for a unified command faded as von Tirpitz continued to fall out of favor with the Kaiser. The command would remain uncoordinated and policy disjointed.

Although the reaction to the new Commander in Chief at high levels was unfavourable, it was very different among the sailors and general populace. They remembered von Pohl's reputation as a practical seaman and his prowess as a tactician during innumerable prewar maneuvers. What is more, his signature to the declaration of unrestricted submarine warfare identified him in the public eye as the most aggressive of the German leaders. The appointment had the temporary effect of convincing both Germany and the Allies that a massive thrust by the High Sea Fleet was at hand. But this was not to be.

Von Pohl was not cast in the heroic mold. He combined a dry and pedantic nature with a considerable arrogance that made him as unpopular among the captains and admirals as his failure to face up to the Kaiser over the use of the fleet. He was happiest in administration, where his precise methods stood him in good stead, although he had proved a capable peacetime fleet commander.

The triumvirate that advised the Kaiser on naval matters fully espoused the policy of preserving the fleet until the war ended rather than "risking the fleet to gain peace." Tirpitz, enraged by the inactivity of his creation, did his best to convince von Muller, the Chief of the Naval Cabinet, von Pohl, and his successor at the Admiralstab, Bachmann, of the error of their ways, but his only success was with the latter.

Officially the policy was to initiate operations in the hope of cutting off a detachment of the Grand Fleet but, as von Pohl was not sanguine as to the possibility of its success, the scheme came to naught. Even though the restrictions on the High Sea Fleet were partially lifted on 30 March, von Pohl would never extend his forays into areas where contact with the Grand Fleet would become at all likely.

The truth was that von Pohl had little interest in the operations of the fleet. His initial excuse for his lack of eagerness was that the High Sea Fleet was not yet fully efficient and needed to undergo lengthy training. He also refused to take the High Sea Fleet out unless all capital ships were available. This put a considerable strain upon both the ships and the dockyards as many repairs were deferred or skimped in order to increase availability, and the dockyards found that they could no longer distribute the load of running repairs and refits over the entire year.

Dissatisfaction began to creep in. The High Sea Fleet made several sorties in March but, as von Pohl continued to have it as his firm policy only to seek action with the Grand Fleet in waters where he could achieve an absolute superiority in light craft and the advantage of precisely sited German mine fields—in other words, around Heligoland Bight—such sorties seemed more in the nature of rats emerging from their holes only to scuttle back at the slightest smell of danger. The expeditions had an unsettling effect which did not take long to spread to the most junior seamen. In addition, von Pohl was beginning to show signs of the cancer that would kill him within eighteen months, and his lackadaisical air became general.

The record of the High Sea Fleet during 1915 and early 1916 is monotonous and dispiriting, in keeping with the mood of its Commander-in-Chief. In the months after Dogger Bank, war weariness and ennui began to set in, which would result in the mutinies of 1917 and 1918. The reservists were the ones who gave most trouble. Many of them mature and successful men in the outside world, they had mobilized with the intention of coming to grips with the British. They were eager to serve their country, but they were not willing to countenance useless activity combined with poor food, harsh conditions and heavy physical work. The burgeoning submarine fleet was already draining off the most experienced and reliable senior personnel and the best and most enthusiastic of the junior officers. The division between officers and men, already marked, became even deeper as men of less experience and poorer quality came to take the places of those who had gone. Even as early as June 1915 there were serious disturbances in the *Derfflinger* and Seaman Richard Stumpf recorded in his diary the hatred of the officers which was beginning to well up amongst the sailors.

The monotony and drudgery of life, unrelieved by the slightest prospect of action, could only mean the inevitable deterioration of the High Sea Fleet as a fighting force. Von Pohl's error was to be fatal. He wasted the year of equality in numbers and material that the High Sea Fleet enjoyed in 1915; once the British new construction had commissioned this time would never return. It was a priceless opportunity missed. Furthermore, it is probable that the inactivity of 1915 damaged the fleet to an extent that could not be repaired, even by the most inspired leader. Scheer might have been able to restore the old feeling after Jutland but, unlike the majority of his officers and men, he knew by just how little his ships had escaped annihilation and that further clashes could only be fought under absolutely favorable conditions or else be resolutely avoided.

The British losses in personnel had been minimal compared with the Germans. *Tiger* had one officer killed and three wounded and nine men killed and eight wounded. *Meteor* suffered four killed and one wounded from the hit in her forward boiler room. *Lion*, in view of her damage, got off extremely lightly with only one man killed and twenty wounded.

It remained to deal with the damage. *Lion* was the most difficult matter. She lay at anchor below Rosyth, still listing badly and almost helpless, with not even steam to her capstans. Her ingenious commander, Fountaine, devised a method of weighing anchor by means of a heavy purchase connected to a heavy electric winch.

Under the direction of Commodore A. H. F. Young of the Salvage Corps, tugs and salvage vessels came alongside the *Lion* and operations to pump out the water began. Jellicoe ordered the fleet repairship *Assistance* down from Scapa to help, there being no other heavy repair facilities immediately available. The damaged sections of the armor belt were enclosed by wooden cofferdams and the affected compartments had concrete poured into them. The temporary work was completed in a matter of days and *Lion* made ready to proceed south. It was here that Admiral Fisher entered the scene. He had no great opinion of dockyard secrecy in the south and he felt that news leaking to the Germans of the *Lion*'s presence in dry dock would negate the attempts which the Admiralty had made to convince them and the neutrals that there had been little or no damage suffered. (They were helped, of course, by the tiny size of the actual casualty list.) Thus, in spite of the fact that there was no dry dock in the area, Fisher ordered that the battle cruiser undergo repair in the Tyne. Beatty and Chatfield heartily cursed the decision. Had the ship been sent to Devonport and dry docked, the repairs would have taken a matter of weeks. The ship was taken in hand by the Armstrong yard of Elswick, and the job proved to be difficult and time-consuming.

The ship had to be drastically lightened and heeled over to expose the damaged areas of plate in a process similar to careening. Newer and larger wooden coffer-dams were then erected to keep the damage free of water and, piece by piece, the armor plate was removed, repaired, and replaced. One special and unexpected difficulty was encountered with the concrete that had been poured into compartments to seal the cracks in the hull. It proved impossible to remove by hand or machinery. Eventually Armstrong had to resort to small charges of dynamite to force its removal.

During the repairs, the opportunity was taken to extend *Lion*'s flagship facilities and accommodation and to fit her with director firing, something, all the gunnery officers appreciated, that should have been done long before. However hard and well Armstrong worked, they could not make up for the lack of a dry dock, and *Lion* did not emerge for nearly four months. It was a good example of how concentration upon one problem can easily create others.

Meteor was quickly repaired and returned to service from Rosyth. *Tiger* joined her sister on the Tyne, to have a new armored roof fitted to her damaged turret. She remained alongside for the duration of the repair, which took less than a fortnight to complete.

And what of the British commanders? Beatty, although the escape of the Germans had not been directly his fault, could feel the trembling of his throne as men harked back to the Nelsonic tradition of total success being the only success acceptable to the British. Beatty need not have worried. Fisher and Churchill both thought very highly of him, and they shared his disappointment at having the cup dashed from his lips. Fisher, in his explosive manner, wrote at intervals to Beatty:

> January 25: "A few lines of sincere gratitude for your good fight!"
> January 27: "I've already written to tell you that you're splendid!"
> [and finally]
> January 31: "I've quite made up my mind. Your conduct was glorious! Beatty beatus!"[12]

The action came as a useful tonic to the British public, reassuring them as it did that the Grand Fleet was not entirely passive and that the Germans could not stand up to it. In Churchill's words:

> The victory of the Dogger Bank brought for the time being abruptly to an end the adverse movement against my administration at the Admiralty

which had begun to gather. Congratulations flowed in from every side, and we enjoyed, once again, an adequate measure of prestige. . . . The neutral world accepted the event as a decisive proof of British supremacy at sea; and even at home the Admiralty felt the benefit in a sensible increase of confidence and good-will.[13]

Beatty did not forget the ratings of the Battle Cruiser Force:

Two days later, Sir David Beatty had all his boys mustered around No 3 Dock at Rosyth, and standing on top of a bollard he addressed us. . . .

Through a megaphone he told us, "You have won the first round so now keep on keeping on." And with a merry smile he quoted a song from a Gilbert and Sullivan opera:

There is a beauty in the howling of the blast,
There is fury in the raging of the gale,
There is a terrific outpouring
When the *Lion* starts a-roaring,
And the *Tiger* starts a-lashing of her tail.[14]

The apt quotation from Gilbert and Sullivan was in fact Fisher's idea, Beatty having lifted it wholesale from a letter of the First Sea Lord's. Beatty was wise enough to see how much it would appeal to his ratings and he also knew that the old man would be delighted by its use.

Neither the Admiralty nor the press were disposed to make anything of Beatty other than the disappointed hero:

. . . Dogger Bank action added tremendously to Beatty's public reputation. An extraordinary photograph of the *Blücher* as she rolled over appeared in the *Daily Mail*—the Admiral was thrust more firmly into the role of the Royal Navy's leading and most successful man of action. He would sink every ship in the German Navy if given the chance. The sole reason why Hipper had "got away" was the fact that Beatty had not been there to finish the job. Beatty was the incarnation of British fighting spirit—a man who could be relied upon for victory.[15]

While Beatty's conduct of the action had been far from perfect, Jellicoe and most of those at the Admiralty felt that he had done very well indeed and would have achieved complete success had he been better served by his subordinates. As Jellicoe wrote to his vice admiral:

The more I hear of the fight the greater is my sympathy with you that you were knocked out in the *Lion* as it seems certain that otherwise you would have had one if not two battle cruisers to your credit in addition to *Blücher*.[16]

Truth to say, Jellicoe was puzzled by certain aspects of the action—notably the British gunnery—but, as none knew better than he how much had to be learnt by bitter experience, he did not press Beatty at the time, perhaps hoping that the latter would profit from his setback. But one danger was preying on Jellicoe's mind, and, in March, he wrote to Beatty:

> I should imagine that the Germans will sooner or later try to entrap you by using their battle cruisers as a decoy. They must know that I am— where I am—and you are—where you are, and they may well argue that the position is one which lends itself into a trap to bring you into the High Sea Fleet, with the battle cruisers as a bait. They know that if they can get you in chase, the odds are that you will be 100 miles away from me, and they can under such conditions draw you well down into Heligoland Bight without my being in effective support. It is quite all right if you keep your speed, of course, but it is the reverse if you have some ships with their speed badly reduced in the fight with the battle cruisers, or by submarines. In that case the loss of some ships seems inevitable if you are drawn into the vicinity of the High Sea Fleet with me still too far off to get to your help, or to their help, so as to extricate them before dark. . . . The Germans also probably know you and your qualities well by report, and will try to take advantage of that quality of "not letting go when you have once got hold" which you possess, thank God [perhaps a jaded reference to Moore—*author*]. . . . The Admiralty and the country's attitude would certainly be one of great praise and laudation in case of success, and one of exactly the opposite should you have ill-luck over such a venture . . . one must concern oneself very seriously with the result to the country of a piece of real bad luck culminating in a serious decrease in *relative* strength. Of course the whole thing is a question of the game being worth the candle and only the man on the spot can decide.[17]

It was a perceptive letter, and a fair warning. Jellicoe had delineated the principal danger to the Grand Fleet and the best way that the Germans could hope to have of reducing the British advantage, but it was meant as nothing more than advice. Beatty could, Jellicoe considered, be relied upon to keep himself only so far out of trouble.

Fisher was enraged by the performance of Beatty's subordinates. In the same letters in which he praised the vice admiral, he wrote:

> . . . *it is simply* ABSOLUTELY INCOMPREHENSIBLE *to me why Moore discontinued the action at* NOON! when the *Seydlitz* and *Derfflinger*, both heavily on fire and badly damaged and they had to scuttle into dock with great urgency and a very great number of killed. It's quite terrible to me that they should have been allowed to go free at noon. WHAT POSSIBLE EXPLANATION IS THERE? What excuse have we to offer!
>
> *Moore's* [conduct] *was despicable! The Captain of the Tiger* (I forget his name) *was a poltroon!* He was a long way ahead, he ought to have gone on, had he the slightest Nelsonic temperament in him, regardless of signals!

like Nelson at Copenhagen and St Vincent! In war the first principle is to disobey orders. Any fool can obey orders!

Is the *Tiger*'s Gunnery Lieutenant efficient? *We cannot have a single inefficient person—OFFICER OR MAN—in the battle cruisers and I call on you to send me a list of everyone who wants replacing, however high or low*! This is wartime and we can't have any damned folly about susceptibilities. Don't you worry about any odium—I will take that and love it![18]

Moore, of course, was the principal target. Beatty kept well out of the controversy, perhaps conscious that he bore some measure of responsibility for the confusion that prevailed. Moore had earned Churchill's regard when, as Director of Naval Ordnance, he had courage enough to stake his professional career on the success of the 15″ gun. But Fisher was never one to count a man's record in his favor, and after the outline of the battle had emerged he was daily demanding Moore's dismissal, court-martial, and even execution.

Churchill did remember and value the Rear Admiral's past services, but it was more than the First Lord's good will that saved Moore from being offered up "pour encourager les autres." In the first place, the court-martial of Rear Admiral E. C. T. Troubridge for failing to engage the German battle cruiser *Goeben* had been held only two months before. The proceedings had been held *in camera*, but the fact of Troubridge's acquittal was well known, and the effect had not been good, since much of the evidence produced had directed blame at the Admiralty. Moore's case would be even less clear-cut than Troubridge's, and any proceedings would be so complex and drawn-out that any salutary effect from a conviction would be lost. Second, although Moore was unpopular in some quarters of the service (notably with Tyrwhitt and Keyes), his record had been good and the other flag officers knew this. Beatty summed up this attitude when he wrote to the C in C, after Moore had been relieved, saying:

Well frankly between you and I he is not of the right sort of temperament for a B.C.S. He is too clever and I fancy his relations in the N.Z. were terribly strained after *Lion* fell out. Halsey is a very loyal man and I got nothing from him but one gets to know things and certainly Moore had a chance which most fellows would have given the eyes in their head for, and did nothing.[19]

Beatty's opinion of Moore had not been so restrained when he wrote to Keyes in September:

. . . I must pick up "that other" cur [?] as you call him. He's a stinker but I've got his measure now. Halsey on the subject is as good as a play.[20]

Despite the fact that, as Beatty noted, Churchill was in "a disturbed frame of mind," the First Lord did not wholly blame Moore, remarking later in *The World Crisis*, that "fortune presented herself to him in mocking and dubious guise." With his politician's mind he saw the value of a victory unsullied by public recriminations, and he was disposed to let Moore off lightly. It is interesting to note that he maintained and indeed expanded his position, for following his comment on Moore in *The World Crisis*, he went on to make one of the most lucid expositions ever written of the difficulties of command at sea and how little it can be compared with command on land. He concluded,

> There are a hundred ways of explaining a defeat on land and of obscuring the consequences of a mistake. Of these, the simplest is to continue the attack next day in a different direction or under different conditions. But on the sea no chance returns. The enemy disappears for months and the battle is over.[21]

Churchill eventually had his way. Moore was removed from the frontline, but not in such a fashion as to cause controversy. He was, in fact, "kicked sideways," for, on 8 February Rear Admiral Sir Archibald Gordon Moore, KCB, CVO, was appointed as Rear Admiral Cruiser Force I, with his flag in the elderly cruiser *Europa*. Operating among the Canary Islands, the command would not require, as the Admiralty delicately put it, "the qualities requisite in an officer commanding battle cruisers in action." Concealed amongst a great reorganization of the Battle Cruiser Force, Moore's departure passed with as little comment as could be expected. Indeed, he did not suffer unduly in the long run, for he went on to become a full admiral. It was left for Jellicoe to close the matter. As Commander in Chief he received all the Reports of Proceedings, together with Moore's own letter of explanation. On 3 March, Jellicoe wrote to the Admiralty:

> When considering the action of Sir Archibald Moore, it is to be observed that his interpretation of the signal made by the Vice Admiral is borne out by an examination of the signal logs of the other ships engaged, and according to his reading of the signal he carried out what he conceived to be the intentions of the Vice Admiral. . . .
>
> The Vice Admiral in his report of the action . . . does not say to what extent it was apparent that enemy's ships other than the *Blücher* had suffered, although he mentions the fact of fires onboard.
>
> Further, in forwarding the Rear Admiral's explanation, he makes no comment on the failure to follow up the retreating enemy. In these circumstances it is difficult for one who was not conversant with the conditions prevailing at the time to give a definite opinion on the correctness or otherwise of the Rear Admiral's procedure.

If as has since been stated two of the enemy's battle cruisers were very severely damaged *and the fact was apparent at the time* [author's italics], there is no doubt whatever that the Rear Admiral should have continued the action. Sir Archibald Moore is not longer under my command and therefore I offer no further comment on his action.[22]

Pelly, though in an even more precarious position, retained his command. Fisher bewailed the fact that the fire-eating Walter Cowan had not been in the *Tiger*, with which Beatty would have heartily agreed, while Keyes who had "for more than a year . . . looked upon the *Tiger* as my ship" found it "almost more than we could bear." But it was Beatty who saved Pelly. He wrote to Jellicoe:

> . . . Pelly did very badly. I think that the shell that landed under the control tower upset them and knocked those in the conning tower out temporarily although he won't say so, but for a time *Tiger* was all over the shop. . . .
> I have said that Pelly has done very well up to then, he has had difficulties to contend with and I don't think he is likely to do the same again, but he is a little bit of the nervous excited type. I am all against changes; it is upsetting and inclined to destroy confidence.[23]

Fisher did not concede the point, but Beatty and Jellicoe, the latter being of much the same opinion as his Vice Admiral, agreed to keep Pelly. Beatty would have preferred Cowan, but he was already required to take command of the *Princess Royal*, and there were not many other senior captains available whom Beatty would have liked under his command. He had little trust in the Admiralty's judgment and was already unhappy at the appointment of Captain Cecil Prowse to the *Queen Mary* in the place of Reginald Hall. In Beatty's view, it was apparently better the devil you know than the devil you don't. *Tiger* had commissioned in a hurry, with an extremely scratch crew. The two months normally devoted by builders to finishing a ship off had been skimped to get her into service, and, as a result, *Tiger* had suffered numerous defects. Although she had been in commission for over three months, she was not yet completely operational. She had never had the chance to settle down, and it had been wrong of Beatty, though he may have wanted to keep her under his eye, to put the ship second in the line—as it proved, a crucial position. In short, *Tiger*'s record had been dismal, and it may be noted that it has many curious parallels with that of the ill-fated *Prince of Wales* in the Second World War. Despite whatever Fisher and Churchill had to say, Jellicoe was quite right to discount brand-new ships as operational units.

So Pelly remained in *Tiger*, and eventually went on to become a full admiral and a knight. His gunnery officer was not, however, so fortunate. The universal opinion of the Grand Fleet, possibly due to *South-ampton's* signal of "salvoes, apparently from *Tiger*," was that the battle cruiser's gunnery had been "villainous," that she had not scored a single hit, and that she had confused the gunnery of the *Lion* and the *Princess Royal* while leaving the *Moltke* unengaged. Evan Bruce-Gardyne was relieved of his appointment, a sacrifice to Fisher's wrath. But *Tiger's* company always swore that they had scored hits on ships other than the *Blücher*.[24]

It will be setting right an injustice to say that *Tiger* did score hits on the German battle cruisers, one on the *Seydlitz* and one on the *Derfflinger*. All things considered, Bruce-Gardyne did as well as could be expected and was not to remain in disgrace forever. He finished the war as the Commander of the *Lion* and retired as a captain. Perhaps, though, he gained more satisfaction from the fact that the ship's company spontaneously manned the side and cheered him as he left the *Tiger*. This step signified more than just the embattled *Tiger* against the world. It was a statement of rectitude and confidence, for the battle cruiser was still the black sheep of the squadron, and one can only hope that somehow Fisher heard of it. Certainly the new gunnery officer was no improvement, for *Tiger's* shooting was no better at Jutland, and even her practice firings continued to be poor.

The principal event after the battle, though largely coincidental, was the reorganization of the battle cruisers and the reconstitution of Beatty's force into the Battle Cruiser Fleet with three separate squadrons. By steady degree, the detached battle cruisers were being brought back into home waters and within weeks all but *Inflexible*, which was in the Mediterranean and whose return would be delayed by her mining in the Dardanelles, were concentrated at Rosyth.

Lion was the fleet flagship, which the battle cruiser squadrons consisted of the First, *Princess Royal* (Flag), *Queen Mary*, and *Tiger*; the Second, *Australia* (Flag), *New Zealand*, and *Indefatigable*; and the Third, *Invincible* (Flag) and *Indomitable*, to which last was attached the *Inflexible* when she eventually returned. In command of a "fleet," though still technically under Jellicoe, Beatty was in an ambiguous position that a lesser man could very easily have abused. Beatty did not do so, and became even more the trusted associate of the Commander in Chief. A bond of mutual respect soon sprang up between the two that would hardly be sullied, even by the bitter controversies of later years.

The flag officers eventually selected for the three squadrons and the new First Light Cruiser Squadron that was to be formed from four of the new *Royalist* class light cruisers (Goodenough's *Towns* became the Second Light Cruiser Squadron) could hardly have been bettered. Osmond de B.

Brock was appointed Commodore First Class, a temporary device until he could become a rear admiral by seniority, in command of the First Battle Cruiser Squadron. Until *Lion* was repaired, he was to share *Princess Royal* with Beatty and her new captain, Walter Cowan. In the crowded flagship the latter had at first a rather thin time of it, "wandering about the ship like a lost soul for a few days."[25]

It had at first been intended to retain Vice Admiral Sir George Patey in the *Australia*, which had been his flagship on the Australian and the North American stations. The relationship between Patey and Beatty, however, would have been too difficult. As a confirmed vice admiral, Patey was the senior, and to get over this difficulty it was necessary to issue an Order-in-Council that granted Beatty acting seniority "for the purpose of command while employed afloat during hostilities." Although, as Jellicoe wrote, "never was promotion better deserved,"[26] it was extremely unfair on Patey, whom Fisher described as having been infallibly correct in his predictions.[27] Patey was a very competent officer who had done extremely well in the early operations in the Pacific, and had his advice been heeded the Coronel disaster would never have taken place. Wasted in the Pacific, he deserved something more, and was soon reappointed to the North American and West Indies Station as Commander in Chief.

Rear Admiral William Pakenham was appointed in his stead. He had endeared himself to Churchill (and, of course, to Beatty and Fisher when they got to hear of it) by drawing the First Lord aside when the latter was on a visit to Rosyth and saying, "First Lord, I wish to speak to you in private, Nelson has come again."[28]

As it would be some time yet before all the older battle cruisers joined, the Third Battle Cruiser Squadron was temporarily combined with the Second under Pakenham's orders. No admiral had yet been found, as the problem of selection was not easy. The officer would have to be both an experienced cruiser commander and acceptable to Beatty—and there were, it must be admitted, few who filled both criteria. Not until May, by a happy combination of circumstances, would the choice fall upon Rear Admiral Horace Hood. Captain E.S. Alexander-Sinclair was appointed Commodore Second Class commanding the First Light Cruiser Squadron. Although a competent officer, he would never display the particular talent for cruiser work possessed by his contemporary, Commodore Goodenough.

With the expansion of command, came an expansion of the staff. Beatty followed Jellicoe's example by dividing his administration into operational and logistic sections. Chatfield was offered the post of Chief of Staff, but he refused it, preferring to remain as Flag Captain. Instead

R. W. Bentinck was appointed. As Chief of Staff, he would be responsible for "everything except the fighting efficiency." As Flag Captain, Chatfield continued to be responsible for this side of affairs, with an extra commander, Sidney Bailey, to assist him with the gunnery. Bentinck was yet another example of Beatty's capacity for employing and gaining the respect of strong and capable men. Rear Admiral W. S. Chalmers wrote of the Captain of the Fleet, "Bentinck's personality inspired confidence . . . a born aristocrat . . . tactful but strong."[29]

There remained the problem of Ralph Seymour, Beatty's "round little flag lieutenant." With any other admiral, the mistakes he had made in the battle, combined with his ambiguous signal during the Scarborough Raid, would have ensured his immediate removal. It must be noted, however, that the notorious signal to turn away was not necessarily Seymour's fault—for if Beatty did give the order to turn away before he informed his staff of the reason, as seems to have been the case, Seymour cannot be blamed. Beatty, however, did not think that he had done so badly, and since Seymour was a pleasant face to have around, he would not be relieved. Few at the Admiralty, or indeed in the Battle Cruiser Fleet, were of the same opinion, but an admiral had to be permitted his foibles. Perhaps the Staff Commander, Reginald Plunkett, and the newly appointed Assistant Flag Lieutenant could keep a close eye on Seymour in the future to see that things did not go too badly wrong. In view of what was to happen at the Battle of Jutland, it might have been better had Beatty sent Seymour to command a destroyer, which would have been no disgrace, and got the very best signal specialist that he could find who would interpret his orders unambiguously. However, if this soft-heartedness was a mistake, it was meant well. Beatty may have been arrogant and very ambitious, but he was rarely one for the knife in the back of a subordinate.

There was one more important personnel change in the wake of the battle. Churchill, Oliver, and Keyes agreed that the position of Commodore (S) was becoming untenable. Matters had come to a head when Moore's signal to Jellicoe indicating that he was withdrawing and that "Commodore (S) reports High Sea Fleet coming out" was read by Fisher who, of course, immediately placed the blame on Keyes. The latter heard of the First Sea Lord's rage and was able to deny that he had made any such signal, but in discussion with Churchill and Oliver, Keyes declared that it would be better if he could go to some other appointment and be out of Fisher's reach. As Keyes wrote:

> It was a great relief to me to get this off my mind, and I think the First Lord was relieved too, for he had expended a good deal of time and energy in fighting my battles, which was all wrong.[30]

Matters had not been improved by a second falling-out between Keyes and Tyrwhitt which occurred just before the Dogger Bank and was not resolved for some days. It developed ostensibly from Tyrwhitt's reaction to the discovery that Keyes had at last managed to get the Admiralty to promise him a light cruiser, the *Inconstant*, which meant one less for the Harwich Force. Tyrwhitt was considerably annoyed, and it seems that the whole matter of their relative seniorities boiled up again. Keyes wrote bitterly to his wife that Tyrwhitt "thought I might be in his way one day" and it is likely that this was so. Their relationship was basically unstable and although the two were soon reconciled, it was well for both that Keyes was going.

On 8 February Keyes was ordered to the Mediterranean, to go as Chief of Staff to Vice Admiral Sackville Carden, who was to lead the attack on the Dardanelles. Delighted by the appointment, Keyes was out of England in a matter of hours, with Tyrwhitt and other friends "only envious, as there was nothing doing in the North Sea." Fisher's protege, S. S. Hall, was appointed to succeed Keyes as Commodore (S)—now a purely administrative job—while Captain Waistell took command of the Overseas Submarine Flotilla.

As far as the Battle Cruiser Force was concerned, the mistakes of the Dogger Bank would not be made again. (With few exceptions, it was now notable as the finest concentration of fighting spirit in the Royal Navy.) Not least among the new arrivals was Captain Walter Cowan. It was said of him that he was one of the few officers who actually enjoyed war and who regarded peace as the worst thing that could happen. Needless to say, he was more notorious than successful in peacetime, but his performance in the *Princess Royal*, as a cruiser squadron commander and in the Baltic after the war, not to say as a septuagenarian commander, RNVR, in the Mediterranean in 1940 and 1941, indicate his mettle as a fighter and war leader.

In the end, perhaps the best thing had been done *pour encourager les autres*. It might have provided a salutary example to send Moore and Pelly ashore with the unfortunate Bruce-Gardyne, but it is important to remember that the repercussions could have been very dangerous, despite the fact that such treatment may have caused certain of the subordinate admirals at Jutland to behave in a more reasonable fashion than they did. The service was not "a youthful and confident David" in the First World War. A distinguished submarine officer had described it as a "wealthy, aged, and puzzled Goliath" and this label has great validity. Callaghan's removal had caused enough of a controversy in the fleet, even when he was replaced by such an "anointed one" as Jellicoe. Had Moore been removed, and it is unlikely that he would have kept silent, the uproar would have been tremendous. It must be remembered that neither Fisher nor Churchill was trusted by large sections of the service. The memory of the Fisher-Beresford dispute, and certain of the First Lord's more iconoclastic prewar activities, were too recent to permit such high-handed behavior. Of course there were many who did think that Moore should go, but there were so many eager for the downfall of Churchill's administration that it is quite possible that the Board would not have survived the controversy. What is more, such a dismissal as Fisher, at least, wanted, would have been "ungentlemanly" and many of the older officers in the navy who had hitherto been neutral would not have stood for it. Had Moore gone, Pelly would almost certainly have had to go too—and he was a man in good standing with the King, no friend of either Churchill or Fisher. Churchill was right to accept the Dogger Bank as a useful little victory—he could not afford the risk of the Royal Navy being sundered by controversy in the middle of the war. Fisher's return meant that the relative calm that had reigned since Wilson became First Sea Lord in 1910 stood in grave danger of being shattered. If that happened, the consequences would be incalculable.

The battle had revealed several grave faults in the Royal Navy's organization and one of these, at least, was hastily dealt with. Even when Lieutenant Commander Seymour's fumblings were taken into account, the signal book and the signal system as a whole could not be said to be adequate. In the hundred years since the end of the Napoleonic Wars, the signal organization had developed to meet all the intricate demands of peacetime operations. It had not, however, kept pace with the needs of the navy in war. So much attention had been concentrated upon new construction and the development of gunnery that signals, along with other specializations, had fallen by the wayside. This had not wholly been the fault of the Admiralty and the senior officers of the day, since there was so much to do before the navy was ready for war and so little time in which to do it, but they did err in attaching so much kudos to the gunnery branch that the brightest, most innovative, and ambitious officers had gravitated toward it at the expense of the other specializations. Signals perhaps suffered most, because in the other specializations improvements always had a much more tangible result in peacetime. In gunnery and torpedo, the target was struck more often at greater ranges. In engineering, ships' machinery became more reliable and capable of running for longer periods at higher speeds. In navigation, ships were able to move in confined and dangerous waters with more confidence. The vast difference between peace- and wartime communications took active service conditions to be discovered. That it was not realized before may also be attributed to the comfortable British habit of conducting maneuvers at the height of summer, when the weather was mild and the visibility excellent.

Five signals were added to the book, one being the old Nelsonic signal "Engage the enemy more closely." Perhaps this signal's original deletion from the signal book may be considered symptomatic of the calm certainty of the Victorian navy in its own fighting abilities against all comers. Pride or not, it was a dangerous thing to have done. The other four signals were:

> The Admiral making the signal is disabled (To signify that the flagship was out of action)
> Admiral unable to make signals by W/T
> Commander in Chief transfers the command
> Commander in Chief has resumed the command.[31]

Richmond, who at Plunkett's behest, "drew the attention of the Powers that be to the omission of 'Engage the enemy more closely,' " ensured that these additions were promulgated with exemplary haste— they were issued on 27 February. It might have been better, in view of the numerous communication failures that were to occur later in the war, had the staff exercised an ounce of prevention and revised the entire signal book. Certainly the five signals would prevent any other subordinate being placed in Moore's position of confusion and uncertainty. But the changes in naval warfare had been too great for these to be the only alterations needed.

The approach to other matters of concern, principally the battle cruisers' protection, their gunnery, and the effectiveness of their shell, was even less satisfactory. Filson Young wrote of the aftermath of the battle:

> Reports on every subject were called for and furnished by the people concerned. Discussions and conferences were held among experts in the various technical branches involved, and a mass of very valuable material, which would have furnished food for a real staff for months, was collected and forwarded to the Admiralty. But it soon became apparent that technical interest in these matters was pretty well confined to our own force. The Admiralty having acknowledged receipt of the masses of material presented to it, made no further sign.[32]

Young paints a somewhat biased picture. The real problem was in fact a complete lack of coordination in analysis. The Battle Cruiser Fleet was not entirely satisfied with its gunnery, putting down the lack of hits to the exceptionally poor conditions, the presence of the untrained *Tiger*, and the lack of directors. These two latter faults could be remedied in time. The question, as Chatfield saw it, was that while there seemed no doubt that our gunnery officers had not succeeded in hitting the enemy sufficiently; *or if they had, then why had they not been put out of action like the Lion and the Blücher?* [Italics supplied] Were our projectiles the cause? But all the experts had faith in them.[33]

On the other hand, in the Grand Fleet proper, Jellicoe came to the conclusion that the German gunnery had been vastly superior to that of Beatty's ships:

. . . thus confirming my suspicion that the gunnery of our Battle Cruiser Squadron was in great need of improvement, a fact which I very frequently urged upon Sir David Beatty.[34]

All were correct, at least partially so. The battle cruisers' gunnery was not good, and the shells were defective. The problem with the Battle Cruiser Fleet was simply a geographical one. Despite the fact that Beatty's ships had some of the finest gunnery personnel in the Royal Navy, the waters around Rosyth were not at all suitable for use as firing ranges, unlike those around Scapa Flow where Jellicoe's main occupation was gunnery practice with his battleships. Jellicoe frequently pleaded with Beatty to bring his ships up to the Flow, at least a squadron at a time, to spend a few weeks undertaking firings, but Beatty would not agree to the risk of having the Battle Cruiser Fleet so far to the north, or his force divided. The problem was not solved until early 1916, when Jellicoe agreed to send the fast *Queen Elizabeth*s to Rosyth to substitute for each Battle Cruiser Squadron as it came up to Scapa Flow. The issue of the defective shells was summed up in Chatfield's sad little sentence, "But all the experts had faith in them." In fact, all the gunnery experts were at sea, and too busy improving their own ships' gunnery to be able to do anything. Not until after Jutland, when Jellicoe went to the Admiralty and took many Grand Fleet officers with him would this matter be dealt with.

At least, however, the installation of director firing and range clocks to all the battle cruisers and battleships was speeded up. *Lion* was fitted during her repair, and the other battle cruisers received it as they came in for refit. Fisher did much to speed this work, and it was largely complete within months. Unfortunately, the system being installed was the austere "Dreyer" version. *Queen Mary* had been the test ship for the original and far more impressive "Pollen" system, which she still carried. The quality of her gunnery, due largely to the advantage she possessed in the Pollen system, would always be far higher than that of the other ships. The controversy, described in Chapter 2, is a sad example of how "in-Service" cabals can influence design and purchase to a damaging extent.

Improvements after Fisher's resignation later in 1915—such as fitting directors to the heavy ships' secondary armaments—took much longer to implement than during his tenure. In war there is much to recommend the approach that "we must 'scrap' everyone who gets in the way." Finally, in gunnery, in spite of his censuring Pelly over his error in the distribution of fire, Jellicoe took good care to have the *Grand Fleet Battle Orders* revised so as to remove any ambiguity and prevent any further confusion in firing.

Although the magazine weakness in the British battle cruisers had not yet been clearly revealed, *Lion*'s structure had not stood up to the German shell fire as well as it should have. The 5" and 6" armor plate had been pierced by 28 cm shells, and thus "the poor side armoring of the British battle cruisers had been unequivocally demonstrated in battle." Furthermore, the 9" side armor had also been driven in by a 30.5 cm shell from *Derfflinger*. This last damage should have been warning enough that the British ships might not face up to 30.5 cm gunfire of any sort.

In the *Lion* herself, possibly chastened by the small fire in "A" turret lobby and the false alarm which had caused "A" magazine to be partially flooded, the Chief Gunner, Alexander Grant, on his own initiative introduced a routine that a strictly limited number of cartridges should be outside the magazine at any one time and that the magazine doors should normally be closed. Strangely enough, although this decision played a major part in saving the *Lion* at Jutland, it does not seem to have been passed on to the other battle cruisers or to the Admiralty.

The problem lay in two areas, the first of which was the propellant itself. The Royal Navy's heavy ships stowed their cordite charges in silk bags. Each quarter charge had a 16-ounce fine-grain black powder detonator, and this meant that such charges "needed very complete flash precautions to be safe in action." In fact, there were no such complete flash precautions and when such a situation was combined with a tendency to have large numbers lying around in the handling spaces in order to ensure a rapid supply to the guns, only disaster could result. It was a highly dangerous policy because any flame could cause a flashback which would spread up to the turret and down to the magazines proper. This was where the major weakness in British design came into play. There had once been self-sealing scuttles which opened only to pass a charge up to the turret, but, in the interests of a faster supply, they had been omitted from the entrance to the magazines. Instead, a "working chamber" was inserted into the chain between gun and magazine. This system was dangerous enough at the best of times, since flash from a cordite explosion can travel hundreds of feet. It was suicidal when large amounts of exposed cordite were left lying about in the working chamber itself. Perhaps the one surprising thing is that only three of the battle cruisers would be lost by this cause.

Churchill and Fisher both now pleaded with Jellicoe to bring the Grand Fleet down to the Firth of Forth and move the Battle Cruiser Fleet to the Humber. Both he and Beatty were set against it. Beatty was unhappy enough with Rosyth because of the length of the passage out into the open sea and its vulnerability to mines. It took so long to sweep a clear channel that, as he complained to Churchill when the latter visited him after the battle, he had several times to sail without any sweeping having been done. Beatty would actually have preferred Cromarty, as a clearer and safer anchorage, but Fisher replied, "It's 150 miles too far off." Churchill apparently raised with Beatty the possibility of the battle cruisers going to the Humber and the Grand Fleet to Rosyth, but, as the Vice Admiral wrote to Jellicoe, he was able to dispose of the idea without difficulty:

> I had made it plain that I did not agree with putting battle cruisers at the Humber. First of all and lastly it is impossible, as there is insufficient water. When I say impossible I mean as a base which one can leave or enter at any time of the tide; this we cannot do three hours each side of low water, i.e. for 6 hours; that I think puts the hat on it. I also think it would be a mistake to move the battle fleet to Rosyth. It no doubt could be made safe with extra craft and extra vigilance, but it seems to me it would be playing into the enemy hands to bring within nearer reach our capital ships, and in a position where going in or out (no matter what precautions we take) they would be far more vulnerable to submarine attack than at Scapa, also destroyer attack if they ever develop it, and most certainly mine-laying, and take them away from a place where they can enjoy some measure of opportunity for gunnery practices.[35]

However, Beatty did suggest that the *King Edward VIIs* with their lesser draught, be sent to the Humber instead as they could operate from the base at all stages of the tide. This proposition would eventually be taken up, but for the rest the First Lord "seemed to concur" and nothing more was said. The other dispositions, all of which would hold for the Battle of Jutland, were to stand.

CHAPTER 13

Summa

The six months discussed in this book can be described as the true beginning of modern naval warfare. Between the outbreak of the Great War and the sinking of the *Blücher*, every aspect of the new technology available was used, albeit with varying degrees of success. Submarines came into their own as weapon systems; aircraft began to play an effective role; open-sea mine laying was commonplace; and surface actions were fought at long range, at high speed, in poor weather, and at least partly under the influence of wireless. Two questions may therefore be asked: How well prepared were the two navies for war, and how well did they react to its challenges?

On the strategic level, the Royal Navy, although having the advantage of an Admiralty in which ultimate responsibility rested, suffered from the lack of an overall plan prepared before the outbreak of war and from a continuing failure to produce a coordinated scheme of operation after hostilities had begun. Unable to delineate specific aims, the Royal Navy was unable to benefit from mistakes so as to proceed more or less steadily toward the fulfillment of its goals. German analysis, and its subsequent effect on operations, was better organized, but the Imperial Navy was rent by contesting factions.

The deficiencies inherent in the Admiralty's outlook have tended to be somewhat obscured by the smooth mobilization of all units, the dispatch of the Grand Fleet to its war station, the institution of the blockade, and the rapid passage of the BEF to France. But the passage of the BEF was an operation dictated by the War Office, not the Admiralty. Mobilization was, even if large scale, a relatively straightforward mechanical undertaking. As for the blockade, its principal purpose was not at first wholly appreciated by the Admiralty. Something of a historical panacea, the blockade was vaguely seen more as a means of bringing the enemy fleet to action than as the ultimate economic weapon at Britain's disposal. This misplaced emphasis resulted in a late decision to implement a distant rather than a close blockade and in a less than energetic pressing of the government to remove the considerable restrictions placed upon the strategy by conventions and agreements of previous decades.

Most important, the War Group made no attempt to define the best overall campaign by which Germany could be defeated at sea. The Group, in essence, functioned as a collection of individuals, each with a particular solution, to which he devoted too much time, and each paying insufficient attention to the greater picture or to the other schemes proposed. The Admiralty, preoccupied by the concept of one decisive battle, little appreciated that the Germans, as the weaker navy, would come out only on their own terms. The offensive sweeps conducted into German waters were, at best, disjointed in their initiation and tended to be the inspiration of the forward commanders, not the Admiralty.

All this was largely the result of the lack of a staff and of knowledge of the proper workings of a staff. Rather than distancing themselves from the details of the naval war so as to turn their attention to the consideration of proposals as part of an overall plan, the members of the War Group espoused individual causes. Such an occupation would have been more appropriate for junior officers. These junior officers of the time should have had the task of preparing detailed appreciations of various proposals so that their seniors could have assessed their suitability to the bigger picture. Instead, the majority of the officers on the staff had little intellectual curiosity and did not expect to be privy to the activities of the War Group. In consequence, although they played a minor part in the implementation of policy, they knew little or nothing of its construction and were given hardly a chance to make suggestions or to advise on practicalities. The change to a staff organization came too late for the Royal Navy in the First World War. Moving from a situation in which the war plans were literally locked within the brain of the First Sea Lord, the British did not have the time to develop a fully functioning staff by the beginning of the war.

Misunderstanding of staff concepts led to tactical and material problems and deprived the Royal Navy of many considerable technological advantages. Since there had been no system before the war to collate and analyze information, or even to devise the questions that would elicit such data, the Admiralty, collectively, had little appreciation of the capabilities of submarines, aircraft, and other technology.

Even the annual maneuvers, conducted on the large scale and with much prior preparation, were not conducive to revealing operational problems. Held in high summer, maneuvers did not test material to its limits or assemble evidence for or against new methods. There was simply no perception of the need to devise trials for such things. Only the 1913 exercises, which displayed the perils of close blockade, were of any real significance in their results.

Thus, in 1914, the Admiralty possessed neither the means nor the inclination to determine tactical doctrine from experimental or operational experience, nor could it thoroughly define and propose remedies for the important material deficiencies which were all too soon apparent. The sinking of *Pathfinder*, for example, was followed, not by intelligent orders setting out the submarine threat and counteracting tactics, but by a bald declaration on the need for higher minimum speeds, which failed, as became obvious from later sinkings, to impress any of the urgency of the matter upon senior officers. Indeed, it is extraordinary that the same navy that operated the E class submarine did not regard submersibles as a seagoing threat.

The division between the designers and the operators of equipment, which it was the Admiralty's duty to prevent, was manifest well before the war. It had shown itself in a number of ways, not only in the tendency of naval architects to site secondary armaments too close to the waterline in cruisers and battleships, but in the notorious and repeated error of placing the spotting top abaft the forefunnel in a number of capital ships. This had the effect of asphyxiating the occupants and making spotting impossible.

The lack of coordinated machinery between analysis and operations hamstrung the fleet at sea. There was little realization of the necessity for the rapid dissemination of operational experience and the improvements this could bring in tactical doctrines and material measures. Because of the lack of a staff and of training in staff methods, intelligent theories based upon the best practical evidence tended to rest in whatever small circle they were devised.

Particularly, small lessons were not made use of. The deficiencies in wireless procedures should have been apparent to every signal and commanding officer, but the practices of the Grand Fleet in 1916 were little better than those of 1914. Similarly, a number of ships, notably the *Lion*, took measures to improve the flash-tight conditions of magazines and turrets, but these were not passed to other units. Furthermore, when efforts (largely at Jellicoe's direction) were made to adjust tactical doctrine and material to the experience of war, as in the *Grand Fleet Battle Orders* and *Gunnery and Torpedo Memoranda*, there was soon ample evidence that too many officers had neither understood the directions nor made their subordinates aware of them. Not merely was there a lack of critical awareness of the general intention of these orders and memoranda, but misunderstanding of even the individual's part in the greater plans was not uncommon.

The Royal Navy was thus weakened, first, by the inefficient operation of the War Group, the supreme directing body, and its supporting arms in the Admiralty, and, second, by the prevailing innocence of officers at sea to the requirements over and above the efficient operation of their own ships or squadrons. Particularly, the latter failed to realize that the command could not function without information and that tactical and material superiority could only be ensured by continual evaluation of experience. Thus, the Royal Navy did not wage war as well as it might have because of its fundamental ignorance of how to go about the job and because it was incapable of defining the basic problems at issue.

The Imperial Navy's preparedness for the war and the reaction to its challenges differed somewhat from that of the Royal Navy. There is no doubt that the Imperial Navy was caught by surprise by many aspects of the early operations of the war. The expectation of a close blockade by the British was based upon hope, not reason. The High Sea Fleet was not as well equipped as it should have been, particularly in the areas of armament and endurance. Apart from the raiding forces, there were few intelligent plans in hand before the outbreak for the employment of the navy as a whole.

Given the German propensity for staff work, ably demonstrated by the Army General Staff, such weaknesses in the Imperial Navy seem incongruous until we remember that the navy was, above all, a political animal. The bulk of the intellectual effort was devoted, not to planning for the war operations of the navy, but to ensuring that the Imperial Navy's budgets, part of von Tirpitz's master plan for the creation of the fleet, passed through the German political system without being gutted. The Admiralstab itself, though possessing the skeleton of an efficient naval staff organization, could not exercise an uninterrupted command function.

The operational employment of the Imperial Navy's units for the first six months of the war was muddled, and the losses at the Heligoland Bight and Dogger Bank actions can be directly attributed to the gravely flawed command organization. With a vacillating Kaiser and a divided and directly competing command structure, the strategic employment of the High Sea Fleet and other units could never be put on a sound footing. One of the greatest opportunities offered to the High Sea Fleet during the entire war was lost when the Germans did not attempt to engage the Grand Fleet during its moment of greatest weakness in 1914. Conversely, the Germans courted disaster by sending unsupported forces into the North Sea that were neither fast enough to run away from, nor powerful enough to stand up to, units of the Grand Fleet. Defeat in detail was not a prospect which ships of the High Sea Fleet should have had to face, working as they did—even in their offensive operations—in such proximity to their own bases.

If there were a fatal defect, it lay in this system of command. The system was fundamentally unworkable because, unlike the British system, it was not governed either by a single dominating personality (unless he were the Kaiser) or by an ideally constituted staff. The British War Group, although it failed to function as a unit, was at least a collection in a single place of those responsible for the overall direction of the navy. The Germans had no such advantage. Eventually, the German deficiencies of command were to prove more damaging than those of the British, if only because they prevented the Germans from embarking upon a policy of coordinated offensive operations when such an offensive was essential for their success at sea. Significantly, however, the German machinery for the analysis and assessment of operational experience worked much more efficiently than that of the British. The Germans were quick to recognize both material and tactical defects and to take steps to remedy them when possible.

The most notable example of the efficiency of the German system was the speedy introduction of improved antiflash precautions to all units after the near-loss of the *Seydlitz* at the Dogger Bank. But large-scale efforts were also made to practice the High Sea Fleet's long-range gunnery, to improve the capabilities of the torpedo craft and, when the weapons became available, to rearm the light cruisers. Unlike the Royal Navy, the Imperial Navy had the bulk of such efforts in hand by early 1915 and, also unlike the Royal Navy, the Imperial Navy developed a particular interest in night fighting. Units of the High Sea Fleet were to prove adept in such techniques at Jutland.

That the Germans could not do more with the High Sea Fleet's capabilities resulted partly from the magnitude of their prewar misjudgments but mainly from the increasing demands put upon German industry by other arms of the forces. Just as the immobility of the warfare on land was to Germany's ultimate disadvantage because of her more limited resources, so the blockade—unlike the submarine, a proven tool—was slowly strangling the Central Powers. As Churchill remarked of a battle fought nearly twenty-eight years later, the Dogger Bank action marked not so much the beginning of the end, but the end of the beginning. The fuse had been lit which would lead inevitably to Jutland and to the surrender of 21 November 1918.

The positions of the Royal and Imperial navies in 1914 have some lessons for the navies of 1984. The progress of technology in the decades preceding the outbreak of the First World War was extraordinary, particularly from the turn of the century on. Similarly, the advent of nuclear submarines, surface-to-surface missiles, and electronic warfare have negated many of the conditions of the 1939–45 war, the most recent major naval conflict.

Development at such speed poses two requirements. The first is for navies to derive sufficient knowledge of the capabilities and limitations of novel technology during peacetime operations so as to minimize the deficiencies of their equipment and to be able to create realistic strategy and tactics for a possible conflict. The second, closely related, is that navies must develop systems by which operational experience at all levels can be assessed effectively and rapidly in order to maintain advantages and remove deficiencies in wartime.

This history has described the extent to which the Royal and Imperial navies met these requirements. Whether the navies of the present day, particularly those of the Western Alliance, are capable of satisfying them is impossible to say. But they will only have done so if they have been realistic in their operations and analyses, testing people and equipment to their limits in exercises that adequately simulate wartime conditions. Maneuvers in fine weather, as the British discovered, are of little value if a blockade must be maintained all year round. Assumptions, of the pattern of the German presumption that ten thousand meters would be the normal maximum fighting range, are of no use if they are never tested. History seems to repeat itself for only so long as its actors are unaware of what has gone before.

Notes

PREFACE

1. *Julian S. Corbett 1854–1922: Historian of British Maritime Policy from Drake to Jellicoe.* Donald M. Schurman, Royal Historical Society, London, 1981.

2. *Former Naval Person: Winston Churchill and the Royal Navy*; Vice Admiral Sir Peter Gretton, Cassell, London, 1968, p. 107.

3. *From Dreadnought to Scapa Flow*, Volume II, *The War Years: To the Eve of Jutland, 1914–1916*. Professor A. J. Marder, Oxford University Press, London, 1965, p. vii.

CHAPTER 1

1. *My Naval Life*. Commander Stephen (Lord) King-Hall, Faber & Faber, London, 1952, p. 87.

2. "The German Official History of the War at Sea," translation in *The Naval Review*, vol. VIII, 1920, pp. 619–20.

3. Admiralty to C in C Home Fleet 24 July 1914, Appendix A to *Naval Staff Monograph (Historical)*, Volume III, Monograph 6, *Passage of the BEF. August 1914*. p. 24.

4. Admiralty to C in C Home Fleet 26 July 1914. Sent 1600. *Ibid.*

5. Admiralty to General & The Press 27 July 1914. *Ibid.*, p. 25.

6. Admiralty to Senior Officers Abroad 27 July 1914. *Ibid.*

7. Admiralty to C in C Home Fleet 28 July 1914. Sent 1700. *Ibid.*, p. 26.

8. Cipher telegram to British Ambassador in Paris 2 August 1914. Sent 1650. *Ibid.*, p. 27.

CHAPTER 2

1. *From Dreadnought to Scapa Flow. The Royal Navy in the Fisher Era 1904–1919*, Volume I, *The Road to War 1904–1914*. Professor A. J. Marder, Oxford University Press, London, 1961, p. 21.

2. Jellicoe to Captain F. C. Dreyer CB, RN, 28 May 1914. *DRYR* 3/2. *Dreyer Papers*, Churchill College Archives, Cambridge.

3. *My Naval Life*, King-Hall, p. 76.

4. *Unpublished Memoirs*, Volume II. Admiral of the Fleet Sir Henry Oliver, National Maritime Museum, p. 99.

5. *Journal* Admiral Sir Herbert Richmond *Richmond Papers* 1/9. National Maritime Museum.

6. *Diary 1906*. Captain Oswald Frewen, *Frewen Papers*.

7. *Diary*. 7 August 1914, Captain C. J. Wintour, RN, Imperial War Museum.

CHAPTER 3

1. Because of the similarity of the translated term to the British titles, the word *Admiralstab* will continue to be used to describe the German staff.

2. For a particularly clear description of the differences between the two systems, see: *Admiral of the Fleet Earl Beatty. The Last Naval Hero: An Intimate Biography*. Captain S. W. Roskill, Collins, London, 1980. p. 62.

CHAPTER 4

1. Beatty to his wife 5 August 1914, quoted in *The Life and Letters of David Earl Beatty*, Rear Admiral W. S. Chalmers, Hodder & Stoughton, London, 1951, p. 137.

2. "The Destruction of the *Königin Luise* and the Sinking of the *Amphion*," Captain C. H. Fox, RN, *The Naval Review*, Volume V, 1917, p. 132.

3. *Ibid.*, p. 134.

4. *Ibid.*

5. *Ibid.*, p. 137.

6. *Ibid.*, p. 139.

7. *Naval Staff Monograph (Historical)*, Volume X, *Home Waters, Part I, From the Outbreak of War to 27 August 1914*, p. 43.

8. *Ibid.*, p. 68.

9. *Ibid.*, p. 75.

CHAPTER 5

1. *The Naval Memoirs of Admiral of the Fleet Sir Roger Keyes*, Volume I, *The Narrow Seas to the Dardanelles 1910–1915*. Thornton Butterworth Ltd, London, 1934, pp. 76–78.

2. *Ibid.*, p. 80.

3. Admiralty to C in C Grand Fleet 26 August 14. Sent 1305. *Naval Staff Monograph (Historical)*, Volume III, Number 11, *The Battle of the Heligoland Bight, August 28th, 1914*. p. 149.

4. C in C Grand Fleet to Admiralty 26 August 14. Sent 1635. *Ibid.*

5. C in C Grand Fleet to Admiralty 26 August 14. Sent 1754. *Ibid.*

6. *Ibid.*, p. 113.

7. Admiralty to C in C Grand Fleet 27 August 14. Sent 0030. *Ibid.*, p. 149.

8. Flag to Battle Cruiser Force 27 August 14. Sent 0800. *Ibid.*

9. *Ibid.*, p. 119.

10. *Ibid.*, p. 142.

11. *The Battle of the Heligoland Bight, 28th August 1914.* Lecture to the Royal Naval Staff College, Greenwich, delivered by Commander John Creswell, RN, 2 May 1932. *Creswell Papers*, Churchill College.

12. Tyrwhitt to his wife, 29 & 30 August 1914. Quoted in *Tyrwhitt of the Harwich Force.* Professor A. Temple Patterson, MacDonald, London, 1973, p. 62.

13. *Cruisers in Battle: Naval Light Cavalry under Fire 1914–18.* Hector C. Bywater, Constable & Co., London, 1939, p. 50.

14. *Naval Staff Monograph (Historical)*, Volume III, Number 11. p. 151.

15. *Ibid.*

16. *Ibid.*

17. *Ibid.*

18. *Ibid.*, p. 129.

19. *The Navy and Defence.* Admiral of the Fleet Lord Chatfield, William Heineman London, 1942, pp. 124–25.

20. *Naval Staff Monograph (Historical)*, Volume III, Number 11. p. 130.

21. *Cruisers in Battle.* Bywater, p. 54.

22. *The German Official History of the War at Sea*, Volume 1, *The War in the North Sea.* Captain Otto Groos, Mittler, Berlin, 1920. Naval Intelligence Department Translation, Admiralty Historical Library, p. 264.

23. *Sea Saga*, Lady L. King-Hall, Victor Gollancz Ltd, London, 1935, p. 382.

24. *Naval Staff Monograph (Historical)*, Volume III, Number 11. p. 135.

25. *Roger Keyes.* Brigadier C. F. Aspinall-Oglander, Hogarth Press, London, 1951, p. 95.

26. *Cruisers in Battle.* Bywater, pp. 62–63.

27. *Ibid.*, p. 70.

28. *The Navy and Defence.* Chatfield, p. 125.

29. *Naval Staff Monograph (Historical)*, Volume III, Number 11. p. 143.

30. *Tyrwhitt of the Harwich Force.* Patterson, p. 61.

31. *Ibid.*, p. 62.

32. Beatty to Arthur Balfour 21 June 1916. Quoted in *From Dreadnought to Scapa Flow*, Volume II. Marder, p. 52.

33. *The Keyes Papers*, Volume I, *1914–1918.* Paul G. Halpern, Navy Records Society, London, 1972, p. 19.

34. *Tyrwhitt of the Harwich Force.* Patterson, p. 65.

35. *The World Crisis*, Volume I. W. S. Churchill, Australasian Publishing Co., Sydney, 1925, p. 309.

36. *Churchill and the Admirals.* S. W. Roskill, Collins Ltd, London, 1977. p. 34.

37. *Admiral von Hipper.* Captain H. Waldeyer-Hartz, Rich & Cowan, London, 1933, p. 114.

38. *Naval Staff Monograph (Historical)*, Volume III, Number 11. p. 148.

CHAPTER 6

1. Admiralty to C in C Grand Fleet 3 September 14. Sent 1945. *Naval Staff Monograph (Historical)*, Volume XI, *Home Waters*, Part II, *September and October 1914*, p. 154.

2. *Ibid.*, p. 37.

3. *The Naval Memoirs of Admiral of the Fleet Sir Roger Keyes*, Volume I. pp. 76–77.

4. *From Dreadnought to Scapa Flow*, Volume II. Marder, p. 57.

5. *The World Crisis*. Churchill, p. 234.

6. Flag *Euryalus* to General 20 September 14. Sent 0504. *Naval Staff Monograph (Historical)*, Volume XI. p. 52.

7. *Bless Our Ship*. Captain Eric Bush, George Allen & Unwin Ltd, London, 1958, p. 37.

8. Tyrwhitt to his sister, 30 September 1914, *Tyrwhitt of the Harwich Force*. Patterson, p. 73.

9. *Ibid.*

10. *The Naval Memoirs of Admiral of the Fleet Sir Roger Keyes*, Volume I. p. 106.

11. *Ibid.*, pp. 106–7.

12. *Naval Staff Monograph (Historical)*, Volume XI. pp. 57–58.

13. Admiralty to General 22 September 14. Sent 2200. *Ibid.*, p. 59.

14. Christian to Jellicoe 29 September 1914. *The Jellicoe Papers*, Volume I, *1893–1916*. Ed. Professor A. Temple Patterson, The Navy Records Society, London, 1966, pp. 70–71.

15. *From Dreadnought to Scapa Flow*, Volume II. Marder, p. 58.

16. Fisher to Mrs. Reginald McKenna, October 1914. *Fear God and Dread Nought. The Correspondence of Admiral of the Fleet Lord Fisher of Kilverstone*, Volume III, *Restoration, Abdication and Last Years 1914–1920*. Professor A. J. Marder, Jonathan Cape, London, 1959, p. 61.

17. *Full Circle: The Biography of Admiral Sir Bertram Ramsay*, Rear Admiral W. S. Chalmers, Hodder & Stoughton, London, 1954, p. 21.

18. *Naval Staff Monograph (Historical)*, Volume XI. p. 65.

19. *Ibid.*, p. 110.

20. *The Naval Memoirs of Admiral of the Fleet Sir Roger Keyes*, Volume I. p. 110.

21. *Ibid.*, p. 113.

22. *Max Horton and the Western Approaches*. Rear Admiral W. S. Chalmers, Hodder & Stoughton, London, 1954, p. 20.

23. *The Naval Memoirs of Admiral of the Fleet Sir Roger Keyes*, Volume I. p. 118.

24. Tyrwhitt to his wife, 17 October 1914. *Tyrwhitt of the Harwich Force*, Patterson, p. 79.

25. Tyrwhitt to his wife, 23 October 1914. *Ibid.*, p. 81.

26. *Naval Staff Monograph (Historical)*, Volume XI. p. 139.

27. *From Dreadnought to Scapa Flow*, Volume II. Marder, p. 86.

28. *A Great Seaman: The Life of Admiral of the Fleet Sir Henry Oliver*. Admiral Sir William James, Witherby, London, 1956, p. 134.

29. *From Dreadnought to Scapa Flow*, Volume II. Marder, p. 88.

30. *The World Crisis*, Volume I. Churchill, pp. 400–1.

31. Battenberg to Hood, 13 November 1914. *The Hood Papers 6/2*. Churchill College Archives, Cambridge.

CHAPTER 7

1. *A Great Seaman*. James, p. 135.

2. *The World Crisis*, Volume I. Churchill, p. 441.

3. See *From Dreadnought to Scapa Flow*, Volume II. Marder, pp. 75–76; *The Jellicoe Papers*, Volume I. Patterson, pp. 75–77; and *The Sea Heritage: A Study of Maritime Warfare*. Admiral Sir Frederick Dreyer, Museum Press, London, 1955, pp. 82–84.

4. Tyrwhitt to his sister, 17 September 1914, *Tyrwhitt of the Harwich Force*. Patterson, p. 69.

5. Fisher to Jellicoe, 3 November 1914, *Fear God and Dread Nought*, Volume III. Marder, p. 65.

6. *A Great Seaman*. James, p. 140.

7. Secretary of the Admiralty to Jellicoe, 7 November 1914, *The Jellicoe Papers*, Volume I. Patterson, p. 79.

8. *The World Crisis*, Volume I. Churchill, pp. 456–57.

9. *The Naval Memoirs of Admiral of the Fleet Sir Roger Keyes*, Volume I. p. 130.

10. Fisher to Jellicoe, 3 November 1914, *Fear God and Dread Nought*, Volume II. Marder, p. 66.

11. C in C Grand Fleet to First Sea Lord 11 November 1914. Sent 1743. *Naval Staff Monograph (Historical)*, Volume XII, *Home Waters*, Part III, p. 191.

12. Admiralty to C in C Grand Fleet 11 November 1914. Sent 2005. *Ibid.*, p. 189.

13. C in C Grand Fleet to Admiralty 11 November 1914. Sent ?. *Ibid.*, p. 190.

14. Jellicoe to Fisher, 11 November 1914, *Fear God and Dread Nought*, Volume III. Marder, p. 69.

15. Admiralty to C in C Grand Fleet 13 November 1914. Sent 1620. *Naval Staff Monograph (Historical)*, Volume XII. p. 192.

16. C in C Grand Fleet to Admiralty 14 November 1914. *Ibid.*, p. 193.

17. Beatty to Fisher, 15 November 1914, *Fear God and Dread Nought*, Volume III. Marder, p. 171.

18. Jellicoe to Fisher, 10 November 1914, *Ibid.*, p. 68.

19. *The World Crisis*, Volume I. Churchill, p. 443.

20. Jellicoe to Fisher, 11 November 1914, *Fear God and Dread Nought*, Volume III. Marder, p. 69.

21. Fisher to Jellicoe, 16 November 1914, *Ibid.*, p. 72.

22. Admiralty to C in C Grand Fleet, 16 November 1914. Sent 1530 & 1615. *Naval Staff Monograph (Historical)*, Volume XII, p. 196.

23. *Ibid.*, p. 42.

24. *The Naval Memoirs of Admiral of the Fleet Sir Roger Keyes*, Volume I, p. 137.

25. *Cryptoanalysis and its Influence on the War at Sea 1914–1918*. Lt. Cdr. Patrick Beesly, RNVR, Fifth Naval History Symposium, Annapolis, MD., 1981.

26. *Diary*. Captain G. C. Harper, RN, 25 October 1914. Imperial War Museum.

27. *Cryptoanalysis*, Beesly.

28. *The Naval Memoirs of Admiral of the Fleet Sir Roger Keyes*, Volume I, p. 139.

29. Tyrwhitt to his wife, 18 November 1914, *Tyrwhitt of the Harwich Force*. Patterson, p. 89.

30. *Ibid.*

31. *Ibid.*

32. *Naval Staff Monograph (Historical)*, Volume XII, p. 77.

33. *The Navy from Within*. Vice Admiral K. G. B. Dewar, Gollancz, London, 1939, p. 165.

34. *The Naval Memoirs of Admiral of the Fleet Sir Roger Keyes*, Volume I, p. 133.

35. *Ibid.*, pp. 133–34.

36. Tyrwhitt to his wife, 6 December 1914, *Tyrwhitt of the Harwich Force*. Patterson, p. 91.

CHAPTER 8

1. *Admiral von Hipper*, Waldeyer-Hartz, p. 133.

2. Admiralty to C in C Grand Fleet, 11 December 1914. Sent 0020. *Naval Staff Monograph (Historical)*, Volume XII, p. 214.

3. *Admiral von Hipper*, Waldeyer-Hartz, p. 133.

4. *Naval Staff Monograph (Historical)*, Volume XII. p. 101.

5. *Ibid.*, p. 102.

6. *The Naval Memoirs of Admiral of the Fleet Sir Roger Keyes*, Volume I. pp. 151–52.

7. *The Sea Heritage*. Dreyer, p. 103.

8. *Ibid.*, pp. 103–104.

9. *The Naval Memoirs of Admiral of the Fleet Sir Roger Keyes*, Volume I. p. 145.

10. *Ibid.*, p. 147.

11. *Ibid.*, p. 151.

12. *Naval Staff Memorandum (Historical)*, Volume XII. p. 124.

13. Jellicoe to Fisher, 18 December 1914, Notation on memorandum of the affair; *The Jellicoe Papers*, Volume I. Patterson, p. 108.

14. Fisher to Jellicoe, 20 December 1914, *Fear God and Dread Nought*, Volume III. Marder, p. 100.

15. Notation on Beatty to Jellicoe letter, 20 December 1914, *The Jellicoe Papers*, Volume I. Patterson, p. 112.

16. Beatty to Jellicoe, 20 December 1914. *Ibid.*, p. 111.

17. *The Papers of Admiral Sir R. A. R. Ernle-Erle-Plunkett-Drax*. DRAX 1/6. Churchill College Archives, Cambridge.

18. C in C Grand Fleet to Admiralty, quoted in *From Dreadnought to Scapa Flow*, Volume II. Marder, p. 145.

19. "D.B. II" by "R.P.D." (Admiral Sir Reginald A. R. Ernle-Erle-Plunkett-Drax). Obituary in *The Naval Review*, Volume 24, No 2, May 1936, p. 215.

20. *Ibid.*

21. Fisher to Jellicoe, 21 December 1914, *Fear God and Dread Nought*, Volume III. Marder, p. 102.

22. Fisher to Jellicoe, 20 December 1914. *Ibid.*, p. 100.

23. *Sea Saga*. King-Hall, p. 420.

24. *A Great Seaman*. James, p. 137.

25. Ballard to Keyes, 23 December 1914, *The Naval Memoirs of Admiral of the Fleet Sir Roger Keyes*, Volume I. p. 78.

26. Churchill to Fisher, 21 December 1914, *Fear God and Dread Nought*, Volume III. Marder, p. 105.

27. *From Dreadnought to Scapa Flow*, Volume II. Marder, p. 147.

28. *The World Crisis*, Volume I. Churchill, p. 478.

29. *Admiral von Hipper*, Waldeyer-Hartz, p. 138.

CHAPTER 9

1. *Tyrwhitt of the Harwich Force*. Patterson, p. 94.

2. *Ibid.*, p. 95.

3. *Ibid.*, pp. 95–96.

4. *Naval Staff Monograph (Historical)*, Volume XII. p. 136.

5. *Ibid.*

6. Tyrwhitt to his sister, 31 December 1914, *Tyrwhitt of the Harwich Force*. Patterson, p. 98.

7. Tyrwhitt to his wife, 29 December 1914. *Ibid.*

8. *A Great Seaman*, James, p. 138.

9. *The Navy from Within*. Dewar, p. 169.

10. Fisher to Chief of the War Staff & First Lord, 6 January 1915, *Fear God and Dread Nought*, Volume III. Marder, p. 126.

11. Churchill to Jellicoe, 11 January 1915, *From Dreadnought to Scapa Flow*, Volume II. Marder, p. 100.

12. *Ibid.*, p. 99. See also *Naval Staff Monograph (Historical)*, Volume XII. p. 153.

13. *Pull Together! The Memoirs of Admiral Sir Lewis Bayly*. George G. Harrap & Co., London, 1939, p. 76.

14. Jellicoe to Bethell, 22 January 1915, *The Jellicoe Papers*, Volume I. Patterson, p. 128.

15. Fisher to Jellicoe, 4 January 1915, *Fear God and Dread Nought*, Volume III. Marder, p. 120.

CHAPTER 10

1. *Tyrwhitt of the Harwich Force.* Patterson, p. 101.
2. Admiralty to Commodore (T), 7 January 1915. Sent 2053. *Naval Staff Monograph (Historical)*, Volume XII, p. 230.
3. *Ibid.*, p. 166.
4. Tyrwhitt to his wife, 17 January 1915, *Tyrwhitt of the Harwich Force.* Patterson, p. 102.

CHAPTER 11

1. *Admiral von Hipper*, Waldeyer-Hartz, p. 148.
2. *The World Crisis*, Volume II. W. S. Churchill, Australasian Publishing Co., Sydney, 1935, p. 129.
3. Admiralty to Commodore (T), 23 January 1915. Sent 1200. *Naval Staff Monograph (Historical)*, Volume III. Monograph 12, *The Action of the Dogger Bank, January 24th, 1915.* p. 219.
4. Admiralty to Vice Admiral *Lion*, 23 January 1915. Sent 1225. *Ibid.*
5. *With the Battle Cruisers.* Filson Young, Cassell & Co., London, 1921, p. 172.
6. *The World Crisis*, Volume II. Churchill, p. 130.
7. *A Great Seaman.* James, pp. 145–46.
8. Admiralty to Commodore (S), 23 January 1915. Sent 1410. *Naval Staff Monograph (Historical)*, Volume III. p. 219.
9. Admiralty to C in C Grand Fleet, Vice Admiral Third Battle Squadron, & Vice Admiral *Lion*, 23 January 1915. Sent 1415. *Ibid.*
10. *With the Battle Cruisers.* Young, p. 173.
11. *Prince Louis of Battenberg, Admiral of the Fleet.* Admiral Mark Kerr, Longmans, London, 1934, pp. 288–89.
12. *With the Battle Cruisers*, Young, pp. 174–75.
13. *Ibid.*, p. 175.
14. *Admiral von Hipper*, Waldeyer-Hartz, p. 151.
15. *Seydlitz* to C in C High Sea Fleet, 24 January 1915. Sent 0745. Received 0750. Received British Admiralty 0753. Deciphered 0815. *The Dogger Bank Action.* Commander John Creswell, RN, Appendix IV, 1932 Session, Royal Naval Staff College.
16. *Admiral von Hipper*, Waldeyer-Hartz, p. 152.
17. Admiralty to Commodore (S), 24 January 1915. Sent 1055. *Naval Staff Monograph (Historical)*, Volume III. p. 221.
18. Senior Officer First Light Cruiser Squadron to C in C Grand Fleet; to Senior Officer First Battle Cruiser Squadron, 24 January 1915. Sent 0823. *Ibid.*, p. 221.
19. Senior Officer First Battle Cruiser Squadron to C in C Grand Fleet, 24 January 1915. Sent 0835. *Ibid.*
20. *Seydlitz* to C in C High Sea Fleet, 24 January 1915. Sent 0844. Received British Admiralty 0850. Deciphered 0919. *The Dogger Bank Action.* Creswell.

21. "'Jacky' Fisher, HMS *Indomitable* and the Dogger Bank Action: A Personal Memoir." Vice Admiral B. B. Schofield, in *Naval Warfare in the Twentieth Century*. Ed. Gerald Jordan, Crane Russak & Co., New York, 1977, p. 68.

22. *Seydlitz* to C in C High Sea Fleet, 24 January 1915. Sent 0905. Received 0907. Received British Admiralty 0908. Deciphered 0929. *The Dogger Bank Action*. Creswell.

23. *Admiral von Hipper*, Waldeyer-Hartz, p. 152.

24. *With the Battle Cruisers*, Young, p. 133.

25. *The Navy and Defence*. Chatfield, p. 133.

26. "The Engagement of the Dogger Bank," HSH Lieutenant Prince George of Battenberg, *The Naval Review*, Volume 5, *1917*, p. 152.

27. *Germany's High Sea Fleet in the World War*. Admiral Reinhard Scheer, Cassel & Co., London, 1920, p. 84.

28. *With the Battle Cruisers*, Young, p. 187.

29. *Ibid.*, p. 189.

30. *Commander Ralph Seymour, RN*. Lady Seymour, The University Press, Glasgow, 1926, p. 65.

31. *300,000 Sea Miles: An Autobiography*. Admiral Sir Henry Pelly, Chatto & Windus, London, 1938, pp. 148–49.

32. The Papers of Admiral Sir R. A. R. Ernle-Erle-Plunkett-Drax. DRAX 1/47. *First Rough Notes*, Churchill College Archives, Cambridge.

33. *300,000 Sea Miles*. Pelly, p. 150.

34. *Admiral von Hipper*, Waldeyer-Hartz, p. 155.

35. *Commander Ralph Seymour, RN*. Seymour, p. 67.

36. The Papers of Admiral Sir William Tennant. TEN/3 *Diary While Serving in HM Ships Lizard and Ferret*. National Maritime Museum, Greenwich. See also *Tyrwhitt of the Harwich Force*, Patterson, p. 107.

37. *With the Battle Cruisers*, Young, pp. 208–9.

38. Tyrwhitt to his wife, 27 January 1915, *Tyrwhitt of the Harwich Force*. Patterson, p. 107.

39. *Naval Battles of the First World War*. G. M. Bennett, Batsford, London, 1965, p. 163.

40. Beatty to Jellicoe, February 1915, *The Jellicoe Papers*, Volume II, *1916–1935*. Ed. Professor A. Temple Patterson, The Navy Records Society, London, 1968, p. 32.

41. *With the Battle Cruisers*, Young, pp. 204–5.

CHAPTER 12

1. "The 24th January 1915," Lieutenant Commander Richard Foerster, in *Auf See Unbesiegt*. Ed. Vice Admiral Eberhard von Manty. J. Flehmanns, Verlag, München, 1921.

2. I am indebted to Dr. N. J. M. Campbell for this information. He made the discovery during his extensive research into the German damage reports produced in the repair yards.

3. *The Private War of Seaman Stumpf*. Ed. Daniel Horn, Leslie Frewin, London, 1969, p. 60.

4. *Admiral von Hipper*, Waldeyer-Hartz, p. 156.

5. *Ibid.*, p. 154.

6. Quoted in *Naval Battles of the First World War*. Bennett, p. 167.

7. *Naval Staff Monograph (Historical)*, Volume XIII, *Home Waters*, Part IV, *February to July 1915*, p. 30.

8. *Ibid.*, pp. 24–25. See *The War in the North Sea*, Volume III, Chapter 6; Volume IV, Chapter 1.

9. *Naval Staff Monograph (Historical)*, Volume XIII, p. 25.

10. *Ibid.*, p. 27.

11. *Ibid.*, p. 29.

12. Fisher to Beatty, 25 January, 27 January & 31 January 1915, *Fear God and Dread Nought*, Volume III. Marder, pp. 146, 147, 150.

13. *The World Crisis*, Volume II. Churchill, pp. 146–47.

14. *HMS* Tiger *at Bay*. Victor Hayward, William Kimber, London, 1977, pp. 70–71.

15. *The Riddle of Jutland*, Langhorne Gibson & Vice Admiral J. E. T. Harper, Cassell, London, 1934, p. 67.

16. Jellicoe to Beatty, 7 February 1915, *The Jellicoe Papers*, Volume I. Patterson, p. 142.

17. Jellicoe to Beatty, 23 March 1915. *Ibid.*, p. 152.

18. Fisher to Beatty, 25 January, 31 January, & 6 February 1915, *Fear God and Dread Nought*, Volume III, Marder, pp. 147, 150–51, 153.

19. Beatty to Jellicoe, 8 February 1915, *The Jellicoe Papers*, Volume I. Patterson, p. 144.

20. Beatty to Keyes, 18 September 1914, *The Keyes Papers*, Volume I. Halpern, pp. 28–29.

21. *The World Crisis*, Volume II. Churchill, p. 141.

22. Jellicoe to the Secretary of the Admiralty, 3 March 1915, *The Jellicoe Papers*, Volume I. Patterson, pp. 147–48.

23. Beatty to Jellicoe, 8 February 1915, *Ibid.*, pp. 144–45.

24. *HMS* Tiger *at Bay*, Hayward, p. 80.

25. *With the Battle Cruisers*, Young, p. 231.

26. Jellicoe to Beatty, 25 February 1915, *The Jellicoe Papers*, Volume I. Patterson, p. 146.

27. Fisher to Jellicoe, 4 April 1915, *Fear God and Dread Nought*, Volume III, Marder, p. 186.

28. *The World Crisis*, Volume II, Churchill, p. 89. See also *From Dreadnought to Scapa Flow*, Volume II, Marder, p. 170.

29. *The Life and Letters of David Earl Beatty*, Chalmers, p. 204.

30. *The Naval Memoirs of Admiral of the Fleet Sir Roger Keyes*, Volume I. p. 173.

31. *Naval Staff Monograph (Historical)*, Volume XIII. p. 4.

32. *With the Battle Cruisers*, Young, pp. 221–22.

33. *The Navy and Defence*, Chatfield, pp. 136–37.

34. *The Grand Fleet 1914–16: Its Creation, Development, and Work.* Admiral of the Fleet Viscount Jellicoe of Scapa, Cassell, London, 1919 p. 181.

35. Beatty to Jellicoe, 8 February 1915, *The Jellicoe Papers*, Volume I. Patterson, pp. 145–46.

Bibliography

PUBLISHED WORKS

Aspinall-Oglander, Brigadier C.F. *Roger Keyes*. Hogarth Press, London, 1951.

Bacon, Admiral Sir Reginald. *The Jutland Scandal*. 2nd ed. Hutchinson, London, 1925.

———. *The Life of Lord Fisher of Kilverstone*. Hutchinson, London, 1929.

———. *The Life of John Rushworth, Earl Jellicoe*. Cassell, London, 1936.

Bayly, Admiral Sir Lewis. *Pull Together! The Memoirs of Admiral Sir Lewis Bayly*. George G. Harrap & Co, London, 1939.

Beatty, Charles. *Our Admiral: A Biography of Admiral of the Fleet Earl Beatty 1871–1936*. W.H. Allen, London, 1980.

Bennett, Captain G. M. *Naval Battles of the First World War*. Batsford, London, 1968.

Bingham, Commander The Hon. Barry. *Falklands, Jutland and the Bight*. John Murray, London, 1919.

Bradford, Vice Admiral Sir Edward. *Life of Admiral of the Fleet Sir Arthur Knyvet Wilson*. Murray, London, 1923.

Brownrigg, Read Admiral Sir Douglas. *Indiscretions of the Naval Censor*. Cassell, London, 1920.

Bush, Captain Eric. *Bless Our Ship*. George Allen & Unwin Ltd, London, 1958.

Buxton, Dr. Ian. *Big Gun Monitors*. World Ship Society/Trident Books, Tynemouth, 1978.

Bywater, Hector E. *Cruisers in Battle: Naval Light Cavalry under Fire 1914–18*. Constable & Co., London, 1939.

Campbell, N.J.M. *Battle Cruisers: The Design and Development of British and German Battle Cruisers of the First World War Era*. Conway Maritime Press, London, 1978.

Carr, W.G. *Brass Hats and Bell-Bottomed Trousers: Unforgettable and Splendid Feats of the Harwich Patrol.* Hutchinson, London, 1939.

Chalmers, Rear Admiral W.S. *The Life and Letters of David Earl Beatty.* Hodder & Stoughton, London, 1951.

―――. *Max Horton and the Western Approaches.* Hodder & Stoughton, London, 1954.

―――. *Full Circle: The Biography of Admiral Sir Bertram Ramsay.* Hodder & Stoughton, London, 1959.

Chatfield, Admiral of the Fleet Lord. *The Navy and Defence.* William Heinemann, London, 1942.

Chatterton, E. Keble. *The Big Blockade.* Hurst & Blackett, London, 1932.

―――. *Fighting the U-boats.* Hurst & Blackett, London, 1942.

Churchill, W.S. *The World Crisis.* Vols. I & II. Australasian Publishing Co., Sydney, 1925.

Coles, Allan. *Three Before Breakfast.* Kenneth Mason, Havant, 1979.

Corbett, Sir Julian; Newbolt, Sir Henry; and Daniel, Lieutenant Colonel E.Y. *History of the Great War: Naval Operations.* Volumes I–V. Longmans, Green & Co., London, 1920–31; revised 1938 (Volume I) and 1940 (Volume III).

Cork and Orrery, Admiral of the Fleet the Earl of. *My Naval Life 1886–1941.* Hutchinson, London, 1942.

Cumminghame-Graham, Admiral Sir Angus. *Random Naval Recollections.* Private Publication, Dunbartonshire, 1979.

Dawson, Captain Lionel. *Flotillas: A Hard Lying Story.* Rich & Cowan, London, 1933.

―――. *Sound of the Guns: Being an Account of the Wars and Service of Admiral Sir Walter Cowan.* Pen-in-Hand, Oxford, 1949.

De Chair, Admiral Sir Dudley. *The Sea is Strong.* Harrap, London, 1961.

Dewar, Vice Admiral K.G.B. *The Navy from Within.* Gollancz, London, 1939.

Dittmar, F.J., and Colledge, J.J. *British Warships 1914–1919.* Ian Allan, London, 1972.

Domvile, Admiral Sir Barry. *By and Large.* Hutchinson, London, 1936.

Dreyer, Admiral Sir Frederick. *The Sea Heritage: A Study of Maritime Warfare.* Museum Press, London, 1955.

Ewing, A.W. *The Man of Room 40: The Life of Sir Alfred Ewing.* Hutchinson, London, 1939.

Fisher, Admiral of the Fleet Lord. *Memories.* Hodder & Stoughton, London, 1919.

―――. *Records.* Hodder & Stoughton, London, 1919.

Fremantle, Admiral Sir Sidney. *My Naval Career 1880–1928.* Hutchinson, London, 1949.

Frewen, Captain Oswald. *A Sailor's Soliloquy.* Hutchinson, London, 1961.

Gibson, Langhorne, and Harper, Vice Admiral J.E.T. *The Riddle of Jutland.* Cassell, London, 1934.

Gibson, R.H. and Prendergast, Maurice. *The German Submarine War 1914–1918.* 2d ed. Constable, London, 1931.

Goodenough, Admiral Sir William. *A Rough Record*. Hutchinson, London, 1939.

Görlitz, Walter, ed. *The Kaiser and His Court: The Diaries, Note Books and Letters of Admiral Georg Alexander von Müller, Chief of the Naval Cabinet 1914–1918*. MacDonald, London, 1961.

Grant, R.M. *U-boats Destroyed*. Putnam, London, 1964.

———. *U-boat Intelligence 1914–1918*. Putnam, London, 1969.

Greger, Rene. *The Russian Fleet 1914–1917*. Ian Allan, London, 1979.

Gretton, Vice Admiral Sir Peter. *Former Naval Person: Winston Churchill and the Royal Navy*. Cassell, London, 1968.

Groos, Captain Otto, and Gladisch, Admiral Walter. *Der Krieg in Der Nordsee* (Volumes I–V, Groos); *Der Krieg in Der Nordsee* (Volumes VI–VII, Gladisch). All volumes are part of the official series *Der Krieg Zur See 1914–1918*, Mitter, Berlin, 1920–1965. British NID translations into English of all except Volume VII are available at the Naval Historical Library.

Halpern, Dr. Paul A. *The Keyes Papers: Selections from the Private and Official Correspondence of Admiral of the Fleet Baron Keyes of Zeebrugge*, Volume I, *1914–1918*, Volume II, *1919–1938*. Navy Records Society, London, 1972 & 1980.

Hampshire, A. Cecil. *The Phantom Fleet*. William Kimber, London, 1977.

———. *The Blockaders*. William Kimber, London, 1980.

Hase, Commander Georg von. *Kiel and Jutland*. Skeffington, London, 1921.

Hayward, Victor. *HMS Tiger at Bay*. William Kimber, London, 1977.

Hezlet, Vice Admiral Sir Arthur. *The Submarine and Sea Power*. Peter Davies, London, 1967.

———. *The Aircraft and Sea Power*. Peter Davies, London, 1971.

———. *The Electron and Sea Power*. Peter Davies, London, 1975.

Holger, Herwig. *"Luxury" Fleet: The Imperial German Navy 1888–1918*. Allen & Unwin, London, 1980.

Horn, Daniel, ed. *The Private War of Seaman Stumpf*. Leslie Frewin, London, 1969.

Hough, Richard. *The Big Battleship: The Curious Career of HMS Agincourt*. Michael Joseph, London, 1966.

———. *First Sea Lord: An Authorised Biography of Admiral Lord Fisher*. Allen & Unwin, London, 1969.

Hoy, H.C. *Room 40 O.B.* Hutchinson, London, 1932.

Hyatt, A.M.J., ed. *Dreadnought to Polaris: Maritime Strategy Since Mahan*. Copp Clark, Toronto, 1973.

James, Admiral Sir William. *The Sky Was Always Blue*. Methuen, London, 1951.

———. *The Eyes of the Navy: a Biographical Study of Admiral Sir Reginald Hall*. Methuen, London, 1955.

———. *A Great Seaman: the Life of Admiral of the Fleet Sir Henry Oliver*. Witheby, London, 1956.

Jameson, Rear Admiral Sir William. *The Fleet that Jack Built: Nine Men Who Made a Modern Navy*. Hart-Davis, London, 1962.

————. *The Most Formidable Thing.* Hart-Davis, London, 1965.

Jellicoe, Admiral of the Fleet the Earl. *The Grand Fleet 1914–16: Its Creation, Development & Work.* Cassell, London, 1919.

Jerrold, Douglas. *The Royal Naval Division.* Hutchinson, London, 1923.

Kerr, Admiral Mark. *Land, Sea and Air: Reminiscences of Mark Kerr.* Longmans, London, 1927.

————. *Prince Louis of Battenberg, Admiral of the Fleet.* Longmans, London, 1934.

Keyes, Admiral of the Fleet Sir Roger. *The Naval Memoirs of Admiral of the Fleet Sir Roger Keyes,* Volume I, *The Narrow Seas to the Dardanelles 1910–1915.* Thornton Butterworth, London, 1934.

King-Hall, Admiral Sir Herbert. *Naval Memories and Traditions.* Hutchinson, London, 1926.

King-Hall, Lady L. *Sea Saga.* Gollancz, London, 1935.

King-Hall, Commander Stephen (Compiler ?). *Photographic Records of the B.C.F. August 1914–December 1916.*

————. *A Naval Lieutenant 1914–1918.* (originally written under the pen name "Etienne"), Methuen, London, 1919.

————. *My Naval Life 1906–1929.* Faber & Faber, London, 1952.

Langmaid, Captain Kenneth. *The Approaches are Mined!* Jarrolds, London, 1965.

Longmore, Air Chief Marshal Sir Arthur. *From Sea to Sky 1910–1945.* Geoffrey Bles, London, 1946.

Lumby, E.W.R. *Policy and Operations in the Mediterranean 1912–14.* Navy Records Society, London, 1970.

March, Edgar J. *British Destroyers 1892–1953.* Seeley Service, London, 1966.

Marder, Professor A.J. *Portrait of an Admiral: The Life and Papers of Admiral Sir Herbert Richmond.* Jonathan Cape, London, 1952.

————. *Fear God and Dread Nought. The Correspondence of Admiral of the Fleet Lord Fisher of Kilverstone.* Jonathan Cape, London; Volume III, *Restoration, Abdication & Last Years 1914–1920,* 1959.

————. *From Dreadnought to Scapa Flow: The Royal Navy in the Fisher Era 1904–1919.* Oxford University Press, London, Volume I, *The Road to War 1904–1914,* 1961; Volume II, *The War Years: To the Eve of Jutland 1914–1916,* 1965.

Moore, Major W. Geoffrey. *Early Bird.* Putnam, London, 1963.

Munro, Captain D.J. *Scapa Flow: A Naval Retrospect.* Sampson Low, London, 1932.

Parkes, Dr. Oscar. *British Battleships.* Seeley Service, London, 1960.

Patterson, Professor A. Temple. *The Jellicoe Papers: Selections from the private and official correspondence of Admiral of the Fleet Earl Jellicoe of Scapa,* Volume I, *1893–1916.* The Navy Records Society, London, 1966.

————. *Jellicoe: A Biography.* Macmillan, London, 1969.

————. *Tyrwhitt of the Harwich Force.* MacDonald, London, 1973.

Pelly, Admiral Sir Henry. *300,000 Sea Miles: An Autobiography.* Chatto & Windus, London, 1938.

Persius, L. *Der Seekrieg.* Verlag der Wettlübine, Charlottenburg, 1919.

Pollen, A.H. *The Navy in Battle*. Chatto & Windus, London, 1918.

Pollen, Anthony. *The Great Gunnery Scandal: The Mystery of Jutland*. Collins, London, 1980.

Raeder, Grand Admiral Erich. *My Life*. U.S. Naval Institute, Annapolis, 1960.

Richmond, Admiral Sir Herbert. *National Policy and Naval Strength and Other Essays*. Longmans, London, 1928.

————. *Statesman and Sea Power*. Oxford University Press, London, 1946.

Robinson, Douglas H. *The Zeppelin in Combat: A History of the German Naval Airship Division 1912–1918*. Revised Edition, Foulis, London, 1966.

Roskill, Captain S.W. *The Strategy of Sea Power*. Collins, London, 1962.

————. *Documents Relating to the Naval Air Service*, Volume I, 1908–1918. Navy Records Society, London, 1969.

————. *Hankey—Man of Secrets*, Volume I, *1877–1918*. Collins, London, 1970.

————. *Churchill and the Admirals*. Collins, London, 1977.

————. *Admiral of the Fleet Earl Beatty: The Last Naval Hero: An Intimate Biography*. Collins, London, 1980.

Scheer, Admiral Reinhard. *Germany's High Sea Fleet in the World War*. Cassell, London, 1920.

Seymour, Lady. *Commander Ralph Seymour, RN*. The University Press, Glasgow, 1926.

Sueter, Rear Admiral Murray F. *Airmen or Noahs*. Pitman, London, 1928.

"Taffrail" (Captain Taprell Dorling). *Endless Story: Being an Account of the Work of the Destroyers, Flotilla Leaders, Torpedo Boats and Patrol Boats in the Great War*. Hodder & Stoughton, London, 1931.

————. *Swept Channels: Being an Account of the Work of the Minesweepers in the Great War*. Hodder & Stoughton, London, 1935.

Taylor, John C. *German Warships of World War I*. Ian Allan, London, 1969.

Tirpitz, Grand Admiral Alfred von. *My Memoirs*. Hurst & Blackett, London, 1919.

Tupper, Admiral Sir Reginald. *Reminiscences*. Jarrold, London, 1929.

Tweedie, Admiral Sir Hugh. *The Story of a Naval Life*. Rich & Cowan, London, 1939.

Usborne, Vice Admiral C.V. *Blast and Counterblast: a Naval Impression of the War*. Murray, London, 1935.

Waldeyer-Hartz, Captain H. von. *Admiral von Hipper*. Rich & Cowan, London, 1933.

Wester-Wemyss, Lady. *The Life and Letters of Lord Wester Wemyss GCB, Admiral of the Fleet*. Eyre & Spottiswoode, London, 1935.

Woodward, E.L. *Great Britain and the German Navy*. Oxford University Press, London, 1935.

Woollard, Commander C.L.A. *With the Harwich Naval Forces 1914–1918*. Private printing, Antwerp, 1931.

Young, Desmond. *Rutland of Jutland*. Cassell, London, 1963.

Young, Filson. *With the Battle Cruisers*. Cassell, London, 1921.

OFFICIAL DOCUMENTS AND PUBLICATIONS

ADMIRALTY WORKS

Serial	Title
OU 6337 (40)	*Review of German Cruiser Warfare 1914– 1918* (1940).
G CB 928	*Grand Fleet Gunnery and Torpedo Memoranda on Naval Actions 1914–1918* (1922).
	The History of British Minefields (Two Volumes by Captain Lockhart Leith 1920).
	Operations off the East Coast of Great Britain 1914–1918 (Naval Staff 1940).

NAVAL STAFF MONOGRAPHS

(Variously edited by Captain A.C. Dewar, Instructor Captain O. Tuck, and Lieutenant Commander J.H. Lloyd-Owen)

No 6 (CB 1585)	*Passage of the British Expeditionary Force, August 1914* (1921).
No 7 (" ")	*The Patrol Flotillas at the Commencement of the War* (1921).
No 8 (" ")	*Naval Operations connected with the Raid on the North-East Coast, December 16th 1914* (1921).
No 11 (" ")	*The Battle of Heligoland Bight, August 28th 1914* (1921).
No 12 (" ")	*The Action of Dogger Bank, January 24th 1915* (1921, revised 1923).
No 18 (CB 917[D])	*The Dover Command: Volume I* (1922).
No 19 (CB 917[E])	*Tenth Cruiser Squadron I* (1922).
No 25 (CB 917[E])	*The Baltic 1914* (1922).
Volume IX [CB 917(G)]	*The Atlantic Ocean, 1914–15, Including the Battles of Coronel and the Falkland Islands* (1923).
Volume X [CB 917(H)]	*Home Waters—Part I. From the Outbreak of War to 27 August 1914* (1924).
Volume XI [CB 917(I)]	*Home Waters—Part II. September and October 1914* (1924).
Volume XII [CB 917(J)]	*Home Waters—Part III. From November 1914 to the end of January 1915* (1925).
Volume XIII [CB 917(K)]	*Home Waters—Part IV. From February to July 1915* (1925).

PUBLIC RECORD OFFICE FILES

Actions in Home Waters 1914 ADM 137 series: 1943, 1949, 1989, 2084, 2134, 2135, 2138, 2139.
Actions in Home Waters 1915 ADM 137 series: 1943, 1949, 1989, 2134, 2135, 2138, 2139.
Orders and Policy Decisions ADM 116 series: 1341, 1348, 1349, 1350, 1351.

PERSONAL MSS

Adams, Commander G.C. Diary Aug–Dec 1914 (IWM).
Archbold, Lieutenant Commander E.L. Diary Aug 1914–Oct 1915 (IWM).
Baldwin, Lieutenant Commander P.N. St J. Journal Sep 1914–May 1915 (IWM).
Blagrove, Rear Admiral H.E.C. Letters, Battle of the Dogger Bank (IWM).
Bradford, Admiral Sir Edward. Letters (NMM).
Brass, Commander J.E.P. Memoirs 1914–15 (IWM).
Childers, Lieutenant Commander R.E. War Diaries (IWM).
Cox, Commander M.L. Journal & Diary Aug 1914–Mar 1915 (IWM).
Crease, Captain T.E. Papers (NHL).
Creswell, Captain John. RNSC Lectures 1931–32 (Churchill College).
De Robeck, Admiral of the Fleet Sir John. Papers (Churchill College).
Dewar, Vice Admiral K.G.B. Papers (NMM).
Dickens, Admiral Sir Gerald. Letters 1914–16 (IWM).
Dixon, Commander C.D.H. Journal 1914–15 (IWM).
Domvile, Admiral Sir Barry. Papers (NMM).
Drage, Commander C.H. Diary 1914 (IWM).
Dreyer, Admiral Sir Frederick. Papers (Churchill College).
Duckworth, Captain A.D. Albums 1914–18 (IWM).
Eody, Commander G.N. Journal 1914–15 (IWM).
Ernle-Erle-Plunkett-Drax, Admiral Sir Reginald A.R. Papers (Churchill College).
Evans, Lieutenant Commander C.E. Memoirs (IWM).
Frewen, Captain Oswald. Diaries 1914–18 (Mrs Oswald Frewen).
Godfrey, Admiral J.H. Memoirs (Churchill College).
———. RNSC Lectures & Papers (NHL).
Grenfell, Captain F.H. Diaries 1914–15 (IWM).
Haigh, Signalman G.E. Diary 1914 (IWM).
Hamilton, Admiral Sir Louis. Diary 1914–15 (NMM).
Heald, Doctor C.B. Short description of Scarborough Raid (IWM).
Hood, Rear Admiral the Hon. Sir Horace. Papers (Churchill College).
Jellicoe, Admiral of the Fleet the Earl. Papers (British Museum).
Langley, Commander A.J.G. Memoirs (IWM).
Lowry, Commander R.G. Diary 1914–16 (IWM).
MacNair, Captain J.H. Memoirs (IWM).
Maloney, J.A. Memoirs (IWM).

Mead, Lieutenant H.P. Letters 1914 (IWM).
Miller, Rear Admiral H. Diary & Memoirs (IWM).
Moore, Gunner T. Diary 1914–16 (IWM).
Oliver, Admiral of the Fleet Sir Henry. Memoirs (NMM).
Paget, Admiral Sir Alfred. Letters 1914 (IWM).
Poole, Commander F. Papers (IWM).
Powell, Petty Officer P. Papers (IWM).
Quantril, Able Seaman R.S. Memoirs 1915–18 (IWM).
Richmond, Admiral Sir Herbert. Papers (NMM).
Rose, Able Seaman R.F. Memoirs 1912–20 (IWM).
Roskill, Captain S.W. Papers (Churchill College).
Snelling, A.G. Diary 1914–17 (IWM).
Spragge, Commander H.E. Diary 1914–15 (IWM).
Stewart, Captain R.R. Diary 1914–15 (IWM).
Sturdee, Admiral of the Fleet Sir Doveton. Papers (Admiral Sir William Staveley).
Tennant, Admiral Sir William. Diary 1914–16 (NMM).
Thursfield, Rear Admiral H.G. Papers (NMM).
Townsend, Leading Signalman T.W. Diary 1914–16 (IWM).
Twigg, Captain A.G.D. Diary 1914–15 (IWM).
Watson, Rear Admiral F.B. Papers 1914 (IWM).
Watson, Vice Admiral B.C. Memoirs 1914–16 (IWM).
Williams, Commander A.M. Memoirs 1914–15 (IWM).
Wintour, Captain C.J. Diary 1914–15 (IWM).
Woolven, F. Memoirs 1914 (IWM).

PERIODICALS

The Navy List (quarterly)
The Naval Review (quarterly)
Jane's Fighting Ships (annual)
The Mariner's Mirror (quarterly)
The Naval Annual (also known as *Brassey's Naval Annual*)
Warship (quarterly)
Warship International (quarterly)
U.S. Naval Institute Proceedings (monthly)

Index

Editor's note: British ships are listed alphabetically by name. German ships are listed alphabetically under German merchant ships; German torpedo boats and minesweepers; German U-boats; and German warships.